Church Reform and
Social Change in
Eleventh-Century Italy

THE MIDDLE AGES SERIES

Ruth Mazo Karras, General Editor
Edward Peters, Founding Editor

A complete list of books in the series is available
from the publisher.

Church Reform and Social Change in Eleventh-Century Italy

Dominic of Sora and His Patrons

John Howe

PENN

University of Pennsylvania Press

Philadelphia

Copyright © 1997 University of Pennsylvania Press
All rights reserved
Printed in the United States of America on acid-free paper

10   9   8   7   6   5   4   3   2   1

Published by
University of Pennsylvania Press
Philadelphia, Pennsylvania 19104-4011

Library of Congress Cataloging-in-Publication Data

Howe, John (John McDonald)
Church reform and social change in eleventh-century Italy : Dominic of Sora and his patrons / John Howe.
    p.   cm.— (Middle Ages series)
Includes bibliographical references and index.
ISBN 0-8122-3412-X (alk. paper)
    1. Dominic, of Sora, Saint, 951–1031 or 2.   2. Christian saints—Italy—Biography.
3. Abbots—Italy—Biography.   4. Patronage, Ecclesiastical—Italy—History.   5. Church history—11th century.   6. Italy—Social conditions.   I. Title.   II. Series.
BX4700.D73H68   1997
274.5′03—dc21   97-20604
                                                                                                                CIP

Contents

Abbreviations

AS	*Acta Sanctorum*, ed. Jean Bolland et al., 1st ed. (Antwerp and Brussels: Société des bollandistes, 1643–); 3rd ed. (Paris: V. Palmé, 1863–69).
ASOSB	*Acta Sanctorum Ordinis Sancti Benedicti*, ed. Luc d'Archery and Jean Mabillon, 2nd ed., 9 vols. (Venice: Sebastian Colet & Joseph Bettinelli, 1733–40).
BAV	Biblioteca Apostolica Vaticana.
BHL	*Bibliotheca Hagiographica Latina Antiquae et Mediae Aetatis*, 3 vols., Subsidia Hagiographica 6 and 70 (Brussels: Société des bollandistes, 1898–1901, 1986).
Bibl. Aless.	Biblioteca Alessandrina, Rome.
Bibl. Vall.	Biblioteca Vallicelliana, Rome.
BS	*Bibliotheca Sanctorum*, 14– vols. (Rome: Istituto Giovanni XXIII della Pontificia Università Lateranense, 1961–70, 1988).
Chron. Casaur.	"Johannes Berardi," *Chronicon Casauriense*, partially ed. in Ludovico Antonio Muratori, *Rerum Italicarum Scriptores* 2(2): 769–920 and 924–1018.
Chron. Cass.	Leo Marsicanus et al., *Chronicon Cassinense*, ed. Hartmut Hoffmann, Monumenta Germaniae Historica *Scriptores* 34 (Hannover: Hahn'sche Buchhandlung, 1980).
Chron. Farf.	Gregory of Catino, *Chronicon Farfense*, ed. Ugo Balzani, as *Il Chronicon Farfense di Gregorio di Catino; precedono la "Constructio Farfensis" e gli scritti di Ugo di Farfa*, 2 vols., Fonti per la storia d'Italia 33–34 (Rome: Istituto Storico Italiano per il Medio Evo, 1903).
Chron. Salern.	*Chronicon Salernitanum: A Critical Edition with Studies on Literary and Historical Sources and on Language*, ed.

	Ulla Westerbergh, Acta Universitatis Stockholmiensis, Studia Latina Stockholmiensia 3 (Stockholm: Almquist & Wiksell, 1956).
Chron. Subl.	*Chronicon Sublacense (AA. 593–1369)*, ed. Raffaello Morghen, Istituto Storico Italiano per il Medio Evo, *Rerum Italicarum Scriptores*, 24 (6) (Bologna: Nicola Zanichelli, 1927).
Chron. Vult.	*Chronicon Vulturnense del Monaco Giovanni*, ed. Vincenzo Federici, 3 vols., Fonti per la storia d'Italia 58–60 (Rome: R. Istituto Storico Italiano per il Medio Evo, 1925–40).
CISAM	Centro Italiano di Studi sull'Alto Medioevo
DBI	*Dizionario biografico degli italiani*, 46– vols. (Rome: Istituto della Enciclopedia italiana, 1960–)
FSI	Fonti per la storia d'Italia.
Gattola, *Accessiones*	Erasmo Gattola, *Ad Historiam Abbatiae Cassinensis: Accessiones*, 2 vols. (Venice: Sebastian Colet, 1734).
Gattola, *Historia*	Erasmo Gattola, *Historia Abbatiae Cassinensis per Saeculorum Seriem Distributa*, 2 vols. (Venice: Sebastian Colet, 1733).
Gregory I, *Dialog.*	Grégoire le Grand, *Dialogues*, ed. Adalbert de Vogüé and Paul Antin, 3 vols. Sources chrétiennes 251, 260, and 265 (Paris, Éditions du cerf, 1978–80).
ISIME	Istituto Storico Italiano per il Medio Evo
J–L	*Regesta Pontificum Romanorum*, ed. Philip Jaffé, rev. S. Loewenfeld et al., under the direction of Wilhelm Wattenbach, 2 vols. (Leipzig: Veit & Comp., 1885–88).
Jacobus de Voragine's *Summary*	Jacobus de Voragine's *De Sancto Dominico Abbati* (1273), a summary of the *Trisulti Life* and *Sora Miracles*, which survives in Biblioteca Alessandrina ms. 91 (2), fols. 347–359v (early seventeenth century).
MC	Miscellanea Cassinese.
MGH	Monumenta Germaniae Historica.

MGH *Const.*	Monumenta Germaniae Historica, *Legum*, Sect. IV, *Constitutiones et Acta Publica Imperatorum et Regum.*
MGH *Dipl. Kar.*	Monumenta Germaniae Historica, *Diplomata Karolinorum.*
MGH *Dipl. Reg. Imp.*	Monumenta Germaniae Historica, *Diplomata Regum et Imperatorum Germaniae.*
MGH *Epp.*	Monumenta Germaniae Historica, *Epistolae.*
MGH *SS*	Monumenta Germaniae Historica, *Scriptores.*
MIÖG	*Mitteilungen des Instituts für Österreichische Geschichtsforschung.*
Monasticon Italiae I	Filippo Caraffa, *Roma e Lazio (eccettuate l'archidiocesi di Gaeta e l'Abbazia Nullius di Montecassino).* Vol. I of *Monasticon Italiae*, Pubblicazioni del Centro Storico Benedettino Italiano (Cesena: Badia di santa Maria del Monte, 1981).
Monte Cassino Life	Anselmo Lentini, "La 'Vita S. Dominici' di Alberico Cassinese," *Benedictina* 5 (1951): 70–77.
PL	*Patrologia Latina*, for Jean-Paul Migne, *Patrologiae Cursus Completus: Series Latina*, 221 vols. (Paris: Migne, 1844–64).
Poncelet, *Cat. Cod. Hag. Lat. Rom.*	Albert Poncelet, *Catalogus Codicum Hagiographicorum Latinorum Bibliothecarum Romanarum praeter quam Vaticanae*, Subsidia Hagiographica 9 (Brussels: Société des bollandistes, 1909).
Poncelet, *Cat. Cod. Hag. Lat. Vat.*	Albert Poncelet, *Catalogus Codicum Hagiographicorum Latinorum Bibliothecae Vaticanae*, Subsidia Hagiographica 11 (Brussels: Société des bollandistes, 1910).
QFIAB	*Quellen und Forschungen aus italienischen Archiven und Bibliotheken.*
RB	Benedict of Nursia, *Regula Benedicti*, ed. Adalbert De Vogüé and Jean Neufville, *La Règle de saint Benoît*, 7 vols., Sources chrétiennes 181–86 bis (Paris: Éditions du cerf, 1971–77).

Reg. Farf.	Gregory of Catino. *Il Regesto di Farfa compilato da Gregorio di Catino*, ed. Ignazio Giorgi and Ugo Balzani, 5 vols. (Rome: Istituto Storico Italiano per il Medio Evo, 1879–1914).
Reg. Petri Diac.	Peter the Deacon, *Registrum*, Archivio di Montecassino ms. 396 (twelfth century).
Reg. Subl.	*Il Regesto sublacense del Secolo XI*, ed. Leone Allodi and Guido Levi (Rome: R. Società Romana di Storia Patria, 1885).
RISS	*Rerum Italicarum Scriptores*, two series: 1st series, ed. Ludovico Antonio Muratori, 25 vols. (Milan: Typographia Societatis Palatinae, 1723–51); 2nd series, a reedition begun by Vittorio Fiorini et al., divides the texts but retains Muratori's volume numbers (Città di Castello, then Bologna: Stamperia di S Lapi, then Istituto Storico Italiano, 1900–).
SH	Subsidia Hagiographica.
Sermon	"In [Festo] Sancti Dominici." *Bibliotheca Casinensis seu Codicum Manuscriptorum Qui in Tabulario Casinensi Asservantur*, 5 vols. (Monte Cassino: Typographia Casinensi, 1873–94), 3:365–66.
Sora Life	François Dolbeau, "Le dossier de saint Dominique de Sora d'Albéric du Mont-Cassin à Jacques de Voragine, *Mélanges de l'École française de Rome: Moyen âge-temps modernes* 102 (1990): 7–78.
SRSP	Società Romana di Storia Patria
Summary	Jacobus de Voragine, *Summary*, Biblioteca Alessandrina ms. 91 (pt. 2), fols. 347–59v (early seventeenth century).
Trisulti Life	"S. Dominici Sorani Abbatis Vita et Miracula a Coaevis Conscripta," *Analecta Bollandiana* 1 (1882): 282–98.
Valva Life	Notes from Monte Cassino ms. 141, published in Anselmo Lentini, "La 'Vita S. Dominici' di Alberico Cassinese," *Benedictina* 5 (1951): 70–77.

Acknowledgments

Many institutions and friends made this project possible. In addition to Texas Tech University, my academic home, it owes much to the University of California at Los Angeles, the University of California at Berkeley, Stanford University, the Biblioteca Apostolica Vaticana, the Biblioteca Alessandrina, the Biblioteca Vallicelliana, the École Française de Rome, the Deutsches Historisches Institut in Rome, and the Archivio di Montecassino. Travel was facilitated by a National Endowment for the Humanities travel-to-collections grant, a Fulbright travel grant, an American Philosophical Society research grant, a TTU faculty development leave, a National Endowment for the Humanities summer stipend, and a grant from the TTU Research Enhancement Fund. TTU helped with publication expenses. Encouragement and aid with particular points came from Bernard S. Bachrach, Herbert Bloch, François Dolbeau, Carmela V. Franklin, the late Baudouin de Gaiffier, Ruth Mazo Karras, Carol Lanham, Francis Newton, Antonio Sennis, and Chris Wickham. Special thanks are due to readers of early manuscript drafts: Patrick Geary, Ruth Mazo Karras, Edward Peters, Jerome E. Singerman, David Troyansky, Chris Wickham, and the anonymous referees recruited by the University of Pennsylvania Press. Amy Troyansky drew the maps. It is not possible to adequately acknowledge the patience of my own family and of Alberto Deflorio and his family, gracious hosts in Italy.

Two now-deceased mentors also deserve thanks. I would never have met Dominic if Gerhart B. Ladner had not patiently allowed me to write a rather unusual doctoral dissertation. Ladner's breadth of historical vision has influenced this work in ways that even I do not fully recognize. I hope that these pages also reflect the gentility and humanity of Lynn T. White, Jr.

Introduction:
A Case Study Approach to
Eleventh-Century Reform

THE HAGIOGRAPHICAL DOSSIER of Dominic of Sora (d. 1032) opens a unique window onto central Italian ecclesiastical and social history. Competing cult centers attempting to establish claims on Dominic's sanctity produced four nearly contemporary *lives* (one followed by extensive *miracles*), a biographically oriented sermon, and five hymns. The only similarly rich, roughly contemporary Italo-Latin hagiographical and historical texts are Peter Damian's *life* of Romuald of Ravenna (d. ca. 1027) and the documents concerning the holy men involved in the battles over simony in Milan and Florence. Nothing comparable survives from central Italy itself. These texts reveal a little known provincial world helping to create the Roman Church of the High Middle Ages.

Dominic's dossier makes possible a case study approach, a method that seeks to illuminate a larger world by examining single, often humble subjects, investigating them exhaustively and analyzing them from different perspectives. Embraced by late medieval and early modern historians, it has resulted in biographical and cultic studies such as Natalie Davis's *The Return of Martin Guerre*, Carlo Ginzburg's *The Cheese and the Worms*, and Jean-Claude Schmitt's *The Holy Greyhound*.[1] Also impressive are geographical microstudies such as Guy Bois's work on Lournand, Maureen Miller's on the church of Verona, and, most famously, Emmanuel Le Roy Ladurie's on Montaillou.[2] The case study method is especially appropriate

1. Natalie Zemon Davis, *The Return of Martin Guerre* (Cambridge, Mass.: Harvard University Press, 1983); Carlo Ginzburg, *The Cheese and the Worms: The Cosmos of a Sixteenth-Century Miller*, trans. John Tedeschi and Anne Tedeschi (Baltimore: Johns Hopkins University Press, 1980); Jean-Claude Schmitt, *The Holy Greyhound: Guinefort, Healer of Children since the Thirteenth Century*, trans. Martin Thom, Cambridge Studies in Oral and Literate Culture 6 (Cambridge: Cambridge University Press, 1979).

2. Guy Bois, *The Transformation of the Year 1000: The Village of Lournand from Antiquity to Feudalism*, trans. Jean Birrell (Manchester: University of Manchester Press, 1992);

for an Italian subject because the current popularity of "microhistory" has its roots in the traditional regionalism of Italy, the historical particularism of Benedetto Croce, and the development of this orientation into a historical method by Italian scholars from the 1970s onward.[3]

The subject of this case study is Dominic of Sora, celebrated in his own age but largely forgotten in ours. Born in Foligno, just north of papal territory, probably around 960, he moved as a young priest to the neighborhood of the imperial monastery of Farfa in the Sabine hills, where he became first a hermit and then a monastic founder. He established a dozen monasteries and churches thoughout the central Apennines before settling down at Sora, just south of Roman territory, where he died in 1032. He owed his success to a complex network of supporters.

Insofar as Dominic can be known, he is an attractive figure, a wandering hermit priest who directed a string of frontier monasteries and hermitages built on awesome natural sites. He was able to flourish among hard people in a hard land. His patrons, on the other hand, evoke horror as well as admiration. They were the nameless people who trailed after him in crowds, men and women who kept alive his memory not only with conventional festivities but also with eery snake-handling rituals. They were also counts and lords, grasping men whose lineages metastasized throughout the central Apennines. In their rise they recreated society, aided by the new ecclesiastical foundations they built for piety and profit. When the wheel of fortune ceased to favor them, they grabbed onto and pulled down with them the monastery of Monte Cassino. Dominic's story has compelling human interest.

Yet it also has broader significance. It reveals neglected dimensions of the so-called Gregorian Reform.[4] This current label for the ecclesiastical

---

Maureen Miller, *The Formation of a Medieval Church: Ecclesiastical Change in Verona, 950–1150* (Ithaca, N.Y.: Cornell University Press, 1993); Emmanuel Le Roy Ladurie, *Montaillou: The Promised Land of Error*, trans. Barbara Bray (New York: George Braziller, 1978).

3. On the development of the case study approach in Italy, see Edward Muir, "Introduction: Observing Trifles," in *Microhistory and the Lost Peoples of Europe*, ed. Edward Muir and Guido Ruggiero, trans. Eren Branch, Selections from *Quaderni Storici* (Baltimore: Johns Hopkins University Press, 1991), viii–xiv; and Giovanni Levi, "On Microhistory," in *New Perspectives in Historical Writing*, ed. Peter Burke (University Park: Pennsylvania State University Press, 1992), 93–113.

4. John Howe, "The Nobility's Reform of the Medieval Church," *American Historical Review* 93 (1988): 319–20, offers a summary definition of "Gregorian Reform." The best extended analyses are Uta-Renate Blumenthal, *The Investiture Controversy: Church and Monarchy from the Ninth to the Twelfth Century* (Philadelphia: University of Pennsylvania Press, 1988); and Gerd Tellenbach, *The Church in Western Europe from the Tenth to the Early Twelfth Century*, trans. Timothy Reuter, Cambridge Medieval Textbooks (New York: Cambridge University Press, 1993).

transformations of the eleventh and early twelfth centuries evokes all too well the dramatic conflicts that erupted during the reign of Pope Gregory VII (1073–1085). It implies that reform was a matter of high politics, a series of battles between popes, emperors, and kings. But the reform movement was more than the investiture controversy. Even Augustin Fliche, the scholar most responsible for the term "Gregorian Reform," saw Gregory at "the center of a vast movement of ideas whose origins are to be found deep in the tenth century and whose manifestations continue on up to the middle of the twelfth."[5] Unfortunately, the emphasis on the later events has tended to devalue the earlier. So too has the dominant interpretive model, set forth in the late 1930s by Gerd Tellenbach, which views earlier reforms as predominantly otherworldly, devoted to fostering ascetic perfection within monastic communities that looked for righteousness in a world to come. Those movements are contrasted to the Gregorian Reform, which is said to have been dedicated to converting the present world and, therefore, to securing the political freedom this mission required. Tellenbach acknowledges that monastic reforms contributed moral influence and personnel to Church reform, but insists on separating the two, emphasizing the novelty of the mid-eleventh-century Roman reform program and giving great weight to the high political struggle.[6] Not everybody has been happy with this dichotomy: H. E. J. Cowdrey has been demonstrating the important role the great monastic houses played in the high reform program;[7] Johannes Laudage has illuminated the development of "Grego-

5. Augustin Fliche, *Études sur la polémique religieuse à l'époque de Grégoire VII: Les Prégrégoriens* (Paris: Société française d'imprimerie et de librairie, 1916); "La formation des idées grégoriennes," in *La Réforme grégorienne*, 3 vols., Spicilegium Sacrum Lovaniense, Études et documents 6, 9, and 16 (Paris: E. Champion, 1924–37), esp. 1:vi–viii, 6, 17, 39–148.

6. Tellenbach, *Libertas, Kirche und Weltordnung im Zeitalter des Investiturstreites* (Stuttgart: W. Kohlhammer, 1936), trans. R. F. Bennett as *Church, State and Christian Society at the Time of the Investiture Controversy* (1959; reprint, New York: Harper Torchbooks, 1970). This English version expands "Appendix V," which distinguishes between Cluniac and Gregorian reform. Note also Tellenbach's "Il monachesimo riformato ed i laici nei secoli XI e XII," in *I Laici nella "Societas Christiana" dei secoli XI e XII: Atti della terza Settimana internazionale di studio, Mendola, 21–27 agosto 1965*, Pubblicazioni dell'Università cattolica del Sacro Cuore Contributi ser. 3, var. 5; Miscellanea del Centro di Studi Medioevali 5 (Milan: Vita e Pensiero, 1968), 118–51, esp. 137–42, which was also published in the original German as "Das Reformmönchtum und die Laien im elften und zwölften Jahrhundert," in *Cluny: Beiträge zu Gestalt und Wirkung der cluniazensischen Reform*, Wege der Forschung 241 (Darmstadt: Wissenschaftliche Buchgesellschaft, 1975), 371–400, esp. 394–400, reprinted in his *Ausgewählte Abhandlungen und Aufsätze*, 4 vols. (Stuttgart: Anton Hiersemann, 1988–89), 3:1067–96, esp. 1090–96. The distinction between Cluniac and Gregorian reforms also animates *The Church in Western Europe*, 161, 293–94, 301–2.

7. H. E. J. Cowdrey, *The Cluniacs and the Gregorian Reform* (Oxford: Clarendon Press, 1970); *The Age of Abbot Desiderius: Montecassino, the Papacy, and the Normans in the Eleventh and Early Twelfth Centuries* (Oxford: Clarendon Press, 1983).

rian" ideology in the first half of the eleventh century;[8] and other scholars have increasingly highlighted the non-elite, amorphous character of much early reform agitation.[9] But Tellenbach still holds the field, leading to what has been described as "the immobilization of interpretative discourse on a central theme of European history."[10]

Dominic's story offers a possible way out of this impasse by giving an Italian perspective on the early stages of reform. Traditional Gregorian historiography is too transalpine. Fliche was French; Tellenbach German. French scholars, maintaining that "the Gregorians elaborated a program starting from the Cluniac enterprise," have spent a century describing how Cluny developed the monastic reforms that led to general ecclesiastical changes (although, from Fliche onward, they have increasingly differentiated between the ultimate forms of Cluniac and Gregorian reform).[11] Ger-

8. Johannes Laudage, *Priesterbild und Reformpapsttum im 11. Jahrhundert*, Beihefte zum Archiv für Kulturgeschichte 22 (Cologne: Böhlau Verlag, 1984), esp. 306–12. Reform outside the investiture controversy is also highlighted in Werner Goez, "Riforma ecclesiastica-Riforma gregoriana," in *La Riforma gregoriana e l'Europa: Congresso Internazionale, Salerno, 20–25 maggio 1985*, Studi gregoriani 13 (Rome: Libreria Ateneo Salesiano, 1989), 167–78.

9. Marxist historians have traditionally emphasized the importance of the crowd in reform, particularly Ernst Werner in such works as *Pauperes Christi: Studien zu sozial-religiösen Bewegungen im Zeitalter des Reformpapsttums* (Leipzig: Koehler & Amelang, 1956). He offered an overview in "Pataria und Virginitas," in *Byzance-Italie: Mélanges réunis en l'honneur de M. Freddy Thiriet*, published in a special issue of *Byzantinische Forschungen* 12 (1987): 489–501.

Italian scholars have joined them, in part because the most conspicuous example was the Milanese *pataria*, analyzed in Cinzio Violante, *La Società milanese nell'età precomunale*, Istituto Italiano per gli Studi Storici in Napoli (Bari: Gius. Laterza & Figli, 1953), and *La Pataria milanese e la riforma ecclesiastica. I: Le premesse (1045–1057)*, ISIME Studi storici 11–13 (Rome: ISIME, 1955); as well as in Paolo Golinelli, *La Pataria: Lotte religiose e sociali nella Milano dell'XI secolo* (Milan: Editoriale Jaca Book, 1984). On the importance of the popular element in eleventh-century Florence, and indeed all Italy, the preeminent scholar has been Giovanni Miccoli, esp. in *Pietro Igneo: Studi sull'età gregoriana*, Studi storici 40–41 (Rome: ISIME, 1960); in *Chiesa Gregoriana: Ricerche sulla Riforma del secolo XI*, Storici antichi e moderni n.s. 17 (Florence: La Nuova Italia, 1966); and in syntheses such as his "La Storia religiosa" in *Storia d'Italia*, 6 vols. (Torino: Giulio Einaudi Editore, 1972–76), 2(1):475–80. The role of local communities in the reform movement is highlighted in Miller, *Formation of a Medieval Church*, 12–14. The importance of the crowd in the Peace of God and other early reform movements has also drawn increasing attention in work on other regions, most recently in Richard Landes, *Relics, Apocalypse, and the Deceits of History: Ademar of Chabannes, 989–1034*, Harvard Historical Studies 117 (Cambridge, Mass.: Harvard University Press, 1995).

10. Karl F. Morrison, rev. of Brigitte Szabó-Bechstein, *Libertas Ecclesiae: Ein Schlüsselbegriff des Investiturstreits und seine Vorgeschichte, 4–11. Jahrhundert*, Studi Gregoriani n.s. 12 (Rome: Libreria Ateneo Salesiano, 1985), in *Speculum* 62 (1987): 998–99.

11. Marcel Pacaut, quoted here from *L'Ordre de Cluny (909–1789)* (Paris: Librairie Arthème Fayard, 1986), 178, exemplifies the dominant tendencies of French Cluniac historiography, balancing an emphasis on Cluny's apostolic outreach to the world against its close connection to the ruling elites, which he insists had led to distinct Cluniac and Gregorian ideological positions by the later eleventh century: see ibid., 178–85, and "Ordre et liberté dans l'église: L'influence de Cluny aux XIe et XIIe siècles," in *The End of Strife: Papers from*

man scholars, on the other hand, maintaining that "there can be no doubt that the Gregorian reform began with the German Popes," have tended to emphasize events within Germany, such as imperial reforms, aristocratic reforms, German penitential and legal developments, and especially the breakthrough that resulted when Pope Leo IX (1049–1054), the former Bishop Bruno of Toul, brought a reform program from the Lorraine to Rome.[12] One would never guess that popular enthusiasm for reform apparently originated in Italy or that during most of the Gregorian period, from 1049 to 1130, the Church was ruled by Italian popes whose cardinals were predominantly Italian monks.[13] Yet the early reform movement has rarely been examined from the perspective of Italy; only in recent decades have Italian scholars begun to play an important role in Gregorian historiography,[14] and in an era of European integration they have generally preferred

the *Colloquium of the Commission internationale d'histoire ecclésiastique comparée (Durham, 1981)*, ed. David Loades (Edinburgh: T. & T. Clark, 1984), 155–79; reprinted with the same pagination in *Doctrines politiques et structures ecclésiastiques dans l'Occident médiéval* (London: Variorum Reprints, 1985). Laudage, *Priesterbild und Reformpapsttum*, 36–41, surveys the positions taken by a variety of French and German scholars on the relationship between Cluniac and Gregorian reform. Barbara H. Rosenwein, *Rhinoceros Bound: Cluny in the Tenth Century* (Philadelphia: University of Pennsylvania Press, 1982), 3–29, indicates the underlying nationalistic biases.

12. Friedrich Kempf, "Die gregorianische Reform (1046–1124)," in *Die Mittelalterliche Kirche*, ed. Kempf et al., vol. 3 of the *Handbuch der Kirchengeschichte*, ed. Hubert Jedin, 10 vols. (Freiburg: Herder, 1962–79), 3:404, quoted here in the English of *The Church in the Age of Feudalism*, ed. Kempf et al., trans. Anselm Biggs, in *History of the Church*, 10 vols., ed. Hubert Jedin and John Dolan (New York: Seabury Press, 1965–81), 3:351. Kempf's perspective is not unique. That "the ideas which would revolutionize the world originated in Burgundy and Lotharingia, not in Rome" is assumed by Hartmut Hoffmann in "Von Cluny zum Investiturstreit," *Archiv für Kulturgeschichte* 45 (1963): 186, reprinted with a "Postscript 1974" in *Cluny: Beiträge zur Gestalt und Wirkung der cluniazensischen Reform*, ed. Helmut Richter, Wege der Forschung 241 (Darmstadt: Wissenschaftliche Buchgesellschaft, 1975), 348. For Blumenthal, "History and Tradition in Eleventh-Century Rome," *Catholic Historical Review* 79 (1993): 186, it is a question of "the reformed, i.e., transalpine, papacy." The scholarly tradition that traces the origins of the Gregorian reform to Lorraine is surveyed in Laudage, *Priesterbild und Reformpapsttum*, 306–7.

13. On the priority of Italian popular reform enthusiasm, see Tellenbach, *Church in Western Europe*, 40, 44. Generalizations about the curial predominance of Italians can be sustained from J. N. D. Kelly, *The Oxford Dictionary of Popes* (New York: Oxford University Press, 1986); and Rudolf Hüls, *Kardinäle, Klerus und Kirchen Roms, 1049–1130*, Bibliothek des Deutschen Historischen Instituts in Rom 48 (Tübingen: Max Niemeyer Verlag, 1977). A similar conclusion is reached in Werner Maleczek, "Rombeherrschung und Romerneuerung durch das Papsttum," in *Rom im hohen Mittelalter: Studien zu den Romvorstellungen und zur Rompolitik vom 10. bis zum 12. Jahrhundert. Reinhard Elze zur Vollendung seines siebzigsten Lebensjahres gewidmet*, ed. Bernhard Schimmelpfennig und Ludwig Schmugge (Sigmaringen: Jan Thorbecke Verlag, 1992), 21.

14. Robert Brentano, "Italian Ecclesiastical History: The Sambin Revolution," *Medievalia et Humanistica* n.s. 14 (1986): 189–97, suggests that until the mid 1950s the best Italian local medieval ecclesiastical history was produced by the German Historical Institute in Rome. See also Fulvio Salimbene, "Introduzione," *Atti della Tavola Rotonda su "Le storie generali*

to adopt a pan-European perspective, avoiding direct challenges to the dominant transalpine nationalistic traditions.[15] The result is that historians continue to underrate Italy's contributions to the reform movement's origins.[16] Dominic's story offers a partial antidote.

Since much of the material for reconstructing his biography is hagiographical, the major texts in his complex dossier—and the problems they pose—require a brief introduction. Underlying the texts are oral traditions, some of which were created by Dominic himself. He would have been the major authority on his early life, from which his hagiographers were separated by many miles and decades. His sayings and stories would have been treasured by his followers because they considered him so holy that upon his death they immediately acclaimed him a saint.[17] The *lives* name individual informants, as well as classes of witnesses such as Dominic's "familiares," the "seniores" at Sora, and the "relatores gestorum Dominici," a group that included the disciple John, who was with the saint for much of his career. Such people must have retold anecdotes countless times. The priority of oral traditions explains anomalies in the written records, such as the existence of divergent versions of the same stories.

---

della Chiesa dopo il Concilio Vaticano II" (28 aprile 1979), published in a special issue of *Ricerche di storia sociale e religiosa* n.s. 11 (1982), 7–13. For descriptions of the subsequent dynamism of Italian research, see Salimbene, ibid., and the other articles in that symposium; Giuseppe Fornasari, "Del nuovo Gregorio VII? Riflessioni su un problema storiografico 'non esaurito'," *Studi medievali* n.s. 3, 24 (1983): 315–53; and the "Gregorian" studies printed in *Benedictina* 33(1) (1986). As note 9 above indicated, Italian historians have particularly distinguished themselves in elucidating the "popular" aspects of the Gregorian Reform.

15. Raffaello Morghen, in *Gregorio VII e la riforma della Chiesa nel secolo XI*, 2nd ed. (Palermo: Palumbo Editore, 1974), 15–19, counters traditional Gregorian historiography's transalpine nationalistic biases not by defining Italy's contributions but by advocating a greater universalism, arguing that what had once been seen as French or German actually characterized the Church as a whole. Only a few scholars have stressed the unique aspects of the Italian experience of reform, as, for example, Miccoli, "La Storia religiosa," in *Storia d'Italia*, 2(1):480.

16. For a striking example of the relative neglect of Italy's role, see Colin Morris, *The Papal Monarchy: The Western Church from 1050 to 1250* (Oxford: Clarendon Press, 1989), 28–33, 79–83.

17. Dominic's sanctity is assumed by a donation made to the monastery of Santa Madre di Dio e Vergine Maria at Sora in 1033, right after Dominic's death, when it identifies that church as the place "ubi beatissimum corpus dompni Dominici abbatis tumulatum est." This text is known from an eighteenth-century copy, ed. Dionigi Antonelli, *Abbazie, prepositure e priorati benedettini nella diocesi di Sora nel medioevo (secc. VIII–XV)* (Sora: Tipografia Editrice Pasquarelli, 1986), 374–75. The copy stemmed ultimately from Casamari's now lost fifteenth-century chartulary, on whose fate see Pierre Toubert, *Les Structures du Latium médiéval: Le Latium méridional et la Sabine du IXe siècle à la fin du XIIe siècle*, 2 vols., Bibliothèque des Écoles françaises d'Athènes et de Rome 221 (Rome: École française de Rome, 1973), 1:37.

The earliest surviving *lives* encapsulate these traditions. They have all been influenced by a now-lost original written version, probably composed at the monastery of San Bartolomeo at Trisulti within several decades of Dominic's death.[18] The closest witness to that lost original may be a rather jejeune abbreviated *Sermon* (*BHL* 2246), the unique copy of which was written in the neighborhood of Monte Cassino around the end of the eleventh century.[19] Dominic is viewed from the Trisulti perspective in the surviving *Trisulti Life* (*BHL* 2241), a long text filled with miracles and local color that, although presumably based on its monastery's ancient oral and written traditions, survives only through an early modern copy whose conclusion bears traces of alterations.[20] The *Valva Life* (*BHL* 2245) is a shorter text, whose readings, attested by early manuscript witnesses, enigmatically bridge the Trisulti and Monte Cassino/Sora traditions.[21]

Dominic's fullest *vita* and *miracula post mortem* were composed between 1067 and ca. 1070 by Monte Cassino's schoolmaster, Alberic the Rhetorician, whose literary career extended from the early 1060s until his

18. Because Dominic's surviving memorials agree about the contours of his career and use similar images, they appear to have a common ancestor. Scholars today postulate a lost original, a "Vita X," because no existing text fits at the head of the tradition. For textual demonstrations, see Anselmo Lentini, "La 'Vita S. Dominici' di Alberico Cassinese," *Benedictina* 5 (1951): 57–77, esp. 67–68, reprinted posthumously in his *Medioevo letterario Cassinese: Scritti vari*, ed. Faustino Avagliano, Miscellanea Casinese 57 (Montecassino: Pubblicazioni Cassinesi, 1988), 140–65, esp. 152–53; François Dolbeau, "Le dossier de saint Dominique de Sora d'Albéric du Mont-Cassin à Jacques de Voragine," *Mélanges de l'École française de Rome: Moyen âge—temps modernes* 102 (1990): 28; and Carmela Vircillo Franklin, "The Restored *Life and Miracles of St. Dominic of Sora* by Alberic of Monte Cassino," *Mediaeval Studies* 55 (1993): 336.

19. *BHL* 2246 was edited from Monte Cassino ms. 146, the sole manuscript witness, by the monks of Monte Cassino in the *Sermon*. More than half of this text is published directly from the manuscript in Franklin, "The *Restored Life and Miracles*," 329–35, but I cite the full edition rather than shift back and forth between it and Franklin's partial text, which differs only orthographically except for two insubstantial textual improvements. The *Sermon*'s author concluded abruptly "for the sake of brevity" when he simultaneously reached both a reasonable sermon length and the bottom of his page.

20. *BHL* 2241 is known by way of a lost transcript made in 1597 by a priest of Anagni, copies of which were secured by two hagiographical collectors. It was published by the Bollandists as "S. Dominici Sorani Abbatis Vita et Miracula a Coaevis Conscripta," *Analecta Bollandiana* 1 (1882): 282–98 (hereafter *Trisulti Life*, although it is often cited in the literature as *John's Life* because of a dubious colophon identifying its author as Dominic's disciple John).

21. The two possibly eleventh-century manuscripts of *BHL* 2245—Monte Cassino ms. 141, fols. 167–70v, and BAV ms. lat. 1197 fols. 133–35—are from San Nicola "de Turre Pagana" in Benevento and from the canons of Corfinio in Valva. This *vita* has never been edited in its own right. A few readings are included in *ASOSB*, 2nd ed., 6(1):315–19, and these are all subsumed in notes given in Lentini, "La 'Vita S. Dominici'," 71–77, made on the basis of the Monte Cassino copy. I cite Lentini's notes, after having cross-checked their readings against the Vatican manuscript. This text is somewhat arbitrarily named the *Valva Life* on the basis of its easterly manuscript distribution.

death between 1094 and 1098/1099.[22] Alberic's work can be reconstructed
to a large extent from the surviving abbreviated *Monte Cassino Life* (*BHL*
2244), the earliest copy of which appears to date from his lifetime,[23] and
from the *Sora Life* (*BHL* 2244 introduction, 2245b, and 2242), a five-times-
longer *life* and *miracles* written for Sora, as its tomb miracles indicate.
Although the *Sora Life* was probably originally written by Alberic, an in-
determinate number of later modifications are included in the surviving
version, the earliest copy of which dates from the late sixteenth century.[24]

None of the *lives* described above can be disregarded because each has
some independent oral or textual source(s). No such authority is demon-
strable for the five surviving hymns,[25] or for a composite *vita* (*BHL* 2243)
by Jacobus de Voragine (d. 1298), the compiler of the *Golden Legend*.[26]

22. The scholarly debates on Alberic and his work are introduced in the ample footnotes
of Franz Josef Worstbrock, "Die Anfänge der mittelalterlichen *Ars Dictandi*," *Frühmittelal-
terliche Studien* 23 (1989): 3–7, 13–14, 20, 30–31; and Franklin, "Restored *Life and Miracles*,"
285. Although wildly differing dates for Alberic's career appear in the literature, Franklin, ibid.,
286–87, solidly justifies those given here. Alberic's authorship of a *life* of Dominic is affirmed
by both *Chron. Cass.* III xxxv, 410; and Peter the Deacon's *De Viris Illustribus Casinensis
Coenobii* xxi, edited in *PL* 173 : 1032–33.

23. Among the copies of *BHL* 2244 is what may be the earliest surviving manuscript of
a *vita Dominici*, Monte Cassino ms. 101, written in a Beneventan hand said to be typical of
the *scriptorium* of Abbot Desiderius (1058–87). *BHL* 2244 was the first Latin version of Dominic's *life* to be printed: early editions appear in *AS* Jan. 2 : 442 (or 3rd ed., Jan. 3 : 56); and in
ASOSB 6(1) : 356–60 (or 2nd ed., 6[1] : 315–19). This present monograph cites the text from
Lentini in the *Monte Cassino Life*. Although Lentini's work was reprinted in *Medioevo letterario Cassinese*, 140–65, that reprint is avoided here because its conversion of his third series of
footnotes into endnotes makes its use slightly more cumbersome.

24. *BHL* 2244 intro/2245b/2242 survives earliest in Antonio Gallonio's late-sixteenth-
century hagiographical collections, in Bibl. Vall. ms. H. 18, where it is identified as "ex Soranae
Civitatis Ecclesiasticis Monumentis." An Italian translation appeared as Gasparo Spitilli, *Vita
di S. Domenico da Fuligno, Abbate dell'Ordine di S. Benedetto* (Rome: Luigi Zannetti, 1604).
The first Latin edition appeared only in the *Sora Life*.

25. Two generic hymns on Dominic, allegedly found in an eleventh-century Monte Cassino breviary, are edited in Guido Maria Dreves, *Hymni Inediti: Liturgische Hymnen des Mittelalters*, 7 vols., Analecta Hymnica Medii Aevi 4, 11–12, 19, 22–23, and 43 (of 55 total vols.)
(Leipzig: O. R. Reisland, 1886–1922), 5 (or 22) : 83–84. Three more are found in J. Paul Getty
Museum ms. IX 1 (formerly Monte Cassino ms. 199), a manuscript probably written at Monte
Cassino in 1153. Editions of this group of hymns on Dominic, all but the last based on early
modern transcripts rather than on Monte Cassino ms. 199, are Mauro Inguanez, "Inni inediti
di Alberico ed il codice Cassinese 199," *Bullettino dell'ISIME e Archivio Muratori* 47 (1932):
191–98; Lentini, "Su tre inni in onore di S. Domenico Abate," *Benedictina* 5 (1951): 185–99;
and now Franklin, "Restored *Life and Miracles*," 340–45. The manuscript attributes at least
the first of these to Alberic.

26. *BHL* 2243 is known through the hagiographical collections of Constantino Gaetani
(d. 1650), found in Jacobus de Voragine's *Summary*. The Bollandists footnoted readings from
this text in their edition of the *Trisulti Life*. Dolbeau, "Le dossier de saint Dominique," 31,
promises an edition. For an introduction to Jacobus's work, see William Granger Ryan, "Introduction," *Jacobus de Voragine: The Golden Legend, Readings on the Saints*, 2 vols. (Princeton, N.J.: Princeton University Press, 1993), 1 : xii–xviii.

These derivative texts are useful for historical reconstruction only insofar as they offer hints about the original readings of the primary texts, some of which survive only in late copies. Additional stories of Dominic's miracles, quite different from the literary tradition, were told at the little village of Cocullo in the high Apennines, where they were recorded in the early modern era—their status is problematic.[27] The arguments underlying all the textual interrelationships of Dominic's *lives* postulated here are set forth in Appendix A, "Dominic's Dossier."

To use such complex hagiographical material for historical reconstruction requires some methodological decisions. Disagreements among the texts of Dominic's surviving interrelated eleventh-century *lives* cannot be settled purely on the basis of literary priority, because they all have independent authority from lost texts and oral traditions. Conflicts have had to be resolved by using logic and/or extrinsic evidence; sometimes they could not be resolved. The several decades stretching between Dominic's career and the earliest surviving *lives* necessitate occasional caveats. Nevertheless, there are reasons for accepting the Dominic they describe as basically an image from the early eleventh century: (1) Dominic's earliest hagiographers would have hesitated to distort radically his reputation for sanctity, which had developed during his lifetime and was still witnessed by surviving contemporaries; (2) when particular hagiographers make their own personal contributions, these tend to be revealed by the discrepancies between their accounts and the parallel *lives*; and (3) the hagiographical Dominic seems to be at home in the world of the early eleventh century, since he fails to embody such High Gregorian concerns as ecclesiastical independence from secular powers and the centrality of canon law. Additional problems are posed by hagiographical commonplaces, which will be analyzed in Chapter 3, "Dominic's Holiness."

27. The earliest references to the Cocullo miracles are in Muzio Febbonio, *Historiae Marsorum: Libri Tres* (Naples: Apud Michaelum Monachum, 1678), 275–76; and in Francesco Tuzii, *Memorie istoriche massimamente sacre della Città di Sora* (Rome: Stamperia di Antonio de-'Rossi, 1727), 58–59. I have not seen a separately published pamphlet, the *Breve notizia del miracolossimo dente di S. Domenico . . . che si conserva nella terra di Cocullo* (1770?; reprint, Naples: Pansa, 1928), which is cited in Alfonso M. Di Nola, *Gli Aspetti magico-religiosi di una cultura subalterna italiana* (Torino: Boringheri, 1976), passim. Giuseppe Celidonio, *La Diocesi di Valva e Sulmona*, 4 vols. (Casalbordino: Casa Tipografica Editrice N. de Arcangelis, 1909–12), 2:98–102, retells the stories. So do eighteenth-century frescoes found in the porch of the chapel of San Domenico in the valley of the Sagittario, panels described in Thomas Ashby, *Some Italian Scenes and Festivals* (London: Methuen, 1929), 112–13. Some have been subsequently repainted, and it would be hazardous to guess what might be seen there today, since when I last visited in 1992 the chapel was "in restauro." Di Nola, ibid., 49–53, describes how the tooth and the muleshoe featured in these stories have become standard elements in Dominic's cult.

Orthography presents difficulties, not only because eleventh-century scribes spelled creatively, but also because their successors, struggling to read the obsolete Beneventan script of their exemplars, made things worse. In this book, personal names that have no universally accepted English spelling are given in Latin, standardized according to what appears to be the dominant spelling of the documents. The place and church names still identifiable today, unless they have a widely accepted English form, are given in Italian; if they cannot be identified, they appear in quotation marks in Latin. This procedure preserves the original names of people and places long gone, while avoiding archaisms involving places still extant. It also helps to distinguish personal from topographical references: for example, Dominic and Berardus were persons; San Domenico and San Berardo are ecclesiastical institutions bearing their names.

What might be learned by studying Dominic? First of all, the concreteness of early reform attempts. People of the tenth and eleventh centuries apprehended ideas and concepts primarily through things. In such a mental world, reform meant restoring lands, building churches, getting the clergy into distinctive costumes, celebrating better liturgies. Property donations did not precede reform, they *were* reform, the most literal possible re-formation of the countryside. If reform involves property as well as ideology, then it can be understood as part of the rebuilding of ecclesiastical institutions that was a natural consequence of Western Europe's tremendous expansion from the mid-tenth century on.

Dominic's story demonstrates the importance of charismatic figures in the early stages of this movement. Scholars who have identified reform with the revival of canon law or the search for pure observance of the Benedictine *Rule* give the impression that texts themselves started revolutions. On the contrary, Dominic's community was centered on him, not on any text. Teaching, as Scripture makes quite clear, can be by word or deed, and Dominic exemplified the latter, catching the popular imagination by his own personal rendition of holiness. He was not alone. A multitude of wandering holy men in the early eleventh century set the stage for the literate, legally oriented, hierarchical reforms of the later eleventh and early twelfth centuries that scholars have often seen as *the* Gregorian Reform.

The ironic aftermath of Dominic's career reveals the extraordinary importance of the communities that reforms such as his fostered. Reforms existed within social contexts, never independently. They were trapped by the very groups they helped create. The ad hoc crowd following a holy man gained identity, power, and purpose. *Castelli* could relate to each other by supporting a common foundation. Familial groups acquired more coherence when their members shared in the responsibilities and benefits of ecclesiastical patronage. Since all things tend toward entropy, these social lumps disintegrated if they were not institutionalized effectively. Yet, even when they were ephemeral, they could determine the course of events. Reform did not exist as an abstraction; for better and for worse, it was incarnated in groups of people.

I

Dominic's World

ITALY DECEIVES THE CASUAL TOURIST who sees the fields, gardens, or-chards, and vineyards surrounding Florence and Rome. These civilized landscapes are atypical pieces in a complex geographical mosaic. Dozens of distinct regions are cut off from each other by hills and mountains, Fernand Braudel's "impressive and demanding presences," part of the Mediterranean's encircling "high, wide, never-ending mountains."[1] The Alps tail off into the Maritime Alps, out of which emerge the Apennines, stretching southeast to flank the Valley of the Po and then extending down the peninsula. Through Tuscany and Umbria they are often pleasant roll-ing hills, but in central Italy the mountains widen as the Italian boot nar-rows, leaving little room for hill country or coastal plain. Here is the Abruzzi, "the highest, widest, and wildest part of the Apennines."[2] Even today, only seventy-five miles east of Rome, there are still bears and wolves.

Dominic and his patrons helped reshape this central Italian landscape, but ultimately it shaped them far more. They had to struggle to prosper, to communicate, sometimes even to survive. They never completely tran-scended its intricate, often harsh geography. Lazio and the Abruzzi are transversed by a series of limestone uplifts. The ridge line is closer to the eastern shore of the Italian peninsula, marginalizing the Adriatic coast. De-pressions at Rieti, L'Aquila, the former Lago Fucino, and Sulmona form broad, isolated valleys with their own inverted weather. Major faults run from the northwest to the southeast, providing channels for swift-flowing rivers such as the Aniene and the Liri. By Mediterranean standards water is relatively plentiful, retained by the local limestone and released gradually through a multitude of springs. Otherwise this is a land of extremes, of

1. Quotation from Fernand Braudel, *The Mediterranean and the Mediterranean World in the Age of Philip II*, 2 vols., trans. Siân Reynolds (New York: Harper & Row, Publishers, 1972), 1:26. Fuller detail in John Robert McNeill, *The Mountains of the Mediterranean World: An Environmental History* (New York: Cambridge University Press, 1992), esp. 13–14.

2. Braudel, *Mediterranean*, 1:40.

severe winters and hot summers, of rivers that flood or trickle. The heights still reveal distinct ecological zones: oak and mixed growth from about 1,500 to 3,200 feet, beech from about 3,200 to 5,200 feet, and rocky high pasture above. Now, however, the woodland survives only in patches, and the lower slopes are often overrun by *macchia*, the scrubby tangles of holm oak, laurel, chestnut, and wild myrtle analogous to the drought-resistant vegetation that Americans call "chaparral." Good farmland, rare today, was rarer still in the Middle Ages. Then the river valleys, whose heavy bottom-lands are now valued highly, were accumulating new fill and becoming marshier. Farmers preferred small, well-drained hillside terraces, located above the malarial lowlands, where they could mix plots of grain, fruit trees, vineyards, and gardens. People were scarce; farms and villages small and relatively isolated.[3]

Rome was the only major city. Even during its tenth-century nadir, poets still hailed "Noble Rome" as "Queen of the world, greatest of all cities."[4] Its bishops, Italy's largest landholders, had income from a vast system of outlying estates. They continually built and rebuilt major churches, palaces, and fortifications. Although Rome's ancient churches no longer corresponded to actual needs in their sizes and locations, those that were superfluous were maintained by monastic communities. Other buildings were continually recycled by a much-reduced population whose center of gravity had shifted west toward the Vatican. There were gardens and vineyards among the ruins. Noble families dominated not only the urban areas surrounding their fortified residences but also regional power bases beyond the city walls.[5]

3. The geographical features of southeastern Lazio are described in Toubert, *Structures*, 1:135–98; those of the Abruzzi in Jean Démangeot, *Géomorphologie des Abruzzes adriatiques*, Centre de recherches et documentation cartographiques et géographiques, Mémoires et documents (Paris: Éditions du Centre national de la recherche scientifique, 1965), esp. 11–14. On recent geological changes, see Claudio Vita-Finzi, *The Mediterranean Valleys: Geological Changes in Historical Times* (Cambridge: Cambridge University Press, 1969), esp. 101–3, 107–8, 114–15, 119–20; and McNeill, *Mountains of the Mediterranean World*, 72–74, 84–93, 272–76.

4. The tenth-century panegyric "O Roma Nobilis" is edited in F. J. E. Raby, *A History of Secular Latin Poetry in the Middle Ages*, 2 vols., 2nd ed. (Oxford: Clarendon Press, 1957), 1: 291. Contemporary images of Rome are discussed in Tellenbach, "Die Stadt Rom in der Sicht ausländischer Zeitgenossen (800–1200)," *Saeculum* 24 (1973): 1–40, reprinted in his *Ausgewählte Abhandlungen*, 1:265–340; and in Rudolf Schieffer, "Mauern, Kirchen und Türme: Zum Erscheinungsbild Roms bei deutschen Geschichtsschreibern des 10. bis 12. Jahrhunderts," in *Rom im hohen Mittelalter*, 129–37.

5. The physical plant of early medieval Rome is described in Richard Krautheimer, *Rome: Profile of a City, 312–1308* (Princeton, N.J.: Princeton University Press, 1980); Étienne Hubert, *Espace urbain et habitat à Rome du Xe siècle à la fin du XIIIe siècle*, Collection de l'École

Outside Rome, the most powerful communities were monastic corporations: Subiaco, Monte Cassino, San Vincenzo al Volturno, Farfa, and others. These were built out of and usually on antique ruins. They were nearly cities themselves. By the end of the ninth century, Farfa's multitowered walls contained a palace for imperial visits, an elaborate monastic cloister, five subsidiary churches, and a grand basilica roofed with lead and boasting an onyx baldacchino over the high altar.[6] San Vincenzo al Volturno had eight churches constructed or rebuilt within its monastic precincts between 792 and 856, among them a large, triple-aisled basilica anchoring a complex that evoked the classical world through fresco work, inscriptions, and Roman spoils.[7] The great monasteries controlled networks of estates donated by Lombard and Carolingian rulers and aristocrats. Farfa under Abbot Peter (890?–920?) possessed not only its territorial core in the Sabina but also churches and farms scattered from Milan to the Abruzzi, a section of Rome which included the whole area now covered by the Piazza Navona and the Palazzo Madama, and even a

---

française de Rome 135 (Rome: École Française de Rome, 1990); and Veronica Ortenberg, "Archbishop Sigeric's Journey to Rome in 990," *Anglo-Saxon England* 19 (1990): 197–246, esp. 208–28. On the use and reuse of Roman buildings, see Bryan Ward-Perkins, *From Classical Antiquity to the Middle Ages: Urban Public Building in Northern and Central Italy, AD 300–850* (Oxford: Oxford University Press, 1984), 203–29. Papal estates are described in Peter Partner, *The Lands of St. Peter: The Papal State in the Middle Ages and the Early Renaissance* (Berkeley: University of California Press, 1972), 6–9, 35–36.

6. Sicard of Farfa, *Libellus Constructionis Farfensis*, edited in *Il Chronicon Farfense di Gregorio di Catino; precedono la "Constructio Farfensis" e gli scritti di Ugo di Farfa*, ed. Ugo Balzani, 2 vols., FSI 33–34 (Rome: ISIME, 1903), 1:3–23; Hugh of Farfa, *Destructio Monasterii Farfensis*, edited in *Chron. Farf.*, 1:28–31. On the remains of the ninth-century construction, see Peter Donaldson, Charles McClendon, and David Whitehouse, "L'Abbazia di Farfa: Rapporto preliminare sugli scavi 1978–80," *Archivio della SRSP* 103 (1980): 5–12; and Charles B. McClendon, *The Imperial Abbey of Farfa: Architectural Currents of the Early Middle Ages* (New Haven, Conn.: Yale University Press, 1987), 54–75, esp. 74.

7. Angelo Pantoni, *Le Chiese e gli edifici del monastero di San Vincenzo al Volturno*, MC 40 (Monte Cassino: Abbazia di Montecassino, 1980), 18–21; *Una grande abbazia altomedievale nel Molise: San Vincenzo al Volturno. Atti del I Convegno di studi sul medioevo meridionale (Venafro-San Vincenzo al Volturno, 19–22 maggio 1982)*, MC 51 (Monte Cassino: Abbazia di Montecassino, 1985), 205–7, 218–19; *San Vincenzo al Volturno: The Archaeology, Art and Territory of an Early Medieval Monastery*, ed. Richard Hodges and John Mitchell, British Archeological Reports International Series 252 (London: B. A. R., 1985), 1–2, 12–15, 27, 125; Mitchell, "Literacy Displayed: The Use of Inscriptions at the Monastery of San Vincenzo al Volturno in the Early Ninth Century," in *The Uses of Literacy in Early Medieval Europe*, ed. Rosamond McKitterick (New York: Cambridge University Press, 1990), 186–225; Hodges, Catherine Coutts, and Mitchell, "San Vincenzo al Volturno," *Current Archaeology* 12 (1994): 244–50; Richard Hodges, "In the Shadow of Pirenne: San Vincenzo al Volturno and the Revival of Mediterranean Commerce," in *La Storia dell'Alto Medioevo italiano (VI–X secolo) alla luce dell'archeologia: Convegno Internazionale (Siena, 2–6 dicembre 1992)*, ed. Riccardo Francovich and Ghislaine Noyé (Florence: Edizioni All'Insegna del Giglio, 1994), 112–16 and 123.

ship exempted from port fees by the emperor.[8] San Vincenzo had a block of land that included the whole upper valley of the Volturno.[9] Subiaco had the upper valley of the Aniene.[10] The heart of Monte Cassino's *Terra Sancti Benedicti* consisted of about 200,000 acres stretching from the mouth of the Garigliano to today's Parco Nazionale d'Abruzzo.[11]

The Latin word *curtis* is used to designate the manorial unit that organized these lands. The *curtes* differed from ideal transalpine manors in that they lacked regular labor services and neat divisions between demesne lands and private plots. Even the greatest tended to be sprawling agglomerations of small fields and orchards. Vineyards were so common, in fact or in wishful imagination, that they appear in more than 85 percent of Farfa's eighth- and ninth-century property descriptions. Despite sparse populations and diffused settlement patterns, the *curtes* were coherent administrative and economic complexes centered on churches, workshops, and other structures. Their names were used by notaries to describe surrounding territories. They dominated the rural Italian landscape until the disruptions that began in the late ninth century.[12]

8. Ildefonso Schuster, "L'Abbate Ugo I e la riforma di Farfa nel secolo XI (998–1030)," *Bollettino della Regia Deputazione di Storia Patria per l'Umbria* 16 (1910): 615; *L' imperiale Abbazia di Farfa: Contributo alla storia del ducato romano nel medio evo* (Rome: Tipografia Poliglotta Vaticana, 1921), 144; Richard Raymond Ring, "The Lands of Farfa: Studies in Lombard and Carolingian Italy," Ph.D. dissertation, University of Wisconsin, 1972, 67, 124–25; Isa Lori Sanfilippo, "I possessi romani di Farfa, Montecassino e Subiaco–secoli IX–XII," *Achivio della SRSP* 103 (1980): 14–21; Hubert, *Espace urbain et habitat à Rome*, 161, 182–84.

9. Chris Wickham, *Il problema dell'incastellamento nell'Italia centrale: L'esempio di San Vincenzo al Volturno*, Studi sullà Società degli Appennini nell'Alto Medioevo 2, Quaderni dell'insegnamento di archeologia medievale della Facoltà di lettere e filosofia dell'Università di Siena (Florence: Edizioni all'Insegna del Giglio, 1985), 12–16, which is partially published in English as "The *Terra* of San Vincenzo al Volturno in the Eighth to Twelfth Centuries: The Historical Framework," in *San Vincenzo al Volturno*, ed. Hodges and Mitchell, 227–58.

10. Wickham, *Il problema dell'incastellamento*, 53–54.

11. Luigi Fabiani, *La Terra di S. Benedetto: Studio storico-giuridico sull'Abbazia di Montecassino dall'VIII al XIII secolo*, 3 vols., MC 33, 34, and 42 (Monte Cassino: Badia di Montecassino, 1968–1980), 1:3–23. Herbert Bloch, *Monte Cassino in the Middle Ages*, 3 vols. (Rome: Edizioni di Storia e Letteratura/Cambridge, Mass.: Harvard University Press, 1986), describes Monte Cassino's dependencies.

12. On the *curtis* system in general, see Toubert, "Il sistema curtense: La produzione e lo scambio interno in Italia nel secoli VIII, IX e X," *Storia d'Italia. Annali 6: Economia naturale, economia monetaria* (Turin: Einaudi, 1983), 5–63, reprinted with the same pagination in Toubert, *Histoire du haut moyen âge et de l'Italie médiévale* (London: Variorum Reprints, 1987); Bruno Andreolli and Massimo Montanari, *L'Azienda curtense in Italia: Proprietà della terra e lavoro contadino nei secoli VIII–XI*, Biblioteca di storia agraria medievale 1 (Bologna: Editrice CLUEB, 1985); Toubert, "L'assetto territoriale ed economico dei territori longobardi: Il ruolo delle grandi abbazie," in *Montecassino dalla prima alla seconda distruzione: Momenti e aspetti di storia cassinese (secc. VI–IX). Atti del II Convegno di studi sul medioevo meridionale (Cassino–Montecassino, 27–31 maggio 1984)*, ed. Faustino Avagliano, MC 55 (Monte Cassino: Abbazia di Montecassino, 1987), 280–95; and Ross Balzaretti, "The Curtis,

As the ability to administer the far-flung *curtes* demonstrates, the ancient infrastructure still functioned. Roman roads survived, although with minor adjustments in some routes. They carried what commerce existed. They were followed by clerks of all types, from monastic estate managers to exalted prelates seeking *pallia* and privileges. Along them marched armies of invaders, domestic and foreign. Most frequent were crowds of pilgrims visiting a network of local and international shrines unparalleled in Western Europe.[13]

Early medieval Italy possessed a surprising amount of central government. Lombard kings had abundant lands and resources, granted by dukes whose infatuation with independence had been cooled by a decade of kinglessness. Pavia's law codes, courts, tax collectors, and archives made it Western Europe's most advanced secular bureaucratic capital (at least after Toledo had fallen to Islam). Below the level of the royal court, the political structures were more nebulous. In each region the multiple, interlocking civil, military, and ecclesiastical systems of antiquity were gradually being replaced by individual lords. Power, which derived from control over land and the soldiers it could support, ultimately resided in those who could establish regional territorial dominance, be they dukes, gastalds (originally royal estate managers), or even bishops who had managed to maintain or regain control over their cities. Charlemagne, after taking the iron crown of Lombardy in 774, built upon the institutions he found. Although he imposed a Frankish military network of nonurban counts and marquesses, he also regularized Lombard authorities. Franks usually received vacant secular posts; the older elites retained most lands and bishoprics.

It must be granted that the first Carolingian kings of Italy were eminently forgettable: Charlemagne crowned his four-year-old son Pippin (781–810), whose death led to another regency for Pippin's son Bernard (812–17); Bernard's revolt left the kingdom to Emperor Lothar (817–55), who was primarily interested in transalpine politics. Yet an absence of monarchical interference may actually have benefitted the legal system. The

---

the Archaeology of Sites of Power," in *La Storia dell'Alto Medioevo italiano*, 99–108. For a concise attempt at definition, see Giovanni Tabacco, *The Struggle for Power in Medieval Italy: Structures of Political Rule*, trans. Rosalind Brown Jensen, Cambridge Medieval Textbooks (New York: Cambridge University Press, 1989), 132–33. Toubert, *Structures*, 1:303–5, 450–73, emphasizes how little is known about agriculture in early medieval Lazio in particular, since few documents survive except from Farfa. The percentage of vineyards found in early Farfa documents is taken from Ring, "The Lands of Farfa," 86–90.

13. Toubert, *Structures*, 1:626–31 and 651–57 describes the road network and the traffic it carried.

state remained so strong that when Charlemagne's great-grandson Emperor Louis II (850–75) did offer dedicated resident leadership, he was able to create a major new imperial monastery (Casauria), repel invaders, and threaten to extend Carolingian power into southern Italy. What broke royal authority was his death without a direct heir, leaving the kings of France and Germany, Louis's two uncles, with equal claims on the Italian crown, and thus leaving Italy almost a century of wars of succession.[14]

Early in the ninth century, Muslim raids began. The independent city states on the shores of Campania—Gaeta, Naples, Amalfi, and Salerno—had routinely traded with Islamic merchants and pirates. Naples used Muslim mercenaries in the 830s, and perhaps in the 820s. Soon Islamic bands in close touch with their cohorts in North Africa, Sicily, and Sardinia became regular features of the southern Italian world. Their full-scale military expeditions captured Taranto, Bari, and the suburbs of Rome itself, ransacking St. Peter's basilica in 846 and destroying the apostle's tomb. Christian Italy fought back: by 852 Leo IV had surrounded the Vatican with the impressive Leonine walls; in 871 Louis II, nineteen years after his first attempt, led the alliance that successfully retook Bari; in 880 the Byzantines regained Taranto; then even Naples was briefly coerced into an anti-

14. The reputation of Lombard and Carolingian central institutions has been rehabilitated to a considerable extent by Tabacco in studies synthesized in *Struggle for Power in Medieval Italy*, and by Wickham, most notably in *Early Medieval Italy: Central Power and Local Society, 400–1000* (1981; reprint, Ann Arbor: University of Michigan Press, 1989), esp. 47–63, but also in "Land Disputes and Their Social Framework in Lombard-Carolingian Italy, 700–900," in *The Settlement of Disputes in Early Medieval Europe*, ed. Wendy Davies and Paul Fouracre (Cambridge: Cambridge University Press, 1986), esp. 112. The problems involved in fitting Carolingian comital institutions into the preexisting Italian order are elucidated in Paolo Delogu, "L'istituzione comitale nell'Italia carolingia (Ricerche sull'aristocrazia carolingia in Italia, I)," *Bullettino dell'ISIME e Archivio Muratoriano* 79 (1968): 53–114; and "Strutture politiche ideologia nel regno di Lodovico II (Ricerche sull'aristocrazia carolingia in Italia, II)," *Bullettino dell'ISIME e Archivio Muratoriano* 80 (1969): 137–89, who emphasizes the personal bases of Carolingian power more than Tabacco and Wickham do. On Carolingian administration in Italy, see Antonio Sennis, "Potere centrale e forze locali in un territorio di frontiera: La Marsica tra i secoli VIII e XII," *Bullettino dell'ISIME e Archivio Muratoriano* 99 (1994): 15–17. On Frankish domination of the aristocracy, see Eduard Hlawitschka, *Franken, Alemannen, Bayern und Burgunder in Oberitalien (774–962): Zum Verständnis der fränkischen Königsherrschaft in Italien*, Forschungen zur Oberrheinischen Landesgeschichte 8 (Freiburg im Breisgau: Eberhard Albert Verlag, 1960), esp. 74. Wickham, *Early Medieval Italy*, 168–81, surveys post-Carolingian struggles for the crown. On the sophistication of the legal system, see Charles M. Radding, *The Origins of Medieval Jurisprudence, Pavia and Bologna 850–1150* (New Haven, Conn.: Yale University Press, 1988), 20, 26, 37–86; and François Bougard, *La Justice dans le Royaume d'Italie de la fin du VIIIe siècle au début du XIe siècle*, Bibliothèque des Écoles françaises d'Athènes et de Rome 291 (Rome: École française de Rome, 1995).

Saracenic league. Yet, after the loss of their urban bases, the Muslim bands became even more mobile and dangerous. In 881 they sacked San Vincenzo al Volturno, leaving its surviving monks to a thirty-three-year Capuan exile. In September of 883, Muslims operating out of a camp at the mouth of the Garigliano destroyed Saint Benedict's monastery on Monte Cassino; its monks then dwelt in San Salvatore, at the base of the mountain, until it fell in October of the same year to Muslim marauders who murdered the aged Abbot Bertharius at the high altar. The remaining monks retreated to their cell in Teano; in 914 they moved to Capua, after electing a well-connected archdeacon from that city as their abbot. Farfa defended its monastic complex for seven years, but by 897 Abbot Peter, recognizing that its position was untenable if it could not secure its estates, dispersed his monks, treasures, and books to Rome, Rieti, and the *castello* of Santa Vittoria in Matenano (diocese of Fermo, in the Marches). Farfa became a temporary Muslim redoubt until one night, while its occupiers were away, some Christian scavengers accidentally burnt it down. The strongest Muslim band, the one controlling the Garigliano, became so entrenched that it took a combined force of papal, Byzantine, Campanian, and Spoletan contingents to annihilate it in 915.[15]

Another menace was the Magyars from Hungary. They encountered little organized opposition after they destroyed, in a battle on the Brenta in 899, what the Venetian chronicler John the Deacon claimed was a 50,000-man royal army. Their most famous depredations were in the Po

---

15. General accounts of the Muslim raids in southern Italy in the ninth and tenth centuries include Nicola Cilento, "I Saraceni nell'Italia meridionale nei secoli IX e X," *Archivio storico per le province napoletane* 77 [n.s. 38] (1959): 109–22, lightly retouched as "Le incursioni saraceniche nell'Italia meridionale," in *Italia meridionale longobarda*, 2nd ed. (Milan/Naples: Riccardo Ricciardi Editore, 1971), 175–89; Partner, *The Lands of St. Peter*, 50–82; and Barbara Kreutz, *Before the Normans: Southern Italy in the Ninth and Tenth Centuries*, Middle Ages Series (Philadelphia: University of Pennsylvania Press, 1991), 18–62, 75–79. For the revised chronology placing the beginning of these raids earlier than the mid-830s, see Paolo Bertolini, "La serie episcopale napoletana nei secoli VIII e IX: Ricerche sulle fonti per la storia dell'Italia meridionale nell'alto medio evo," *Rivista di storia della Chiesa in Italia* 24 (1970): 439–40. Armand O. Citarella sketches the economic context in "The Relations of Amalfi with the Arab World before the Crusades," *Speculum* 42 (1967): 299–312, and details the background of the fall of Monte Cassino in "The Political Chaos in Southern Italy and the Arab Destruction of Monte Cassino in 883," in *Montecassino dalla prima alla seconda distruzione*, 163–80. On the destruction of the tomb of St. Peter and on Roman responses to this catastrophe, see Federico Marazzi, "Le 'città nuove' pontificie e l'insediamento laziale nel IX secolo," in *La Storia dell'Alto Medioevo italiano*, 252–68. The major document on the Garigliano battle of 915 is a charter edited and analyzed in Otto Vehse, "Das Bündnis gegen die Sarazenen vom Jahre 915," *QFIAB* 19 (1927): 181–204.

Valley, but at various times they also attacked Tuscany, the suburbs of Rome, and even Apulia. Since their goal was booty, they kept to the Roman roads, the better to cart things home. Although Italy offers no definite evidence that the Magyars ever conquered a defended city, no archeological traces of their artifacts, and few toponymic indications of their passing, they certainly contributed to a widespread sense of insecurity.[16]

According to the laments of Italian chroniclers, the destruction was total. Saracens "completely depopulated Calabria" as well as "the regions of Naples, Benevento, and Capua"; "they depopulated nearly all the cities of Apulia, and mowed down all the men who had grown up in the fields," until "not only the monastery [of Monte Cassino] but all the plains around it were so deserted because of the assaults of the Saracens that only a rare man—or no man at all—could be found there who would give due allegiance to the monks." At San Vincenzo al Vulturno, 900 monks were allegedly killed, like the martyrs of the Theban legion, and in its possessions there was "no dwelling place of man, but everything was the possession of beasts . . . you would see cities deserted, churches destroyed, and the whole earth soaked with the blood of Christians, nor was there any refuge by flight since slaughter was likewise carried to the mountains and hills. People were thinking that the end of the world had already arrived."[17]

Close reading of such descriptions reveals hyperbole. For example, it is hard to accept literally the Salernitan chronicler's account of how Amalfi had been captured by Salerno, and "depopulated . . . and everything

16. Scholars debate the severity of the Hungarian raids. The catastrophic view is preeminently championed by Gina Fasoli in studies that include *Le incursioni ungare in Europa nel secolo X*, Biblioteca storica Sansoni, n.s. 12 (Florence: G. C. Sansoni, 1945), esp. 224; "Points de vue sur les incursions hongroises en Europe au Xe siècle," *Cahiers de civilisation médiévale, Xe–XIIe siècles* 2 (1959): 17–35, esp. 24–26; and "Encore des Hongrois?" *Cahiers de civilisation médiévale, Xe–XIIe siècles* 5 (1962): 461–62. A revisionist approach, involving a more skeptical attitude toward the sources, is exemplified in Albert d'Haenens, "Les incursions hongroises dans l'espace belge," *Cahiers de civilisation médiévale, Xe–XIIe siècles* 4 (1961): 423–40; and Aldo A. Settia, "Gli Ungari in Italia e i mutamenti territoriali fra VIII e X secolo," in *Magistra Barbaritas: I barbari in Italia*, ed. Giovanni Pugliese Carratelli (Garzanti: Scheiwiller, 1984), 185–218 (Settia includes a bibliography on the Hungarian raids in Italy). On the psychological impact of the Hungarians, see Fasoli, "Unni, Avari e Ungari nelle fonti occidentali e nella storia dei paesi d'Occidente," in *Il Secolo di ferro: Mito e realtà del secolo X, 19–25 aprile 1990*, 2 vols., Settimane di studio del CISAM 38 (Spoleto: CISAM, 1991), 1:32–43.

17. Erchempert, *Historia Langobardorum Beneventanorum* xxxv, ed. Georg Waitz, MGH *SS Rerum Langobardorum et Italicarum, Saeculi VI–IX* (Hannover: Hahnsche Buchhandlung, 1878), 248; *Chron. Salern.* lxxx, 79; *Chron. Cass.* II i, 166; *Chron. Vult.*, 1:359, 362, 368, 370.

around it depopulated," since the next few lines describe the attempts made by the prince of Salerno to promote intermarriage between the peoples of the two cities. The Monte Cassino chronicler's claim that the Hungarians were "burning and depopulating everything in the region of the Marsi" is similarly suspicious, given that the Marsi successfully attacked the baggage train of those same Hungarians on their way home.[18] Archeological investigations document damage,[19] but even the Duchy of Gaeta, the harassed western neighbor of the Garigliano Muslims, still had most of its preinvasion settlements in place after 915.[20] Perhaps the chroniclers are especially apocalyptic because the raiders hit their monasteries hardest. The great rural houses were destroyed, their monks dispersed, their *curtes* lost to monastic control.

The most significant damage may have been psychological. Today's historians, blessed with excellent hindsight, know that after 915 "the Arab peril in central Italy was past" and that after Otto I's victory at the Lechfeld in 955 there was "no great threat from the East."[21] Contemporaries had no such confidence. Salerno's late-tenth-century chronicle offers no hint that Muslim raids are over. Liutprand of Cremona (d. 972), who begins his *Antipodasis* with an account of the Saracen devastation at La Garde-Freinet, is anxious about hostile neighbors in all his literary works.[22] The same fears animated Rodulfus Glaber, who in a section of his *Histories* revised in the late 1030s still awaits the next Muslim onslaught.[23] In fact, North African rulers did continue to support piracy and raids on the "Land of Rome" until Pisan counterattacks finally overwhelmed them in the late eleventh

18. *Chron. Salern.* lxxiv, 73: *Chron. Cass.* I lv, 141–42.

19. Hodges, "The San Vincenzo Project: Preliminary Review of the Excavation and Surveys at San Vincenzo al Volturno and in Its *Terra*," in *Castrum 2: Structures de l'habitat et occupation du sol dans les pays méditerranéens: Les méthodes et l'apport de l'archéologie extensive,* ed. Ghislaine Noyé, Collection de l'École française de Rome 105; Publications de la Casa Velázquez, sér. arch. 9 (Rome: École française, 1988), 425.

20. Jean François Guiraud, "Le réseau de peuplement dans le Duché de Gaete du Xe au XIIIe siècle," *Mélanges de l'École française de Rome: Moyen âge–temps modernes* 94 (1982): 497–98.

21. Partner, *Lands of St. Peter,* 82; R. W. Southern, *The Making of the Middle Ages* (New Haven, Conn.: Yale University Press, 1953), 25.

22. Karl J. Leyser, "Ends and Means in Liutprand of Cremona," *Byzantinische Forschungen* 13 (1988): 119–43, esp. 143.

23. Rodulfus Glaber, *Historiarum Libri Quinque* I v, ed. and trans. John France as *Rodulfi Glabri Historiarum Libri Quinque,* Oxford Medieval Texts (Oxford: Clarendon, 1989), 33–47; or ed. and trans. Guglielmo Cavallo and Giovanni Orlandi, as *Rodolfo il Glabro: Cronache dell'Anno Mille,* 3rd ed., Scrittore Greci e Latini (Milan: Fondazione Lorenzo Valla, 1991), 39–53. Note also France, "War and Christendom in the Thought of Rodulfus Glaber," *Studia Monastica* 30 (1989): 105–19, esp. 109–10 and 113.

century.[24] The result was a lethal legacy—the crusades would be created by Italian popes.[25]

Northern Europeans responded to barbarian attacks by building internal fortifications, especially castles, that is, fortified lordly residences. In Mediterranean Europe people built *castelli* (in Latin, *castra*), fortified set-

24. Overviews can be found in Hilmar C. Krueger, "The Italian Cities and the Arabs before 1095," in *A History of the Crusades*, ed. Kenneth M. Setton, 6 vols. (Madison: University of Wisconsin Press, 1969–89), 1:40–53; Cowdrey, "The Mahdia Campaign of 1087," *The English Historical Review* 92 (1977): 8–9, reprinted with the same pagination in *Popes, Monks, and Crusaders* (London: The Hambledon Press, 1984); and Giuseppe Scalia, "Contributi pisani alla lotta anti-islamica nel Mediterraneo centro-occidentale durante il secolo XI e nei primi decenni del XII," in *Actas del Primo congreso internacional de historia mediteranea*, published in a special issue of *Anuario de Estudios Medievales* 10 (1980): 135–44.

25. The 1095 call to battle given by Urban II to his fellow Franks was actually the logical culmination of initiatives taken by his Italian predecessors:

Leo IV (847–55), in the aftermath of the Muslim sack of Saint Peter's, pledged a heavenly reward to Franks killed in battle (*PL* 115:656–57 and 161:720).

On the spiritual rewards that John VIII (872–82) promised to opponents of the Saracens, see Kenneth Baxter Wolf, *Making History: The Normans and Their Historians in Eleventh-Century Italy* (Philadelphia: University of Pennsylvania Press, 1995), 64–65.

Sergius IV (1009–12), following the destruction of the Church of the Holy Sepulchre in Jerusalem, participated in a crusading project memorialized in an altered bull, ed. Harald Zimmermann, *Papsturkunden 896–1046*, 3 vols., Österreichische Akademie der Wissenschaften, Philosophisch-historische Klasse, Denschriften 174, 177 and 198 (Vienna: Verlag der Österreichische Akademie der Wissenschaften, 1984–89), 2:845–48. On the problems connected with this document, the authenticity of which has been repeatedly challenged and defended, see Carl Erdmann, *The Origin of the Idea of Crusade*, ed. Marshall W. Baldwin and Walter Goffart (Princeton, N.J.: Princeton University Press, 1977), 113–16, esp. 113n; Hans Martin Schaller, "Zur Kreuzzugsenzyklika Papst Sergius' IV," *Papsttum, Kirche und Recht im Mittelalter. Festschrift für Horst Fuhrmann zum 65. Geburtstag*, ed. Hubert Mordek (Tübingen: Max Niemeyer Verlag, 1991), 135–53; and Marcus Bull, *Knightly Piety and Lay Response to the First Crusade: The Limousin and Gascony, c. 970–c. 1130* (Oxford: Clarendon Press, 1993), 64–66.

Benedict VIII in 1016 promised divine aid to soldiers who would defend Luni against Muslim attack, an incident recorded in Thietmar, *Chronicon* VII xlv, ed. Robert Holtzmann, MGH *SS Rerum Germanicarum* n.s. 9 (1935, reprint, Munich: MGH, 1980), 452–55.

Alexander II in 1063 and subsequent popes promised to commute the penances, and pardon the sins, of men who would fight the Muslims in Spain. See Erdmann, *Origin of . . . Crusade*, 138–39n; and Giovanna Petti Balbi, "Lotte antisaracene e 'militia Christi' in ambito iberico," in *'Militia Christi' e Crociata nei secoli XI–XIII: Atti della undecima Settimana internazionale di studio, Mendola, 28 agosto–1 settembre 1989*, Miscellanea del Centro di Studi Medioevali 13 (Milan: Vita e Pensiero, 1992), 519–49. For an unconvincing attempt at minimizing the influence of the Spanish theater on the development of crusade ideology, see Bull, *Knightly Piety*, 70–114.

The Norman campaigns in Sicily were interpreted in crusade terms, at least according to later sources described in Wolf, *Making History*, 106–9.

Gregory VII in 1074 proposed a military expedition against the Turks. See Erdmann, *Origin of . . . Crusade*, 164–69; Cowdrey, "Pope Gregory VII's 'Crusading' Plans of 1074," *Outremer: Studies in the History of the Crusading Kingdom of Jerusalem Presented to Joshua Prawer*, ed. Benjamin Z. Kedar, Hans Eberhard Mayer, and R. C. Smail (Jerusalem: Yad Izhak Ben-Zvi Institute, 1982), 27–40; reprinted with the same pagination in *Popes, Monks, and Crusaders*.

The role played by Victor III in the Pisan/Genoese expedition against Mahdia on the coast of Tunisia is treated in Cowdrey, "The Mahdia Campaign," 1–29, esp. 4, 6, and 17–18.

tlements for large numbers. These were located on naturally defensible hill-top sites, protected by rough stone walls, and sometimes provided with a second fortified level, a house for the lord or his agent. The surviving records suggest that the *castelli* were pioneered by the great monasteries, often in partnership with lay magnates. By the end of the eleventh century, Monte Cassino had about forty, Subiaco thirty, Farfa sixty.[26] By then the scattered households of the *curtes* had been replaced by the tightly defined hilltop communities that still dominate the central Italian countryside. English-speaking medievalists, groping for a word analogous to the Italian "*incastellamento*," have dubbed this process "encastellation."

Was encastellation a military response to foreign invaders? So thought medieval writers.[27] So also thought most contemporary historians up until the mid-1950s, when Mario Del Treppo, on the basis of the incomparable San Vincenzo resettlement records, began to stress other aspects of encas-tellation, tying it to repopulation, land clearing, and more intensive culti-vation. He claimed that, insofar as encastellation was a military measure, it was aimed not against foreign invaders but against aggressive lay lords.[28] Pierre Toubert went further, and, dismissing military considerations al-most entirely, treated encastellation as a means of seignorial exploitation of the peasants, emphasizing that there was no clear chronological cor-relation between real external military threats and the encastellation of particular regions (which often occurred much later).[29] After subsequent debate he retreated slightly, acknowledging that the original purpose of the fortified settlements was to protect the lands of the *curtes*, admitting that he may have overreacted against traditional military explanations.[30]

26. The statistics on monastic ownership of *castelli* are from Toubert, "Pour une histoire de l'environnement économique et social du Mont-Cassin (IXe–XIIe siècles)," in *Comptes rendus de l'Académie des Inscriptions et Belles-Lettres, nov.–déc. 1976* (Paris: Académie des In-scriptions et Belles-Lettres, 1976), 698; reprinted with the same pagination in *Histoire du haut moyen âge et de l'Italie médiévale* (London: Variorum Reprints, 1987).

27. *Chron. Vult.* I, 1:231.

28. Mario Del Treppo, "La Vita economica e sociale in una grande abbazia del Mez-zogiorno: San Vincenzo al Volturno nell'alto medioevo," *Archivio storico per le province na-poletane* n.s. 35 (1955), 31–110, excerpts reprinted as "Frazionamento dell'unità curtense, incas-tellamento e formazioni signorili sui beni dell'abbazia di San Vincenzo al Volturno tra X e XI secolo," in *Forme di potere e struttura sociale in Italia nel Medioevo*, ed. Gabriella Rossetti (Bologna: Società Editrice il Mulino, 1977), 285–304.

29. Toubert, *Structures*, passim, esp. 1:330–38 and 367.

30. Toubert, "Pour une histoire de l'environnement économique . . . du Mont-Cassin," 698, reprinted with the same pagination in *Histoire du Haut Moyen Age*; "Les destinées d'un thème historiographique: 'Castelli' et peuplement dans l'Italie médiévale," in *Flaran 1: Actes des premières journées internationales d'histoire de Flaran (Flaran, 20–22 septembre 1979)* (Auch: Comité départemental de tourisme du Gers, 1980), 25–26, reprinted with the same pagination in *Histoire du Haut Moyen Age*. For criticisms of his initial position, see Hoffmann,

Chris Wickham nuances the problem further by distinguishing between the military functions of the *castello*, which could have been served by a castle without concentrated settlement, and its economic functions, which encouraged group cohesion for land development. This dichotomy explains encastellation's regional diversity in terms of variations in the relative importance of military and economic factors.[31] Yet such distinctions may isolate the motives of the fortifiers better than they themselves could.

Perhaps there is still wisdom in the "external threat" explanations. Few things can better motivate people to modify traditional customs and accept expensive changes than an alleged menace from abroad. Preparing for the last war rather than the current one is an ancient tradition. Encastellation was certainly stimulated by fears of Muslim and Magyar invasions long after these had actually ceased. Then, once the process of fortification and resettlement was well underway, it would have taken on a life of its own as insecure proprietors attempted to counter their competitors' *castelli*.

Encastellation was the most important economic, military, and social development in Dominic's world. It enabled monasteries to reorganize and reclaim their estates. It gave power to those nobles who could take the lead in developing monastic and public lands. It increased population and prosperity. Toubert claims that "There is not the least doubt of the fact that the first encastellation signalled the beginning of the process of recovery, of the 'Renaissance of the Tenth Century.'"[32]

Yet encastellation proved to be a mixed blessing for the great monasteries, because their ability to control the process had been eroded by years of deleterious exile. The monks of Monte Cassino, according to a com-

"Der Kirchenstaat im hohen Mittelalter," *QFIAB* 57 (1977): 1–45, esp. 12–13, 42; and Giovanni Tabacco, rev. of Toubert, *Structures*, in *Studi medievali* 3rd ser., 15 (1974): 901–18, esp. 908–9.

31. Wickham, *Il problema dell'incastellamento . . . San Vincenzo al Volturno*, 25, 58, 61–71, and 82–86; *The Mountains and the City: The Tuscan Appennines in the Early Middle Ages* (Oxford: Clarendon Press, 1988), 303–6.

32. Toubert is quoted from "L'Assetto territoriale," 286. To gain some impression of scholarship on encastellation, note the series of conferences signaled in his introduction to *Castrum 3: Guerre, fortification et habitat dans le monde méditerranéen au moyen âge: Colloque organisé par la Casa de Velázquez et Madrid, 24–27 novembre 1985*, ed. André Bazzana, sér. arch. 12; Collection de l'École française de Rome 105 (Madrid: Casa de Velázquez, 1988); and his sketch of the debate in "L'Assetto territoriale," 276–95. Note also Wickham, "L'incastellamento et i suoi destini, undici dopo il *Latium* di P. Toubert," in *Castrum 2*, 411–20; Francesco Bosco, "Incastellamento, territorio e popolamento dell'Italia centro-meridionale nella recente storiografia," *Bullettino della Deputazione Abruzzese di Storia Patria* 78 (1988): 55–83; and *Archeologica medievale* 16 (1989), a special issue devoted to "incastellamento."

plaint by Pope Agapitus II (946–55), were scattered all over their remaining possessions, conducting themselves dishonestly and shamefully ("inhoneste et turpiter").[33] Tenth-century Farfa seems to have been even worse. Abbot Ratfredus did succeed in reestablishing monks there between 930 and 933, but he was promptly poisoned by two of them: Campo, who ruled at Farfa (936?–943?), and Hildebrand, abbot of Farfa, ca. 939, who, after dividing its lands with Campo, established his headquarters at Fermo, where he was still claiming to be Farfa's abbot as late as 971. Attempts at Cluniac reform were frustrated when the monks refused to admit Abbot Odo of Cluny around 937; when they expelled Cluniac visitors in 947; and when they poisoned Abbot Dagibert of Cuma (947?–953?), a reformer installed by force by Prince Alberic of Rome (932–54). As Jean Décarreaux once observed, Farfa's custom of poisoning abbots was "unquestionably faithful to a tradition that goes back to the first disciples of St. Benedict."[34] Yet the unfortunate community lacked similar fidelity to Benedictinism's more positive aspects. Farfa sold its library books to raise money. It alienated some estates to abbots' children and divided others among its monks.[35]

Disorganization put the landholdings of the great monasteries at risk. Central Italian noble families found acquisitiveness expedient, even necessary, because they practiced partible inheritance, dividing lands and often titles among all male heirs and transferring considerable wealth to daughters. If a family with many children failed to increase its landed possessions, the result could be disastrous, but if it could gain control over new resources it could become a great lineage. Italian nobles did not take power for granted. They were quick to exploit weaknesses in the central govern-

---

33. Agapitus II, *Epistula* (J–L 3664), in *Papsturkunden 896–1046*, ed. Zimmermann, 1: 191–93 (no. +110). Most studies of papal correspondence treat this letter as a forgery by Peter the Deacon, who includes it in his *Register*. For full references see Zimmermann, *Papstregesten, 911–1014*, vol. 2 (5th part) of J. F. Boehmer, *Regesta Imperii* (Vienna: Hermann Böhlaus Nachf., 1969), 75. Yet the letter must antedate Peter, since Leo Marsicanus used it in *Chron. Cass.* I lviii, 146–47. Its picture of tenth-century Monte Cassino's degradation may be a little one sided: see Leccisotti, "Il secolo X e l'influsso della riforma monastica romana a Montecassino," *Archivio della SRSP* 103 (1980): 79–89; and Penco, *Storia del Monachesimo in Italia: Dalle origini alla fine del Medioevo*, 2nd ed. (Milan: Jaca Book, 1983), 180.

34. Jean Décarreaux, *Normands papes et moines: Cinquante ans de conquêtes et de politique religieuse en Italie méridionale et en Sicile (milieu du XIe siècle–début du XIIe)* (Paris: Éditions A. et J. Picard, 1974), 44.

35. Gregory of Catino, *Chron. Farf.*, 1:324–29. Hugh of Farfa, *Destructio Monasterii Farfensis*, ed. Balzani, in *Chron. Farf.*, 1:33–47. Commentary on these chronicles by Ildefonso Schuster can be found in "L'abbate Ugo I e la riforma di Farfa," 617–20; and *L'imperiale Abbazia di Farfa*, 96–100. On the alienation of Farfa's books, see Giorgio Brignoli, "La biblioteca dell'Abbazia di Farfa," *Benedictina* 5 (1951): 5 and 9–10.

ment and in the great monastic corporations. Public lands were privatized. Abandoned or poorly defended monastic ones were appropriated or, to the same effect but with better grace, "leased." [36]

An excellent example of this dynamic is offered by the lineage of the counts of Marsica, a family that figures prominently in this book because of its support of Dominic of Sora. Their county is named after the Marsi, an ancient Italian tribe that once dwelt around the Lago Fucino, about fifty-five miles east-northeast of Rome. In an extended sense, however, the name "Marsica" was applied to the whole southern part of the Duchy of Spoleto. Monte Cassino's chronicle, well informed about Marsican affairs because its first author was Leo Marsicanus, describes the origins of these counts as follows: "Along with [King] Hugh there came to Italy Count Azzo, uncle of that Berardus who is called the Frank, a relative of the king himself, from whom the counts of the Marsi arose." Hugh of Arles (926–47), the most effective post-Carolingian king, was notorious for placing his Burgundian and Provençal kinsmen in high positions whenever he got the chance.[37] His relative Berardus, founder of the first documented *hereditary* line of Marsican counts, was still living in 954. He appears to have had seven sons. They and their descendents, seeking spheres of influence and bases for new counties, spread throughout the southern part of the duchy of Spoleto and even into the Sabina and the Molise, absorbing all public lands, gaining control over episcopal sees, and acquiring monastic estates from Farfa, Subiaco, Monte Cassino, San Vincenzo al Volturno, and Casauria. From Berardus the Frank would descend the counts of Marsica, Valva, Rieti, Balsorano, Sangro, Collimento, and so forth.[38]

36. David Herlihy, *Medieval Households*, Studies in Cultural History (Cambridge, Mass.: Harvard University Press, 1985), 88–89, describes inheritance practices. The emergence of new tenth-century extended lineages in Tuscany is detailed in Cinzio Violante, "Le strutture familiari, parentali e consortili delle aristocrazie in Toscana durante i secoli X–XII," in *I Ceti dirigenti in Toscana nell'età precomunale. Comitato di studi sulla storia dei ceti dirigenti in Toscana: Atti del 10 Convegno: Firenze, 2 dicembre 1978* (Pisa: Pacini Editore, 1981), 2–10. Atto of Vercelli's *Polypticum* documents the insecurity of the comital elite, in passages analyzed in Suzanne Fonay Wemple, *Atto of Vercelli: Church, State, and Christian Society in Tenth Century Italy*, Temi e testi 27 (Rome: Edizioni di storia e letteratura, 1979), 90–95. See also Wickham, *Early Medieval Italy*, 175.

37. Hugh's partiality for foreigners, especially for his relatives, is analyzed in Hlawitschka, *Franken, Alemannen, Bayern und Burgunder*, 85–86; and in Wemple, *Atto of Vercelli*, 87–91.

38. Two monographs early in this century dealt extensively with the counts of the Marsi: Cesare Rivera, *I Conti de'Marsi e la loro discendenza fino alla fondazione dell'Aquila (843–1250): Cronistoria medioevale dell'Abruzzo e della Sabina de Rieti*, Biblioteca abruzzese publicazione periodica 1 (Teramo: Giovanni Fabbri Editore, 1913–15) [never finished]; and Hermann Müller, *Topographische und genealogische Untersuchungen zur Geschichte des Herzogtums Spoleto und der Sabina von 800 bis 1100: Inaugural-Dissertation zur Erlangung der Dok-*

The counts of Marsica had many competitors. In the domains of Farfa and Subiaco, for example, their major rivals as feudatories were the Crescenzi, another lineage that would support Dominic. Although their exact origins are debated, their power is connected to the Theophylact who, in Roman records from the early tenth century, rose from knight to "magister militum" to "gloriosissimus dux" to "consul et dux" at the time of his death, acquiring titles resembling those used by independent rulers of southern Italian cities. His ascent was presumably aided not only by sections of the Roman aristocracy, but also by the favor of the dukes of Spoleto, who were then actively interested in Rome. Popes from the time of Sergius III (904–11) worked closely with Theophylact and his daughter Marozia, whose succession of politic marriages was ended by a coup that brought into power her son Alberic II (932–54). Scholars have now rehabilitated Theophylact's family to some extent, looking beyond the invective of Liutprand of Cremona, a propagandist for Emperor Otto I who deposed them, and paying more attention to the Romans who hailed Alberic as "Princeps Omnium Romanorum" and "Cultor Monasteriorum." Yet the last years of the dynasty have no defenders. It is to be expected that Liutprand would vilify Alberic's son, Prince John-Octavian, who was only about eighteen years old when he became Pope John XII, but the *Liber Pontificalis* treats him little better, claiming that he "passed his days in vanities and adulteries." Even Benedict of Sant'Andrea of Monte Soratte (fl. ca. 980), who despised the Germans, still describes their opponent John XII as a "*homo ferus*," a wild man who "blazed with passions." John was deposed in absentia by the emperor in 962, and his efforts to return to Rome were stopped by his death in 964. Yet his downfall did not end his family's power.[39]

---

torwürde der Philosophischen Fakultät der Universität Greifswald (Greifswald: Buchdruckerei J. Herper, 1930), 54–57, 58–68, and 70–75. Much of Rivera's research on the early history of the descendents of Berardus is recapitulated in his "Valva e i suoi conti," *Bullettino della R. Deputazione Abruzzese di Storia Patria* ser. 3, 17 (1926): 79–91. Unfortunately, Müller did not have access to Rivera's work. A "*tesi di laurea*" on "La Contea dei Marsi fino al XII secolo" submitted by Antonio Sennis to the University of Rome "La Sapienzia" in 1992, which I have not seen, is presumably subsumed into his "Potere centrale e forze locali."

Leo Marsicanus is quoted from *Chron. Cass.* I lxi, 153–54. That Berardus was still alive in 954 is witnessed by two charters in the *Liber Largitorius vel Notarius Monasterii Pharphensis*, ed. Giuseppe Zucchetti, 2 vols., ISIME/Istituto Storico Prussiano Regesta Chartarum Italiae 11 and 17 (Rome: Hermann Loescher, 1913 and 1932), 1:114–15 (nos. 159 and 160).

39. Overviews of the house of Theophylact are given by Willi Kölmel, *Rom und der Kirchenstaat im 10. und 11. Jahrhundert bis in die Anfänge der Reform: Politik, Verwaltung; Rom und Italien*, Abhandlungen zur mittleren und Neueren Geschichte 78 (Berlin-Grunewald: Verlag für Staatswissenschaft und Geschichte, 1935), 1–25; Paolo Brezzi, *Roma e l'Impero medioevale, 774–1252*, Storia di Roma 10 (Bologna: Licinio Cappelli Editore, 1947), 97–134; Partner, *Lands of St. Peter*, 77–90; and Toubert, *Structures*, 2:974–98. Vehse, "Das

The Crescenzi relatives of the Theophylact clan became dominant when Otto I, groping for a way to govern the Romans, accepted as pope John XIII (965–72). John quickly established a certain Benedict, who was related to Theophylact's family and who may also have been a papal nephew, as Count of the Sabina, and arranged Benedict's marriage to Theodoranda, daughter of "Crescentius a Caballo." Soon after the death of John XIII, the Crescenzi launched the first of a number of attempts to put their candidates on the papal throne. Despite some bloody reversals at the hands of the emperors, this lineage dominated Rome for nearly two generations and the Sabina for more than a century. Its survival graphically illustrates how much power had fallen into the hands of aristocratic factions organized in family arrays, power so great that even emperors generally found it easier to compromise with them than to root them out of their fortified strongholds.[40]

Bündnis gegen die Sarazenen," 185, examines Theophylact's early titles; Toubert, *Structures*, 2:963–64, urges caution in interpreting them. The family's role as monastic patrons is described in Bernard Hamilton, "The Monastic Revival of Tenth-Century Rome," *Studia Monastica* 4 (1962): 35–68; and "The House of Theophylact and the Promotion of Religious Life among Women in Tenth-Century Rome," *Studia Monastica* 12 (1970): 195–217, both reprinted with the same pagination in his *Monastic Reform, Catharism and the Crusades (900–1300)*, Variorum Collected Studies Series (London: Variorum Reprints, 1979). Praises of Alberic II are quoted from Benedict of San Andrea di Monte Soratte, *Chronicon*, ed. Giuseppe Zucchetti, FSI 55 (Rome: ISIME, 1920), 166–67. Disparagements of John XII can be found in Liutprand of Cremona, *Liber de Rebus Gestis Ottonis Magni Imperatoris*, edited in Joseph Becker, *Die Werke Liudprands von Cremona*, 3rd ed., MGH *SS Rerum Germanicarum in Usum Scholarum* (Hannover: Hahn, 1915), 159–75; *Liber Pontificalis* cxxxiii, edited in Louis Duchesne, *Le Liber Pontificalis: Texte, introduction et commentaire*, 2nd ed. Bibliothèque des Écoles françaises d'Athènes & de Rome, 3 vols. (Paris: E. de Boccard, Editeur, 1955–57), 2:246; and Benedict of Sant'Andrea di Monte Soratte, *Chronicon*, 173.

40. Crescenzi family history is analyzed in Vehse, "Die päpstliche Herrschaft in der Sabina bis zur Mitte des 12. Jahrhunderts," *QFIAB* 21 (1929/1930): 120–75; Kölmel, *Rom und der Kirchenstaat*, 25–46; Brezzi, *Roma e l'Impero medioevale*, 137–95; Partner, *Lands of St. Peter*, 90–103; and Toubert, *Structures*, 2:1009–22. Scholars have long debated the family's precise origin. Gaetano Bossi, "I Crescenzi di Sabina: Stefaniani e Ottaviani (dal 1012 al 1106)," *Archivio della R. SRSP* 41 (1918): 111–70, considered Pope John XIII a nephew of Alberic II, a notion accepted, for example, in Vehse, "Die päpstliche Herrschaft in der Sabina," 137–38. This and other alleged early genealogical links were challenged by Carlo Cecchelli, "Note sulle famiglie romane fra il IX e il XII secolo," *Archivio della R. SRSP* n.s. 58 (1935): 75–79, who did, however, identify residential and political connections between the pope and the family of Crescentius. Brezzi, in *Roma e l'Impero medioevale*, 138, 142–46, and 148–52, carefully addresses the issues raised and outlines the unknowns. For a revised perspective that treats the Crescenzi as a lineage formed by the combination of several different families (a "consorteria" that became a family), see Harald Zimmermann, "Parteiungen und Paptswahlen in Rom zur Zeit Kaiser Ottos des Grossen," *Römische historische Mitteilungen*, 8/9 (1964/65 and 1965/66), 29–88, reprinted with bibliographical additions in *Otto der Grosse*, ed. Zimmermann, Wege der Forschung 450 (Darmstadt: Wissenschaftliche Buchgesellschaft, 1976), 325–414. Toubert, *Structures*, 2:1016–17, doubts that this group constituted a "family," but his arguments, based on the diverse policies followed by different branches, seem hypercritical.

To appreciate how such ruling elites could disrupt monasteries, one need only look at what happened to several of the greatest abbots around the year 1000. Abbot Manso of Monte Cassino (986–96) was fatally blinded by agents of Bishop Alberic of Marsica, one of the sons of Count Berardus the Frank.[41] Almost simultaneously, Abbot Roffridus of San Vincenzo al Volturno and most of his monks were driven out for ten months by an unnamed "invasor" who had to be removed by Emperor Otto III (d. 1002).[42] Between 1003 and 1005, Abbot Peter III of Subiaco, who had refused to cede power over certain *castelli*, was captured, blinded, and imprisoned until his death by the counts of Monticelli, a branch of the Crescenzi.[43] These were bad years, but even in better ones counts continually encroached upon the landholdings of the great monasteries.

Could anyone check the predatory lineages and the regionalism they abetted? Decades of fighting had resulted in ruined central authority, alienated public lands, and subinfeudated military forces. Although it has been claimed that "The Italian state in 950 was still . . . the most sophisticated in Western Christendom, with a complex legal-administrative system that ran courts and collected dues across the Po plain and Tuscany in a more systematic manner than any other part of the Carolingian empire," whatever coherence it retained came from its semiautonomous court system, not from monarchical power. Italian kings had been chosen from outside first because the Carolingian heirs were outsiders; then because neutral outsiders might not provoke internal rivals; and finally because, by the mid-tenth century, the native Italian candidates were just too weak. None had the power and prestige of King Otto I of Germany, who, in 951, made his first foray into Italy, during which he defeated King Berengar II, declared himself king, and rescued and married Adelaide, the wealthy widow of King Hugh of Arles' son, King Lothar II (d. 950). Political troubles in Germany and difficulties in securing the cooperation of Prince Alberic II

41. The details of the plot against Manso are said to have been divulged by the priest Andrew, one of the co-conspirators, to John, a former archpriest of Marsica, who, after a short stint as a Monte Cassino monk, became bishop of Sora (1073–1086). He apparently told the story both to his nephew, Leo Marsicanus, the Monte Cassino chronicler, and to Peter Damian. The major sources are *Chron. Cass.* II xvi, 196–200; and Peter Damian, *Epistula* 157 (old numbering IV viii), in *Die Briefe des Petrus Damiani*, ed. Kurt Reindel, 4 vols., MGH *Briefe der Deutschen Kaiserzeit* 4(1–4) (Munich: Hahnsche Buchhandlung, 1983–93), 4:79–84.

42. *Chron. Vult.* II, 1:325–26.

43. For an overview, see Benedetto Cignitti, "Pietro III," *BS* 10:787–90. The principal sources are Hugh of Farfa, *Relatio Constitutionis*, ed. Balzani, 1:55–56; and *Chron. Subl.*, 7. The dates of Peter and other abbots are established from the eleventh-century *Register* by Pietro Egidi, *I Monasteri di Subiaco* (Rome: Ministero della Pubblica Istruzione, 1904), 207–18.

of Rome led to a reprieve for Berengar, but a decade later further troubles in Italy prompted Otto's return, and on 2 February 962 he received from the pope an imperial crown.[44]

A Western Roman emperor ruled again. Yet his authority was essentially military, superimposed over preexisting secular and ecclesiastical jurisdictions. Great landholders were independent within their own localities, a fact concealed by the way they swore oaths of loyalty to the emperor, participated in his court ceremonies, and supported his military expeditions when it suited them. After the royal palace in the old Lombard capital of Pavia was destroyed during a riot in 1024, it was not rebuilt—its elaborate system of judges and archives had ceased to be relevant. Saxon and Salian emperors concentrated on controlling their personal possessions and attempting to control the Church (never entirely successfully). They were able to destroy individual enemies, and sometimes even to shuffle properties around, but only the most talented mastered the art of using force in occasional well-timed applications. Calamities such as a disputed regency nullified central power. While in theory the emperors were the divinely appointed guardians of peace, in fact they were significant only when present with their armies. The arrival of an emperor in Rome was a portentous event, awesome as a comet, destructive as an earthquake. But almost as soon as he had recrossed the Milvian bridge, the local factions reasserted themselves.

The attempt by Otto III to end the impasse by living in Rome failed to quell discontent. From then on the city saw its emperors only in armed processions marred by bloody riots such as those associated with the coronations of 1014 and 1027. Central Italian hatred found its spokesman in Benedict of Sant'Andrea of Monte Soratte, for whom German rule failed in theory because it humiliated Rome's proper dignity and failed in practice because its sporadic manifestations were marked by plague, bloodshed, and cattle rustling.[45]

44. Wickham, *Early Medieval Italy*, 168–93, esp. 171, surveys the late and post-Carolingian Italian kings. He is quoted here from "Lawyer's Time: History and Memory in Tenth- and Eleventh-Century Italy," in *Studies in Medieval History Presented to R. H. C. Davis*, ed. Henry Mayr-Harting and R. I. Moore (London: Hambledon Press, 1985), 54; reprinted with revisions in his *Land and Power: Studies in Italian and European Social History, 400–1200* (London: British School at Rome, 1994), 276. An unannotated narrative survey, emphasizing economic and social history, is given by Vito Fumagalli, *Il Regno italico*, vol. 2 of *Storia d'Italia* (Torino: UTET, 1978). A concise overview of current scholarship on the transformation of the kingdom of Italy is found in Tabacco, "Regno, Impero e aristocrazie nell'Italia postcarolingia," in *Secolo di ferro*, 1:243–71. Note also Barbara H. Rosenwein, "The Family Politics of Berengar I, King of Italy (888–924)," *Speculum* 71 (1996): 247–89.

45. For general studies of the workings of the Empire, see Timothy Reuter, "The Imperial Church System of the Ottonian and Salian Rulers: A Reconsideration," *Journal of*

An imperial alternative was the eastern "Emperor of the Romans." Constantinople was not much farther from Rome than Aachen or Paderborn and was easier to reach by sea. Perhaps it was not as distant culturally as Western scholars tend to assume. Rome had Greek monasteries, and among their philhellene supporters was one of the most important families, the Tuscolaners, direct decendents of Alberic II. Their family chapel was the Greek monastery of Grottaferrata located in their seat at Tuscolo, an ancient hill town about twelve miles from Rome.[46] The Italo-Greek hermits who made regular pilgrimages to Rome were saints esteemed even by the ascetical connoisseurs of the East.[47] The duke of Gaeta, whose territory

Ecclesiastical History 33 (1982): 347–74; Heinrich Fichtenau, *Lebensordnungen des 10. Jahrhunderts: Studien über Denkart und Existenz im einstigen Karolingerreich*, 2 vols., Monographien zur des Mittelalters 30 (Stuttgart: Anton Hiersemann, 1984), 1:224–25; trans. (without notes) by Patrick J. Geary as *Living in the Tenth Century: Mentalities and Social Orders* (Chicago: University of Chicago Press, 1991), 164–65; and Benjamin Arnold, *German Knighthood, 1050–1300* (Oxford: Clarendon Press, 1985), 1–14. The ideological structure of the Empire is discussed in Percy Ernst Schramm, *Kaiser, Könige und Päpste: Gesammelte Aufsätze zur Geschichte des Mittelalters*, 4 vols. in 5 (Stuttgart: Anton Hiersemann, 1968–71), 3:33–437. On the City of Rome's hostility to the Germans, see Brezzi, *Roma e l'Impero medioevale*, 130, 132, 133, 138, 145, 148, 155–56, 175–77, 196, and 203. Benedict of Sant'Andrea, *Chronicon*, 162, 177, and 186, compares Bavarians to Saracens.

46. On the Greek monastic presence in Rome, see Anton Michel, "Die griechischen Klostersiedlungen zu Rom bis zur Mitte des 11. Jahrhunderts," *Ostkirchliche Studien* 1 (1952): 32–45; and Guy Ferrari, *Early Roman Monasteries: Notes for the History of the Monasteries and Convents at Rome from the V through the X Century*, Studi di Antichità cristiana pubblicati per cura del Pontificio Istituto di Archeologia Cristiana 23 (Vatican City: Pontificio Istituto di Archeologia Cristiana, 1957), 449. Greek influence is described in Hamilton, "The City of Rome and the Eastern Churches in the Tenth Century," *Orientalia Periodica Christiana* 27 (1961): 5–26; Patricia M. McNulty and Hamilton, "*Orientale Lumen et Magistra Latinitas:* Greek Influences on Western Monasticism (900–1100)," in *Le Millénaire du Mont Athos, 963 – 1963: Études et mélanges*, 2 vols. (Chevetogne/Venice: Éditions de Chevetogne, 1963–64), 1: 184–90; and "The Monastery of S. Alessio and the Religious and Intellectual Renaissance in Tenth-Century Rome," *Studies in Medieval and Renaissance History* 2 (1965): 265–310—all three reprinted with the same pagination in Hamilton's *Monastic Reform, Catharism and the Crusades*. The links between the Crescenzi and the Greeks are sketched in Brezzi, *Roma e l'impero medioevale*, 131, 132, and 167; and in Zimmermann, "Parteiungen und Papstwahlen in Rom," 78–80, reprinted in *Otto der Grosse*, 406–7. The relationship between the counts of Tuscolo and Grottaferrata is briefly described in Brezzi, "Aspetti dell vita politica e religiosa di Roma tra la fine del sec. X e la prima metà del sec. XI," *Bollettino della Badia Greca di Grottaferrata*, n.s. 9 (1955), 115–26. On Byzantine features of Grottaferrata's architecture, see Luigi Devoti, "L'Abbazia di Grottaferrata dalla fondazione alle fine del medioevo," in *Tra le Abbazie del Lazio*, ed. Renato Lefevre (Rome: Gruppo Culturale di Roma e del Lazio, 1987), published as a special issue of *Lunario Romano* 17 (1988): 127–43.

47. General surveys of the expansion of Italo-Greek monasticism include G. da Costa-Louillet, "Saints de Sicile et d'Italie méridionale aux VIIIe, IXe et Xe siècles," *Byzantion* 29–30 (1959–60): 89–173; Silvano Borsari, *Il monachesimo bizantino nella Sicilia e nell'Italia meridionale prenormanne* (Naples: Istituto Italiano per gli Studi Storici in Napoli, 1963), 37–76; and McNulty and Hamilton, "*Orientale Lumen*," 181–90, 196–206. On some particular aspects, see Francesco Russo, "La 'peregrinatio' dei santi italo-greci nelle tombe degli Apostoli Petro e Paolo a Roma," *Bollettino della Badia Greca di Grottaferratta*, n.s. 22 (1968): 89–99;

bordered Rome's, still bore the Byzantine title of "hypatos" ("consul").[48] Naples was a bilingual city, an active center of Greek/Latin translation between 875 and 975.[49] The Lombard princes had protected their jealously guarded political independence from the Franks by forging cultural and political links with the Byzantines.[50] The Greek emperor held the south more tightly than the German emperor held the north; during the late tenth and early eleventh centuries he was expanding his territories at the expense of the Lombard princes, even making serious plans for the reconquest of Muslim Sicily.[51] The wealth he needed to support such projects came in part from Southern Italy's silk industry.[52] Yet he was hated at least as much as his western colleague. He faced not only jealousy, xenophobia, and religious suspicion, but also general hostility to all centralized political authority—Western or Eastern. Regionalism had triumphed.

In theory, the bishops of Rome could have provided overlordship. But first they had to establish an independent position against the major secular authorities. The hostility between the Crescenzi and the German emperors resulted in violence, bloodshed, and the imposition of bishops from

Enrica Follieri, "Il culto dei santi nell'Italia greca," *La Chiesa greca in Italia dall'VIII al XVI secolo*, 3 vols., Italia Sacra 20–22 (Padua: Editrice Antenore, 1969), 2:553–57; and Annabel Jane Wharton, *Art of Empire: Painting and Architecture of the Byzantine Periphery: A Comparative Study of Four Provinces* (University Park: Pennsylvania State University Press, 1988), 127–60.

48. Patricia Skinner, *Family Power in Southern Italy: The Duchy of Gaeta and Its Neighbours, 850–1139* (Cambridge: Cambridge University Press, 1995).

49. Bibliography on the Greek element in Neapolitan life can be accessed through François Dolbeau, "Le rôle des interprètes dans les traductions hagiographiques d'Italie du sud," *Traduction et traducteurs au Moyen Âge: Actes du Colloque international du CNRS organisé à Paris, Institut de recherche et d'histoire des textes, les 26–28 mai 1986*, ed. Geneviève Contamine (Paris: Éditions du Centre national de la recherche scientifique, 1989), 145–68, esp. 145–46; and Brunhölzl, *Geschichte der lateinischen Literatur*, 2:339–47. For the larger context of this activity, see Walter Berschin, *Griechisch-lateinisches Mittelalter: Von Hieronymus zu Nikolaus von Kues* (Bern: Francke Verlag, 1980), esp. 204–7, 252–55.

50. On the relationship between the princes of Salerno and Byzantium, see Huguette Taviani-Carozzi, *La Principauté lombarde de Salerne (IXe–XIe siècle): Pouvoir et société en Italie lombarde méridionale*, 2 vols., Collection de l'École française de Rome 152 (Rome: École française, 1991), 1:183–87 and 221–26.

51. Jules Gay, *L'Italie méridionale et l'Empire byzantin depuis l'avénement de Basile Ier jusqu'à la prise de Bari par les Normands (867–1071)*, Bibliothèque des Écoles françaises d'Athènes et de Rome 90 (Paris: Albert Fontemoing, Éditeur, 1904), 229–429. For proposed Sicilian campaigns, see the *Annales Barenses* for 1027, ed. Georg Heinrich Pertz, MGH SS 5: 53; and the accounts of the expedition of 1038–40 cited in Wolf, *Making History*, 12–13. Yet weaknesses existed in southern Italian Byzantine government, intensifying in the early eleventh century, which are treated in France, "The Occasion of the Coming of the Normans to Southern Italy," *Journal of Medieval History* 17 (1991): 185–205.

52. André Gillou, "Production and Profits in the Byzantine Province of Italy (Tenth to Eleventh Centuries): An Expanding Society," *Dumbarton Oaks Papers* 28 (1974): 89–109; "La soie du Katépanat d'Italie," *Recherches sur le XIe siècle*, Centre de recherche d'histoire et civilisation de byzance, travaux et mémoires 6 (Paris: Éditions E. de Boccard, 1976), 69–84.

abroad, including Gregory V (996–99) and Sylvester II (999–1003), the first German and French popes. The Crescenzi appeared to triumph when Otto III and Sylvester II died within a year of each other, but then their own faction fell victim to the same fate in 1012 when their patrician and pope both died in the same week. The Tuscolan counts seized the city.

Historians have long accepted Ferdinand Gregorovius's characterization of the Tuscolaners as "diese wilden Barone," but a more favorable picture is beginning to emerge. Benedict VIII (1012–24), a son installed by the family patriarch, was a great success. He coopted potential opposition by working closely with the German emperor (he even made an archbishop of Cologne Rome's honorary "Bibliothecarius") and with the deposed Crescenzi faction (he kept members as rector of the Sabina and count of Campania). He supported moderate reforms, consistently strengthened papal authority in southern Italy, and increased Rome's international activity. After his death, his office was inherited by his brother, John XIX (1024–32). The dynasty only faltered when the papal crown was handed down to a miscast nephew, Benedict IX (1032–44, 1045, 1047–48). Although historians normally begin the story of papal reform with the reign of Leo IX (1049–1054), he was greatly indebted to the Tuscolaners, who kept the emperors at a distance and established precedents for an active, reforming, independent papacy.[53]

Much of the dynamism of the Italian Church was found at a level below the papacy and the great abbeys. Aristocrats were building private monasteries in record numbers.[54] Crowds of hermits were reappearing throughout Italy. Perhaps there had always been hermits living anony-

53. Ferdinand Gregorovius, *Geschichte der Stadt Rom im Mittelalters*, 2nd ed., 8 vols. (Stuttgart: J. G. Cotta'schen, 1869–74), 4:11. For current interpretations, see Toubert, *Structures*, 2:1015–38 and 1226; and Klaus-Jürgen Herrmann, *Das Tuskulanerpapsttum (1012–1046): Benedikt VIII., Johannes XIX., Benedikt IX*, Päpste und Papsttum 4 (Stuttgart: Anton Hiersemann, 1973), who offers a narrative treatment (1–24) and an evaluation of Tuscolaner importance (166–78). Cowdrey, *Cluniacs and the Gregorian Reform*, 36–43, stresses their role in promoting Cluniac monasticism. Laudage, *Priesterbild und Reformpapsttum*, 52–56, 78–87, 115–19, examines their reform councils. G. A. Loud, *Church and Society in the Norman Principality of Capua, 1058–1197* (Oxford: Clarendon Press, 1985), 10–11, argues that the Tuscolaners often handled local administration better than the popes of the Gregorian Reform. Although Tellenbach, *The Church in Western Europe*, 159 and 163–64, invokes various *argumenta ex silentio* against this more positive appraisal of the Tuscolaners, he does not convincingly undermine it.

54. The wave of private monastic foundations that swept Italy around the year 1000 has been especially well studied for Tuscany. See Miccoli, *Chiesa Gregoriana*, 47–73; Wilhelm Kurze, "Adel und Klöster im frühmittelalterlichen Tuszien," *QFIAB* 52 (1972): 90–115, invoking themes he takes up again in "Nobilità toscana e nobilità aretina," *I Ceti dirigenti: Atti del 1° Convegno*, 257–65, and in "Monasterium Erfonis, I primi tre secoli di storia del monastero e la loro tradizione documentaria," *950° [anno] della consecrazione della nuova chiesa dell'Ab-*

mously during the hagiographical dark ages that lie between the *Dialogues* of Gregory I (d. 604) and its eleventh-century imitation, the *Dialogues* of Abbot Desiderius of Monte Cassino (1058–87).[55] Yet most scholars believe that radical asceticism at least revived during the eleventh century. Various theories attempt to explain why. One links the rise of hermitism to the prestigious example of the Italo-Greek monks, a group whose continuous eremitical tradition is well documented and whose prominence in Rome was greatest in the late tenth century.[56] Another credits Romuald of Ravenna (d. ca. 1027), an organizer driven "to turn the whole world into a hermitage,"[57] although to attribute the revival of hermitism to him alone necessarily oversimplifies, since he was part of a tradition manifesting itself independently in many areas.[58] Some scholars suggest the influence of the

---

bazia di San Salvatore al Monte Amiata, 1035–1985 (Rieti: Monaci Cistercensi dell'Abbazia di San Salvatore, 1986), 27 [studies presented in Italian, in *Monasteri e nobiltà nel senese e nella toscana medievale: Studi diplomatici, archeologici, genealogici, giuridici e sociali* (Siena: Ente provinciale per il turismo di Siena, 1989), 155–64, 295–318, and 357–74]; Werner Goez, "Reformpapstum, Adel und monastische Erneuerung in der Toscana," *Investiturstreit und Reichsverfassung*, Vorträge und Forschungen Herausgegeben von Konstanzer Arbeitskreis für mittelalterliche Geschichte 17 (Sigmaringen: Jan Thorbecke Verlag, 1973), 211–16; and Wickham, *The Mountains and the City*, 185–94. For Europe in general, see Howe, "The Nobility's Reform," 321–24.

55. The frequency of hermits at each end of the centuries that span the period from the close of late antiquity to the eleventh century revival of communal life is obvious from a cursory reading of Gregory I, *Dialog.* and of Desiderius, *Dialogi de Miraculis Sancti Benedicti* xxii, ed. Gerhard Schwartz and Adolf Hofmeister, in MGH *SS* 30(2):1111–51.

56. Enrico Morini, in "Eremo e cenobio nel monachesimo greco dell'Italia meridionale nei secoli IX e X," *Rivisti di storia della Chiesa in Italia* 31 (1977): 354–90, analyzes the monastic and eremitical lifestyles of Italo-Greek saints. On their possible role in the eleventh-century Western revival of hermitism, see Howe, "Greek Influence on the Eleventh-Century Western Revival of Hermitism," 2 vols., Ph.D. dissertation, University of California at Los Angeles, 1979, esp. 1:2–9; 2:365–69; and Pasquale Corsi, "Studi recenti sul monachesimo italo-greco," *Quaderni medievali* 8 (1979): 244–61. The evidence is greater than indicated in Derek Baker, "'The Whole World a Hermitage': Ascetic Renewal and the Crisis of Western Monasticism," in *Medieval Church and Society: Studies for Denis Bethell*, ed. Marc A. Meyer (London: Hambledon Press, 1993), 207–23.

57. The quotation is taken from Peter Damian's *Vita Romualdi* xxxvii, ed. Giovanni Tabacco, *Petri Damiani Vita Beati Romualdi*, FSI 94 (Rome: ISIME, 1957), 78. Romualdian hermitism is competently surveyed, and the relevant literature invoked, in Christian Lohmer, *Heremi Conversatio: Studien zu den monastischen Vorschriften des Petrus Damiani*, Beiträge zur Geschichte des alten Mönchtums und des Benediktinertums 39 (Münster: Aschendorff, 1991), 1–35. On the alleged primacy of this Romualdian tradition, see Tabacco, "Romualdo di Ravenna e gli inizi dell'eremitismo camaldolese," in *L'Eremitismo in Occidente nei secoli XI e XII: Atti della seconda Settimana internazionale di studio, Mendola, 30 agosto–6 settembre 1962*, Pubblicazioni dell'Università Cattolica del Sacro Cuore, Contributi ser. 3, var. 4; Miscellanea del Centro di Studi Medioevali 4 (Milan: Società Editrice Vita a Pensiero, 1965), 73–121, esp. 95–96, 100–103; Penco, *Storia del Monachesimo in Italia*, 197–204; and Baker, "'Whole World a Hermitage,'" 207–8, 216–20.

58. Romuald was only one of many contemporary hermits. He himself began life in the desert as a pupil of the uneducated Venetian hermit Marinus (Damian, *Vita Romualdi* iv, 20–

ascetic side of Cluniac spirituality, with which Romuald himself had some connections.[59]

Whatever the reason, hermits were becoming more visible in the first half of the eleventh century. The best known illustration is the career of the Ravenna scholar Peter Damian, who had joined a Romualdian community in the 1030s, had begun to identify himself as the "ultimus heremitarum servus" by at least 1043, and had become a leader of the papal *curia* by 1057.[60] Dominic of Sora's career is an early manifestation of this wider movement.

---

21). Pietro Palazzini, "Fonte Avellana e Pier Damiani," in *Le Abbazie delle Marche: Storia e Arte. Atti del Convegno internazionale, Macerta, 3–5 aprile 1990*, ed. Emma Simi Varanelli, Pubblicazioni della Facoltà di Lettere e Filosofia dell'Università di Macerata 66, Sezione "Atti di Convegni" 20 (Cesena: Badia di S. Maria del Monte, 1992), 127–58, esp. 150, treats the Fonte Avellana community that Peter Damian joined as a pre-Romualdian milieu. The monastery of Chiusa in the Alpine Valley of Susa seems to have originated out of late tenth-century hermitism, although its hagiographic records present problems surveyed in Giuseppe Sergi, "Culto locale e pellegrinaggio europeo: Un'interferenza nel medioevo piemontese," *Luoghi sacri e spazi della santità*, ed. Sofia Boesch Gajano and Lucetta Scaraffia (Torino: Rosenberg & Sellier, 1990), 6–73. On Bononius of Lucedio (d. 1026), trained as a hermit near Mount Sinai, see Patrizia Cancian, *L'Abbazia di S. Genuario di Lucedio e le sue pergamene*, Deputazione subalpina di storia patria Biblioteca storica subalpina 93 (Torino: Palazzo Carignano, 1975), 20–21. For hints of a Tuscan pre-Romualdian eremitical tradition, see Miccoli, *Chiesa Gregoriana*, 61–64; and, more generally, his "Storia Religiosa," 470–75. On Aldemarius of Monte Cassino (d. early eleventh century), see Laurent Feller, "Pouvoir et société dans les Abruzzes autour de l'an mil: Aristocratie, *incastellamento*, appropriation des justices (960–1035)," *Bullettino dell'ISIME e Archivio Muratoriano* 94 (1988): 11–25, and "L' 'Incastellamento' inachevé des Abruzzes," *Archeologia medievale* 16 (1989): 133–35. On Adalbertus of Casauria (d. post 1047), see Renato Aprile, "Adalberto, monaco di Casauria," in *BS*, 1:180–81. Dominic of Sora, almost an exact contemporary of Romuald, obviously belongs on this list. Other examples are noted in Penco, "Eremitismo irregolare," 201–21. Romuald is better understood not as the cause of the new eremitical enthusiasm but as one of its most conspicuous symptoms.

59. Kassius Hallinger, "Progressi e problemi della ricerca sulla riforma pre-Gregoriana," *Il Monachesimo dell'alto medioevo e la formazione della civiltà occidentale, 8–14 1956*, Settimane di studio 4 (Spoleto: CISAM, 1957), 268; Tabacco, "Romualdo di Ravenna," 104–6, 111–12; Federico Farina and Benedetto Fornari, *Storia e documenti dell'Abbazia di Casamari, 1036–1152* (Casamari: Edizioni Casamari, 1983), 4.

60. Quotation from Peter Damian, *Epistula* 3 (old numbering III ii), 1:106.

2

Hermit Errant

FOR DOMINIC TO SERVE as an example of the achievements and ambiguities of the early reform movement, it is necessary to reconstruct his career. Fortunately, by correlating data from his hagiographical dossier with information from chronicles, charters, and tithe lists, it is possible to identify his foundations, his patrons, and even some solid chronological reference points. The mountains and *castelli* of central Italy also help illuminate his environmental and social contexts. The results are sometimes surprising. Much of what was "known" about Dominic derives ultimately from the work of Lodovico Jacobilli (1589–1664), an Umbrian antiquary whose studies remain "worthy of our respect and admiration" but not of our "unconditional belief."[1] If we return to the sources, if we treat Jacobilli's reconstructions skeptically, our images of Dominic and his patrons suddenly come into sharper focus. Map 1 presents Dominic's progress from his birthplace at Foligno to his tomb near Sora as an itinerary, indicating his foundations as stops on route. The complexities it reduces to dotted lines are this chapter's subject.

Dominic was born in the city of Foligno.[2] Its Umbrian neighborhood,

1. Lodovico Jacobilli wrote on Dominic in *Vite de' santi e beati di Foligno* (Foligno: Appresso Agostino Alterij, 1628); *Vita di S. Domenico da Foligno, Abbate dell'Ordine di S. Benedetto* (Foligno: Agostino Alterii, 1645); and *Vite de' santi e beati dell'Umbria*, 3 vols. (Foligno: Appresso Agostino Alterij, 1647–61). For warnings about his work, see Pier Lorenzo Meloni, "Monasteri benedettini in Umbria tra VIII e XI secolo nella storiografia di Lodovico Jacobilli," *Aspetti dell'Umbria dall'inizio del secolo VIII alla fine del secolo XI: Atti del III Convegno di Studi Umbri, Gubbio, 23–27 maggio 1965* (Gubbio: Facoltà di lettere e filosofia dell'Università degli studi de Perugia, 1966), 321; and Antonio Buoncristiani, "Il culto dei santi e delle loro reliquie nelle opere agiografiche di Ludovico Iacobili (1589–1664)," *Bollettino storico della Città di Foligno* 6 (1982): 107–25.

2. Dominic's *lives* differ on the geographical coordinates for Foligno. The *Sermon*, 365, and a variant of the *Trisulti Life* attested in Jacobus de Voragine's *Summary*, fol. 326, correctly place Dominic's native city in the Duchy of Spoleto. Yet the surviving early modern copy of the *Trisulti Life* i, 282, has Foligno in "Hetruria," following the tradition of the *Valva Life* xi, 71; the *Monte Cassino Life* xi, 71; and the *Sora Life* xi, 36. Perhaps this alternative version reflects the influence of the dukes of Tuscany in the region around Foligno during the mid- and later eleventh century.

today a sleepy Italian backwater, once linked the imperial capitals of Rome and Ravenna. Exarchs and popes strove to control the Via Flaminia, the major north–south road that ran through Narni, Terni, Spoleto, Foligno, Nocera, and out to the coast. But after invading Lombards had established a ducal capital in Spoleto traffic had to be rerouted through the upper Tiber Valley, reducing the road through Foligno from national to local importance.[3] Although the city found itself just inside the Lombard border, it maintained its old Roman site and its independence from the acquisitive diocese of Spoleto. It would have become less isolated when the dukes of Spoleto were transformed into Carolingian marquesses and involved themselves in papal politics.[4] Jacobilli claims that in 840 Foligno survived a Muslim raid, and in 915 and 924 Hungarian raids, but his testimony cannot be verified.[5] In 970 the city unpleasantly felt the ascendency of its new German emperor when one of Otto's relatives who had been collecting relics along the Via Flaminia, Bishop Theoderic of Metz, confiscated the body of Foligno's patron saint, Felicianus.[6] Did Dominic as a young boy watch the Germans carry off his city's celestial protector? Whether he personally saw or not, he must have sensed that his home was becoming part of a more integrated, intrusive world.

3. Donald A. Bullough, "La *Via Flaminia* nella storia dell'Umbria (600–1100)," in *Aspetti dell'Umbria*, 211–33, and "Dalla Romanità all'alto medioevo: L'Umbria come crocevia," in *Orientamenti di una regione attraverso i secoli: Scambi, rapporti, influssi storici nella struttura dell'Umbria: Atti del X Convegno di Studi Umbri, Gubbio, 23–26 maggio 1976* (Perugia: Centro di Studi Umbri, 1978), 177–92; Lorenzo Quilici, "La rete stradale del Ducato di Spoleto nell'alto medioevo," in *Il Ducato di Spoleto: Atti del 9° Congresso internazionale di studi sull'alto medioevo, Spoleto, 27 settembre–2 ottobre 1982*, 2 vols. (Spoleto: Centro Italiano di Studi sull'Alto Medioevo, 1983), 1:399–420; and Giulio Schmiedt, "Contributo della foto-interpretazione alla conoscenza della rete stradale dell'Umbria nell'alto medioevo," in *Aspetti dell'Umbria*, 177–210. On the Lombard duchy of Spoleto in general, see Pier Maria Conti, *Il Ducato di Spoleto e la storia istituzionale dei Longobardi*, Quaderni di "Spoletium" 2 (Spoleto: Edizioni dell'Accademia spoletina, 1982).

4. Bruno Ruggiero, "Il ducato di Spoleto e i tentativi di penetrazione dei Franchi nell'Italia meridionale," *Archivio storico per le province napoletane* 84–85 (1966–67): 77–116. So active were the dukes of Spoleto in Roman affairs that they are misidentified as viceroys for Italian kings and emperors in the *Libellus de Imperatoria Potestate in Urbe Roma*, ed. Zucchetti (appended to Benedict of San Andrea's *Chronicon*), 193–94.

5. Jacobilli, *Discorso della Città di Foligno* (Foligno: Appresso Agostino Alterij, 1646), 16. The absence of supporting evidence is signaled in Fasoli, *Le incursioni ungare*, 152.

6. The sources for Theoderic's journey are analyzed in Eugenio Dupré-Theseider, "La 'grande rapina dei corpi santi' dall'Italia al tempo di Ottone I," *Festschrift Percy Ernst Schramm zu seinem siebzigsten Geburtstag von Schülern und Freunden zugeeignet*, 2 vols. (Wiesbaden: Franz Steiner Verlag, 1964), 1:420–32, esp. 427. Yet local patriots continued to claim the relics, among them Jacobilli, whose "Vita di San Feliciano M. V. e Protettore della Città di Foligno insieme con le vite dè vescovi successori a esso santo," has been republished, in its 2nd ed., by Mario Sensi in the *Bollettino storico della Città di Foligno* 13 (1982): 121–204, esp. 167–69. The seventeenth-century Bollandists suggest tactfully that Theodericus could have divided up the holy bodies (*AS* Jan., 3rd ed., 3:203).

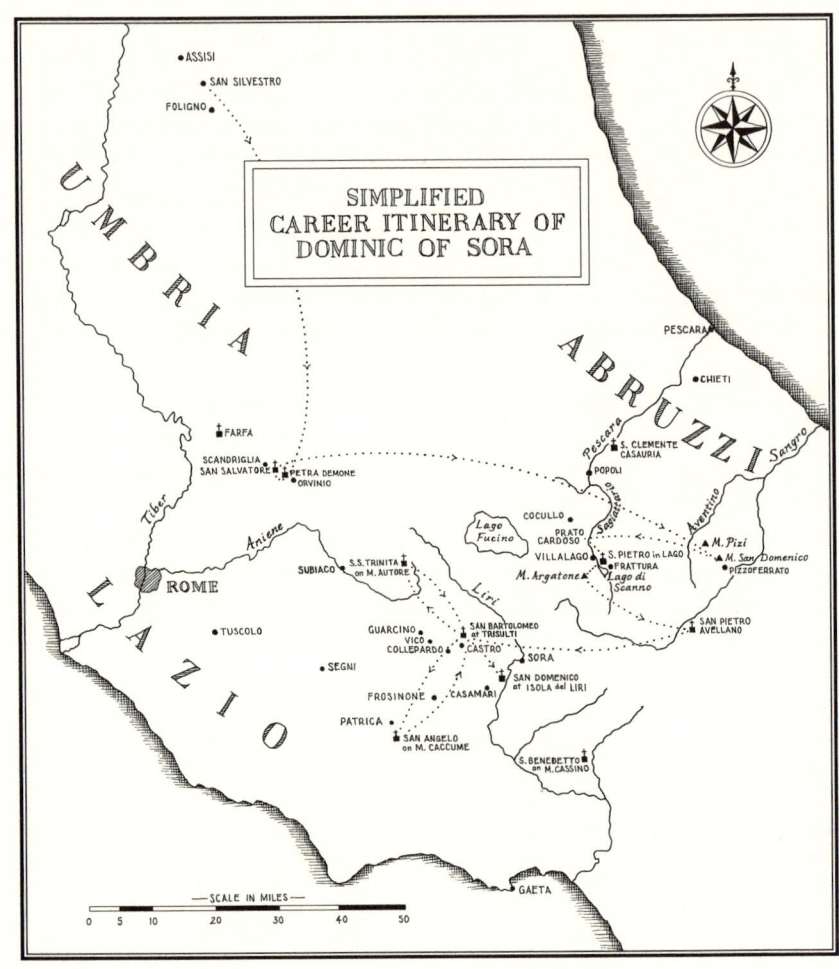

Map 1

Dominic's *lives* name his father and mother as John and Apa.[7] The name John suggests Romano-Italian rather than Lombard ethnic stock, but this would be hazardous to infer, since by the tenth century John was the most common personal name in central Italy. Alberic of Monte Cassino claimed that Dominic's parents were "illustrious both in birth and religion."[8] Here he presumably does not use the word "illustris" as a technical noble honorific, since nothing else in Dominic's *lives* suggests parental nobility. Right after this passage, Italian translations of the *Sora Life* made by Spitilli and Jacobilli add, respectively, that John was "di professione legista" and "dottor de leggi."[9] Did the manuscripts these authors claim to have translated identify Dominic's father as an urban notary or judge? More likely, Spitilli, when reading Alberic's claim that Dominic was born to "viris et genere et religione illustribus," misread "viris" as "iuris" and interpreted his words as indicating illustriousness in legal studies; Jacobilli, who knew Spitilli's work, could have followed his error.[10] All that can be said with certainty is that Dominic's parents must have been city dwellers with some disposable income, since, as will be seen, they were able to take the initiative in arranging for a son's education.[11] Dominic's social status may have resembled that of later bourgeois ecclesiastical reformers such as Peter Damian and Gregory VII.

Dominic was probably born around 960. The traditionally cited birthdate of 951 is a year produced by subtracting Dominic's alleged eighty-year

7. The texts name Dominic's mother either "Apa" or "Ampa." The *Sermon* gives no name. The original Trisulti tradition probably read "Apa." Although the published *Trisulti Life* i, 282, renders the mother's name as "Ampa," its ultimate manuscript source, Bibl. Aless. 91(2), fol. 326, is unclear; Jacobus de Voragine's *Summary*, which has independent Trisulti tradition readings, gives "Apa" (fol. 347). The *Valva Life* xi, 71, also reads "Apa." "Ampa," favored by the Alberician texts, is found in the *Monte Cassino Life* xi, 71; and the *Sora Life* xi, 36.

8. *Monte Cassino Life* xi, 71; and *Sora Life* xi, 36 (where Dolbeau's edition fails to indicate that the line of text including this phrase is added in the margin of Vall. ms. H. 18, fol. 407). Yet Dominic's original *life* probably did contain a phrase relating to the high piety and status of Dominic's parents, since some other texts hint at it: the *Sermon*, 365, specifies "religiosi parentes"; and, although the surviving Trisulti tradition texts have no qualifiers, the *Valva Life* xi, 71, with "genere et religione illustribus," is close to the Alberician tradition.

9. Spitilli, *Vita di S. Domenico*, 7. Jacobilli, *Vita di S. Domenico*, 3; *Vite de'santi e beati di Foligno*, 25; and *Vite de' santi e beati dell'Umbria*, i : 114.

10. Cf. *Monte Cassino Life* xi, 71, with *Sora Life* xi, 36. See Franklin, "Restored *Life and Miracles*," 300.

11. If Dominic were an oblate, destined to live at San Silvestro for life, his parents would have been expected to offer a substantial gift at the time of his entrance: see Joseph H. Lynch, *Simoniacal Entry into Religious Life from 1000–1260: A Social, Economic and Legal History* (Columbus: Ohio State University Press, 1976), esp. xvii, 50, 61–81. If he were simply a student there, which seems more likely given his subsequent career, then his parents were presumably able to compensate the monastery in some way for the expenses involved.

lifespan from 1031, the heretofore universally accepted year of his death. One problem with this date is that it depends on a literal reading of the claims of the Trisulti tradition, which has him die as an "octogenarian"; other *lives* less assuredly specify that at his death he was "almost eighty." [12] The eighty-year figure is likely to err on the side of longevity since unusual old age was considered a sign of sanctity.[13] Also problematic is the *obit* upon which the calculation hinges. Although all sources agree that Dominic died on 22 January 1031, a recently published charter shows him completing a property exchange the following June.[14] Fortunately, thanks to the idiosyncracies of medieval calendars, it is not necessary to postulate posthumous real estate dealings. Farfa, for example, whose connections with Dominic will soon be described, began its year on 25 March, the feast of the Annunciation.[15] Under this system Dominic could have been trading land in June of what would have been today's year 1031 and then died on 22 January in what would have been his year 1031 but our year 1032. If the traditional date for Dominic's death must be nudged forward, then so must that for his birth. Yet his birthdate cannot be advanced too many

12. *Trisulti Life* xxxv, 298; *Valva Life* lxviii, 76; *Monte Cassino Life* lxviii, 76; *Sora Life* cciv, 61. The postscript in *Trisulti Life* xxxiii, 297, also presumes an eighty-year life span; if one adds up the 44½ years Dominic is said to have spent building his monasteries, the 15 years at San Bartolomeo, and the 20½ years at Sora, the exact total is eighty. But since this scheme does violence to Dominic's actual chronology, it appears to be nothing more than an arbitrary attempt to allocate his alleged eighty years.

13. On the venerable qualities of old age, see Isabelle Cochelin, "*In Senectute Bona*: Pour une typologie de la viellesse dans l'hagiographie monastique des XIIe et XIIIe siècles," *Les Âges de la vie au moyen âge: Actes du Colloque du Département d'études médiévales de l'Université de Paris-Sorbonne et de l'Université Friedrich-Wilhelm de Bonn, Provins, 16–17 mars 1990*, Cultures et civilisations 7 (Paris: Presses de l'Université de Paris-Sorbonne, 1992), 135–36. Examples of "age inflation" in eleventh-century Italian hagiography are given in Walter Franke, *Romuald von Camaldoli und seine Reformtätigkeit zur Ottos III*, Historische Studien 107 (Berlin: E. Ebering, 1913), 46–49.

14. Scholars have failed to recognize the significance of the date of the June 1031 charter commemorating the exchange of lands between Dominic and Lord Peter of Sora because they refuse to believe it. Although Farina and Fornari, *Storia e documenti . . . di Casamari*, 154–56, published the charter from a copy made from Casamari's lost late-medieval chartulary, they presumed the date must be a scribal error since Dominic was supposed to have died in January 1031. Dionigi Antonelli, *Abbazie . . . di Sora*, 214–15, argued that an error had been made by Farina and Fornari, who, confronted with the date "Anni sunt mille trigesimo primo mense iunii tertia decima indictione," should have construed "primo" not with the year but with the month, thus assigning the charter to the first day of June in 1030. But here Antonelli errs, because his reading does not conform to the practice of Sora charters, which indicate years and months but not days (see, for example, the documents in Farina and Fornari, *Storia e documenti . . . di Casamari*, 151–63). No one heretofore has been willing to envision the possibility that the date is correct.

15. Schuster, "Martyrologium Pharphense ex Apographo Cardinalis Fortunati Tamburini O. S. B. Codicis Saeculi XI," *Revue bénédictine* 26 (1909): 433–63, esp. 448; 27 (1910): 75–94 and 363–85.

years beyond 951, since, as will be seen below, he had become a priest, served apprenticeships as a monk and as a hermit, and begun to found monasteries well before the turn of the millennium. His early career becomes improbably compressed if his birth is placed later than the start of the 960s.

Dominic's hagiographers relate that when he was just a boy (an "infans," a "puer," "in annis adhuc puerilibus," or in "pueritia"), his parents decided to send him for literary studies to a monastery dedicated to St. Sylvester. The *lives* confusingly render the name of that house as "S. Silvester Subaserus" or "cui Aseri cognomentum est" or "Curaserus." [16] Jacobilli resolved this muddle by claiming that San Silvestro was Santissima Trinità, Foligno's first monastery, differently named at that time. [17] Since he does not cite any evidence for this identification, he may have invented it on the basis of the following premises: (1) Dominic was from Foligno, (2) Dominic went to a monastic school dedicated to St. Sylvester, (3) the only monastery known to have existed in Foligno in the mid-tenth century was Santissima Trinità, and, therefore, (4) Dominic must have entered Foligno's ancient monastery, which must then have been named San Silvestro. Thanks to Jacobilli's assertion, this "San Silvestro" has been accepted as Dominic's school, has entered major indexes of monasteries, and has even had a manuscript attributed to it. [18]

16. The *Sermon*, 365, reads "in cenovio scilicet Sancti Silvestris quod dicitur subaseri"; the *Trisulti Life* i, 282, does not specify where Dominic was trained; the *Valva Life* xiii–xiv, 71, notes literary studies but not the school's name; the *Monte Cassino Life* xiii, 71–72 has Dominic sent "in monasterio Sancti Silvestri, cui Aseri cognomentum est"; the *Sora Life* xiii, 37, places him "in monasterio Sancti Silvestri cui Curaseri cognomentum est" (Dolbeau has here amended Vall. ms. H. 18, fol. 407, which reads "in monasterio quod Sancti Silvestri Curaseri cognomentum est"). This mess has frustrated scholars: the Maurists, for example, gave up trying to reconcile the readings and conjectured "*Sub-Aseri*, vernacule *Curassero*" (*ASOSB* 6[1]:316n).

17. Jacobilli, *Vite de' santi e beati di Foligno*, 26; *Vite de' santi e beati dell'Umbria*, 1:114; and *Vita di S. Domenico*, 10, 57–58.

18. Jacobilli's identification of San Silvestro was accepted by subsequent historiographers, including, for example, Francesco Tuzii, *Memorie istoriche massimente sacre della Città di Sora* (Rome: Stamperia di Antonio de'Rossi, 1727), 44; Giuseppe Bragazzi, *Compendio della Storia di Fuligno*, Biblioteca istorica della antica e nuova Italia 85 (1858; reprint, Bologna: Forni Editore, 1973), 53; and Luigi Tosti, "La Leggenda di San Domenico Abate," in his *Opere Complete*, ed. Loreto Pasqualucci, 5 vols. (Rome: L. Pasqualucci, Editore, 1886–90), 2:299–300. It entered standard inventories of monasteries such as Augustin Lubin, *Abbatiarum Italiae Brevis Notitia* (Rome: Typis Jo. Jacobi Komarek Boëmï, 1693), 152; Ferdinand Ughelli, *Italia Sacra sive de Episcopis Italiae*, 2nd ed., 10 vols. (Venice: Sebastian Colet, 1717–22), 1:686–87; and Laurent-Henri Cottineau, *Répertoire topo-bibliographique des abbayes et prierés*, 3 vols. (Macon: Protat Frères Imprimeurs-Éditeurs, 1936–70), 1:1166–67. As a result, the secondary literature boasts a plethora of citations concerning San Silvestro at Foligno, but none of these antedate Jacobilli. Failure to recognize this has led to errors, including the assignment of a manuscript to this hypothetical house by Leo Eizenhöfer, in "Die Feier der Ostervigil in der

No one heretofore has recognized that a better documented candidate for Dominic's school is the monastery of San Silvestro on Monte Subasio.[19] Located high above the Flaminian Way, about four and a half miles directly north of Foligno, it offers the region's only secure dedication to St. Sylvester. Perhaps Jacobilli did not consider this solution because in his time San Silvestro on Monte Subasio was not in the diocese of Foligno (then it was in a narrow strip of the diocese of Spoleto stretching up between Assisi and Foligno).[20] Or perhaps he rejected the identification as chronologically impossible, because of a tradition that the monastery on Monte Subasio was founded in the early eleventh century by St. Romuald, the illustrious founder of the Camaldolese monks.[21] That tradition, however, is almost certainly false. The crypt of San Silvestro has been dated to the tenth century.[22] Moreover, Romuald's alleged foundation is not mentioned either in Peter Damian's *Vita Romualdi* or in the 1152–53 letter by which Eugenius III donated San Silvestro to Camaldoli.[23] The association with Romuald appears to be an anachronistic backdating of the 1152–53 affiliation. Thus nothing prohibits identifying Dominic's San Silvestro with San Silvestro on Monte Subasio, an identification that elegantly explains the otherwise unintelligible qualifiers found in the *vitae* as progressively deteriorated readings from "Subasio" to "Subasero" to "cui aseri cognomentum est" to "Curaseri."

It is a surprising coincidence that Dominic was trained on Monte Su-

Benediktinerabtei San Silvestro zu Foligno um das Jahr 1100 nach Ms. 379 der Pierpont Morgan Library, New York City," *Archiv für Liturgiewissenschaft* 6 (1960): 339–71.

19. For bibliography on San Silvestro near Collepino, see Sensi, "Monasteri benedettini in Assisi: Insediamenti sul Subasio e abbazia di S. Pietro," in *Aspetti di vita benedettina nella storia di Assisi: Atti del convegno, 12–13 settembre 1980*, Atti Accademia Properziana del Subasio, ser. 6, 5 (Assisi: Accademia Properziana, 1981), 29, 35–43; and "San Silvestro di Collepino fra storia e mito," *Spoletium: Rivista di arte storia cultura* 34–35 (1990): 181–86.

20. That San Silvestro was originally within the borders of the diocese of Spoleto is demonstrated by tithe records in *Rationes Decimarum Italiae nei secoli XIII e XIV: Umbria*, ed. Pietro Sella, 2 vols., Studi e Testi 161 and 162 (Vatican City: Biblioteca Apostolica Vaticana, 1952), 1:420, 430, and 458. Yet it probably always maintained close contacts with Foligno. A twelfth-century missal, Pierpont Morgan Library ms. 379, described in Eizenhöfer, "Feier der Ostervigil," 339–71, esp. 342, invokes as patrons both Silvester and Felicianus. The bishops of Foligno participated in San Silvestro's sixteenth-century reform attempts noted in Agostino Fortunio, *Historiarum Camaldulensium Libri Tres* II xxii (Florence: Bibliotheca Sermartelliana, 1575), 176. The geographical logic of such contacts probably explains why the territory was transferred to the diocese of Foligno in the eighteenth century.

21. Jacobilli, *Vite de'santi e beati dell'Umbria*, 3:305.

22. Gisberto Martelli, "Le più antiche cripte dell'Umbria," in *Aspetti dell'Umbria*, 344–48 (figs. 55 and 56) and 352.

23. Eugenius III, *Epistula* (J–L 9671), edited in *PL*, 180:167–68; noted in Paul Fridolin Kehr, *Italia Pontificia*, 10 vols. (Berlin: Weidmann, 1906–75), 3:179–80; 4:15–16.

basio, because there, a little more than two centuries later, God and nature would also become immanent to young Francis of Assisi. Subasio is a rocky hump over 4000 feet high, with ilex and holm oak on its slopes and pasture on top, tapering off in the west into the range of hills where Assisi sits, pink-hued from Subasio stone. The first permanent retreats of Francis and his followers are said to be the "Carceri," a series of ancient hermitages partially cut into the rock.[24] About four miles to the east of them is Dominic's church of San Silvestro, today gleamingly restored. Its nearest neighbor, below and to the east, is Collepino, a walled mountain village typical of the rural aristocratic order. The "Rocca Paida" towered close by, a former stronghold of the lords of Armenzano, a family that produced some of Francis's early recruits.[25] Perhaps long before they helped Francis, they supported Dominic's San Silvestro, a hypothesis bolstered not only by the proximity of monastery and castle but also by the monastery's ownership of property in Armenzano itself.[26] The extent of San Silvestro's dependencies and possessions indicates that it once had powerful patrons.[27]

What type of monastic life would Dominic have experienced? Greek influence might be postulated if one were willing to accept the claims of local antiquarians that many odd toponyms in this mountain region, such as "Rocca Paida," and even the earliest lords of Armenzano themselves, were Greek in origin, a result of refugee resettlement after the 969 Apulian campaigns of Otto I and Prince Pandulf I Ironhead of Capua—but little documentation supports this scenario.[28] San Silvestro has been identified as a Camaldolese foundation, but that tradition is discounted above. Most probably it was Benedictine, like many other monasteries created in central Italy in the late tenth and early eleventh centuries. What is certain is that there Dominic would have learned institutional pioneering. San Silvestro

24. For the traditions linking Francis to these retreats, see Arnaldo Fortini, *Nova Vita di San Francesco*, 4 vols. [in 5] (Assisi: Edizioni Assisi, 1959 [1960–68]), 3:155–62.

25. Fortini, *Nova Vita di San Francesco*, 2:430–36.

26. Fausti, "Le chiese della diocesi spoletina nel XIV secolo," 168–70 and 213, cites a list of Spoletan churches, whose original is said to go back at least to 1393, which claims in a section "De Plebatu Armenzano," that the church of Sta. Maria de Montefano was subject to San Silvestro.

27. Property lists for San Silvestro, produced as a result of complicated suppression proceedings, are described in Sensi, "Il patrimonio monastico di S. Maria di Vallegloria a Spello," *Bollettino della Deputazione di Storia Patria per l'Umbria* 81 (1984): 77–149; and Giovanna Casagrande, "Inventario-regesto delle pergamene della chiesa parrochiale di S. Maria Maggiore a Spello (1187–1844), *Bollettino della Deputazione di Storia Patria per l'Umbria* 83 (1986): 9. Tithe lists showing San Silvestro heavily assessed are edited in *Rationes Decimarum Italiae . . . Umbria*, 1:420, 430, and 458.

28. Fortini, *Nova Vita di San Francesco*, 1:399, 2:430–37.

was surrounded by a forest important enough to trigger a fatal thirteenth-century legal dispute between its monks and some of their dependents.[29] In a new monastery surrounded by mountain forest, close to a new castle and fortified village, young Dominic would have directly experienced both environmental conquest and community building.

Dominic had been sent to San Silvestro to study. The *Trisulti Life*, which glosses over his boyhood, observes only that his parents had made arrangements for him to learn sacred letters: it perfunctorily mentions progress in hymns, prayers, fasts, and the perpetual wearing of a hair shirt.[30] The *Valva, Monte Cassino*, and *Sora Lives* use similar *topoi* but add that after Dominic had quickly become skilled, according to the rite of the region, in reading and singing, he was advanced through the lower orders to the priesthood.[31] It would help to establish Dominic's chronology if it could be ascertained that his ordinations followed the ancient canons concerning the required ages for ordinands and the required time intervals between the reception of different orders—their punctilious observance would have kept Dominic at San Silvestro until he was twenty-five, twenty-six, or perhaps even thirty.[32] Unfortunately, the specification that the intervals of promotion were "proper" ("congrua") seems to have been added by Alberic, the author most concerned about the technical correctness of Dominic's career. All *lives* agree that Dominic learned quickly and possessed wisdom and understanding beyond his years.[33] They evoke the pre-Christian image of the *puer senex*, a hagiographical commonplace that reconciles opposites by balancing youth against old age.[34] It is

29. Gregory IX, on 25 April 1236, gave the nuns of Santa Maria di Vallegloria at Spello the right to gather wood from San Silvestro's forests; several months later he suddenly attempted to suppress San Silvestro entirely, opening up generations of legal conflict and violence. See Casagrande, "Inventario-regesto . . . di S. Maria Maggiore a Spello," 9.

30. *Trisulti Life* i, 282.

31. *Valva Life* xiii–xiv, 72; *Monte Cassino Life* xiii–xiv, 72; *Sora Life* xiii–xiv, 37.

32. The ancient canons concerning the age of ordinands might have been observed in Dominic's Italy: Peter Damian, *Epistula* 40 (old numbering, *Opusculum* VI), 1:399, writing around 1052, presumes as an institutional norm that no one should be admitted to the priesthood until he is thirty. On the tradition involved, see J. Delmaille, "Âge," *Dictionnaire de droit canonique*, 7 vols. (Paris: Letouzey et Ané, 1935–65), 1:338–41.

33. *Sermon*, 365; *Trisulti Life* i, 282; *Valva Life* xiii–xiv, 71–72; *Monte Cassino Life* xiii, 72; *Sora Life* xiii, 37.

34. The *puer senex* topos is described in Ernst Robert Curtius, *European Literature in the Latin Middle Ages*, trans. Willard R. Trask, Bollingen Series 36 (1953; reprinted with "Epilogue" by Peter Godman, New York: Pantheon Books, 1990), 98–101; and in Teresa C. Carp, "*Puer Senex* in Roman and Medieval Thought," *Latomus* 39 (1980): 736–39. On its influence see Donald Weinstein and Rudolph M. Bell, *Saints and Society: The Two Worlds of Western Christendom, 1000–1700* (Chicago: University of Chicago Press, 1982), 29; and Shulamith Shahar, *Childhood in the Middle Ages* (London: Routledge, 1990), 15–16.

striking that even though Dominic had studied at San Silvestro for many years and was ordained to the priesthood, he does not appear to have received the monastic habit there.[35] Was his initial vocation priestly rather than monastic? Priests could be trained in monasteries, even in Rome.[36] Or did Dominic intend to become a monk, but not at San Silvestro?

Soon after his ordination, he traveled more than sixty miles south, evoking from his hagiographers echoes of Abraham's faith journey "out of his country and from his kindred" (cf. Genesis 12:1). His new home was an obscure "Monasterium Sanctae Dei Genitricis Mariae Virginisque Perpetuae" (the *lives* do not agree on the exact wording of the dedication). It was located at "Petra Daemonis" ("Rock of the Demon"), a name so sinister that Alberic felt compelled to supply a more classical etymology, deriving it from "Petra Dei Amonis" and identifying it as a former site of pagan worship.[37] Perhaps it was connected with the hill named "Pietra," rising to about 4000 feet, which is located west of the town of Orvinio, a place whose medieval name, as unattractive as Petra Demone's, was "Canemorto," that is, "Dead Dog."

The records of nearby Farfa do not mention a community at Petra Demone until the eleventh century, when they note its "pertinentia" in 1011 and its "castellum" in 1083/1084.[38] Yet the *castello* must already have existed in 1011, since the "pertinentia," presumably fields and possessions,

35. Dominic's *lives* present the sequence of ordination and monastic entrance in two opposed ways. The *Sermon*, 365, in a moralizing, nonchronological passage, has the expected sequence of monk, priest, and hermit; the *Trisulti Life* i, 282, which is truncated here, omits San Silvestro and puts the ordination at Dominic's next stop, after monastic vows. The more surprising order, placing priestly ordination before monastic vows, is found in the *Valva Life* xiv–xvi, 72; the *Monte Cassino Life* xiv–xvi, 72; and the *Sora Life* xiv–xvi, 37. The latter sequence has been accepted here because (1) the *Valva*, *Monte Cassino*, and *Sora Lives* give fuller information on Dominic's studies, and (2) the reversal of the normal sequence for a monk is the *lectio difficilior*, and Alberic, who struggled to assimilate Dominic's career to a customary Benedictine pattern, would have not unnecessarily reversed the expected order.

36. Little is known about how secular priests were trained in Italy around the year 1000. Cathedral choirs and *scholae* were apparently traditional: for the arrangements at Verona, see Miller, *Formation of a Medieval Church*, 42–50. Yet would-be Roman priests were educated initially in the *scholae cantorum* of the Vatican and the Lateran, both of which were run by monks. Prior monastic formation might help explain the way that some priests who were Dominic's contemporaries, after having been ordained at their parents' urging, suddenly jumped into monastic life: see, for examples, the *lives* (*BHL* 1147 and 2239) of Benedict of Benevento (d. 1003) and Dominic Loricatus (d. 1060).

37. *Trisulti Life* ii, 282; *Valva Life* xv, 72; *Monte Cassino Life* xv, 72; *Sora Life* xv–xvi, 37. The little that is known about the monastery at Petra Demone is described in *Monasticon Italiae* 1:167.

38. *Reg. Farf.*, 4:15–16, 5:78 and 90 (docs. 617, 1083, 1095); cf. *Chron. Farf.*, 2:122 and 170–71.

presuppose it.[39] Dominic's hagiographical texts may push its origin back
further, perhaps to the late 980s or 990s, since his "familiares" used it as a
reference point for his activity during those years. Petra Demone did not
prosper. Today the hill named Pietra is covered with *macchia*. That brush
must have been a problem early on, since the Farfa property donation from
1011 and its subsequent confirmations name a place called "maccla felcosa"
that bounded the "pertinentia" of Petra Demone; a list of Farfa properties
from 1119 mentions a "casalis de Maccla . . . in Petra Demonis."[40]

Why would Dominic have traveled sixty miles south to a brushy area
near "Rock of the Demon," just west of "Dead Dog?" Was this his own
unlikely inspiration? Or had he been recruited? The one obvious link between his old and new residences is the monastery of Farfa. Farfa had
grazing rights throughout the Duchy of Spoleto.[41] In Foligno it claimed
ownership of the church of "Sancta Maria in Fullonica"; in Assisi, at least
in the eleventh century, it had not only fields, vineyards, and churches,
but also the monastery of "Sancti Benedicti in comitatu Asisinato," the
ecclesiastical establishment that dominated Monte Subasio.[42] Moreover,
Dominic's new monastery, about ten miles from Farfa, bore a Marian dedication very similar to Farfa's own "Congregatio Sanctae Dei Genitricis
Semperque Virginis Mariae." Was this monastic community subordinate to
Farfa, imitating or using directly the name of the motherhouse? If Dominic
was recruited by Farfa, this suggests a new line of inquiry in regard to encastellation: while it has long been recognized that the monastic and noble
developers of the new *castelli* hunted far afield to find the peasant farmers
they needed, Dominic's move suggests that they might also have recruited
clergymen for their related ecclesiastical foundations.

39. Toubert, *Structures*, 1:501.

40. *Reg. Farf.*, 4:15–16 and 5:313–15 (docs. 617 and 1320); cf. *Chron. Farf.*, 2:90 and 297.

41. Farfa's Spoletan grazing rights were granted by Louis the Pious and confirmed by
Lothar. See *Reg. Farf.*, 2:199 and 238 (docs. no. 242 and 282 [the second of two of this num-
ber]), reiterated in *Chron. Farf.*, 1:189 and 205; analyzed in Ring, "The Lands of Farfa," 103–5.

42. Farfa's contested claim to Foligno's church of Santa Maria is found in a confused
and broken passage in *Chron. Farf.*, 1:253. On its Assisi holdings, see Sensi, "Monasteri benedettini in Assisi," 32–35. Especially relevant is Farfa's claim to San Benedetto al Subasio, which
owned much of Monte Subasio. The crypt of San Benedetto is dated to the tenth century in
Martelli, "Le più antiche cripte dell'Umbria," 344–52. Unfortunately, literary evidence earlier
than 1041 has not survived: see Angelo Pantoni, "San Benedetto al Subasio," *Benedictina* 2
(1948): 47–74, esp. 47–48. Both Leo IX in 1051 and Henry IV in 1067 confirm Farfa's ownership of San Benedetto: *Reg. Farf.*, 4:281 and 356 (docs. 884 and 976); cf. *Chon. Farf.*, 2:137
and 153. Yet previous Farfa general property confirmations do not mention this house, the
charters cited above list it together with new acquisitions, and it disappears again from Farfa's
lists of dependencies at the end of the eleventh century. Thus how the two monasteries were
related in the late tenth century remains unknown.

Dominic would have found monastic life at Petra Demone familiar. He had persevered in a long course of priestly training at San Silvestro on the forested slopes of Monte Subasio, not far from Collepino. His new monastery was on the slopes of a mountain, in the neighborhood of the recently founded *castello* of Petra Demone. It apparently had an impressive abbot. The Trisulti and Valva accounts report that abbot "Dionysius" or "Domnisus" clothed Dominic in the monastic habit; Alberic describes abbot "Domnosus" as "outstanding in marvelous sanctity."[43] If the correct name form were "Dionysius," a rare name in tenth-century Latin Italy, it might suggest Greek origin, but neither the name nor the nationality can be confirmed. This spiritual father is the only man whom Dominic's *lives* cite as an influence on him.

Dominic's hagiographers claim that he was a monk for a considerable period of time ("aliquantulum temporis" or "per annos aliquot").[44] The monastic virtues he developed are conflated in the *Trisulti Life* and only obliquely hinted at in the *Valva Life*. Alberic, however, praises Dominic's fasts, vigils, prayers, and readings, finding him "remarkable, in short, in the observation of the whole discipline of monastic life."[45] Jacobilli goes even further: he makes Dominic a perfect seventeenth-century Benedictine by claiming that his superiors sent him off for training at Monte Cassino, an anachronistic novitiate whose lack of historicity was not signaled until the 1950s.[46]

43. The sources present the name of Dominic's abbot in varied fashion. The *Trisulti Life* ii, 282, reads "Dionysius," as does Jacobus de Voragine's *Summary*, fol. 347. The *Valva Life* xv–xvii, 72, reads "Domnisus." Alberic appears to have used "Domnosus": *Monte Cassino Life* xvi, 72, reads "Domnosus"; the *Sora Life* xvi, 37, may read "Domnosus" (Dolbeau's reading of a word where the second and third letters have been illegibly crossed out by the corrector of Vall. ms. H. 18, fol. 407, who has made it "Donnosus"). Dolbeau, "Dossier de saint Dominique," 27, who prefers "Domnosus," uses this name to illustrate what he sees as "the progressive impoverishment of information" proceeding from Alberic's work, which he sees as the *Monte Cassino Life*, to the *Valva Life*, and the *Trisulti Life*. This argument only works if there is a compelling reason for accepting "Domnosus" as the original form. The odd "Domnisus," found in both eleventh-century manuscripts of the *Valva Life*, is a well-attested *lectio difficilior*.

44. *Sermon*, 365; *Trisulti Life* ii, 282; *Valva Life* xviii, 72. Here the Alberician texts sacrifice chronology for rhetorical elaboration.

45. The *Sermon*, 365; the *Trisulti Life* ii, 282; and the *Valva Life* xviii, 72, contrast with the rhetoric of the *Monte Cassino Life* xvii, 72; and the *Sora Life* xvii, 37.

46. Dominic's alleged stay at Monte Cassino is mentioned in Jacobilli, *Vite de'santi e beati dell'Umbria*, 1 : 115; and *Vita di S. Domenico*, p. 11. It did not appear in his first account of Dominic, written more than a dozen years earlier, in *Vite de'santi e beati di Foligno*, 25–35. From Jacobilli the story was taken up by writers such as Tuzii, *Memorie istoriche . . . di Sora*, 45; Bragazzi, *Compendio della storia di Fuligno*, 53; and Tosti, "La Leggenda di San Domenico," in *Opere Complete*, 2:302–3. Its lack of historicity was not signalled until Lentini, "S. Domenico Sorano e Montecassino," *Benedictina* 5 (1951): 185–91.

Then Dominic became a hermit. His hagiographers all echo the *Rule of Benedict* here, linking Dominic's entry into the desert to the desire to advance out of the monastic battleline in order to seek the eremitical life; some specify that Dominic had secured the permission of his abbot before he climbed to the top of a nearby mountain and led the solitary life for what the *Valva Life* describes as "many days."[47] All *lives* proclaim that a city on a mountain cannot be hidden (Matthew 5:14–15, cf. Mark 4:21 and Luke 11:33). In fact, they turn Dominic's mountain into a virtual city, claiming that, after he had been discovered there, everyone in the area began to visit, bringing him necessities of earthly life while he gave them sustenance for eternal life.[48] Alberic embellishes the narrative with alliteration, swift-flying "rumor," and a tag from Horace: "Dominic's reputation took wings" and the news went "through farms and cities" and was known "in the towers of the wealthy, in the taverns of the poor, even in the huts of the shepherds." The other hagiographers less eloquently convey the same message: Dominic, his training complete and his contact with the mountain wilderness established, had become a celebrity.[49] As a result of his fame, he was asked to build monasteries.

The establishment of Dominic's first foundation, San Salvatore at Scandriglia, highlights a paradox characteristic not only of Dominic's career but also of early reform efforts in general—the patrons of reform are often those most in need of it themselves. Dominic built San Salvatore not far from where he had received the monastic habit. In fact, today Petra Demone's site is not far from the commune of Scandriglia, located about 1700 feet above sea level, occupying a long, narrow ridge overlooking the Via Salaria. In 764 Farfa's records treat Scandriglia as a "curtis"; in 1023 they note "pertinentia," suggesting a more concentrated population; in 1083–84 they specify a "castellum," presumably the present town.[50] Domi-

---

47. *Sermon*, 365; *Trisulti Life* ii, 282; *Valva Life* xvii, 72; *Monte Cassino Life* xviii, 72; *Sora Life* xviii, 37–38. Cf. *RB* i, 1:436–39. While the *Valva Life* xviii, 72, specifies "non paucis diebus," the *Monte Cassino Life* xviii, 72, and the *Sora Life* xviii, 37–38, sacrifice the time referent in favor of a more explicit citation of Benedict's *Rule*.

48. *Sermon*, 365–66; *Trisulti Life* ii, 282–83; *Valva Life* xix–xxii, 72; *Monte Cassino Life* xix–xxii, 73; *Sora Life* xix–xxii, 38.

49. *Monte Cassino Life* xxiii, 73; *Sora Life* xxiii, 38. Compare Horace, *Carmen* I iv, edited in Kenneth Quin, *Horace: The Odes*, Classical Series (New York: Macmillan Education Limited, 1985), 7.

50. *Reg. Farf.*, 2:63, 3:260, 5:78 and 90, (docs. 63, 551, 1083, 1095); reiterated in *Chron. Farf.*, 1:154; 2:48; 168; and 171. A full survey of the documentary evidence is found in Schuster, "Il Monastero del Salvatore e gli antichi possedimenti farfensi nella 'massa torana'," *Archivio della R. SRSP* 41 (1918): 5–58.

nic's monastery of San Salvatore lay about three and a half miles outside this new town, between it and Petra Demone, on the side of a canyon in a protected location halfway up the slopes of Monte Pendente. Its ruins, now incorporated into a villa, are at about the same elevation as Scandriglia, but set back into the mountains, farther away from the Tiber Valley, looking out from the wilderness onto the *castello*.[51]

Not all *lives* agree on why Dominic founded San Salvatore. The *Trisulti Life* cites popular initiative, claiming that "many men invited sweetly by the reputation of his sanctity began to give up their secular habit and pledge themselves to divine service; and so, after a monastery . . . had been constructed, he established a father for them." It may be more than coincidence that by describing the foundation of Dominic's first monastery as a popular enterprise, the Trisulti author gives it the same history as his own monastery. The *Sermon* on Dominic also mentions popular enthusiasm. The other *lives*, however, which present more detailed information about Dominic's early career, claim that he was induced to found the monastery by the "potentissimus marchio Hubertus," whose enthusiastic entreaties Alberic elegantly elaborates.[52]

Who was this "extremely powerful marquess?" In Carolingian Italy a marquess was at the top of the social pyramid, the ruler of one of a small number of super counties—Friuli, Tuscany, and Spoleto—that guarded the realm against the Avars, the sea-going Saracens, and menaces from the south; a later addition to this list was Ivrea, created in Western Lombardy to oppose the Muslims.[53] But in seeking Dominic's Marquess Hubert, it is necessary to bear in mind that the rank had evolved, or perhaps devolved. More and more marquesses were appearing. Partible inheritance meant that brothers could share titles. Pretensions to the rank may have been en-

51. Giuseppe Sacchi Lodispoto, "L'Abbazia di S. Salvatore di Scandriglia," in *Tra le abbazie del Lazio*, 285, describes the remains of San Salvatore. The site is reached by an unpaved, unmarked road. Most of what may have been part of the walls of the monastery has been incorporated into the present villa.

52. In its account of San Salvatore, the *Sermon*, 366, emphasizes the role of the people; the *Trisulti Life* ii, 282–83, names Scandriglia, but not Hubert. Hubert's role is described in the *Valva Life* xxiii–xxxi, 73. Alberic's rhetorical amplifications are revealed by the *Monte Cassino Life* xxiv–xxvii, 73, and the *Sora Life* xxiv–xxvi, 38–39. In the versions Alberic inspired, the marquess encourages Dominic to select any part of his domain for his new monastery, and Dominic chooses a generous endowment.

53. The genesis of the title "marchio" is treated in J. Dhondt, "Le titre du Marquis à l'époque carolingienne," *Archivum Latinitatis Medii Aevi* 19 (1948): 407–17; its Italian application in Katherine Fischer Drew, "The Carolingian Military Frontier in Italy," *Traditio* 20 (1964): 437–47, reprinted with the same pagination in *Law and Society in Early Medieval Europe: Studies in Medieval Legal History* (London: Variorum Reprints, 1988).

hanced when territories were redefined in ways that gave nobles lands and powers in more than one county.[54] By Dominic's day, a marquess was not necessarily a pillar of the old Carolingian order; he could be a junior son or even an aristocratic parvenu.

The key to identifying Dominic's Marquess Hubert is a charter from Farfa originally written in July 1003. Guido, the recording notary, describes what transpired "in the fortified settlement which is called Toffia, within the house which belonged to Lord Hubert, . . . in front of the bed where Lord Hubert, son of the former Marquess Theobaldus, was lying in infirmity." Also present were thirteen good men serving as witnesses ("*boni homines*"), including two monks from Farfa and "Remedius, who was priest, monk, and prior of San Salvatore." The monks exhorted Hubert to "remember the properties which you hold that belong to our monastery, so that you might give them back for the redemption of your soul." Hubert then restored to Farfa all its former houses, vineyards, fields, orchards, and woodlands, together with all that appertained to them. "And so it was done and defined." The care taken to witness and record this donation suggests that the men around the sickbed wanted to be absolutely certain it would still be honored if Hubert recovered.[55]

They were right to be cautious. "Lord Hubert," insofar as he can be identified from the hints given by this charter, was a notorious character even by the standards of tenth-century Farfa. The "Marquess Theobaldus" named as Hubert's father was probably the man of that name who received the Duchy of Spoleto in 929 from his uncle King Hugh (a ruler whose egregious nepotism has already been noted), and who held this honor until his death ca. 937.[56] One link between the two is Hubert's place of residence, the *castello* of Toffia, which is supposed to have been founded by

---

54. Mario Nobili, "L'evoluzione delle dominazioni marchionali in relazione alla dissoluzione delle circoscrizioni marchionali e comitali e allo sviluppo della politica territoriale dei comuni cittadini nell'Italia centro settentrionale (secoli XI e XII)," in *La Cristianità dei secoli XI e XII in Occidente: Coscienza e strutture di una società: Atti della ottava Settimana internazionale di studio, Mendola, 30 giugno–5 luglio 1980*, Pubblicazioni dell'Università Cattolica del Sacro Cuore, Miscellanea del Centro di Studi Medioevali 10 (Milan: Vita e Pensiero, 1983), 235–58.

55. *Reg. Farf.*, 3:125 (doc. 415).

56. Adolf Hofmeister, "Markgrafen und Markgrafschaften im italischen Königreich in der Zeit von Karl dem Grossen bis auf Otto den Grossen (774–962)," *MIÖG: Ergänzungsband* 7 (1907): 407–9; Antonio Falce, *Il Marchese Ugo di Tuscia*, Pubblicazioni del R. Istituto di Studi Superiori Pratici e di Perfezionamento in Firenze, Sezione di filologia e filosofia n.s. 2 (Florence: R. Bemporad & Figlio, 1921), 419–24; Hlawitschka, *Franken, Alemannen, . . . in Italien*, 86, 131, 208, 262.

Theobaldus.[57] Another link is the career of Marquess Theobaldus II of Spoleto (after 956–967?) who was also "Rector of the Sabina."[58] Of him, Abbot Hugh of Farfa (d. 1039) complained, in his *Destructio* (a lament about catastrophes Farfa had suffered), that after the death of Abbot Adam (whose last signed document is from 963):

> Marquess Theobaldus invaded and seized the monastery. He arranged for his brother Hubert to dwell there, a learned canon with debilitated limbs, who held it for some space of time. He shamefully dissipated the monastic property by living there daily with prostitutes, dogs, and all manner of worldly obscenities. Then Pope John who was called "from Narni" [John XIII, 965–972] took the monastery away from him and gave it to an abbot of Sant'Andrea on Monte Soratte.[59]

The pieces of the puzzle fit together if the Hubert whom Theobaldus II had established at Farfa after 963 was the same man who later launched Dominic's career as a monastic founder and who last appears in July 1003 on his sickbed (deathbed?) at Toffia.[60] If this identification is correct, then

57. Toffia sits on a ridge about a third of the way between Farfa and Scandriglia. It appears from 940 on as a *castellum* claimed by Farfa: note especially *Reg. Farf.*, 3:80 and 81 (docs. 373, 374); reiterated in *Chron. Farf.*, 1:313–14 and 2:222. The circumstances of its foundation are unclear. Giuseppe Marocco, *Monumenti dello Stato pontificio e relazione topografica di ogni paese*, 14 vols. in 5 (Rome: Boulzaler, 1833–37), 3:49, on the authority of a now lost document from the collegiate church of San Lorenzo at Toffia, claims that Toffia was founded by Theobaldus, Duke of Spoleto. Francesco-Paolo Sperandio, *Sabina sagra e profana, antica e moderna* (Rome: G. Zempel, 1790), 330–31, arguing from a now lost 964 San Lorenzo document, claims that Toffia had been founded ca. 900 by the bishop of Foronovo. Toubert, *Structures*, 1:410, considers foundation by Theobaldus more consonant with Farfa's development.

58. The rectorship of the Sabina was instituted by Prince Alberic of Rome. The expansive view of this office offered by Vehse, "Die päpstliche Herrschaft in der Sabina," 120–75, esp. 129–31, 150–52, is deconstructed to a considerable extent by Toubert in *Structures*, 2:988–95. The rectorship certainly never gave Rome unchallenged control, since the holders of the office tended to be local nobles, as listed in Kölmel, *Rom und der Kirchenstaat*, 154–55.

On Theobaldus as rector, see Hugh, *Destructio*, 1:42; *Chron. Farf.*, 1:329. Note also Hofmeister, "Markgrafen und Markgrafschaften im italischen Königreich," 424; and Vehse, "Päpstliche Herrschaft in der Sabina," 131, 133, and 137. Although earlier historians treated Theobaldus II, the Marquess of Spoleto, and Theobaldus, the Rector of the Sabina, as two separate individuals, historians today accept Vehse's conclusion that there is no need to multiply entities here unnecessarily.

59. Hugh of Farfa, *Destructio*, 1:44.

60. Schuster in "L'abbate Ugo I," 746–47; "Il monastero del Salvatore," 26–28; and *L'Imperiale Abbazia di Farfa*, 141, first identified Farfa's Hubert with Dominic's Marquess Hubert. Because this identification has been largely overlooked by commentators on Dominic, no one heretofore has signaled a problem: Hubert's father is identified as Marquess Theobaldus [I of Spoleto?] in the Farfa charter of 1003; but Theobaldus II's father is named as Duke Boniface of Spoleto (946–953/954) in a Farfa charter of 947 found in *Reg. Farf.*, 3:56–58 (doc. 354).

If Hubert and Theobaldus had different fathers, how were they brothers? Of the various

Hubert would have survived his eviction by Pope John XIII, whose success in handing the Sabina over to his own Crescenzi relatives has already been noted. He would have remained encysted in Farfa's patrimony, in possession of, at minimum, his residence in Toffia, the endowments he later gave to Dominic, and the lands he restored to Farfa in 1003. Such a luxurious retirement does not seem so incredible if one examines the fates of other Farfa ex-abbots. Abbot Wigbertus, deposed in 769, retained a mill and a lifetime tenancy of a monastery near Rieti, all of which, albeit with considerable dispute, reverted back to Farfa after his death.[61] Abbot Hugh's *Destructio* describes how ex-abbots Campo, who reigned sporadically from 936 through the early 960s, and Hildebrand, who appeared around 939 and kept alive his claims into the 970s, remained in control of chunks of Farfa's territory and attempted to gain more as opportunities arose.[62] Emperor Otto I himself approved a 971 settlement that formally retired Hildebrand onto Farfa lands; even Hildebrand's consort Inge received three *mansi* for her use.[63] Farfa's ex-abbots lived comfortably. The monastery had anticipated the sort of generous executive buyout that in the 1980s would be called a "golden parachute." Thus Marquess Hubert was left able to plan his campaign of repentence.

Dominic must have received his lands from Hubert many years before 1003. Missing at Hubert's bedside are not only Dominic himself but also

scenarios that could explain the relationship, one fits all the fragmentary data. It is known that the widow of Marquess Theobaldus I, i.e., the probable mother of Hubert, was remarried to Sarlio, a Burgundian nobleman who then assumed the titles of "Marquess" and "Rector of the Sabina," dominating Farfa in the mid 940s. His household would therefore have included any minor children of Theobaldus I. After Sarlio's death, a certain Boniface proclaimed himself marquess on the basis of no known hereditary right. If Boniface's rule had also been legitimized by marriage to Theobaldus's widow (now also Sarlio's widow), then Hubert and Theobaldus II would have been step-brothers. Or they could have been full brothers if Theobaldus II had been a royal-blooded son of Theobaldus I, had entered Boniface's household through his mother's marriages, and then had been adopted as Boniface's heir in order to legitimize his rule, a scenario that explains both the unusual way that Boniface and "son" are treated as corulers in the 947 Farfa charter and the appearance of a second marquess of Spoleto with the name Theobaldus. The little known about Sarlio and Boniface is discussed in Hofmeister, "Markgrafen und Markgrafschaften im italischen Königreich," 421–25; and Hlawitschka, *Franken, Alemannen, . . . in Italien*, 262–64.

61. The proceedings concerning the lands of Wigbertus are in Ring, "The Lands of Farfa," 207–10. The sources are *Constructio Monasterii Farfensis* xii, 1:18–19; and *Reg. Farf.*, 2:93–94, 94, 94–95, 109–10, 113–15 (i.e., docs. 103, 104, 105, 129, 135); some of which are reiterated in *Chron. Farf.*, 1:155, 161, 163–64.

62. Hugh of Farfa, *Destructio*, 1:37–42, 45–47; *Chron. Farf.*, 1:289–90, 324–27, 329, 343–44.

63. *Reg. Farf.*, 3:97 (doc. 395); also published in MGH *Dipl. Reg. et Imp.*, ed. Theodor Sickel, 2nd ed., 1:551–52 (doc. 405). Note also Hugh of Farfa, *Destructio*, 1:45–47; *Chron. Farf.*, 1:343–44.

his designated successor, whom the Alberician texts name "Constantius."[64] Speaking instead for San Salvatore is Remedius the Prior ("Praepositus"), whose loyalties are clearly revealed by his presence in the crowd of Farfa witnesses urging the return of lands to "our" monastery. Back in the years when Dominic and Hubert were building San Salvatore, presumably in the late 980s or 990s, they seem to have operated with relative independence. By the start of the eleventh century, however, Farfa was consolidating its territory. Although Abbot John (966–997) had made progress in this direction, the principal hero was Abbot Hugh (998–1039), whose efforts to regularize the patrimony are memorialized in the surviving texts of 220 charters.[65] His success may be reflected both by Farfa's apparent absorption of San Salvatore and by its delegation around Marquess Hubert's bed.

If Farfa controlled San Salvatore in 1003, then who really "owned" the land in the 980s or 990s when Dominic built his monastery? Hubert seems to have had effective control, but the location was in Farfa's traditional territory. Did Farfa welcome Dominic's monastic initiative? Its records ignore him. To complicate matters further, Petra Demone and Scandriglia were also claimed, at least on occasion, by the counts of Rieti, Farfa's neighbors to the northeast. These counts were a branch of the family of the counts of Marsica: Count Theodinus, attested in Farfa records from 982 to 1000, was one of the sons of the lineage founder, Berardus the Frank.[66] The border between them and Farfa cannot always be defined precisely, but it certainly ran very near the places associated with Dominic.[67] Dominic's hagiographers make no mention of the counts of Rieti, but their knowledge about this stage of Dominic's life is particularly limited.

---

64. Only the texts based on Alberic, who tries both to provide names for all Dominic's appointees and to assimilate Dominic to St. Benedict, name "Constantius" as Dominic's successor at San Salvatore: see the *Sermon*, 366; the *Trisulti Life* ii, 283; the *Valva Life* xxiii–xxxi, 73; the *Monte Cassino Life* xxix, 73; and the *Sora Life* xxix, 39. This raises the possibility that the name "Constantius" may be an artifact since it is the name of Benedict's first successor at Monte Cassino: see Gregory I, *Dialog.* II prol., 2:128–29; and *Chron. Cass.* I ii, 20.

65. Schuster, "L'Abbaye de Farfa et sa restauration au XIe siècle sous Hugues I," *Revue bénédictine* 24 (1907): 17–35, 374–402, esp. 390–93; "L'abbate Ugo," 662–65, 804; and *L'Imperiale Abbazia di Farfa*, 119–25, 140–43. On the multiplication of agrarian contracts during Hugh's reign, see Anna Margherita Civitarese, "I contratti agrari in Abruzzo nei secoli X e XI," *Clio* 20 (1984): 23–24.

66. Müller, *Topographische und genealogische Untersuchungen*, 47–49.

67. Müller, *Topographische und genealogische Untersuchungen*, 37–39, describes Rieti's borders. The charters consistently place Petra Demone and Scandriglia "in territorio sabinensi." However, they place "Macla Felcosa," which bordered Petra Demone, in the county of Rieti—see *Reg. Farf.*, 5:290, (doc. 1303), and *Chron. Farf.*, 1:139. Wherever the border ran, it was theoretical rather than practical inasmuch as the counts of Rieti were among Farfa's major leaseholders.

The counts could have been involved in the construction of the *castelli*, or they could have acquired power over them later by lease or usurpation. What is known is that by 1083/1084 they claimed rights not just over Petra Demone and Scandriglia, but also specifically over San Salvatore.[68]

After San Salvatore had been handed over to "Constantius," Dominic "migrated" to a place called "Domus," to "a mountain called Pizi," where he and a disciple named John built a hermit's hut in the style of the desert fathers (a "tugurium") and "meditated day and night on the law of God."[69] Such a relationship between master and disciple, long characteristic of Greek monasticism, was becoming common in Latin Italy.[70] Jacobilli thought "Domus" must have been somewhere in the Sabine hills, and subsequent commentators have acquiesced.[71] Yet this assumption overlooks the fact that all the *vitae* use forms of the verb "migrare," suggesting long-distance travel rather than relocation within the same neighborhood. Closer examination reveals that Dominic actually "migrated" nearly a hundred miles east, all the way over the crest of the Apennines to the province of Chieti in the Abruzzi, where the twelfth-century *Catalogus Baronum* locates an undefined territory of "Domo."[72] At "Domus" Dominic founded two monasteries: one on the plain next to the "fluvius Aventinus," the other on the mountain "qui Pizzi dicitur"; he dedicated these, respectively, to the Holy Mother of God and the Holy Trinity.[73]

68. *Reg. Farf.*, 4:78 and 90–91 (docs. 1083 and 1095); *Chron. Farf.*, 2:169–71. A puzzling restatement of this charter, from 1089 or 1090, is found in *Reg. Farf.*, 5:235 (doc. 1255); reiterated in *Chron. Farf.*, 2:192–93.

69. *Sermon*, 366; *Trisulti Life* iii, 283; *Valva life* xxxi, 73; *Monte Cassino Life* xxx, 73; *Sora Life* xxx–xxxi, 39.

70. Parallels are cited in Tabacco, "*Privilegium Amoris*: Aspetti della spiritualità romualdina," *Il Saggiatore* 4 (1954): 327.

71. Jacobilli has Dominic moving by stages toward the Abruzzi in *Vite de' santi e beati di Foligno*, 27–28; and in *Vita di S. Domenico*, 13. This model was incorporated into, among other works, Tuzii, *Memorie istoriche . . . di Sora*, 46; Tosti, "Leggenda di San Domenico Abate," in *Opere complete*, 2:305; Celidonio, *Diocesi di Valva e Sulmona*, 2:97; and Dolbeau, "Vie e miracles de S. Dominique," 40n.

72. On "Domo," see Errico Cuozzo, *Catalogus Baronum: Commentario*, Fonti per la storia d'Italia 101** (Rome: ISIME, 1984), 303–4, 324, 370. Cuozzo's sources indicate the general area of Chieti where "Domus" was located, but not its exact boundaries.

73. *Valva Life* xxxii, 73, is the sole *life* that transmits the name of the Aventino clearly. The whole section was omitted in the *Monte Cassino Life*. The name was present in the *Sora Life*, but it cannot be read in the authoritative surviving copy, Vall. ms. H. 18, fol. 408, which has a hole where a form was erased that apparently ended in "-inum." Spitilli, who worked extensively from that copy, omits the word (*Vita*, 9–10). Yet the "fiume Aventino" is named by Jacobilli, in a section he translates from the *Sora Life*, so it may have been present in the now lost Sora chancery copy he cites in the margin (*Vita*, 13). The names of Dominic's foundations appear only in the *Sora Life*, in repetitive phrases that read as if they had been added as glosses.

This geography fits the wild country not far from Pizzoferrato in the Abruzzi, where the Fiume Aventino flows out of the Monti Pizi. Although today there is no trace of the mountain monastery of Santissima Trinità, perhaps its name was changed to honor Dominic and its site relates to Monte San Domenico outside of Pizzoferrato. The people of the district claim that a ravine with ancient trees and a spring was one of Dominic's original hermitages and have erected a little chapel in his honor.[74] Local tradition also claims that Dominic founded the monastery of Santa Maria dello Spineto, located near Castello di Quadri, a house whose twelfth-century remains are on the podium of an Italic temple.[75] But this identification is not a perfect fit, for Santa Maria is on the Sangro, one valley over from the Aventino. Support for a link between Dominic and the general region around Pizzoferrato comes from the fact that it is on the very eastern edge of the diocese of Valva-Sulmona, Dominic's next known theater of operations.[76]

Dominic had crossed the Apennines to go to a place where the eremitical life was particularly lively. His hagiographers claim that while he resided at the place called "Domus," he was frequently importuned to found monasteries by the "magnates" of the "terra Credenderii [or 'Credendei'] et Zaterii."[77] Heretofore no one has attempted to identify these obscure characters. In the Abruzzi, however, there are traditions concern-

74. In addition to the chapel, the local citizens have named a ski lift after San Domenico. His cult at Pizzoferrato is described in Di Nola, *Gli Aspetti magico-religiosi*, 52. An "Ecc. S. Domynici de Silvis" was already noted in a pre-1350 tithe list, *Delle Antiche Decime Valvensi (Notizie e Documenti)*, ed. Giuseppe Celidonio (Sulmona: Tipografia P. Colaprete, 1903), 46.

75. Ugo Pietrantonio, *Il Monachesimo benedettino nell'Abruzzo e nel Molise*, Documenti e storia 5 (Lanciano: Editrice Rocco Carabba, 1988), 263–64; Paolo Favole, *Abruzzo e Molise*, vol. II of *Italia Romanica* (Milan: Jaca Book, 1990), 184.

76. The location of Pizzoferrato and Quadri in the diocese of Valva is demonstrated by the Valva tithe lists, *Rationes Decimarum Italiae. Aprutium-Molisium. Le Decime dei secoli XIII–XIV*, ed. Sella, Studi e testi 69 (Vatican City: BAV, 1936), 63, 65, 78, 91, 101, 107, 112–13 (for S. Maria). The "Ecc. S. Domynici de Silvis" is situated within the diocese of Valva in *Delle Antiche Decime Valvensi*, 46. Perhaps the regional elite also linked the Pizzoferrato region to Valva. Cuozzo, *Catalogus Baronum Commentario*, 303 and 370, speculates that the occurrence of the names Oderisius and Berardus among the twelfth-century feudatories at Quadri and Pizzoferrato might signify that these men were connected to the family of the counts of Valva, where these are *Leitnamen*. Evelyn Jamison, "The Significance of the Early Medieval Documents from S. Maria della Noce and S. Salvatore di Castiglione," in *Studi in onore di Ricardo Filangieri*, 3 vols. (Naples: L'Arte tipografica, 1959), 1:55, suggests that the Borelli, who, as will be seen, were also from the line of the counts of Valva, had their links to "Domo."

77. The *Valva Life* xxxii, 73, reveals only that while Dominic was at "Domus" he was visited by the "*magnates*" of the region; the *Sora Life* xxxii, 39, goes on to specify that they were from the "terra Credenderii et Zaterii." This same place would have been the ultimate homeland of the "Benedictus Crassus," who appears in Sora's miracle collection as a refugee "servus Signulfi Credendei de loco cui *Domui* proprium vocabulum" (*Sora Life* cxxxvii, 53).

ing a "Credindeus Credindei" who is supposed to have been "Lord of Chieti." He is connected with the Greek abbot Hilary and his seven followers, who, according to their legends, sought to avoid Muslim raiders by establishing a monastery in the upper valley of the Aventino, and who then, after the death of their second abbot, Nicholas the Greek, dispersed to various hermit caves, ultimately to become the patron saints of small towns around Chieti. There are no contemporary *lives* of these saints, who for many years were misdated by four centuries.[78] Nevertheless, their cultic geography locates them in the upper valley of the Aventino, where local tradition says land was given them by Credindeus of Chieti and his mother Teodoranda.[79] The story goes back many centuries, since it is invoked in a bull issued by Honorius III on 10 November 1221 confirming ownership of property that the monastery of San Martino in Valle claimed to have received from Credindeus in a deathbed donation, allegedly in 1044.[80] Thus the "*magnates*" of the "terra Credenderii" or "Credendei" were presumably followers of this shadowy overlord, who was protecting Greek hermits in the exact region where Dominic and John established themselves.

The *Sora Life* also claims that Dominic was visited by the "magnates" of "Zatterii." These might have been citizens of Frattura, a *castello* on a mountainside high above the Lago di Scanno. At first this conjecture seems ludicrous, since formidable mountains separate the Lago di Scanno from

78. Cesare Rivera, "Valva e i suoi conti," 92, names the seven alleged followers of Abbot Hilary: Nicholas the Greek, who died at Prati but whose body was translated to Guardia-grele; Rinaldo, who settled at Falascoso; Franco of Francovilla; Stephan of Santa Spirito della Maiella; John of San Giovanni in Venere; Orante, who died at Ortucchio; and Falco, born at Taverna, who retired to San Egidio near Palena. Little is said about these saints in the standard reference works (*AS* Maii 2:382–83 and Aug. 2:475; *BS* 5:445–46 and 1251–52; 9:920–22). The popular tradition is set forth in Pietro-Antonio Corsignani, *Reggia Marsicana ovvero memorie topografico-storiche di varie colonie e città antiche e moderne della provincia dei Marsi e di Valeria*, 2 vols. (Naples: Presso il Parrino, 1738; reprint, Bologna: Lithografia S. I. R. A. B., 1971), 2:199–208. Perhaps the best overview is in Celidonio, *Diocesi di Valva e Sulmona*, 2:66–75, who notes churches dedicated to these saints before the early fourteenth century.

79. Cesare Rivera, "Valva e i suoi conti," 92.

80. Honorius III, *Epistula* (10 November 1221), ed. César Auguste Horoy, *Honorii III Romani Pontificis Opera Omnia*, 5 vols., Bibliotheca Patristica seu Eiusdem Temporis Patrologia 1–5 (Paris: Imprimerie de la Bibliothèque ecclésiastique, 1879–82), 4:19–21; described in *Regesta Honorii Papae III: Iussu et Munificentia Leonis XIII Pontificis Maximi ex Vaticanis Archetypis Aliusque Fontibus*, ed. Pietro Presutti, 2 vols. (Rome: Typographia Vaticana, 1888–95), 2:9.

The date of 1044, which is absent in the charter of Honorius, was added, from the notes of an eighteenth-century antiquarian, by Cesare DeLaurentiis, "Il gastaldato e la Contea di Teate con la serie de' suoi conti," *Bollettino della Società di Storia Patria Anton Ludovico Antinori negli Abruzzi* 16 (1904): 1–37 and 231–38, esp. 36–37. On the monastery itself, see Ugo Pietrantonio, "Fara S. Martino," *Il Monachesimo Benedettino nell'Abruzzo*, 161–64, who cites, not altogether clearly, many local studies; and Pietrantonio, *Monachesimo benedettino nell'Abruzzo*, 161–64.

lands further east. Yet I can testify that it is possible—albeit absolutely inadvisable—to climb by car up the poorly maintained gravel road from Frattura around the flanks of Monte Genzana, follow the ridge, drop down to the neighboring valley, and ascend the Monti Pizi to the site of San Domenico "in Silvis," all in less than thirty-one miles.[81] Horsemen proceeding more directly might have been able to make this journey in a day. The fact that Dominic's next foundations were near Frattura suggests prior contact with the region.

Dominic's journey to the area around Pizzoferrato had taken him to high meadows so rocky and rugged that, centuries later, they would appall the professional poet and traveler Edward Lear (d. 1888), who claimed that "nothing could be wilder or less interesting than . . . [this] treeless country."[82] Lear would become lyrical, however, about Dominic's next venue, Prato Cardoso, a solitude located to the west in the county of Valva[83]: "The Gole or Foce di Scanno . . . might be drawn as the Poet's Inferno . . . the stupendous rocks which enclose the path are . . . beyond imagining. . . . the Lago di Scanno . . . is really one of the most beautiful spots in nature, and the more so for being in so desert a place."[84] About a mile north of the Lago di Scanno and the present town of Villalago lies a valley named Prato Cardoso, west of the Sagittario. Today a cave identified as Dominic's hermitage, fronted by an early modern chapel dedicated to him, is located on a picturesque artificial lake at the beginning of a sheer-walled canyon.[85] Although the *lives* do not specify Dominic's residence as a cave, the local tradition is bolstered by a mention of caves in a 1067 (or 1069?) charter designating Prato Cardoso as a "monasterium heremitarum."[86] Further

81. The route from Frattura to San Domenico lies largely on unpaved, unmarked, rock and gravel roads, some of Italy's infamous "strade bianche." Most of these tracks are not mapped; most of those that are should not be. My thanks to the Alberto DeFlorio family for helping me to demonstrate the possibility of travel east from Frattura, a feat none of us will attempt again.

82. Edward Lear, *Illustrated Excursions into Italy*, 2 vols. (London: Thomas M'Lean, 1846), 1:99. Although today Lear is remembered more for such children's poetry as "The Owl and the Pussycat," his income came largely from travel literature. On his stay in the Abruzzi, see Susan Chitty, *That Singular Person Called Lear: A Biography of Edward Lear, Artist, Traveller and Prince of Nonsense* (New York: Atheneum, 1989), 59–74.

83. The *Trisulti Life*, truncated here, takes Dominic directly to the foundation of San Pietro in Lago. The *Valva Life* xxxiv, 73, the *Monte Cassino Life* xxxv, 74, and the *Sora Life* xxxvi–xxxviii, 40, name Prato Cardosa in the county of Valva.

84. Lear, *Illustrated Excursions into Italy*, 1:85 and 93.

85. Celidonio, *La Diocesi di Valva e Sulmona*, 2:97; Pietrantonio, *Monachesimo benedettino nell'Abruzzo*, 284–85. In the grotto, Dominic's alleged wooden bed was displayed until 1988, when some careless pilgrim set it afire and destroyed it. By 1992, however, it had reappeared.

86. Cave hermitages are associated with San Pietro in Lago in a 1067 charter entered into a Monte Cassino register compiled by Peter the Deacon (d. post 1159), in *Reg. Petri Diac.*,

south, halfway up a mountain to the northeast of the Lago di Scanno, less
than two miles north of Frattura, Dominic built the monastery of San Pietro in Lago.[87] Little of it remains today except some materials recycled into
nearby Villalago.[88]

In this region, Dominic's principal patrons were the counts of Valva,
another part of the family of the counts of Marsica. Their founder was
Oderisius I, one of the seven sons of Berardus the Frank. Oderisius is well
attested in documents dating from 972 to 1001—one obituary tradition
places his death in 1002.[89] His *obit* is the *terminus post quem* for Dominic's
foundation of San Pietro in Lago, or rather for its now lost formal foundation charter, since the patrons who signed that document were counts
of the next generation, presumably Oderisius's sons. Their names—Beraldus, Theodinus, and Randisius—were introduced into Dominic's hagiographical tradition by Alberic of Monte Cassino, whose precision here
suggests that his source was the otherwise unknown foundation charter
whose existence he mentions.[90] Randisius's wife, Giseltrudis, appears in

---

fol. 210r (no. 496); edited in Gattola, *Accessiones*, 1:179–80; noted in Hartmut Hoffmann,
"Chronik und Urkunde in Montecassino. I. Das Register des Petrus Diaconus. II. Gefälschte
Herrscherdiplome und Papsturkunden in der Klosterchronik und in den Registern des Petrus
Diaconus," *QFIAB* 51 (1971): 135.

87. *Trisulti Life* iii, 283; *Valva Life* xxxv–xxxviii, 74; *Monte Cassino Life* xxxv–xxxviii, 74;
Sora Life xl, 40.

88. On San Pietro in Lago, see Bloch, *Monte Cassino*, 1:338–42; and Pietrantonio, *Monachesimo benedettino nell'Abruzzo*, 325–27. Few traces of walls remain on what the people of
Villalago identify as the site. Celidonio, *Diocesi di Valva e Sulmona*, 2:123, indicates that the
ruins were more extensive at the start of the century; he claims that the former monastery was
the source of Villalago's church bell and altar.

89. On the early counts of Valva, see Cesare Rivera, "Per la storia delle origini dei Borrelli
conti di Sangro," *Archivio storico per le province napoletane*, n.s. 5 [= 44] (1919): 67, and also
"Valva e i suoi conti," 85–93; Müller, *Topographische und genealogische Untersuchungen*, 74;
and Wickham, *Studi sulla società degli appennini nell'alto medioevo: Contadini, signori e insediamento nel territorio di Valva (Sulmona)*, Università degli Studi di Bologna, Quaderni del
Centro studi Sorelle Clarke 2 (Bologna: Editrice CLUEB, 1982), 117. These genealogies supersede Celidonio, *Diocesi di Valva a Sulmona*, 2:126–51.

90. The *Trisulti Life* iii, 283, does not name Dominic's Valva patrons; the *Valva Life*
xxxv, 74, lists them only as the "comites terrae illius." Alberic seems to have gotten more
precise information from the foundation charter he mentions: the *Monte Cassino Life* xxxv,
74, names "counts Beraldus, Theodinus, and Randisius"; the *Sora Life* xxxviii, 40 names
only "Beraldus and Randisius." Dolbeau, "Vie et miracles de saint Dominique," 40, in
keeping with his view of the relative priority of the texts, suggests that the name "Theodinus"
was interpolated into the list of the founders, and observes that this man alone has no
children listed in the group of 1067. The historical reality of a Count Theodinus of Valva
in Dominic's era can be confirmed, however, since he was a party in a 1022 judgement
included in *Chron. Vult.* V, 3:30–34; also edited in Cesare Manaresi, *I Placiti del "Regnum Italiae"*, 3 vols., FSI 92, 96, and 97 (Rome: ISIME, 1957), 2:640–43 (doc. 314). Another possible reference to this Theodinus is signalled in Wickham, *Studi sulla Società degli
Appennini*, 63–64.

one of Dominic's miracle stories.[91] In a 1067 (1069?) charter, Randisius and Berardus are invoked as the deceased fathers of the men who were then the patrons of San Pietro in Lago.[92] Presumably it was in the very first years of the new century that the three counts commemorated their support for Dominic's efforts in a charter, since, as will be seen, he had moved on to Trisulti by 1003/1004.[93]

At this time Dominic received a series of heavenly visions. He had appointed a superior to oversee San Pietro, and had retired to a nearby hermitage called "Plataneta," located on the heights of the mountain which is called "Argometa" (or "Argoneta"). There, except for certain fixed days when he descended to supervise the monastery, he lived in a small cell dedicated to the Holy Trinity.[94] The site was probably on Monte Argatone, which towers nearly 7,000 feet above sea level, rising abruptly more than 3,000 feet above the Lago di Scanno. It is close enough for Dominic to have been able to visit San Pietro and for his monks to have brought him supplies. On one night when Dominic was praying there, he allegedly saw columns of colored light in the sky; on another occasion he felt himself transported above the clouds so that he could see the whole earth.[95] Reductionists might observe that the columns of light could have been the *aurora borealis* and that one can see a long way indeed from the top of Monte Argatone. In any case, the events described were spiritual experiences for Dominic, whose choices of impressive hermitage sites indicate his proficiency at finding God in nature.

Dominic is next said to have gone to the Valley of the Sangro, where "Borrellus Major" asked him to build the monastery that came to be called

91. *Sora Life* lxxix, 46.

92. *Reg. Petri Diac.*, fol. 210r (no. 496); edited in Gattola, *Accessiones*, 1:179–80; summarized in Hoffmann, "Chronik und Urkunde," 135. This donation was mentioned in *Chron. Cass.* III xvii and xxxix, 382, 416. Its elements disagree: 1067 is the date from the incarnation; 1069 is the date from the indiction.

93. A date of ca. 1010 is often cited for Dominic's foundation of San Pietro in Lago, but this probably originated as a conjecture in Cesare Rivera, "Per la storia delle origini dei Borelli," 64, perhaps based on his interpretation of the implicit chronology of Jacobilli, *Vita di San Domenico*, 14–17.

94. *Trisulti Life* iii, 283; *Valva Life* xxxv–xxxviii, 74. The geographical specifications absent in the *Monte Cassino Life* xxxvii–xxxviii, 74, are found in the *Sora Life* xlii–xliv, 41. There is no reason to equate "Plataneta" with "Prato Cardoso," as does Celidonio in *Diocesi di Valva e Sulmona*, 2:97 and 119.

95. *Trisulti Life* iv–v, 283–84; *Valva Life* xxxix–xliv, 74; *Monte Cassino Life* xxxix–xliv, 74; *Sora Life* li–lv, 42 (here a misreading of "columnas" as "columbas" has been restored by the corrector).

San Pietro Avellana (located in the province of Isernia in Molise).[96] Borellus was also from the family of the counts of Marsica: he was a grandson of
Berardus the Frank; a son of the first Valva count, Oderisius I; and thus a
brother of Dominic's Valva patrons, counts Beraldus, Theodinus, and Randisius.[97] By strategically positioning himself on the southeastern frontier of
the family holdings, Borrellus would ultimately be able to extend his power
beyond the Duchy of Spoleto—he became the progenitor of the counts of
Sangro and other dynasties.[98] Doubts had been raised about Dominic's
role in the founding of San Pietro Avellana, because the charter surviving
in the Monte Cassino archives does not mention him when it describes
how Borellus formally granted the monastery to an Abbot Peter in September of 1026.[99] That problem is solved by the now published *Sora Life*, which
identifies Peter as Dominic's appointee.[100]

Since the foundation charter of 1026 is the last notice of Borellus, its
date probably reflects his efforts to put his own affairs into final order rather
than any specific stage in the development of the monastery. In fact, the
dates of the events with which Dominic's *lives* bracket the founding of San
Pietro Avellana leave little time for Dominic's work: a *terminus post quem*
appears to be the death of Count Oderisius I of Valva after 1001, since the
subsequent counts formally sponsored San Pietro in Lago; a *terminus ante
quem*, explicitly placed "post haec" by the *lives*, is the establishment of San
Bartolomeo in Trisulti, for which Dominic received donations in 1003/
1004 and 1006 (discussed below). Perhaps the building of San Pietro in

96. *Trisulti Life* vi, 284; *Valva Life* xxxix–xliv, 74; *Monte Cassino Life* xxxix–xliv, 74;
Sora Life lxi, 43. On the location, see Pietrantonio, *Monachesimo benedettino nell'Abruzzo*,
457–60; and Bloch, *Monte Cassino*, 1 : 362–63.

97. Much of the literature concerning the genealogy of Borrellus is misleading because
a major charter was long misdated. See Howe, "*Monasteria Semper Libera*: Cluniac-Type Monastic Liberties in Some Eleventh-Century Central Italian Monasteries," *Catholic Historical
Review* 78 (1992): 25.

98. On the descendents of Borrellus, see Howe, "*Monasteria Semper Libera*," 24–25.
One of the studies cited there, "The Significance of the Earlier Medieval Documents from S.
Maria della Noce and S. Salvatore di Castiglione," has been reprinted in Evelyn M. Jamison,
Studies on the History of Medieval Sicily and South Italy, ed. Dione Clementi and Theo Kölzer
(Aalen: Scientia Verlag, 1992), 437–66.

99. Archivio di Montecassino aula III, caps. XIV, no. 35; edited in Gattola, *Historia*, 1 :
238–40; noted in Tommaso Leccisotti, *I Regesti dell'archivio*, Pubblicazioni degli Archivi di
Stato 54, 56, 58, 60, 64, 74, 78, 79, 81, 86, 95 (Rome: Ministero dell'Interno, 1964–77) [the last
three acknowlege Faustino Avagliano as coeditor], 2:137. This charter must have been available
when Leo of Marsica wrote *Chron. Cass.* III xxxix, 416. Its omission of Dominic was signalled
by Leccisotti, "Per la storia della Diocesi Cassinese: S. Pietro Avellana," *Diocesi di Montecassino: Bollettino Diocesano* 1 (1973): 69; and by Bloch, *Monte Cassino*, 1 : 362–63.

100. *Sora Life* lxi, 43.

Lago had already begun under Oderisius I, so that its charter represents an end rather than a beginning. Or perhaps the foundations commissioned by the comital brothers in the adjacent valleys of the Sagittario and the Sangro were built simultaneously. One consequence of heavy destruction at San Pietro Avellana in World War II was the discovery of the ruins of what might be Dominic's monastery, now situated under the present church.

Led "by an angel" or "by revelation," Dominic moved next to the other side of the Marsican world, to a place called "Trisaltus" in the Monti Ernici in the province of Frosinone in Campania; there he took up residence in a cave by a spring "in radice montis qui 'Porche' vocatur."[101] Although the cave on Monte Porca is almost 2,600 feet above sea level, it is overwhelmed by Monte Rotonaria, which rises above 5,700. The cave is natural, about thirty feet deep, and has been incorporated into a chapel, for which a plenary indulgence was secured in 1703.[102] It is surrounded by a forest of beech, oak, and chestnut. According to the *Trisulti Life*, Dominic hid here for three years, like St. Benedict in his cave, until a deer miraculously led hunters to him, but that three-year interval is chronologically impossible, since Dominic must have become known very quickly to the citizens of Collepardo, who gave him the forest of Ecio in 1003/1004.[103] There he founded a monastery dedicated to the Apostle Bartholomew and to the Holy Trinity, and constructed three altars: one to St. Bartholomew and to all the Apostles; one to the Blessed Virgin Mary Mother of God and

101. As one would expect, the *Trisulti Life* vi–xxii, 284–92, presents an elaborate account of Trisulti's origins, even including a founding prayer. On the other hand, the *Valva Life* liv–lv, 75; the *Monte Cassino Life* liv–lv, 75; and the *Sora Life* lxiii–lxv, 43–44, dispense with this material in a few lines.

102. The geography of Trisulti is described in Luigi De Persiis, *Tecchiena e il suo statuto* (Frosinone: Tipografia di Claudio Stracca, 1895), 12; A Benedictine Monk [Beda Castelli], *La Certosa di Trisulti* (Tournai: Tipografia Notre Dame des Près, 1912), 5–8; Benedetto Fornari, "I monasteri di San Domenico e di San Nicola presso Trisulti," *Rivista Cistercense* 2 (1985): 127–35; and James Hogg, "The Charterhouse of Trisulti," in *La Certosa di Trisulti*, ed. Hogg, Giovanni Leoncini, and Michele Merola, *Analecta Cartusiana* 74(2) (Salzburg: Universität Salzburg Institut für Anglistik und Amerikanistik, 1991), xi–xiii.

103. A text commemorating Collepardo's donation, based on a transcription contained in an unpublished *Annales Trisultani* begun by the Carthusian Vincenzo Marucci in 1692, is edited and translated in Atanasio Taglienti, *Il monastero di Trisulti e il castello di Collepardo: Storia e documenti* (Casamari: Tipografia di Casamari, 1984), 88–91. Taglienti's version places the event in the first year of Pope John XIX (i.e., 1024/1025), but the papal number, which may have been contributed by a later scribe, is probably wrong, since the charter is dated to the second year of the indiction, which corresponds to the first year of John XVIII (1003/1004). De Persiis, who also knew the text by way of Marucci, dated it to 1003/1004 (*Tecchiena*, 13).

to all the saints; and one to Michael the Archangel and to all the angels (an additional chapel to the Most Holy Trinity is attested only by Jacobilli).[104]

Other properties were given in 1006 by nineteen citizens of the neighboring *castello* of Vico, along with their unnamed relatives and heirs. These founders were listed in a lost donation charter whose text is partially known by a confirmation of 1215, in which the original has been rewritten because "the Latin was extremely corrupt due to the simplicity of the scribe."[105] The surviving *Trisulti Life* describes the monastery as a joint venture by the citizens of Vico, Guarcino, Collepardo, and Castro, the first appearances these towns make in the historical record.[106] They are all about 2,000 feet above sea level, hugging the upper limits of olive and vine cultivation and maintaining good access to the higher forested zones favored by Dominic. According to the *Trisulti Life*, Dominic secured papal guarantees for the new foundation.[107] Its ruins survive today, formerly buried in

104. The *Trisulti Life* x, 286, as befits a local production, carefully names the dedicatees of the tripartite church. The *Valva Life* lxv, 75; the *Monte Cassino Life* lxv, 75; and the *Sora Life* lxiv–v, 43–44, have this monastery dedicated only to "the name and memory of the Apostle Bartholomew." The additional information in Jacobilli, *Vita di S. Domenico*, 9, may be anachronistic. For further bibliographic information on Trisulti, see *Monasticon Italiae*, 1:137.

105. Innocent's corrected text is edited in Alfred A. Strnad, "Zehn Urkunden Papst Innocenz' III. für die Kartause San Bartolomeo zu Trisulti (1208–1215)," *Römische historische Mitteilungen* 11 (1969): 55–57; and in Antonietta Angela Sechi, *La Certosa di Trisulti da Innocenzo III al Concilio di Costanza (1204–1414) (Note e documenti)*, *Analecta Cartusiana* 74(1) (Salzburg: Universität Salzburg Institut für Anglistik und Amerikanistik, 1981), 81 and 152–53. Honorius III also transmitted this donation, apparently repeating Innocent's version: see Franciscus Liverani, *Spicilegium Liberianum* (Florence: Ex Officina Augusta Sumptibus et Cura Equitis F. Cambiagi, 1864), 719–21. This document has been misattributed to the second year of Pope John XIX (i.e., 1025–26), but the year of the indiction does not fit. If it is presumed to have been issued during the reign of John XVIII, like the parallel donations from the citizens of Collepardo, then the fourth year of the indiction would have been 1006. This charter must be contemporary with the Collepardo charter, since both were written in similar language by the same notary from Alatri.

106. *Trisulti Life* xv–xvi, 288–89. The early histories of Vico, Guarcino, and Collepardo are described in *Lazio medievale: Ricerca topografica su 33 abitati delle antiche diocesi di Alatri, Anagni, Ferentino, Veroli* (Rome: Multigrafica Editrice, 1980), 25–27, 41–50, and 67–70. Although in *Lazio medievale* the records of the *castrum* of Guarcino are begun with a bull of 1175 (ibid., 41), Dominic's dossier enables that date to be pushed back more than a century and a half.

"Castro" is a generic name. On today's map, the nearest known "Castro" is "Castro dei Volsci" (ibid., 233–39), but since this is 18 miles from Collepardo, separated by the major towns of Ceccano and Alatri, it would not have been the "Castro" of the *Trisulti Life*, whose citizens, like those of the three immediately surrounding towns with which it is associated, are part of the inner circle of Dominic's patrons. Dominic's "Castro" was almost certainly a *castello* of Trisulti that once existed across the valley from the monastic site itself: see De Persiis, *Tecchiena*, 10, for references to "Monte Castello" and the "Castello di Trisulti"; and Taglienti, *Il Monastero di Trisulti e il Castello di Collepardo*, 159–60; and *La Certosa di Trisulti: Ricostruzione storico-artistica*, 2nd ed. (Casamari: Tipografia di Casamari, 1987), 9.

107. *Trisulti Life* xv–xvi, 288–89. See Kehr, *Italia Pontificia*, 2:152–53.

rock and debris fallen from the mountain above but now partially restored thanks to sporadic, insecurely financed campaigns by the Cistercians of Casamari.[108] A doubtful local tradition, unconfirmed in the hagiographical sources, attributes to Dominic the nunnery of San Nicola at Trisulti, the ruins of which can still be seen.[109]

There are confused reports about the "oratorium" or "monasterium" Dominic subsequently founded "on the side of the mountain which is called Cacume" or "near a river at the foot" of it, and dedicated to "Michael the Archangel" or to "the holy angel."[110] On Monte Cacume, which rises above the ancient city of Patrica in the province of Frosinone, there is a local tradition about a monastic site at a place not far from the ruins of a castle in a forested high mountain zone near a spring.[111] An abbot of Sant'Angelo de Cacume witnessed a Ceccano charter in 1209; an "ecclesia S. Angeli de Cacumine" appears in fourteenth-century tithe lists (classified as insolvent in the final mention from 1333–35).[112] The *Trisulti Life* and the *Sora Life* mention a patron, Count Amatus of Segni, who the latter says gave considerable movable and real property, witnessed by a charter. This man is otherwise known from records of a papal judicial assembly in 1011, where he bears the grand title of "Count of Campania," and from donations he made to Monte Cassino in 1015(?).[113] Perhaps he saw some

108. Taglienti, *La Certosa di Trisulti*, 16–20; Fornari, "I monasteri di San Domenico e di San Nicola," 127–37.

109. De Persiis, *Tecchiena*, 13; Fornari, "I monasteri di San Domenico e di San Nicola," 132–33; Antonelli, *Abbazie . . . di Sora*, 315. On the lack of evidence, see Caraffa, *Monasticon Italiae*, 1:137–38. The dedication to Nicholas is possible prior to the 1087 translation of the body of St. Nicolas to Bari, but more probable afterward. Moreover, the *lives* list no other houses Dominic founded for women.

110. *Trisulti Life* xi, 286; *Valva Life* lvi, 75; *Monte Cassino Life* lvi, 75; *Sora Life* cxvi–cxvii, 49.

111. Toubert, *Structures*, 1:192; Gioacchino Giammaria, "Note preliminari sul *Castrum Cacuminis*: Rassegna documentaria per una ricerca archeologica," *Atti del III Convegno dei gruppi archeologici del Lazio: Roccagorga (Lt), 8–9–10 dicembre, 1978* (Rome: Gruppi archeologici d'Italia, 1980), 93–109; *Monasticon Italiae*, 1:155–56; Maria A. Scarpignato, "Patrica," *Lazio medievale*, 179–80.

112. *Annales Ceccanenses* 1209, ed. L. C. Bethmann, in MGH *SS*, 19:299; *Rationes Decimarum Italiae nei secoli XIII e XIV: Latium*, ed. Giulio Battelli, Studi e Testi 27 (Vatican City: BAV, 1946), 216, 232, and 242.

113. Count Amatus of Segni is known earliest through a *placitum* held in 1011, whose text is found in *Reg. Farf.*, 4:14–15 (doc. 616). The dating elements of the two donations he made to Monte Cassino disagree. One is in *Reg. Petri Diac.*, fols. 122v–123r, no. 268; edited in Gattola, *Historia*, 1:486; summarized by Hoffmann, "Chronik und Urkunde," 119; noted in *Chron. Cass.* II xxxii, 226. Another is also in *Reg. Petri Diac.*, fol. 143v (no. 331); edited in Gattola, *Historia*, 1:497; summarized by Hoffmann, "Chronik und Urkunde," 124. The position of Amatus as "count of Campania" is analyzed in Giorgio Falco, "L'amministrazione papale nella Campagna e nella Marittima dalla caduta della dominazione bisantina al sorgere dei comuni," *Archivio della R. SRSP* 38 (1915): 688–94. He appears to have been connected

strategic value in a new foundation sited right on the border of Roman Campania.

After a while Dominic left his base at San Bartolomeo and "was traveling around the mountains and hills and unknown places of the forests until he came to the river which is called 'Flaternus,' where he constructed a church in honor of the Blessed and Ever Virgin Mary and stayed for two and a half years."[114] "Flaturnus" is a medieval name for the Sagittario.[115] Although only the Trisulti hagiographer mentions this foundation, he is unlikely to have invented it gratuitously, since Dominic's sojourn there undercuts his major theme—Trisulti's central importance. The accounts of Dominic's earlier stay in the Valley of the Sagittario mention Prato Cardoso, San Pietro in Lago, and the hermitage on Monte Argatone, the major sites associated with him there. The one local cult center unaccounted for is Cocullo, a small, walled village high in the mountains that separate the broad valleys of the Lago Fucino and of Sulmona. Its most distinctive feature is a cult of Dominic that includes relics, an oral tradition of miracle stories about how Dominic would come out of his nearby hermitage to help its citizens, and a feast day on the first Thursday of May featuring pilgrimage, snake handling, and other exotic festivities. Jacobilli claimed that Dominic founded a monastery there at the time he founded San Pietro in Lago, but this appears to be unsupported speculation.[116]

Cocullo's early history is obscure.[117] Its traditions could have a historical basis if Dominic had built a hermitage nearby; certainly its site on a hill extending out of a rising mountain system, adjacent to a stream, parallels others Dominic chose. Cocullo, however, is on a tributary of the Sagittario, not directly on the river itself. A further complication is that its church of San Domenico, the cult headquarters, appears on the earliest

---

with the Crescenzi, judging from *Reg. Farf.*, 4:286 (doc. 891): see Bossi, "I Crescenzi di Sabina," 133 and 158; Kömel, *Rom und der Kirchenstaat*, 62 and 167; and Herrmann, *Das Tuskulanerpapsttum*, 8.

114. *Trisulti Life* xi, 286.

115. Giovanni Alessio, "Per una toponomastica dell'Abruzzo e del Molise," *Abruzzo: Rivista dell'Istituto di Studi Abruzzesi* 2 (1964): 217–18.

116. Jacobilli, *Vita di S. Domenico*, 15.

117. On Cocullo itself, documentation is scarce. In the middle of the twelfth century, it is mentioned in the *Catalogus Baronum*: see Cuozzo, *Catalogus Baronum Commentario*, 335, 336. A Sulmona charter of 1196 involving a Cocullo resident is published in Nunzio Federigo Faraglia, *Codice Diplomatico Sulmonese* (Lanciano: R. Carabba Editore, 1888), 57–58 (doc. 62); note also 59–61. The *castello* might well have been contemporary with Dominic, since the settlement patterns around Sulmona were generally established by the eleventh century: see Wickham, *Il problema dell'incastellamento*, 67; with more detail in *Studi sulla società degli Appennini*, 72–86 and 103.

tithe lists under the name of a different patron, Aegidius (St. Giles).[118] Perhaps Dominic's original connection with Cocullo involved some other local site—such as San Giovanni in Campo at Cocullo, a property attested from the 1390s on as a grainary of San Pietro in Lago—from which the cult of Dominic was later shifted to the parish church.[119] Ultimately, however, Dominic's hermitage near the Sagittario remains unidentifiable because the Trisulti hagiographer was interested not in Dominic's sojourn away from San Bartolomeo but rather in his return and subsequent miracles.

One of Dominic's last foundations was an oratory dedicated to the Holy Trinity, which he built on the summit of a mountain called "Petra Imperatoris." This is attested by the *Trisulti Life* and, even more fully, by the *Sora Life*, which adds that a church dedicated to the holy angel was established at the foot of the mountain.[120] Jacobilli and most subsequent scholars identified "Petra Imperatoris" as Monte Montano near Sora.[121] However, Filippo Caraffa, in studying the hermitages and memorials above Subiaco around Vallepietro in the upper valley of the Aniene, argued that "Petra Imperatoris" was actually Monte Autore (6,022 feet), which bears that name more than a dozen times in Subiaco documents. Although Caraffa knew information from the *Sora Life* only by way of Spitilli and Jacobilli, he argued that Dominic's church of the Holy Angel might have inspired the name of the locality of Sant'Agno below Monte Assalonne, which is connected with Monte Autore. He equated Dominic's oratory to the Holy Trinity with what is today the shrine of Santissima Trinità, centered on a grotto near the top of the mountain.[122] The *Sora Life* specifies

118. The evidence for Egidio as the original patron of San Domenico at Cocullo is set forth in Di Nola, *Aspetti magico-religiosi*, 49–50. Tithe information confirming this conclusion is given in *Rationes Decimarum Italiae: Aprutium-Molisium*, 63, 72, 84, 100, 109, and 120. The change to the name "San Domenico" had been made by the sixteenth or seventeenth century according to Marsican archival fragments alluded to in Angelo Melchiorre, "La Diocesi dei Marsi dopo il Concilio di Trento," *Bullettino della Deputazione Abruzzese di Storia Patria* 75 (1985): 297.

119. Celidonio, *Diocesi di Valva e Sulmona*, 2:113–14.

120. *Trisulti Life* xxii, 292; *Sora Life* cxxii–iv, 51.

121. Jacobilli, *Vita di S. Domenico*, 29; Tuszii, *Memorie istoriche . . . di Sora*, 54; Tosti, "Leggenda di San Domenico," in *Opere Complete*, 2:318.

122. Caraffa, "S. Domenico di Sora e l'origine del santuario della SS. Trinità sul Monte Autore presso Vallepietra," *Alma Roma* 19 (1978): 31–37; and "S. Domenico di Sora e il santuario di Vallepietra," *Il Sacro Speco* 2 (1979): 31–36. These studies supplement Caraffa's earlier work on the region, esp. "Vallepietra e il santuario della Santissima Trinità sul Monte Autore," *Bollettino dell'Istituto di Storia e di Arte del Lazio Meridionale* 2 (1964): 9–37; 3 (1965): 135–65; and *Vallepietra dalle origini al secolo XIX con una appendice sul Santuario della Santissima Trinità sul Monte Autore*, published as a dedicated issue of *Lateranum* n.s. 35 (1969). In his identification of "Petra Imperatoris," Caraffa was aided by Guglielmo Salvi, "La "Petra Imperatoris" nell'alta valle dell'Aniene," *L'Osservatore Romano* 93, no. 234 (9 October 1953), 3.

that Dominic's patrons were "Humbert the Great" and "John son of Atto," the "illustrious optimates of the land."[123] Although Humbert's identity remains unknown, "John, son of Atto," who has not heretofore been identified, was almost certainly a grandson of the Octavian who founded the Ottaviani Crescenzi, the family that then dominated the Sabina and had interests reaching down into the Subiaco area.[124]

Santissimà Trinità is an impressive local pilgrimage center. Although even today no paved highway extends all the way to the oratory, brave buses leave the narrow, winding road behind Subiaco and then thread their way through clumps of pine along a track that ends a little below the shrine ledge itself; other pilgrims enter from the Marsican side, driving a dozen miles of gravel road through high Alpine meadows of extraordinary beauty. The site itself is a ledge leading into a grotto protected by overhanging rock. In recent years, a series of confessionals and votive chapels have replaced a nineteenth-century facade surrounded by an awkward clutter of votive offerings and corrugated-aluminum-roofed hawkers' huts. One of the chapels still contains some eleventh/twelfth-century fresco fragments, attesting to the age of the cult and its focus on the Trinity. The human constructions do not detract too much from the awesome view of the valley far below, whose sheer rock walls bottom out into the green fields of the *castello* of Jenne. The surrounding mountains are the Simbruini, so high and fierce that they were able to provide an absolute eastern border

123. Bibl. Vall. ms. H. 18, fol. 412, reads "ecclesia ab Huberto [amended by a corrector to "Humberto"] Malore, Ioanne Actone illustribus optimatibus terrae, dotata est." Dolbeau, in the *Sora Life* cxxiv, 51, corrects and punctuates the passage as though it were a question of three founders: "ab Humberto Maiore, Iohanne, Actone, illustribus optimatibus terrae." I read "Joanne" and "Actone" together as a single personal name with patronymic, equivalent to "Joanne Actonis," because (1) this is the punctuation of the manuscript; (2) Spitilli, *Vita S. Domenico*, 20, who may have had direct access to a Sora lectionary source, construed the name as "Giovanni Attone"; and (3) at this point the text consistently gives a name and an additional qualifier for each person introduced, e.g., "Humberto Maiore" and "Petrus Rainerii."

124. On the Sabine Crescenzi in general, see pp. 97–99 below. The genealogy of John is given in Müller, *Topographische und genealogische Untersuchungen*, 27–29 and 33; and Hansmartin Schwarzmaier, "Zur Familie Viktors IV. in der Sabina," *QFIAB* 48 (1968): 64–65, 74 (a genealogical stemma), and 75–77; also "Der *Liber Vitae* von Subiaco: Der Klöster Farfa und Subiaco in ihrer geistigen und politiischen Umwelt während der letzten Jahrzehnte des 11. Jahrhunderts," ibid., 95–103. For additional commentary and context, see Toubert, *Structures*, 2:903–4; Hoffmann, "Zur Abtsliste von Subiaco," *QFIAB* 52 (1972): 788; Paolo Delogu, "Territorio e cultura fra Tivoli e Subiaco nell'alto medio evo," *Atti del Convegno "L'Eredità medievale nella regione tiburtina,"26–27 maggio 1979 — Villa d'Este Tivoli*, published in a dedicated issue of *Atti e memorie della Società Tiburtina di storia e d'arte* 52 (1979): 36–37; and Annibale Ilàri, "I possessi monastici sublacensi in Anticolo di Campagna (Fiuggi) e gli Abati Umberto (1050–69) e Giovanni V (1069–1121)," *Benedictina* 27 (1980): 432–39.

to the papal state during all of its existence. From here flow lively rivers such as the Simbrivio and the Aniene; to the south is Trevi, the *castello* whose waters an aqueduct conveys to the Bernini-designed fountain in Rome into which foreign tourists toss their coins.[125]

Dominic's final monastery was San Domenico in Isola del Liri near Sora. His life gains a certain symmetry from his last years here, because Sora resembles his birthplace, Foligno: both are cities with Roman Republican roots, situated gracefully below mountains on pleasant plains irrigated by rivers; both are just across the border from papal territory. The *lives* present this return to origins as accidental. They describe how, while Dominic was traveling to visit his monasteries, he encountered the penitent lord of Sora, Peter son of Rainerius, whom he advised to construct and endow a monastery; how Peter without consulting Dominic established a convent of nuns instead, whose conduct was soon a public disgrace; and how Dominic got the nuns expelled by agreeing to organize the monks who would replace them.[126] The result was the monastery originally dedicated to Santa Maria Madre di Dio e Vergine, but which soon, after the addition of Dominic's own name, became popularly known as San Domenico. It was situated at the confluence of the Liri and the Fibreno, on the ruins of a Roman villa that local antiquaries identify as the birthplace of Cicero.[127] Dominic's work here is often misdated. The postscript added to the surviving form of the *Trisulti Life* contains a chronological scheme that has him arriving at Sora in 1011, a date still favored by Sora's historians.[128] Yet San Domenico cannot have been founded before the late 1020s, because if the project originated when Dominic met Lord Peter at a time when he was already ruling Sora, then that meeting must have occurred after the death

125. Caraffa, *Vallepietra*, 1–3, 217–53 describes the site and its history. The fresco fragments are analyzed in Anna Maria d'Achille, "Gli affreschi del santuario della SS. Trinità sul Monte Autore presso Vallepietra," *Atti e memorie della Società Tiburtina di Storia e d'Arte* 8 (1980): 42–63.

126. *Trisulti Life* xxii, 292–93; *Valva Life* lvii–lxvi, 76; *Monte Cassino Life* lvii–lxvi, 76; *Sora Life* cxviii–xxi, cxxv–xxxi, 51–52.

127. The debate over Cicero's birthplace, an argument not free from *campanilismo*, is summarized in Achille Lauri, "Le origini del distrutto monastero di Santa Chiara in Sora," *Benedictina* 3 (1951): 79–83; and in Antonelli, *Abbazie . . . di Sora*, 212–13.

128. *Trisulti Life* xxxiii, 297. Perhaps in part as a matter of local pride, an early foundation date for San Domenico at Sora still appears in such works as Cesare D'Onofrio and Carlo Pietrangeli, *L'Abbazie del Lazio* (Rome: Staderini Editore, 1971), 296; Farina and Fornari, *L'Architettura cistercense e l'abbazia di Casamari*, 2nd ed. (Casamari: Edizioni Casamari, 1981), 56; and Sophia Boesch Gajano, "Domenico di Sora, santo," in *DBI*, 40:676.

of Peter's father, the gastald Rainerius, who was still alive in 1021, though deceased by 1024.[129] It is also necessary to allow time for monastic construction and the aborted nunnery.

The Sora *life* specifies that after Peter had enriched the place with "farms, villas, mills, pastures, gardens, woodlands, forests, etc.," he confirmed his generosity with legal documents.[130] Cesare Baronio, the great Counterreformation historian who was also a proud Sora native, personally examined the foundation charter of 1030 and inserted part of it into his *Annales Ecclesiastici*.[131] Of the seven known texts commemorating Lord Peter's donations, only the three for San Domenico are issued jointly with his wife, "Doda, daughter of Count Oderisius of blessed memory."[132] A daughter of the counts of Marsica was naturally a partner in Dominic's work.[133]

129. In 1021 Rainerius, as gastald of Sora, donated a church to Monte Cassino, in a transaction commemorated in *Reg. Petri Diac.*, fol. 123r (no. 269), ed. Alessandro Magliari, "Documenti," *Bollettino storico volsco* 3 (1899): 33–34; analyzed in Hoffmann, "Chronik und Urkunde," 119; and Bloch, *Monte Cassino*, 1:304–5, 821. Antonelli, *Abbazie . . . di Sora*, 210–12, has anticipated this argument for a 1021 *terminus post quem* for Sora's foundation, but his attempt to advance it even further, to 1025, depends on misattributing a San Bartolomeo document to Pope John XIX (1024–32) rather than to John XVIII (1003–9). See note 105.

Rainerius had died before a 1024 charter was issued by his son, "Domnus Petrus Filius quondam Domni Rayneri de Civitate Sorana," whose text is preserved in an early modern Casamari chartulary copy, edited in Farina and Fornari, *Storia e documenti . . . di Casamari*, 151–53. Peter also appears as an independent agent in the mid-1020s in Amatus of Monte Cassino, *L'Histoire de li Normant* xxxiii, ed. Vincenzo de Bartholomaeis as *Storia de' Normanni di Amato di Montecassino volgarizzata in antico francese*, FSI 76 (Rome: Tipografia del Senato, 1935), 43–44.

130. *Sora Life* cxxxi, 51–52.

131. Cesare Baronio, *Annales Ecclesiastici*, 26 vols., ed. Augustino Theiner (Bar-le-Duc: L. Guerin, 1864–83), 16:544–45. Farina and Fornari, *Storia e documenti . . . di Casamari*, 7–8, edit a text supposedly taken from the lost Casamari chartulary and published in Filippo Rondinini, *Monasterii Sanctae Mariae et Sanctorum Johannis et Pauli de Casaemario Brevis Historia* (Rome: Fr. Gonzaga, 1707), 40–44 (it reads suspiciously like the version of Baronio, and even has a similar truncation).

132. Peter, son of Rainerius confirmed two donations to the church of San Elia at Castagnieto in 1024 and 1027, in texts that are edited in Farina and Fornari, *Storia e documenti . . . di Casamari*, 151–53, from transcripts made from the lost fifteenth-century Casamari chartulary. He gave the church of San Silvestro "in territorio Arpinensi loco" to Monte Cassino in February of 1028, a transaction recorded in *Reg. Petri. Diac.*, fols. 131r–131v (doc. 289), ed. Magliari, "Documenti," *Bollettino Storico Volsco* 2 (1898): 33–34; a transaction noted in *Chron. Cass.* II lx, 273, and discussed in Hoffmann, "Chronik und Urkunde," 121; and Bloch, *Monte Cassino*, 1:305–7. Peter's foundation charter for San Domenico is noted immediately above. His exchange of property with Dominic in June of 1031 is also edited in Farina and Fornari, *Storia e documenti . . . di Casamari*, 154–56, from an early modern Casamari copy. After Dominic's death, Peter and Doda confirmed an additional donation to San Domenico, dated to January of 1033, and gave portions of some mills to Monte Cassino, in June 1034, in documents whose late Casamari copies are edited in Antonelli, *Abbazie . . . di Sora*, 374–77.

133. The "Count Oderisius" who was Doda's father would have been Oderisius I of Marsica (attested 995–1012), the son of the Count Rainaldus (attested 968–1000), who was the son of Berardus the Frank. See Rivera, *Conti de' Marsi*, 54–60; and Müller, *Topographische und genealogische Untersuchungen*, 60–63 and 70. This genealogy is supported by the fact that

The written sources do not support an anachronistic local tradition that Dominic helped found the nunnery of Santa Chiara.[134] Nor do they verify that he established a hermitage in the nearby mountains.[135] Founding San Domenico may have been work enough. Details of the endowment were still being settled as late as June of 1031, when Dominic and Peter exchanged two pieces of property.[136] Perhaps such business affairs inspired his last journey to Tuscolo, a *castello* important as the family stronghold of Pope John XIX. Dominic fell ill en route and had to be rushed back to Sora, where he died on 22 January 1032.[137] He was buried in his monastery, and over his tomb a basilica was soon constructed.

"Doda" is a recurring lineage name, popular in the family of the counts of Marsica ever since it was borne by Berardus's wife. The *Sora Life* blames Doda for the attempt to turn the future monastery into a nunnery, which it says Peter did "coniuge consulente." This is closely followed by a phrase describing women as the weaker sex. In Dominic's dossier such misogynism is confined to *Sora Life* cxxv, 51. If Doda had actually turned her husband away from his high purpose, then it is surprising that other *lives* would have ignored this juicy *exemplum*.

134. Sora's local historians traditionally attributed the founding of Santa Chiara to Dominic—for example, see Lauri, "Le origini . . . di Santa Chiara in Sora," 87–93. This is denied by Caraffa, *Monasticon Italiae*, 1:170, and Antonelli, *Abbazie . . . nella diocesi di Sora*, 251–58, who believe the convent was actually a mendicant foundation, emphasizing the dedication to Clare of Assisi and the absence of any documentation prior to 1260.

135. Antonelli, *Abbazie . . . di Sora*, 11, 215–16, edits an unpublished archival scrap from Baronius, which claims that local tradition identifies a hermitage of Dominic in the mountains around Sora. Hermitages certainly were associated with some of Dominic's monasteries: for example, Settefonti, on which see Farina and Fornari, *Storia e documenti . . . di Casamari*, 154–56; and Antonelli, ibid., 66, 214, 226, 228, and 321. Popular traditions could have personalized such relationships.

136. *Copi Permutationis Cuiusdam Septem Fontium Possessionis*, ed. in Farina and Fornari, *Storia e documenti . . . di Casamari*, 154–56.

137. *Trisulti life* xxxiv, 298; *Valva life* lxviii, 76–77; *Monte Cassino Life* lxviii, 76–77; *Sora Life* cciv–xiii, 61. On the date of the *obit*, see p. 28 above.

3

Dominic's Holiness

DOMINIC AND OTHER ECCLESIASTICAL REFORMERS at the start of the High Middle Ages are remembered today because they were charismatic figures. To understand their significance, it is necessary to understand their holiness. This is not easy. Holiness is indefinable according to human standards. Of course, by using scholastic remotion, one could argue that the sacred is the "not secular," but that is not much help. Nor is looking at the "experience of the holy," the psychological perspective adopted by historians of religion, since cross-cultural phenomenological generalizations do not elucidate the uniqueness of specific cases. To describe holiness poses theoretical and methodological problems.

Yet Dominic's holiness is central to his *lives*: "God, who works miracles, is glorious in His saints, wonderful in His 'sanctitas'"; an abbot of wonderful *sanctitas* bestowed the monastic habit on Dominic; Dominic's *sanctitas* impressed Marquess Hubert; after a mysterious deer had led hunters to Dominic's cave, they recognized his *sanctitas*.[1] All hagiographical texts describe the holiness of their subjects, but Dominic's *lives* are especially explicit. To traditional *topoi* used traditionally, they add detailed anecdotes linking Dominic to a variety of sacred roles and to an entire spectrum of holy resonances. What they describe is not "holiness" or even "Christian holiness" but "Dominic's holiness."

Sociologists of religion, following Max Weber, use the term "charisma" to designate the prestige a leader gains from a special connection with the divine. They differentiate between official charisma, based on the holding of a sacred office within an organized ecclesiastical body, and personal charisma, the result of a direct gift of grace.[2] Clerics in eleventh-

---

1. *Trisulti Life* v and vii, 284; *Monte Cassino Life* xvi and xxiv–xxvi, 72 and 73; *Sora Life* xvi and xxiv–xxvi, 37 and 38.

2. *Max Weber on Charisma and Institution Building: Selected Papers*, ed. S. N. Eisenstadt (Chicago: University of Chicago Press, 1968), passim, esp. 253–54; Brian R. Wilson, *The Noble Savages: The Primitive Origins of Charisma and Its Contemporary Survival* (Berkeley: University of California Press, 1975), 4–13.

century Italy could have understood this distinction—it is evoked with dangerous ambiguity in Gregory VII's *Dictatus Papae* xxiii, where the pope is declared to be "sanctus"; and more precisely in Peter Damian's contrast between a person "called holy on the basis of a ministerial position" and one "said to be holy on the basis of the merits of his life."[3]

Dominic's hagiographers were convinced that their hero was perfectly holy in both senses. This is clear from a miracle story that describes how a priest from Arpino named Benedict, "unable to stand the great reputation of the holy man, began to attack his way of life, and was claiming that his 'sanctitas' consisted only in the celebration of Masses, so that otherwise he was like a layman." Father Benedict was willing to credit Dominic with the institutional sanctity derived from his priesthood, but not with personal charisma. Perhaps he considered the latter a threat to a clerical monopoly over the sacred. But then, "one day, while he was barking out against the man of God, illness suddenly struck him," and his death "closed the mouths of many of Dominic's detractors."[4] Indeed, "swift retaliations were frequently inflicted on men of this sort in order to demonstrate to everyone, more clearly than the light of the sun, how greatly divine honor valued Dominic."[5] In striking down Father Benedict, God Himself affirmed that Dominic's holiness was both institutional and personal. Dominic simultaneously fulfilled official sacred roles and yet was a "holy man" in his own right.

Dominic's *lives* emphasize his priesthood. He had been ordained only after becoming "skilled in singing and reading according to the rite of the region."[6] The author of the *Trisulti Life* mentions four separate Masses. The citizens of the surrounding *castelli* assembled at the church of San Bartolomeo in order to donate properties to Dominic "for their own souls and the souls of their relatives," and after Dominic had conducted Mass in his priestly vestments, he took their hands in his, accepting their promises

3. Gregory VII, *Registrum*, ed. Erich Caspar, MGH *Epp.*, 2(1):207; Peter Damian, *Liber Gratissimus*, ed. L. de Heinemann, in MGH *Libelli de Lite*, 3 vols. (Hannover: Hahnsche Buchhandlung, 1891–97), 1:31. Commentary can be found in Walter Ullmann, "Romanus Pontifex Indubitanter Efficitur Sanctus: *Dictatus Papae* 23 in Retrospect and Prospect," *Studi Gregoriani* 6 (1959–61): 229–64, esp. 238–39; and Giuseppe Ruggieri, "Santità ed ecclesiologia al sorgere della Cristianità gregoriana," *Cristianesimo nella storia* 6 (1985): 245–61.

4. *Sora Life* clxviii–clxxi, 57. A variant version from the *Trisulti Life* xviii, 290, places Fr. Benedict in Vico, has him suggest that Dominic's custom of offering daily Mass is the source of his sanctity, and ends more happily when Dominic restores his now chastened critic to health.

5. *Sora Life* clx, 56.

6. *Valva Life* xiv, 72; *Monte Cassino Life* xiv, 72; *Sora Life* xiv, 37.

that what was contributed would not be taken back.[7] A Mass sung at the church of Sant'Angelo at Vico was followed by a sermon and a blessing.[8] All along Dominic's road, from Vico to Collepardo, men, women, and children waved palms and flowers; then they heard a Mass and sermon at the church of San Salvatore.[9] After a Mass celebrated for the contentious citizens of Vico, Guarcino, Collepardo, and other surrounding places at Santa Maria in Carapignana, a neutral site half a mile northwest of Collepardo, Dominic preached a sermon, exorcized a possessed woman in a three-hour ceremony, and then made the sign of the cross over all the people, blessing them and sending them home.[10] That three-hour ceremony may not have been unique. The *Sora Life* describes the ill-fated attempt of another rival priest named Benedict, son of a priest named Hermus, who began his Mass at daybreak and tried to stretch it out to midafternoon, "thinking that in prolonging the Mass he would easily be able to equal Dominic or . . . even surpass him." [11]

The accounts of the liturgies cited above emphasize Dominic's sermons. The *lives* proclaim his "burning eloquence" and "mellifluous admonitions." [12] Five paragraphs of the *Trisulti Life* offer what purports to be an actual sermon by Dominic in which he exhorts citizens of competing *castelli* to practice mutual charity and to strive for personal conversion, a concept used precociously to denote a change of life within the world rather than entry into a monastery.[13] This peace emphasis must have been timely, given that one of the earliest Italian "Truce of God" documents, written down a decade or so after Dominic's death, is known to us through a Trisulti copy.[14] In the *Sora Life* Dominic urges laymen to fight against sin with tears, prayer, fasting, and almsgiving—a traditional emphasis on externally manifested piety.[15] That *life* also tells how, at Arpino, Dominic gave "an exhortatory sermon to the people according to his custom," de-

7. *Trisulti Life* xiv, 287–88.

8. *Trisulti Life* xvii, 289. San Angelo heads the fourteenth-century Vico tithe lists published in *Rationes Decimarum . . . Latium*, 128, 143, 159.

9. *Trisulti Life* xvii, 289. San Salvatore heads Collepardo's fourteenth-century tithe lists published in *Rationes Decimarum . . . Latium*, 130, 145, 149, 161.

10. *Trisulti Life* xxvii, 294. On the church of Santa Maria in Carapignana, which was located outside of the competing *castra*, see *Rationes Decimarum . . . Latium*, 131, 145, 161.

11. *Sora Life* clxx, 57.

12. *Monte Cassino Life* xxii, 72; *Sora Life* xxii, 38; *Trisulti Life* xvii, 289.

13. *Trisulti Life* xxvi–xxx, 294–96.

14. Roger E. Reynolds, "Odilo and the *Treuga Dei* in Southern Italy: A Beneventan Manuscript Fragment," *Mediaeval Studies* 46 (1984): 450–62.

15. *Trisulti Life* xvii, 289.

livered after a eucharistic service that must have been far from customary, since he had refused to celebrate it at all until the archpriest had taken the pulpit and excommunicated and expelled all the married clergymen and their wives.[16] The *lives* mention several sermons in which Dominic exhorted clergy to practice the chastity proper to their station.[17]

These texts strongly emphasize liturgy. The Mass unites people. John Bossy has described how in the later Middle Ages the Mass created a community of the living and the dead.[18] In Dominic's Italy the Mass did well to create a community out of the living, to help people transcend, even temporarily, their sexual, social, and geographical divisions. The increased emphasis on seeing and reverencing the Eucharist, so characteristic of the High Middle Ages, has often been treated by scholars as an epiphenomenon of the eucharistic controversies that reemerged in the mid-eleventh century.[19] Yet, if Dominic's *lives* are not anachronistic here, customs such as the elongated Mass appear to have been part of central Italian rural spirituality a generation earlier. It may be more than coincidence that in 1022 the fathers at the Council of Seligenstadt felt compelled to forbid priests from celebrating more than three Masses per day.[20] Perhaps in Eucharistic piety, as in many other areas of the medieval Church, learned theory followed rather than led popular enthusiasms.

The virtues appropriate to a good priest are ascribed to Dominic. He was accessible to penitents needing spiritual direction, even when he was traveling.[21] According to his *lives*, he was so merciful that, thanks to his intercessions, there were no permanent ill effects from two-thirds of the miracles of retribution that they describe.[22] Dominic's chastity is to be presumed not only from his frequent criticism of womanizing clerics, but also from the way that an opponent who had accused him of hypocrisy in this matter was turned into an irrational beast.[23] Dominic's campaigns against

---

16. *Sora Life* cxcvi–cxcviii, 60.

17. *Trisulti Life* xvii, 289; *Sora Life* clxxii, cxc, cxcvii, 57, 59, 60.

18. John Bossy, " Essai de sociographie de la messe," *Annales, E. S. C.* 36 (1981): 44–70, revised as "The Mass as a Social Institution, 1200–1700," *Past and Present* 100 (1983): 29–61.

19. Émile Bertaud, "Dévotion eucharistique," in *Dictionnaire de spiritualité*, 4(2): 1623–24; Miri Rubin, *Corpus Christi: The Eucharist in Late Medieval Culture* (Cambridge: Cambridge University Press, 1991), 14–20.

20. *Concilium Salegunstadiense* v, edited in Johannes Mansi, *Sacrorum Conciliorum Nova et Amplissima Collectio*, 53 vols. (Venice: Antonio Zatta et al., 1759–1927), 19:397.

21. *Trisulti Life* xxii, 292; *Valva Life* lvii, 76; *Monte Cassino Life* lvii, 76; *Sora Life* cxviii, 50.

22. *Trisulti Life* xvi, xviii, xx, xxi, 288–89, 290, 290–91, 291–92; *Sora Life* lxxxvii–lxxxviii, xcii–xciii, cvii–cviii, cxiii–cxiv, cxxix–cxxx, cxl, clxii–clxv, clxix, clxxi, clxxx–clxxxv, cxcv, cc–ccii, cxxxviii–cxxxix, xxxliv–xxxlx, 47(2x), 48, 49, 52, 54, 56, 57(2x), 58, 59, 60, 64, 75.

23. *Sora Life* clxi–clxvii, 56.

less virtuous priests are one of the most striking features of his *lives*. If one
were to judge from the standard historiography of the Gregorian Reform,
one might suspect that this was a hagiographical anachronism reflecting
the concerns of the later eleventh century. Yet such "Gregorian" themes
were an early part of Italian reform mentality. Far more explicit than any of
Dominic's denunciations are the attacks on womanizing clergy and their
illegitimate offspring made in 1022 by Benedict VIII at the Council of
Pavia.[24] Toubert's study of Farfa's rental contracts indicates that in the early
eleventh century the number of clerical families was low and getting lower,
suggesting that hostility to priestly marriage was a potent force.[25] Dominic's public opposition to the abuses of his fellow clergymen probably placed
him in the forefront of the progressive priestly culture of his day.

The monastic life, as defined by Dominic's hagiographer Alberic, was
the life led "by those renouncing the world."[26] Benedict's *Rule* indicates
two ways this renunciation could properly be made: life in community and
life as a hermit.[27] One of the many contributions of Jean Leclercq to medieval ecclesiastical history was to demonstrate that "Benedictine hermitism" was a vital tradition in the early Middle Ages. He showed that monks
viewed the cenobitical and eremitical lives not as mutually exclusive alter-
natives but rather as ends of a spectrum of possible monastic practices.[28]
Each had its characteristic virtues: in cenobitical life a monk served under
a rule and an abbot, developed obedience and humility, and participated
in community prayer; in the solitude of eremitical life he perfected individual prayer. Dominic, his hagiographers agree, excelled at both.

24. Benedict VIII, "Praefatio" and "Decretum" for the Synod at Pavia on 1 August
1022, ed. Ludwig Weiland, in MGH *Leges*, 11–vols. (Hannover: Hahnsche Buchhandlung,
1843–), 1:70–76. Although the pope seems especially concerned about the possible loss of
Church property to clerical families, he also raises issues of ecclesiastical purity and leadership
and attacks the married clergy personally, invoking, among other analogies, Epicurus and stal-
lions maddened by desire to mount their mares.

25. Toubert, *Structures*, 1:779–83.

26. *Monte Cassino Life* xxxvi, 74; *Sora Life* xxxix, 40. On the ancient universal tradition
behind the definition of monasticism as world renunciation, see de Vogüé, *La Communauté
et l'abbé dans la Règle de saint Benoît: Textes et études théologiques* (Paris: Desclée de Brouwer,
1960), 151–52; trans. Charles Philippi and Ethel Rae Perkins as *Abbot and Community in the
Rule of St. Benedict*, 2 vols., Cistercian Studies Series 5 (Kalamazoo, Mich.: Cistercian Publications, 1979–1988), 1:117–18.

27. *RB* i, 1:436–41.

28. Leclercq, "Pierre le Vénérable et l'érémitisme clunisien," *Studia Anselmiana* 40
(1956): 99–120; "'Eremus' et 'Eremita': Pour l'histoire du vocabulaire de la vie solitaire,"
Collectanea Ordinis Cisterciensium Reformatorum 25 (1963): 8–30; "Solitary Life and Common Life," *Contemplative Life*, trans. Elizabeth Funder, Cistercian Studies 19 (Kalamazoo,
Mich.: Cistercian Publications, 1978), 46–57.

Alberic's decription of Dominic's progress at the monastery near Petra Demone itemizes the virtues connected with monastic discipline: "It is almost incredible to recall how the life of Dominic then stood out—how restrained in his diet, how constant throughout the night in his vigils, how frequent in his prayers, how assiduous in his readings, how remarkable, in short, in the observation of the whole discipline of monastic life."[29] Dominic did not have much time to shine as a cenobitical star, for after he left Petra Demone he had no further recorded contacts with monastic superiors. Yet he wore a monastic habit throughout his life.[30]

Given Dominic's short career as a simple monk, a more convincing way to establish his cenobitical credentials was to make him an "alter Benedictus," to assimilate him to the patriarch of Western monasticism.[31] Dominic's life parallels Benedict's. Like the young Benedict, the young Dominic is a *puer senex*.[32] Both saints, when they are first revealed in their eremitical retreats, evoke "light of the world" themes (Matthew 5:14–15; cf. Mark 4: 21 and Luke 11:33).[33] Both give spiritual nourishment in return for earthly food.[34] Both receive a celestial vision, a "cosmic sign."[35] A phrase concern-

29. For Alberic, see *Monte Cassino Life* xvii, 72; and *Sora Life* xvii, 37. The less ornate original tradition is witnessed in the *Sermon*, 365; *Trisulti Life* ii, 282; and *Valva Life* xiii–xiv, 72.

30. Dominic received the monastic habit at the monastery near Petra Demone, as described above. The *Sermon*, 365, affirms that he "enhanced it with wonderful acts." According to the *Sora Life* clxi, 56, a hostile priest claimed that Dominic too would have had a family if he had not been prohibited by the propriety monastic garb required.

31. On Benedict as a hagiographical model, see Penco, "S. Benedetto nel ricordo del medio evo monastico," *Benedictina* 16 (1969): 173–87; reprint, *Medioevo monastico*, Studia Anselmiana 96 (Rome: Pontificio Ateneo S. Anselmo, 1988), 215–33. The importance of this model for Dominic's hagiography has been signaled in Franklin, "Restored *Life and Miracles*," 336–39.

32. Gregory I, *Dialog.* II prol. 1, 2:126–27.

33. On the "light of the world" image, compare Gregory I, *Dialog.* II i vi, 2:134–35, with *Valva Life* xix–xxii, 72; *Monte Cassino Life* xix, 72; and *Sora Life* xix, 38. The *Sermon*, 366, and the *Trisulti Life* ii, 283, hint at it when they claim that "suaeque vitae radiis plurimos illustraret."

34. Compare Gregory I, *Dialog.* II viii, 2:136, with *Valva Life* xix–xxii, 72; *Monte Cassino Life* xxii, 72; *Sora Life* xxii, 38.

35. Compare Gregory I, *Dialog.* II xxxv and IV viii, 2:236–43 and 3:42–43, with Dominic's two visions as described in the *Trisulti Life* iv–v, 283–84; the *Valva Life* xxxix–xli, 74; the *Monte Cassino Life* xxxix–xliii, 74; and the *Sora Life* li–liv, 42. On the ancient *topos* of an elevated observer comprehending the whole world in a glance, and the way this became part of Benedict's image, see Pierre Courcelle, "La vision cosmique de Saint Benoît," *Revue des études augustiniennes* 13 (1967): 97–117, esp. 114–17; Françoise Monfrin, "Voir le monde dans la lumière de Dieu: A propos de Grégoire le Grand, *Dialogues*, II, 35," *Les fonctions des saints dans le monde occidental (IIIe–XIIIe siècle): Actes du Colloque organisé par l'École française de Rome avec le concours de l'Université de Rome "La Sapienza," Rome, 27–29 octobre 1988,* Collection de l'École française de Rome 149 (Rome: École française de Rome, 1991), 37–49; and additional bibliography in Penco, *Storia del monachesimo in Italia*, 2nd ed., 55.

ing Dominic's "spirit of prophesy" is borrowed from the *Dialogues*.[36] Dominic's miracles involving food offerings that were stolen, hidden, and then, as he predicted, turned into serpents are like a wonder worked by Benedict.[37] The most egregious echo is found in the foundation story of San Bartolomeo at Trisulti already noted, which describes how there Dominic had lived unknown in a cave for three years, an evocation of Benedict at Subiaco that contradicts Dominic's actual chronology.[38] For the Trisulti hagiographer, the advantage of this ahistorical event was that just as Benedict had emerged from his cave and begun his public career, so also Dominic came forth and embarked on his greatest public mission—the founding of San Bartolomeo. Hagiographers wove into Dominic's *life* echoes of the Benedictine *Rule* concerning the entrance of hermits into the desert and the arrangement of monastic facilities.[39]

The eremitical life was a search for solitude. The *Trisulti Life* hails Dominic as an "appetitor dilectae solitudinis."[40] "Thinking only about solitude he circled around looking for a place where he might more comfortably dwell," and finally he and his disciple John discovered Prato Cardoso, where they could live "tranquille et quiete."[41] He built a hermitage on Monte Argatone because he was "needing solitude."[42] All Dominic's hagiographers—but Alberic especially—stress the antisocial nature of his dwellings by using diminutive forms such as *tuguriolum, tuguriunculum, humilis cellula, habitaculum, cellam parvulam,* and *latibulum*.[43] Yet he sought solitude for the sake of prayer, not as an end in itself. The *Trisulti Life* emphasizes that at Scandriglia, a place Dominic had chosen for "eremiticum laborem," he was meditating daily.[44] On Monte Pizi Dominic and John passed their days and most of their nights meditating on the law of God.[45] On the remotest parts of Monte Argatone, after Dominic had built a little cell that he never wanted to leave, he was looking up to the sky while praying (or, in one version, while singing hymns), and it was then

36. Compare Gregory I, *Dialog.* II xi 3, 2:174–75, with *Sora Life* lxvi, 44.

37. Compare Gregory I, *Dialog.* II xviii, 2:194–95, with *Sora Life* lxxxvii, 47.

38. Compare Gregory I, *Dialog.* II i, 2:130–37, with *Trisulti Life* vi–vii, 284.

39. Compare *RB* i, 1:436–39, with *Monte Cassino Life* xviii, 72; and *Sora Life* xviii, 37–38. Compare also *RB* lxvi, 2:660–61, with *Sora Life* cxxi, 50–51.

40. *Trisulti Life* iii, 283.

41. *Valva Life* xxxiii, 73 [a section not found in the *Monte Cassino Life*]; *Sora Life* xvxvi–xxxvii, 39–40.

42. *Trisulti Life* iii, 283.

43. *Trisulti Life* iii, 282; *Valva Life* xxiii–xxxi, 73; *Monte Cassino Life* xx, xxxi, xxxvi, 72, 73, 74; *Sora Life* xx, xxxi, xxxix, xliii, 38, 39, 40, 41.

44. *Trisulti Life* ii, 283.

45. *Valva Life* xxiii–xxxi, 73; *Monte Cassino Life* xxxi, 73; *Sora Life* xxxi, 39.

that he received his vision of the columns of light; he was in this same hermit cell thinking about heavenly things when he saw the whole earth laid out before him.[46]

In hermit *lives*, especially those written for noneremitical audiences, the solitary life includes a social dimension. The hermit's sacred isolation draws people to him. Greater holiness obtained in the desert leads to greater care of the people of God; increased love of God to increased love of neighbor. Peter Brown's famous 1971 article on the holy man in Late Antiquity brought into focus the charismatic, liminal dimension of radical asceticism.[47] Its social dimensions in Antiquity are now increasingly studied.[48] Similar models have been applied to eleventh- and twelfth-century hermitism.[49] The range of possible social relationships goes from the grubbily concrete to the ethereally abstract. The hermit can be a grounded earthly figure, an economic developer of waste land, a person who offers hospitality to travelers and help to the poor.[50] Or he can be an otherworldly power, a model of holiness, almost sacramental in his ability to channel the sacred to earth.[51] Or he can be both. Dominic's hagiographers follow a traditional model when they connect his search for solitude to his creation

46. *Trisulti Life* iv, 283; *Valva Life* xxxv–xxxviii, 74. The *Monte Cassino Life* xxxix, 74, lacks the desert background of the visions, but the *Sora Life* xlvii–l, 41–42, introduces them with a miracle of feeding in the desert.

47. Peter Brown, "The Rise and Function of the Holy Man in Late Antiquity," *Journal of Roman Studies* 61 (1971): 80–101, reprinted in Peter Brown, *Society and the Holy in Late Antiquity* (Berkeley: University of California Press, 1982), 103–52. His later reflections are in "The Saint as Exemplar in Late Antiquity," *Representations* 1 (1983): 1–25; and "Arbiters of the Holy: The Christian Holy Man in Late Antiquity," *Authority and the Sacred: Aspects of the Christianization of the Roman World* (Cambridge: Cambridge University Press, 1995), 55–78.

48. Examples include Han J. W. Drijvers, "Hellenistic and Oriental Origins," *The Byzantine Saint: University of Birmingham Fourteenth Spring Symposium of Byzantine Studies*, ed. Sergei Hackel, *Studies Supplementary to 'Sobornost'* 5 (London: Fellowship of St Alban and Sergius, 1981), 25–33; Joan M. Petersen, "Dead or Alive? The Holy Man as Healer in East and West in the Late Sixth Century," *Journal of Medieval History* 9 (1983): 91–98; Susan Ashbrook Harvey, *Asceticism and Society in Crisis: John of Ephesus and the Lives of Eastern Saints* (Berkeley: University of California Press, 1990).

49. Colin Phipps, "Romuald—Model Hermit: Eremitical Theory in Saint Peter Damian's *Vita Beati Romualdi*, Chapters 16–27," *Monks, Hermits and the Ascetic Tradition: Papers Read at the 1984 Summer Meeting and the 1985 Winter Meeting of the Ecclesiastical History Society*, Studies in Church History 22 (Oxford: Basil Blackwell for the Ecclesiastical History Society, 1985), 65–75; Henry Mayr-Harting, "Functions of a Twelfth-Century Recluse," *History* 60 (1975): 337–52.

50. For the economic dimensions of hermitism in the High Middle Ages, see Henrietta Leyser, *Hermits and the New Monasticism: A Study of Religious Communities in Western Europe, 1000–1150* (New York: Saint Martin's Press, 1984); and Ann K. Warren, *Anchorites and Their Patrons in Medieval England* (Berkeley: University of California Press, 1985).

51. On the hermit's embodiment of sacred categories, see Howe, "The Awesome Hermit: The Symbolic Significance of the Hermit as a Possible Research Perspective," *Numen* 30 (1983): 106–19.

of monastic foundations. They specifically link the attractive power of his sanctity to the founding of his monasteries near Scandriglia, near Pizzoferrato, in the Valley of the Sagiattario, and at Trisulti.

In summary, then, Dominic's hagiographical image effectively combines the holinesses of priest and monk, cenobite and hermit. This conflation has parallels. Just as the high nobility, lesser nobles, and knights were all beginning to merge into a common chivalric culture of "those who fight," so also priests and monks were becoming a common class of "those who pray." Perhaps some of the hostility Dominic encountered from secular priests was because they were competing for the same territory. The combination of monk and pastor was a potent threat to the old order. It was the engine behind the success of the High Gregorian Reform, which was dominated by monks who were bishops, cardinals, and popes. Yet this combination of roles was not without problems. It blurred important distinctives and distinctions. Ultimately reformers would try to separate out and reestablish the sometimes contradictory strengths of the sacerdotal and monastic orders. The twelfth century's drive for definition would separate them, at least in theory, and would give ecclesiastical leadership to the lawyers who did the separating.

Beyond the institutional charisma(s) that Dominic embodied, he also had personal charisma. He was a holy man in his own right. Hagiographers portray holiness, which is not directly definable, by comparing their subjects to known sacred images and models. I call such allusions to holy persons, places, and things "hagiographic light." This heavenly glow suffuses all hagiographic narrative, frustrating any would-be Leopold Von Ranke who wishes to reconstruct the life of a saint "as it actually happened." Hagiographic light at best tends to overwhelm individual details, reducing earthly events to silhouettes against a golden backdrop. At worst it distorts the narrative so that major incidents are misrepresented or lost.[52]

---

52. Although the theory of hagiographical light is implicit in critical hagiographical work, it is rarely explicit. For a more detailed explication, see Howe, "The Awesome Hermit," 106–19. The effect of this mentality on sacred biography is analyzed in Thomas J. Heffernan, *Sacred Biography: Saints and Their Biographers in the Middle Ages* (New York: Oxford University Press, 1988), 122–84.

On hagiographical images themselves, see Jean Leclercq, *La Vie parfaite: Points de vue sur l'essence de l'état religieux*, Tradition monastique 1 (Paris: Brepols, 1948); and Marc van Uytfanghe, *Stylisation biblique et condition humaine dans l'hagiographie mérovingienne [600 – 750]*, Verhandelingen van de Koninklijke Academie voor Wetenschappen, Letteren en schone Kunsten van België, Klasse der Letteren, Jahrgang 49, 120 (Brussels: Paleis der Academiën, 1987), 71–102. Gregorio Penco has long studied how monastic hagiography uses particular

Does hagiographic light have any objective referent? Or does it reveal nothing more than the mentality of hagiographers and their audiences? Historians often try to eliminate sacred patterns and paradigms, resorting to the source criticism characteristic of the nineteenth-century "historical" interpreters of the Bible who blithely discarded all stereotypes, sometimes leaving nothing more than a jumbled pile of odd detritus. Such hypercriticism is not necessary here. Dominic himself probably tried to conform to sacred models, not only because he was pious, but also because he would have known that his celebrity was due to his *sanctitas*, and that therefore his public projects required a saintly persona. Dominic's hagiographers—writing for lively, diverse, and knowledgeable cultic communities—would have found it necessary to use the more appropriate images of their literary repertoires and to avoid the more incongruous ones. Thus, while it is important to identify stereotypes and emphasize their problematic nature, in Dominic's case hagiographical light may well embody objective historical information.

The analogies Dominic's hagiographers applied to their hero certainly indicate how they perceived and conceptualized his holiness. Angels provide one image. The theme of angelic life as an ideal, especially as a monastic ideal, goes back to the desert fathers, and, while it was most fully developed in the Greek Church, it was also found in post-Carolingian Western monasticism, particularly in the Cluniac tradition.[53] Yet it plays little part in Dominic's hagiography. Perhaps he was implicitly assimilated to angels, when he was raised above the earth and shown heavenly things in his cosmic vision. He is also said to have associated with angels—the *Trisulti Life* specifies angelic guidance in regard to two of his foundations, and most *lives* situate a choir of angels at his deathbed.[54] His personal devotion to the cult of the angels is shown by several church dedications.[55]

Prophets were exemplars of the holy life, not only because they taught

---

sacred images, and many of his relevant articles are reprinted in *Medioevo monastico*, Studia Anselmiana 96 (Rome: Pontificio Ateneo S. Anselmo, 1988).

53. Leclercq, *Vie parfaite*, 19–56; Karl Suso Frank, ΑΓΓΕ ΙΚΟΣ ΒΙΟΣ: *Begriffsanalytische und Begriffsgeschichtliche Untersuchungen zum "Engelgleichen Leben" in frühen Mönchtum*, Beiträge zur Geschichte des alten Mönchtums und des Benediktinerordens 26 (Münster, Wf.: Aschendorffsche Verlagsbuchhandlung, 1964); John Bugge, *Virginitas: Essays in the History of a Medieval Ideal*, International Archives of the History of Ideas, Series Minor 17 (The Hague: Martinus Nijhoff, 1975), 30–35; Penco, "La figura dell'abate nella tradizione spirituale del monachesimo," *Medioevo monastico*, 379.

54. On angelic guidance, see the *Trisulti Life* vi and xi, 281 and 286. Angels present at death are noted in *Trisulti Life* xiii, 306; *Valva Life* lxxvi, 77; *Monte Cassino Life* lxxvi, 77; and *Sora Life* ccix–ccxii, 61.

55. *Trisulti Life* x, xi, 286; *Sora Life* cxxiv, 51.

righteously, but also because their careers allegorically foreshadowed Christ's. The assimilation of saint and prophet is a common hagiographical theme, East and West.[56] According to the *Sora Life*, Dominic spoke out in a "prophetic spirit" when he warned the wife and son of Count Berardus II of Marsica of the count's impending doom if he did not stop ruling tyrannically and seizing tithes, a "prophesy" that was fulfilled.[57] Comparisons are made to the patriarchs and prophets of the Hebrew Bible: Dominic went "out from his homeland and kinsmen" like Abraham (cf. Genesis 12:1)[58]; he was steadfast like Job[59]; he echoed David's acclamations (cf. Ps 76:15)[60]; and he was continually saying with the prophets that he would rather be abject in the house of the lord than dwell in the tabernacles of sinners (cf. Ps 83:11).[61] There are prophetic resonances in the way an anecdote introduced in the *Sora Life* makes the first wonder associated with Dominic the provision of food in the wilderness.[62] In a word omitted from the published edition of the *Sora Life*, Dominic's warning to servants who stole wine was "prophetic."[63]

The imitation of Christ is a common hagiographical theme, which is what one would expect, since "the cult of the saints is nothing if it is not centered on him for whom the saints lived and suffered."[64] Yet the use of Christic referents and imagery varies considerably, not only because there are many alternative Christian sacred models and images but also because

56. Leclercq, *La vie parfaite*, 57–81; Jacques Fontaine, "Une clé littéraire de la *Vita Martini* de Sulpice Sévère: La typologie prophétique," in *Mélanges offerts à Christine Mohrmann* (Utrecht: Spectrum Éditeurs, 1963), 84–95; Penco, "Le figure bibliche del *Vir Dei* nell'agiografia monastica," *Benedictina* 15 (1968): 1–13.

57. *Sora Life* lxvi–lxxvii, 44–46.

58. The paradigm of Abraham's migration is omitted in the *Sermon* and is only vaguely invoked in the *Trisulti Life* ii, 282, and *Valva Life* xv–xvii, 72. In Alberic's work it was much more explicit, as can be seen from *Monte Cassino Life* xv, 72, and *Sora Life* xv, 37.

59. *Sermon*, 365.

60. *Trisulti Life* iv, 283.

61. *Sermon*, 365.

62. *Sora Life* xlvii–l, 41–42.

63. *Sora Life* cxiii, 49, should read "interminatione prophetica." In Vall. H. 18, fol. 411v, the original reading, obscured by the corrector, is "propha" with an abbreviation stroke above.

64. Quotation from Hyppolyte Delehaye, *Cinq leçons sur la méthode hagiographique*, Subsidia Hagiographica 21 (Brussels: Société des bollandistes, 1934), 146. For the tradition of imitating and following Christ, see Jaroslav Pelikan, *The Growth of Medieval Theology, 600–1300*, vol. 3 of *The Christian Tradition: A History of the Development of Doctrine* (Chicago: University of Chicago Press, 1978), 23–24. On the monastic tradition, see Leclercq, *La Vie parfaite*, 126–60; Penco, "Gesù Cristo nella spiritualità monastica medievale," *Gesù Cristo, mistero e presenza* (Rome: Teresianum, 1971), 407–45, reprinted in *Medioevo monastico*, 133–70; and "L'imitazione di Cristo nell'agiografia monastica," *Collectanea Cisterciensia* 28 (1966): 17–34, reprinted in *Medioevo monastico*, 133–70, 171–91.

there are different images of Christ himself.[65] Dominic's career is sometimes paralleled to Christ's: when he instructs his followers not to reveal
his mountain visions, he acts as Christ did after the Transfiguration; when
he quotes Christ's words, he places himself in the position of Christ as
teacher; and when he encounters crowds of people lining his road waving
palms, he resembles Christ entering Jerusalem.[66] Dominic's hagiographers
most frequently associate Christic qualities with miracle working. Dominic
healed a woman with a flow of blood; he enabled the blind to see, the deaf
to hear, and the lame to walk.[67] In the *Trisulti Life* he specifically prays for
Christ's help during two exorcisms and the healing of a blind man.[68] All
the tomb miracles are attributed to Christ through Dominic's prayers.[69]

The apostles are traditional models. They preach and work miracles;
they exemplify community life in the early Church at Jerusalem.[70] To
Dominic, as to the apostles, could be applied Christ's words about the
city on the mountain and the light under the bushel basket that could not
be hidden.[71] Dominic's preaching, already described, had apostolic resonances, especially when it was linked to conversion in passages such as

65. The limitations of considering sacred biography solely as a recapitulation of the life
of the founder are indicated in Howe, "Awesome Hermit," 109–11. On the multitude of
"Christs," see William A. Clebsch, *Christianity in European History* (New York: Oxford University Press, 1979); and Pelikan, *Jesus through the Centuries: His Place in the History of Culture*
(New York: Harper & Row, 1985).

66. *Sora Life* lvi, 41; *Trisulti Life* xvii, xxi, 289, 292.

67. The healing of the woman with the flow of blood is found in *Trisulti Life* xii, 287;
Valva Life xlvi–xlix, 75; *Monte Cassino Life* xlvi–xlix, 75; and *Sora Life* ccxiv, 62. Its importance
is suggested by the way hagiographers have moved the story around: the *Trisulti Life* places it
at San Bartolomeo, the *Valva Life* and *Monte Cassino Life* leave the location unclear, but the
Sora Life has shifted the whole block to Sora.

The phrases involving sight to the blind, etc. (cf. Math 11:5 and Luke 7:22) are found in
the *Trisulti Life* vii and xxxiii, 285 and 297. The final citation, an awkward doubling of the
reference, is found in a section of the text that may have suffered alteration.

68. *Trisulti Life* xix, xxx, and xxxii, 290, 296, and 297.

69. *Valva Life* lxxx, 77; *Monte Cassino Life* lxxx, 77; *Sora Life* ccxiv, 62.

70. Leclercq, *La vie parfaite*, 82–105. Studies on early manifestations include Felix
Haase, *Apostel und Evangelisten in den orientalischen Überlieferung*, Neutestamentliche Ab-
handlungen 9 (1–3) (Münster, Wf.: Aschendorffschen Verlagsbuchhandlung, 1922); Frank,
"*Vita Apostolica*: Ansätze zur apostolischen Lebensform in der alten Kirche," *Zeitschrift für
Kirchengeschichte* 82 (1971): 145–66; and Frank, "Vita apostolica als Lebensnorm in der Alten
Kirche," *Internationale katholische Zeitschrift* 8 (1979): 106–20. For medieval developments,
see Marie-Humbert Vicaire, *L'Imitation des apôtres: Moines, chanoines, mendiants (IVe–XIIIe
siècles)* (Paris: Éditions du Cerf, 1963). The whole question of the topos of the "primitive
Church" at Jerusalem and its relationship to the apostolic life theme is extremely complex—
see Howe, "Greek Influence," 169–74. Glenn W. Olsen (Utah) has a comprehensive study in
progress.

71. *Trisulti Life* vii, 284; *Valva Life* xix–xxii, 72; *Monte Cassino Life* xix, 72; *Sora Life*
xix, 39.

"he converted the inhabitants of this place away from many crimes."[72] His ability to detect partially withheld donations implicitly recalled Peter's dealings with Annias and Saphira. In the *Trisulti Life* some greedy Monte Cassino monks appear as apostolic antitypes, whom Dominic has to instruct, "Don't possess gold and silver" (Math. 10:9), and "Be content with food and clothing" (1 Tim. 6:8).[73] The *Sora Life* explicitly makes Dominic "an imitator of the apostles."[74]

Dominic was hailed as "an imitator of the ancient saints in his life, in his miracles, and in his teaching."[75] The careers of many saints are invoked by such things as the *puer senex* topos, the miraculous feeding of a holy man in the wilderness, a vision of heavenly light, an ecstatic experience of being lifted above the world, miracles of retribution, miraculous healings called forth by the sign of the cross, prayers that cure a woman's infertility, the falling tree miraculously diverted, the deathbed colloquy with angels, and so forth. A historian armed with E. Cobham Brewer's *Dictionary of Miracles*, or exploiting the *Acta Sanctorum*'s "Index Moralis," can accumulate dozens of parallels. Such a procedure, however, fails to convey the vitality of stories that circulated freely in a predominantly oral culture. For example, it would be easy to multiply hagiographic parallels for the several stories in Dominic's memorials in which his wash water was the agent of miraculous healings.[76] Yet such stories evoked not only ancient deeds of power but also contemporary wonders. Bishop Anselm I of Lucca (1056–61), ill with a fever, had wash water brought to him from John, a local holy man, a cure that succeeded so well that he survived to become Pope Alexander II (1061–73). As pope his own wash water helped a lame man. Bruno of Segni (d. 1123) was thought to have used his wash water to exorcize a possessed woman.[77]

Such miracles linked past and present in a way made clear by an interlocutor in Desiderius's *Dialogues* who connects the miraculous recovery of a lost item from the water, made by the monks of a Monte Cassino dependency in Gaeta, with the miracles "worked in the Old Testament [period] by Elisha and in the New by our most holy father Benedict." Such wonders, he notes, "are pleasing because they are marvelous, but, even more,

72. *Valva Life* liv, 75; *Monte Cassino Life* liv, 75; *Sora Life* lxiii, 43.
73. *Trisulti Life* xxi, 292.
74. *Sora Life* cxxxv, 53.
75. *Valva Life* li, 75; *Monte Cassino Life* li, 75. This is a different form, perhaps Alberic's original form, of the passage quoted immediately above from *Sora Life*.
76. *Trisulti Life* xiii, 287 (three instances); *Valva Life* xlv–xlix, 74–75; *Monte Cassino Life* xlv–xlix, 74–75; *Sora Life* lvii, clii, clv–clviii, 42–43, 55, 55–56.
77. *Chron. Cass.* II xc, III xxxvi, and III lvi, 344, 412–13, 437.

because they are recent."[78] Peter Damian advises that "it is more effective to use recent examples than older ones."[79] The wondrous deeds of the saints, far from being confined to books or limited to some sort of marginal "popular culture," were the living world of the Church.

Yet, altogether, Dominic's *lives* make relatively modest use of hagiographic light. The sacred patterns, subtlely and infrequently invoked, do not run away with the narrative. Perhaps this is a matter of taste and style. Or perhaps the existence of a knowledgeable cult community and the presence of still-living witnesses encouraged writers to maintain a more down-to-earth narrative tone that emphasized specific deeds over panegyric. The one exception, the only text in which hagiographic light predominates, is the *Sermon*, whose unwieldy digressions and vague imagery read as though they were part of a school exercise. One striking aspect of the sacred images in Dominic's memorials is their relative lack of emphasis on the great late-eleventh- and twelfth-century reforming themes of "imitatio Christi" and "vita apostolica." There is no counterpart here to the Christic imagery found, for example, in Peter Damian's *life* of Dominic Loricatus (d. 1060).

Dominic's memorials and, even more strikingly, his cult also contain pre-Christian sacred resonances. Dominic Christianized the numinous geography of the central Apennines. This thesis will be received skeptically by some. Robert Markus, for example, argues that ancient Christianity had an "undifferentiated . . . spatial universe" until it created a new sacred geography through the cult of the martyrs, that in this process there was "no simple substitution of a Christian for a pagan religious topography," that "between the two lies a slow attrition of Christian belief in the unholiness of pagan holy places, and the emergence, only slightly faster, of a readiness to envisage the possibility of holiness attached to particular spots." But even then, Markus says, "Christianity was—and, perhaps, is, or ought to be—deeply hostile to allowing any place to become holy."[80] As I argue elsewhere, Christianity has a continuous tradition of sacred geography, one that expands in frontier areas as the Church itself expands.[81] Yet Mar-

78. Desiderius, *Dialog.* II xiii and III iii, 1134 and 1145. The references are to 4 Kings 6: 5–7 and to Gregory I, *Dialog.* II vi, 2:154–57 (cf. ibid. II viii, 164–65).

79. Peter Damian, *Epistula* 50 (old numbering, *Opusculum* XV), 2:126.

80. Robert Markus, *The End of Ancient Christianity* (New York: Cambridge University Press, 1990), 139–55; "How on Earth Could Places Become Holy? Origins of the Christian Idea of Holy Places," *Journal of Early Christian Studies* 2 (1994): 257–71.

81. Howe, "The Conversion of the Physical World: The Creation of a Christian Landscape," in *Varieties of Religious Conversion in the Middle Ages*, ed. James K. Muldoon (Gainesville: University Presses of Florida, 1997), 63–78.

kus is correct in asserting that such expansion is not a question of "simple substitution," whereby, for example, a pagan cult might metamorphose into a Christian one. Rather, the development of Christian geography serves both to neutralize demonic residues by setting up countershrines and to exploit, as did the pre-Christian sacred geography before it, the "hierophanies" presented by particular geographical and natural features.

In the Apennine wilderness, the sacred geography of the martyrs was not particularly evident. There were no famous relics except for a few holy bodies treasured in the remains of cities along the Roman roads. Dominic did not change this. There is no record of any translations of saints made for his churches, which usually did not have saints as patrons. His foundations on mountain tops tended to be dedicated to the Trinity, to Michael, or to the angels; those in valleys to Mary (a pattern that parallels cross-cultural associations of heaven/male and earth/female). The only saints besides Mary who received dedications were apostles: Peter, who was Italy's preeminent local and universal patron; and Bartholomew, who was enjoying a wave of popularity as a result of Otto III's translation of his body to Rome. Did relic-centered devotions seem ill-advised to a man who, as a pious boy in Foligno, may have seen the Germans carry off his city patron? Did other focuses of the sacred seem unnecessary to a priest who emphasized the centrality of the Mass? Or did Dominic find relic-centered sacred geography redundant precisely because he had selected sites with their own preexisting sacred qualities?

Dominic's most obvious use of natural symbolism involves his predilection for caves. Some of the most sacred sites of the Greco-Roman world had been caves.[82] In Germanic and Celtic paganism they had offered a way to enter the earth and communicate with the underworld.[83] In the mountains of Italy the two most important Christian pilgrimage centers were grottos: Benedict's hermitage at Subiaco and Michael's shrine on Monte Gargano. In addition, there were less celebrated caves such as those dedicated to Michael at Monte Tancia (near Farfa at the end of the chain of mountains that separates the Tiber valley from the Rieti area)[84] and to San

82. Robin Lane Fox, *Pagans and Christians* (New York: Alfred A. Knopf, 1986), 204–6.

83. H. R. Ellis Davidson, *Myths and Symbols in Pagan Europe: Early Scandinavian and Celtic Religions* (Syracuse: Syracuse University Press, 1988), 26.

84. Francesco Gandolfo, "Luoghi dei Santi e luoghi dei demoni: Il riuso dei templi nel medio evo," *Santi e demoni nell'alto medioevo occidentale (secoli V–XI), 7–13 aprile 1988*, 2 vols., Settimane di studio del CISAM 36 (Spoleto: CISAM, 1989), 2:890–93; Poncelet, "San Michele al Monte Tancia," *Archivio di R. SRSP* 29 (1906): 541–48; Schuster, *L'Imperiale Abbazia di Farfa*, 37–38, 174–76, 193; Immacolata Aulisa, "Le fonti e la datazione della *Re-*

Angelo at Balsorano (a few miles northeast of Sora).[85] The sacrality of caves would have transferred to Dominic when he took up residence within them at Prato Cardoso, Trisulti, and Vallepietra. Except for the shrines that boast of Dominic's physical relics, these caves became his most revered cult sites. In fact, since the connection between Dominic and the hermitage of Santissima Trinità at Vallepietra has only recently been rediscovered, the holiness experienced there by believers surely owes more to site than saint.

There were other numinous places. Mountain peaks had sacred resonances.[86] Fountains had been major sites for worship—and for miracles—in the pagan world.[87] Forests were awesome.[88] The power of these features of the natural landscape increased when they occurred together. Historians of religion have analyzed how, cross-culturally, a perfect spatial image embodying completeness, solitude, and even paradisal resonances can be created by juxtaposing features such as mountains, water, trees, and grottos.[89] In Classical nature description, water, trees, and cliffs form a perfect landscape so common that Ernst Robert Curtius named the *topos*, adopting a constantly recurring phrase, the "locus amoenus."[90] When such sites actually occurred near cities, churchmen tended to appropriate them.[91] Those further afield could reveal God to hermits: for example, Peter Damian tells how the young Romuald, whenever he went hunting in the woods and entered a "locus amoenus," would soliloquize, "O how well hermits could live in these recesses of the forest, how well they would be

velatio seu Apparitio S. Michaelis Archangelis in Monte Tancia," *Vetera Christianorum* 31 (1994): 315–331.

85. Antonelli, *Abbazie . . . nella diocesi di Sora*, 309–13.

86. Davidson, *Myths and Symbols in Pagan Europe*, 115; Diana L. Eck, "Mountains," *Encyclopedia of Religion* 10:130–34.

87. Holy wells have received considerable antiquarian attention. To enter into this literature, see Aline Rouselle, *Croire et Guérir: La foi en Gaule dans l'Antiquité tardive* (Paris: Librairie Arthème Fayard, 1990), 31–49, 181–86; and Francis Jones, *The Holy Wells of Wales* (Cardiff: University of Wales Press, 1954). Limited bibliography is found in Arthur Gribben, *Holy Wells and Sacred Water Sources in Britain and Ireland: An Annotated Bibliography*, Garland Folklore Bibliographies 17 (New York: Garland Publishing, 1992), esp. 15–16.

88. Réginald Grégoire, "La foresta come esperienza religiosa," *L'ambiente vegetale nell'alto medioevo, 30 marzo–5 aprile 1989*, 2 vols., Settimane di studio del CISAM 37 (Spoleto: CISAM, 1990), 2:663–703; Roland Bechmann, *Trees and Man: The Forest in the Middle Ages*, trans. Katharyn Dunham (New York: Paragon House, 1990), 276–82. Vito Fumagalli, *Landscapes of Fear: Perceptions of Nature and the City in the Middle Ages*, trans. Shayne Mitchell (Cambridge, England: Polity Press, 1994), 127–28 and 147, argues that forests became increasingly more mysterious as people were cut off from them by encastellation and its accompanying concentrated settlement.

89. Mircea Eliade, *The Sacred and The Profane: The Nature of Religion*, trans. Willard R. Trask (New York: Harcourt, Brace, & World, 1959), 151–55.

90. Curtius, *European Literature*, trans. Trask, 92–94, 183–202.

91. Poly and Bournazel, *Feudal Transformation*, trans. Higgitt, 265.

able to contemplate quietly here, away from all the disturbance of worldly noise."[92]

Dominic's establishments were awesomely sited. Seven of the dozen monasteries and hermitages he founded were on mountains. Although these tended to be at springs located about half to two-thirds of the way toward the summits, isolated hermitages could be even higher, as on Monte Argatone where Dominic had his visions. A price was paid for such geographical sacrality inasmuch as mountaintop hermitages had to be supported by lower-altitude communities. Life in them could be difficult. Once when Dominic was on Monte Argatone, a snowstorm struck on the vigil of St. Martin [November 10], isolating him for forty days.[93] The *lives* specifically associate half his sites with rivers, springs, and lakes. Obviously monks and hermits had a biological need for water, but, since their habitations always had to be located accordingly, literary mentions of their water sources must also relate to some higher perfection of the sites.

The *lives* frequently refer to forests. The woods around San Bartolomeo, still impressive today, are invoked in the account of its foundation. At Pizzoferatto the traditional hermitage site is San Domenico "in silvis." Etymologies derive the name "Plataneta" from plane trees (*platanus*), and "Sancti Petri de Avellana" from hazelnuts (*avellana*), the latter perhaps questionably, since the foundation charter reads "de Obellana." The texts praise the woods and forests donated to San Domenico at Sora by Lord Peter. A hollow oak tree appears in the *Sora Life* in an eery miracle where fish are turned into serpents.[94]

The Trisulti hagiographer glorified San Bartolomeo by juxtaposing all the major natural elements into a coherent *locus amoenus*. Although he had previously indicated that Prato Cardoso was a "locus congruus" for hermitism, his geographical information was standard until the point in his story where Dominic entered Campania. Then, he says, Dominic took up residence in a certain cave "in the place which is called Trisulti, at the base of the mountain which is called Porca, where a stream of water rises abundantly"—it was here that the miraculous deer led hunters to Dominic. The same geographical particulars are reiterated when Dominic is asked by an angel to put a monastery on this site, and his prayer on this occasion evokes the world-creating power of God. Then the inhabitants of the sur-

92. Peter Damian, *Vita Romualdi* i, 14.
93. *Sora Life* xlvii–l, 41–42.
94. *Trisulti Life* x and xiv, 285–86, 287. *Valva Life* xxxv–xxxviii and lii, 74 and 75; *Monte Cassino Life* liv, 75; *Sora Life* xlii, lxi, xcv, cxxxi, 41, 43, 47, 52.

rounding *castelli* give Dominic mountains, forests, and fishing rights in the river. Thus San Bartolomeo becomes an archetypal paradise.[95]

Hermit saints can blend into their wildernesses like wild men or silvan deities.[96] When shepherds discovered the hermitage of Benedict of Nursia and saw him clothed in rough skins, "they mistook him for some wild animal"; Romuald of Ravenna, after too much time in a swamp, temporarily lost his hair and turned green.[97] Dominic also merged into the wilderness. At Trisulti the hunters who were led by the mysterious guiding deer "uncovered" his cell when the deer entered the cave "in which the saint was hiding" and then vanished.[98] Dominic found his hermitage on the Sagiattario while he was circling the mountains and hills and "hidden places" of the forest.[99] Alberic most extensively develops the theme of hiding. He describes how outside of Petra Demone, "Dominic was hiding in the hidden places," and employs three more variant forms of *latere* before he finally has Dominic "discovered by the inhabitants"; he tells how Dominic, known to hide in his "beloved hiding places" on "Monte Pizi," was discovered by the local magnates; he has Dominic "discovered" at Prato Cardoso."[100] Like the wild man, Dominic has powers over nature. Although this is most obvious from the miraculous guiding deer, additional miracles stop falling stones and trees. To chastise those who would cheat him, Dominic called down a cat upon a fisherman's catch, and three times he knew that stolen goods would be turned into serpents.[101]

Most deliciously shocking to the nineteenth-century travelers who came to admire the wild scenery and colorful folkways of the Abruzzi, however, was Dominic's feast at Cocullo, which is celebrated in early May, the traditional time for pagan festivals. As part of the celebration, local snake handlers (*serpari*) drape his statue with wriggling snakes and parade

95. *Trisulti Life* ii, vi–vii, ix, xiv, 283, 284, 285, 287.

96. Charles Allyn Williams, *Oriental Affinities of the Legend of the Hairy Anchorite: The Theme of the Hairy Solitary in Its Early Forms with Reference to "Die Lügend von Sanct Johanne Chrysostomo,"* 2 vols., University of Illinois Studies in Language and Literature 10 (2) and 11 (4) (Urbana: University of Illinois Press, 1925, 1927); Richard Bernheimer, *Wild Men in the Middle Ages: A Study in Art, Sentiment, and Demonology* (Cambridge, Mass.: Harvard University Press, 1952), 16–17, 192.

97. Gregory I, *Dialog.* II i, 2:136–37; Peter Damian, *Vita Romualdi* xx, 45–46.

98. *Trisulti Life* vii, 284.

99. *Trisulti Life* xi, 286.

100. *Monte Cassino Life* xix–xx and xxxv, 72 and 74; *Sora Life* xx–xxii, xxxii, xxxviii, 38, 39, 40.

101. *Trisulti Life* xxi, 291–92; *Sora Life* lxxxix–xciii, xciv–cviii, cix–cxiv, 47, 47–48, 48–49.

with it after Mass, while Dominic's devotees toss more live snakes at it, praying all the while for protection against snakebite, rabies, and toothache.[102] According to one of the more creative folklorists:

The old religion of nature lingers on. In this remote region pagan and Christian are harmoniously amalgamated worlds, and San Domenico is representative of a far older age than the one in which he lived. He substituted an ancient cult, and naturally he became accredited with the powers of the replaced divinity, who was undoubtedly the ancient Marsian goddess, Angitia. . . . [After indicating alleged parallels involving healing, power over nature, fertility associations, and totemic thought:] There is enough left to ensure us of the continuity of the ancient cult until the present day transformed by new currents of thoughts, and containing elements that bring widely separated ages together. [103]

In reality, what is known about Angizia's cult does not parallel Dominic's.[104] Yet the prominence of serpents at his feast is probably related to ancient Marsican traditions. In the Roman world, the Marsi were notoriously expert with snakes.[105] Marsican snake handlers remained recognizable vagrants in the Kingdom of Naples well into the nineteenth century.[106] There would have been no doctrinal problem in integrating snake-handling rituals into Dominic's cult, because power over serpents, whatever part it may once have played in pagan ritual, was an aspect of sanctity for which considerable biblical support could be adduced (cf. Mark 16:10, Luke 10:19,

102. The longest detailed description of Dominic's festival at Cocullo is given in Di Nola, *Aspetti magico-religiosi*, 35–44, but many observers of the nineteenth and twentieth centuries have left accounts. Perhaps the first modern Englishman to allude to it was Keppel Craven, in his *Excursions in the Abruzzi and Northern Provinces of Naples*, 2 vols. (London: Richard Bentley, 1838), 1:146, 2:36. Particularly full reports are in a W. H. Woodward article in the *Manchester Guradian* (1 June 1910), reprinted in Ashby, *Italian Scenes and Festivals*, 115–21; and in Estella Canziani, *Through the Apennines and the Lands of the Abruzzi: Landscape and Peasant Life* (New York: Houghton Mifflin Company, 1928), 293–318. On the biases of such observers, see Bianca Maria Galanti, *Vita tradizionale dell'Abruzzo e del Molise: Saggi storico-critici*, Biblioteca di "Lares" 7 (Florence: Leo S. Olschki, Editore, 1961), 16–45; and Di Nola, *Aspetti magico-religiosi*, 45–47.

103. Linda Clarke Smith, "A Survival of an Ancient Cult in the Abruzzi," *Studi e materiali di storia della religioni* 4 (1929): 106–19, esp. 110 and 118.

104. Di Nola, *Aspetti magico-religiosi*, 107, 114–16.

105. Classical references to the Marsi as snake charmers are surveyed in Erminia d'Ignazio, "I Serpari e la Marsica," *Studi meridionali* 4 (1971): 361–65. For references in *passiones*, see Baudouin de Gaiffier, "Les *Marsi* dans quelques textes hagiographiques," in *Miscellanea in onore di Luciano De Bruyne e Antonio Ferrua*, published in *Rivista di archeologia cristiana* 48 (1972): 167–72, reprinted with the same pagination in *Recueil d'hagiographie*, Subsidia Hagiographica 61 (Brussels: Société des bollandistes, 1977).

106. Craven, *Excursions in the Abruzzi*, 1:145–46; Octavian Blewitt, *Handbook for Travellers in Southern Italy*, John Murray Handbooks for Travellers (London: John Murray, Ablemarle Street, 1853), 18; Anne MacDonell, *In the Abruzzi* (London: Chatto & Windus, 1908), 183.

Acts 28:3). Local snake handlers may not have found the jump difficult, if, as Carlo Ginzburg maintains, there is a "convergence of orthodox and diabolical religion in common piety . . . especially in rural areas where the faith was often mixed with superstitious elements or even pre-Christian residues."[107]

Alfonso di Nola, the author of the only monographic study on Dominic's snake-handling rituals, dates the link between the Marsican *serpari* and Dominic's cult to the seventeenth century, when he thought that the earliest literary witnesses and the first dated artifacts appeared.[108] He did not know additional sources suggesting that the fusion occurred much earlier. One piece of indirect evidence, which pertains to the cult of a rival saint in Cocullo's diocese of Valva and Sulmona, indicates that power over serpents was a major issue in the diocese long before the seventeenth century. There is nothing concerning apotropaic power over snakes in the eleventh-century *life* (*BHL* 6418d) of Bishop Pamphilus of Sulmona and Corfinio (d. late seventh century), the patron of the cathedral chapter at Corfinio.[109] Yet in offices written for Pamphilus in a fourteenth-century hand, he is praised for "warding off injuries from serpents" and is the hero of an undated posthumous miracle story in which he extracts a snake from inside a Sulmona woman sleeping at his tomb.[110] This new twist in Pamphilus's cult, unrelated to his written *life*, can be explained most easily as a response to claims of protection against snakes being made by Dominic's followers at nearby Cocullo. The canons of Corfinio, whose cathedral no

107. Carlo Ginzburg, *Clues, Myths, and the Historical Method*, trans. John Tedeschi and Ann C. Tedeschi (Baltimore: Johns Hopkins University Press, 1989), 15.

108. Di Nola, *Aspetti magico-religiosi*, 49–50, 78, 84–85, 109, 140.

109. The early *life* of Pamphilus (*BHL* 6418d) is found in Archivio Capitolare di Benevento ms. 4 (once III), fols. 169–176, a parchment volume of the eleventh or twelfth century written in Beneventan script. It is described in "Catalogus Codicum Hagiographicorum Latinorum Bibliothecae Capituli Ecclesiae Cathedralis Beneventanae," *Analecta Bollandiana* 51 (1933): 348–53, esp. 353; Elias Avery Loew, *The Beneventan Script: A History of the South Italian Minuscule*, 2nd ed., ed. Virginia Brown, Sussidi Eruditi 33 and 34 (Rome: Edizioni di storia e letteratura, 1980), 2:18; and Jean Mallet and André Thibaut, *Manuscrits en écriture béneventaine de la Bibliothèque capitulaire de Bénévent*, 2–vols., Documents, études et répertoires publiés par l'Institut de recherches et d'histoire des textes (Paris: IRHT, 1984–), 1:135–43, esp. 141. Celidonio, *Diocesi di Valva e Sulmona*, 1:87–92, edited it and placed its composition in the eleventh century because of its particular local political concerns (1:107–18).

110. Vatican BAV ms. lat. 7810 [not 7818, as in Celidonio, *Diocesi di Valva e Sulmona*, 1: 85], fols. 4–9, contains an office ed. *AS* Apr., 3rd ed., 3:590–91. Manuscript descriptions are in Poncelet, *Cat. Cod. Hag. Lat. Vat.*, 218–24, esp. 218; and Loew, *Beneventan Script*, 2nd ed., 2:153.
A slightly different office, which also concludes with the story of the snake extracted from the Sulmona woman, is found in a section of a Sulmona cathedral manuscript written in a sixteenth-century hand. Its responses are published by Celidonio, ibid., 1:83 and 92–94, who claims that the whole was originally printed in a seventeenth-century edition.

longer had a city, could not afford to be complacent about competing saints. Other evidence comes from Dominic's dossier. Di Nola had believed that, except for the *Trisulti Life*'s single story of stolen fish that were turned into snakes, no evidence in the hagiographic tradition linked Dominic to power over serpents.[111] He did not know the *Sora Life*, and so did not know that it presented two additional versions of such stories, revealing a prominent association between Dominic and serpents back in the eleventh century.[112] The link between Dominic's cult and snake handling could have begun early, perhaps facilitated by Dominic's strong association with other pre-Christian sacralities such as caves.

Dominic's hagiographers saw his holiness as amazingly universal. They claim for him almost all the aspects of *sanctitas* found in his world. According to the *Valva, Monte Cassino*, and *Sora Lives*, "Dominic . . . was not only a servant of God, not only a just man and devout (cf. Luke 2:25), but truly a saint, truly a friend of God, truly in his life, in his miracles, and in his teaching to be considered an imitator of all of the ancient saints (*al.* apostles)."[113] Max Weber and his interpreters tend to postulate an exclusionary relationship between institutional charisma and the charisma of the prophet, but Dominic's followers were quick to credit him with both. Moreover, they were willing to assimilate him not only to conventional orthodox models of piety but even to the natural sacralities of the Abruzzi. This strategy worked for a time. While Dominic was alive, his palm-waving followers sang praises to God because "we have merited to have in our country such a defender."[114] In the generation or two after his death, hagiographers continued to sing his praises. But in later ages dominated by ecclesiastical lawyers, the indiscriminate mixing of all categories of sacrality would not be so well received.[115]

---

111. Di Nola, *Aspetti magico-religiosi*, 63–65 and 120.
112. *Sora Life* xciv–cxiv, 47–49.
113. *Valva Life* li, 75; *Monte Cassino Life* li, 75; *Sora Life* cxxxv, 53.
114. *Trisulti Life* xvii, 289.
115. On the tendency of the later Middle Ages to separate institutional and prophetic charisma, see André Vauchez, "Les pouvoirs informels dans l'Église aux derniers siècles du moyen âge: Visionnaires, prophètes et mystiques," *Mélanges de l'École française de Rome* 96 (1984): 281–93, esp. 281.

4

A "Benedictine" Monastic System

THE SCINTILLATING CHARISMATIC AURA of a living saint, no matter how bright, was of little earthly consequence unless its energy could be harnessed. Holiness is known because it was used. Wandering hermit saints such as Dominic were remembered thanks to their churches, monasteries, confraternities, and crowds of followers. This chapter looks at the structure of Dominic's formal creations, his monasteries. The following chapter examines the patronage networks behind them. Study of both these aspects of Dominic's monastic system can provide a better understanding not only of Dominic's "Benedictinism," but also of Western monasticism as a whole at the start of the High Middle Ages.

Dominic's foundations were Benedictine. When he was given the monastic habit at the community near Petra Demone in the ambient of Benedictine Farfa, he himself probably vowed to live "according to the law of the *Rule*."[1] The *Sora Life* claims that the counts of Valva heard that Dominic had founded monasteries "according to the order of St. Benedict," a phrase crossed out by a later corrector of the Vallicelliana manuscript and inadvertently omitted in the unique published edition.[2] Two of Dominic's three surviving foundation charter texts specify that the monks should live "secundum regulam et normam beati Benedicti," and the phrase could originally have been in the third.[3] It therefore seems paradoxical that the

---

1. *RB* lviii, 2:626–33, requires that novices vow to observe the *Rule*. Note the commentaries by de Vogüé in *RB* 6:1322–33; and by Hubertus Lutterbach, in *Monachus Factus Est: Die Mönchwerdung im frühen Mittelalter zugleich ein Beitrag zur Frömmigkeits- und Liturgiegeschichte*, Beiträge zur Geschichte des alten Mönchtums und des Benediktinertums 44 (Münster: Aschendorffsche Verlagsbuchhandlung, 1995), 134–44.

2. The overstruck phrase "ab ordine Sancti Benedicti" is still legible in Bibl. Vall. ms. H. 18, fol. 408, and belongs between "aliis" and "ab eo" in *Sora Life* xxxix, 40.

3. The *RB* is invoked in the related charters for San Pietro Avellana (Gattola, *Historia*, 1:238) and San Domenico near Sora (Baronius, *Annales Ecclesiastici* 16:544–45), the latter of which is echoed in 1205 in Innocent III, *Privilegium*, edited in Farina and Fornari, *Storia e documenti . . . di Casamari*, 156. It is not mentioned in the charter text written for San Bartolomeo at Trisulti, which is known through Innocent III's confirmation, edited in Strnad,

letter of the *Rule* is contradicted by Dominic's actual customs and by many of the internal and external features of his monasteries.

One obvious difference in terms of monastic organization is that Benedict wrote about a single abbot ruling a single community, not about an administrator such as Dominic who governed many monasteries, oratories, and churches. Yet in this regard Dominic's system was far from novel. Pachomius (d. 346), the founder of cenobitic monasticism, is said to have directed 3,000 monks—all of his organizational skills as an ex-soldier must have been required to oversee the subordinate general superiors, the heads of communities, and the monks themselves in their scattered cells! Extended monastic families were the basis of the Irish ascetical tradition. Benedict himself, before establishing his community on Monte Cassino, ruled a dozen houses simultaneously. Monastic confederations were always accepted and often typical: a single abbot could direct several monasteries, a monastic founder could oversee individual abbots in each of his foundations, or a secular ruler or other monastic patron might grant one reformer authority over several houses. Monastic reforms of the tenth and eleventh centuries based upon such confederations included groups of monasteries directed by Gerard of Brogne and other Gorze reformers (ca. 933–1015), by Dunstan (d. 988), by Romuald of Ravenna (d. ca. 1027), and by William of Volpiano (d. 1031). Even the "Order of Cluny" now appears to have been united not so much by laws as by personal links to outstanding abbots.[4]

Such a system depended to a large extent on the person of the abbot.

"Zehn Urkunden," 56–57 (doc. 9); and in Sechi, *Certosa di Trisulti,* 152–53 (doc. 10), but, since Innocent's version was rewritten after the monastery had been handed over to the Carthusians, there would have been no incentive to preserve a Benedictine allusion.

4. Joël Letellier, "L'*Urbs monastica*: Du *Locus terribilis* à la *Visio pacis,*" *Collectanea Cisterciensia* 56 (1994): 294–98, documents the organizational complexity of early desert monasticism. Máire Herbert, *Iona, Kells, and Derry: The History and Hagiography of the Monastic "Familia" of Columba* (Oxford: Clarendon Press, 1988), 5, 13–16, and 124–26, offers an Irish example. For a plethora of others, see *Naissance et fonctionnement des réseaux monastiques et canoniaux: Actes du Premier Colloque International du CERCOM, Saint-Etienne, 16–18 Septembre 1985* (Saint-Etienne: Publications Université Jean Monnet, 1991).

Cluniac organization has been reevaluated. Barbara H. Rosenwein, *Rhinoceros Bound: Cluny in the Tenth Century* (Philadelphia: University of Pennsylvania Press, 1982), 3–29, describes how in the 1950s the assumption that tenth- and eleventh-century "Cluny" was a coherent corporation was called into question. On the shift from a centralized institutional model to an emphasis on personal and local affiliations, see Giles Constable, "Cluny in the Monastic World of the Tenth Century," in *Il Secolo di ferro: Mito e realtà del secolo X, 19–25 aprile 1990,* 2 vols., Settimane di studio del CISAM 38 (Spoleto: CISAM, 1991), 1:391–448, esp. 411–14; and Bouchard, "Merovingian, Carolingian, and Cluniac Monasticism: Reform and Renewal in Burgundy," *Journal of Ecclesiastical History* 41 (1990): 365–88. On the current status of the question, see Tellenbach, *The Church in Western Europe,* 109–10.

He had to be able to oversee both spiritual and administrative affairs. He had to represent both the authority of God and the political power of the founding families. He needed power in personality. Dominic's hagiographers describe an attractive sensitivity to the needs of others. When messengers came with offerings from Monte Cassino, "the saint went out to meet them in the open space in front of the gates."[5] When young Count Oderisius II of Marsica met Dominic and bent down to kiss him on the knee, Dominic lifted him up, took his hand in his, gave him the kiss of peace, and then prophesied the good things that were to happen to him.[6] Dominic responded to a whole series of thieving messengers with thanks, patience, smiles, jokes, and, after their transgressions had been revealed and confessed, pardons.[7] These anecdotes are commonplaces, but Dominic's hagiographers believed that they were characteristic of the saint himself and appropriate to a man in his position. Geniality is not generally associated with the tenth-century "age of iron," but it may have been especially important in an era where personal relationships were more significant than legal structures.[8]

Controlling a monastic empire through personal authority presented logistical difficulties. Dominic's *lives* hint at the travel required. One anecdote begins at a time "when blessed Dominic had abundantly constructed churches, monasteries, and oratories, and was traversing the villas and farms of the monasteries to oversee them and handle their business."[9] Some geographical references reveal the extent of this travel. When the adolescent Count Oderisius first met Dominic, it was at a place called "Veneris," presumably today's Venere in the province of L'Aquila in the Abruzzi, a site located on the shore of the Lago Fucino on a somewhat indirect route that Dominic would have been traveling to cross through the mountains north of the Valley of the Sagittario.[10] Peter, lord of Sora, likewise first met Dominic at a time "when the man of God was traveling from San Pietro in Lago to visit San Bartolomeo."[11] Amatus, a depraved

5. *Trisulti Life* xix, 291.

6. *Sora Life* lxxi–lxxii, 44–45.

7. *Sora Life* lxxix–cxiv, 46–49, most fully transmits the stories about thieving messengers.

8. On the importance of being "affabilis" and "iucundus," see Fichtenau, *Lebensordnung*, 1:190–91, trans. Geary, *Life in the Tenth Century*, 138–39.

9. *Trisulti Life* xxii, 292.

10. *Sora Life* lxxi, 44. On Venere, see Bloch, *Monte Cassino*, 1:338; Pietrantonio, *Monachesimo benedettino nell'Abruzzo*, 276; and Sennis, "Potere centrale e forze locali," 62.

11. *Trisulti Life* xxii, 292; *Valva Life* lvii, 76; *Monte Cassino Life* lvii, 76; *Sora Life* cxviii, 50. The *Sora Life* locates the meeting of Peter and Dominic "in the place which is called

priest from Arsoli, lay in ambush for Dominic at the place called "Campus Artinace," which may have been at the Altopiano di Arcinazzo, on the route from Subiaco to Trisulti or Sora.[12]

Dominic must often have walked, since some of his hermitages were on rugged peaks where horses would have been impractical to ride or maintain. Yet he and his successors did not object to riding: he agreed to ride ("equitare") with Lord Peter of Sora to look for a monastic site; when the priest Amatus tried to attack Dominic with shield and lance, he was employing a method of attack that would make more sense if Dominic himself was also mounted; three *post mortem* miracles involved horses belonging to the monastery of San Domenico at Sora.[13] The proper mounts of Western holy men would soon be donkeys and mules, animals easily distinguished from the horses ridden by warriors: hermit saints would evoke Christ's entrance into Jerusalem by riding donkeys; Archdeacon Hildebrand (the future Gregory VII) rode a mule; subsequent popes ostentatiously adopted the style.[14] The only suggestion that Dominic followed such a custom is in an orally transmitted story from Cocullo.[15]

If Dominic failed to maintain contact with his monks, they sought him out. After he had been away for two and a half years in the valley of the Sagittario, the brothers of San Bartolomeo at Trisulti, "lacking his supervision and sweet admonition and mellifluous consoling words, sent messengers with letters saying that he should swiftly return to care for the servants and sons he had planted there."[16] After he had not communicated with San Pietro Avellana for several years, three brothers, "came to him by order of the community to visit and to ask about things" ("gratia visitandi et requirendi"). Dominic received them kindly, and, after kisses of peace given to each other in turn with joy, they ate together in charity the foods that Dominic himself served.[17]

Furca," a generic name for any geographical "fork," but which here could refer to the "Forca Carusa," a pass on a route connecting the Lago Fucino with the Sulmona basin.

12. *Sora Life* clxxii–clxxxv, 55–56. On the identification of Arcinazzo, see Dolbeau, "Le dossier de saint Dominique," 57.

13. Dominic's equitation is noted in the *Trisulti Life* xxii, 292; *Valva Life* lix, 76; *Monte Cassino Life* lix, 76; and *Sora Life* cxx, 50. An armed, mounted priest lies in wait to attack him in *Sora Life* clxxix, 58. Horses are associated with San Domenico in the *Sora Life* cxxxiii, ccclxiv, and ccclxxv, 52, 75, and 77.

14. The ubiquity of hermits with mules in the late eleventh century is discussed by Jean Becquet, "L'Érémitisme clérical et laïc dans l'ouest de la France," and Charles Dereine, "Discussione," in *Eremitismo*, 194 and 203. Peter the Hermit demonstrated how effective this symbolism could be. Hildebrand rides a mule in *Chron. Subl.*, 12.

15. Celidonio, *Diocesi di Valva*, 2:99.

16. *Trisulti Life* xi, 286.

17. *Trisulti Life* viii, 285.

Dominic extended his physical presence through nepotism. His hagiographers do not emphasize this, presumably because they do not consider it part of otherworldly sanctity. Yet the *Sora Life* reveals that Dominic made his cousin Liutus abbot of San Pietro in Lago, an unhappy choice, since six years later Dominic had to relieve him of command and send him to Scandriglia.[18] Alberic's prologue mentions another relative, "the revered abbot Benedict [of San Domenico at Sora, who reigned from 1064 or earlier to some time prior to 1097/1098], near to Dominic in blood as well as in sanctity."[19] There is no reason to suppose that these two chance references include all the family members involved in Dominic's enterprises.

Command authority could also be enhanced by moving trusted monks from one house to another. This would have been done in the cases of the relatives mentioned above, who presumably came from Foligno. If Liutus's ultimate destination was a reversion, then Dominic would have accepted him into his first monastery at Scandriglia, assigned him to command San Pietro in Lago, and then sent him back to his former house. Alberic claimed that the old monk John whom he had met at Sora had become Dominic's disciple when he was still a boy: presumably he was the disciple John who had accompanied Dominic to the Pizzoferrata area around the 990s and had traveled with the saint from then on.[20] At Sora, Alberic also spoke with "the revered old men of that place, educated long ago under the instruction of Dominic," men who might well have been instructed by Dominic elsewhere, since he had actually spent very little time at Sora.[21] There were potential advantages in shifting monks around. Brothers in isolated rural monasteries might have appreciated the chances for relocation and promotion provided by an expanding system. Pioneering monks who specialized in construction could have helped build churches and monasteries on new sites. This might explain why the Trisulti *life* designates a limited group of Dominic's monks as "ejus condiscipuli," using the

---

18. *Sora Life* xlii and lx, 41 and 43.

19. *Monte Cassino Life* iii, 70; *Sora Life* iii, 35. The dates of this abbot Benedict are poorly known. He is mentioned in charters from 1064 and 1077, edited in Farina and Fornari, *Storia e documenti . . . di Casamari*, 160–62. The calendar written by Leo Marsicanus in 1097/1098, edited in Hoffmann, "Der Kalender des Leo Marsicanus," *Deutsches Archiv* 21 (1965): 131, lists an Abbot Benedict who died on 3 December. In favor of the speculative assumption that this entry refers to Abbot Benedict of San Domenico is Leo's known interest in Sora, where his beloved uncle John was bishop, a relationship described in Francis Newton, "Leo Marsicanus and the Dedicatory Text and Drawing in Monte Cassino 99," *Scriptorium* 33 (1979): 186–90, 199–203.

20. *Monte Cassino Life* vii and xxx, 71 and 73; *Sora Life* vii and xxx, 35 and 39.

21. *Monte Cassino Life* vii, 71; *Sora Life* vii, 35.

phrase to refer to a group of monks who were somehow particularly close to him.[22]

Once Dominic had established a monastery, he chose a superior for it. At Scandriglia, according to Alberic, "after the monastery had been built and no small multitude of brothers collected, Dominic appointed one of them to take charge as father, a man named Constantius, extremely suitable in equal measure in life, knowledge, and speech."[23] In the Monti Pizi, the *Sora Life* relates, once "a multitude of monks had been collected," the monasteries on the mountain and on the plain were both entrusted to Brother Humbert, "splendid in religion and learning."[24] San Pietro in Lago, as has already been noted, was ruled for six years by Dominic's relative Liutus, "whom he had judged suitable enough for that office," but whom he later replaced, "for a certain cause," with an abbot drawn from among the brethren.[25] San Pietro Avellana, as its foundation charter confirms, was given to Abbot Peter, whom the *Sora Life* calls "illustrious in knowledge and morals."[26] This same source identifies the first abbot of San Bartolomeo as a monk named Albertus, "outstanding in his birth, in his way of life, and in his teaching."[27] Conflicting stories are told about the disposition of the Campanian oratory dedicated to Michael the Archangel, which the Trisulti tradition says was placed in the custody of "Peter, a religious and fine man," while the Sora tradition has it entrusted to "Cofredus, a man recommended by his innocence of life and knowledge of letters and of the world."[28] The *Trisulti Life* affirms that the oratory to the Trinity at "Petra Imperatoris" was given to "a certain religious monk."[29] Although Dominic did not appoint an abbot at Sora, where he directly assumed the "paternal care" of his monks, the *lives* present this as an exceptional case, to which he only reluctantly agreed.[30] These portraits have a pattern: the Trisulti tradition praises the religious virtues of Dominic's

22. *Trisulti Life* viii, ix, 285.

23. *Monte Cassino Life* xxix, 73; *Sora Life* xxix, 39.

24. *Sora Life* xxxvi, 39.

25. The *Trisulti Life* iii, 283, does not name the superior of San Pietro, whom it calls a "prior." The *Valva Life* xxxvii–xxxviii, 74, and the *Monte Cassino Life* xxxvii–xxxviii, 74, are silent about the whole arrangement. The *Sora Life* xxxxii and lx, 41–43, which makes Liutus an "abbot," has the fullest information on this episode.

26. *Sora Life* lxii, 43.

27. *Sora Life* lxv, 43–44.

28. *Trisulti Life* xi, 286; *Sora Life* cvii, 49.

29. *Trisulti Life* xxii, 292.

30. *Trisulti Life* xxiii, 293; *Valva Life* lxv, 76; *Monte Cassino Life* lxv, 76; *Sora Life* cxxix–cxxx, 52.

abbots, whereas the Monte Cassino tradition emphasizes not only their piety but also their education. Here one sees the hand of Alberic, Monte Cassino's schoolmaster.

Although the Benedictine *Rule* gives communities the right to elect their own abbots, Dominic chose the superiors himself.[31] The *Trisulti Life* obviates any irregularity by claiming that this procedure had been approved for San Bartolomeo by the pope, who had empowered Dominic to name a new abbot if he should go elsewhere (no such privilege is attested in the surviving ameliorated thirteenth-century copy of the papal foundation charter).[32] Yet here again Dominic's practice has many parallels. Even though no early medieval monastic rule except the *Rule of the Master* advocates that abbots choose their successors, hagiography offers so many well-attested cases of this system of election that Adalbert de Vogüé has described it as "a kind of variant on the periphery of the more common practice sanctioned by law, a variant admitted at least tacitly in every period."[33] It is best known from the practice of the abbots of Cluny, whose careful management of succession produced a splendid string of talented and long-lived rulers.[34] It was also in vogue in Italian reform circles: for example, shortly before 1044, Peter Damian was designated by his mentor as his successor at Fonte Avellana, and in 1057 Desiderius was chosen by Fridericus (then Pope Stephen IX) to succeed him at Monte Cassino.[35]

Did the abbots Dominic chose have the power and independence envisioned in the Benedictine *Rule*? Or were they just glorified priors serving at his pleasure? Dominic's *lives* assume that he continued to provide spiritual and material oversight, but it is not clear how much intervention this actually entailed. The already cited case of the dismissal of Dominic's nephew, Abbot Liutus, does not prove that all abbots served at his pleasure, since Dominic had familial as well as ecclesiastical authority over Liutus. There is a hint of considerable independence for Dominic's abbots in the fact that the 1026 foundation charter of San Pietro Avellana, issued

---

31. *RB* lxiiii, 2:648–49.

32. Compare *Trisulti Life* xv, 288, to Innocent III's confirmation, edited in Strnad, "Zehn Urkunden," 56–57 (doc. 9); or edited in Sechi, *Certosa di Trisulti*, 152–53 (doc. 10). Since the *vita* contains the *lectio difficilior* and fits better with other hagiographical testimony on this matter, it is possible that Innocent's "improved" charter dropped what would have been an obsolete and questionable privilege.

33. de Vogüé, *Communauté et l'abbé*, 351–52, trans. Philippi and Perkins, *Abbot and Community*, 2:311–13.

34. Constable, "Cluny in the Monastic World," 1:407–9.

35. John of Lodi, *Vita B. Petri Damiani* vii, edited in *PL* 144:124; *Chron. Cass.* III ix, 370.

while Dominic still lived, names only his appointee, Abbot Peter. Yet perhaps it is futile to seek a precise constitutional basis, or even a customary
pattern, for the authority Dominic wielded. So long as both his monks and
his powerful lay patrons continued to respect him, he could intervene in
the affairs of his foundations whenever he wished.

Another divergence between Dominic's practice and the Benedictine
Rule relates to monastic stability. The first chapter of the *Rule* defines
cenobites as monks who "live in monasteries and serve under a rule and
an abbot," and contrasts them with the "gyrovagues" who "spend their
whole lives tramping from province to province . . . always on the move,
with no stability." [36] Dominic's career seems more like that of the gyrovagues. Perhaps this disturbed some of his monastic hagiographers. The
lives reflecting Alberic's work take every opportunity to indicate that Dominic's moves were involuntary, undertaken for the sake of prayer at times
when crowds forced him to seek new hiding places. The *Sermon* avoided
the problem by following Dominic's career only up to the point where he
had founded his first monastery and reentered the desert. Jacobilli, who
wrote in an era when Counter-Reformation authorities were particularly
sensitive about such points, eliminated the problem entirely by adding that
Dominic had "obtained the permission (the 'facoltà') from Pope John XV
and from the superior of the Benedictine Order to be able to build as many
churches and monasteries as he wished." [37]

Yet Dominic's peregrinations did have some Benedictine justification.
Benedict assumed that abbots, unlike simple monks, had responsibilities
that might require considerable travel. [38] Furthermore, even though Dominic stretched the limits of Benedict's theory, he conformed uncannily to
his practice. Benedict was born at Nursia, went south to study in Rome,
and then became a hermit at Subiaco, where, after he was discovered and
acclaimed, he became abbot of twelve Apennine monasteries; at the end of
his life he founded Monte Cassino on the edge of the coastal plain. Dominic was born at Foligno, went south to study at Petra Demone, and then
became a hermit there, where, after he was discovered and acclaimed, he
became the head of about a dozen Apennine monasteries and hermitages
(including one just above Subiaco) before he founded his monastery near

36. *RB* i, 1:436–41.
37. Jacobilli, *Vite de'santi e beati dell'Umbria*, 1:115.
38. de Vogüé, *Communauté et l'Abbé*, 427, trans. Philippi and Perkins, *Abbot and Community*, 2:376.

Sora on the edge of the coastal plain. It would be difficult to find another abbot who followed Benedict's actual footsteps so closely.

A major problem presented by Dominic's career involves his relationship to his original abbot. Whereas the first chapter of Benedict's *Rule* appears to presume that hermits, once they have graduated out of the *cenobium*, were still considered forward contingents of the monastic battle line subordinate to the abbot, Dominic, once he had gotten permission to enter the desert, had no further recorded contact with his former abbot or any other monastic superior. This deviation also has parallels: during these same years Romuald of Ravenna worked entirely on his own once he had received his abbot's permission to undertake the eremitical life.[39]

Another anomaly involves the abbot's place of residence. The *Rule* envisions an abbot living within the monastic compound (even though he might have to withdraw on occasion from the daily life of the community because of travel, guests, private prayer, and reading).[40] Dominic, however, after building San Pietro in Lago, lived in a hermitage on a nearby mountain, and only returned on fixed days to supervise the community.[41] This arrangement had a long tradition in Italo-Greek ascetic circles, where it was anchored in customs extending back to early Palestinian monasticism.[42] It appeared elsewhere in Latin Italy during Dominic's lifetime, especially in Romuald's milieu and around Pomposa.[43]

Benedict did not envision monasteries filled with priests. Probably he himself was never ordained. Although he was innovative in his willingness to accept priests as full members of his communities, he was conservative in insisting that they provide sacramental services only for other monks.[44] But already in the Carolingian era, priests were becoming numerous in monastic communities.[45] In later centuries, just as more and more rural

---

39. Peter Damian, *Vita Romualdi* iiii, 20. For an explication, see Phipps, "Romuald—Model Hermit," 65–75.

40. *RB* lvi, 3:622–23. For commentary see de Vogüé, *RB*, 6:1285–87.

41. *Trisulti Life* iii, 283; *Valva Life* xxxv–xxxviii, 74; *Sora Life* xliv–xlv, 41.

42. Morini, "Eremo e cenobio," 357, 366–67, 371, 373, and 380–88.

43. Fasoli, "Incognite della storia dell'Abbazia di Pomposa fra il IX e l'XI secolo," *Benedictina* 13 (1959): 202; Tabacco, "*Privilegium Amoris*," 343, and "Romualdo di Ravenna," 100, 108–11.

44. *RB* lx, lxii, 2:634–37, 640–43. Commentary by de Vogüé, in *RB*, 7:400–407, trans. John Baptist Hasbrouck as *The Rule of Saint Benedict: A Doctrinal and Spiritual Commentary*, Cistercian Studies Series 54 (Kalamazoo, Mich.: Cistercian Publications, 1983), 289–300.

45. Many priests and deacons appear in the Carolingian monastic rosters edited in Otto Gerhard Oexle, *Forschungen zu monastischen und geistlichen Gemeinschaften im westfränkischen Bereich*, Münstersche Mittelalter-Schriften 31 (Munich: Wilhelm Fink Verlag, 1978).

monasteries were being founded and monks were receiving many churches as gifts, ordained monks become a majority. It seems likely that this increase relates in part to increased involvement with pastoral care, but causality is hard to demonstrate because monasteries could staff the churches they owned with hired priests, a compromise so common that it became the generally accepted practice after long episcopal and monastic jurisdictional battles in the early twelfth century.[46]

Did Dominic's little churches and monasteries provide pastoral care? This would not have been unparalleled in Marsica, where in 1114 Pope Paschal II protested against customs established by "the depraved presumption of monks," who he claims were baptizing, anointing the sick, hearing confessions, and even failing to respect episcopal excommunications.[47] If Dominic's establishments had undertaken such ministries, monastic life within them would have been greatly affected, since it is doubtful that they could have afforded separate "parish" and "monastic" churches. If they had public ministries, one would expect to find evidence of such telltale signs as possession of burial rights, "first fruits," and tithes.

At least some of Dominic's churches did receive permission to officiate at burial services. According to the *Trisulti Life*, when San Bartolomeo was founded, the pope granted its personnel the rights to visit the sick and to conduct funerals; allegedly he also established its church as the "foremost church of all the churches of the adjacent *castelli*" and "confirmed these privileges with letters and documents."[48] No such documents survive. Yet the very fact that the *life* claims rights of visitation and burial proves the monastery either was involved in these ministries or else wished to be. Its rights to visit the sick and to bury the dead are confirmed in a letter from Alexander III, written between 1160 and 1176.[49] Burial rights enjoyed by

46. Constable, "Monasteries, Rural Churches and the *Cura Animarum* in the Early Middle Ages," *Cristianizzazione ed organizzazione ecclesiastica delle campagne nell'alto medioevo: Espansione e resistenze, 10–16 aprile 1980*, 2 vols. Settimane di studio del Centro Italiano di Studi sull'Alto Medioevo 28 (Spoleto: Centro italiano di Studi sull'Alto Medioevo, 1982), 1: 349–95, esp. 359–65, 380–81; Thomas L. Amos, "Monks and Pastoral Care in the Early Middle Ages," *Religion, Culture, and Society in the Early Middle Ages: Studies in Honor of Richard E. Sullivan*, Studies in Medieval Culture 23 (Kalamazoo, Mich.: Medieval Institute Publications, 1987), 165–80; Martin Dudley, "The Monastic Priest," *Monastic Studies II: The Continuity of Tradition*, ed. Judith Loades (Bangor, Gwynedd: Headstart History, 1991), 183–92, esp. 186–91. For Lazio, see Toubert, *Structures*, 2:909–912. The trend's monastic context is set forth in de Vogüé, *Community and Abbot*, 1:109, 2:298–300; see also de Vogüé in *RB*, 7:408, trans. Hasbrouck, *Rule of Saint Benedict*, 319.

47. Paschal II, *Epistula* ccclxxvii (J–L 6371), edited in *PL* 163:338–40.

48. *Trisulti Life* xv, 288.

49. Alexander III, *Epistula*, ed. Kehr, "Papsturkunden in Campanien," *Göttinger Nachrichten* (1900): 329–30; noted in Kehr, *Italia Pontificia*, 2:153.

San Domenico at Sora are mentioned by Innocent III in a document from 1205.[50] Nevertheless, since private churches in early medieval Italy occasionally possessed burial rights, these do not necessarily prove that Dominic's churches had parochial functions.[51]

Whether or not Dominic's foundations received "first fruits" is an even more complex question. Six miracle stories concern food offered to Dominic: fish donated by Monte Cassino, by a fisherman who fished on Sunday, and by a cadet member of the counts of Marsica; wine from the great men of Arpino; and fancy breads from the wife of Randisius I of Valva, a gift that included what is apparently the first recorded mention of "calzoni."[52] The importance of these tales is indicated by the fact that they constitute nearly an eighth of the text of the *Sora Life* (excluding the *post-mortem* material). Several designate the gifts by the Graecism "exenia," which in this region meant expected offerings.[53] These "gifts," however, were offerings not from local farmers but from important patrons and clients. They could have been part of an ongoing patronage relationship. Or they could have been "rents" for the use of major properties. They were not necessarily routine ecclesiastical offerings.

Partial control over canonical tithes is often assumed to have been one of the benefits of church foundation. Yet not until well after Dominic's death do the residents of central Italy's Apennine wilderness appear to have been bound by the Carolingian and post-Carolingian legislation that made tithes compulsory. Such customs as did exist tended to respect the ancient rights of the baptismal churches. Italian monks at the start of the eleventh century were more likely to be paying tithes than receiving them. Thus it is not surprising that the only tithes mentioned in Dominic's memorials have no relation to his own foundations, but appear in a list of charges

50. Innocent III, *Privilegium*, ed. Farina and Fornari, *Storia e documenti . . . di Casamari*, 165–68, esp. 167.

51. Settia, "Pievi e capelle nella dinamica del popolamento rurale," *Cristianizzazione*, 1: 453–58.

52. *Sora Life* lxxix–cxiv, 46–49, which specifies that Giseltruda's gift included "cibosque quosdam quos uulgus nuncupat calciones, qui uidelicet fiunt in speciem lunae corniculatae." "Calciones" are absent in the list of medieval terms for breads assembled in A. M. Bautier, "Pain et pâtisserie dans les textes médiévaux latins antérieurs au XIIIè siècle," *Manger et boire au moyen âge: Actes du Colloque de Nice (15–17 octobre 1982)*, 2 vols., Publications de la Faculté des lettres et sciences humaines de Nice 27 (Nice: Les Belles lettres, 1984), 1: 33–65.

53. The local usage of "xenia" or "senia" or exaenia" for obligatory donations of plants and animals can be determined from records at Veroli, seven miles from Sora. See Giorgio Falco, "Note in margine al cartario di Sant'Andrea di Veroli," *Archivio della SRSP* 84 (1961): 198 and 224, reprinted in Falco, *Studi sulla storia del Lazio nel medioevo*, 2 vols., Miscellanea della SRSP 24 (Rome: SRSP, 1988), 2: 708 and 735.

against a "tyrannical" count of Marsica who collected tithes unjustly.[54]

Overall, this survey of the evidence for the public ministries of Dominic's churches leaves a cloudy picture. Rights to burial and to visit the sick are documented for his larger churches, albeit rather late; evidence for "first fruits" is doubtful; evidence for tithes is nonexistent. The most convincing argument for pastoral ministry is Dominic's own career, which featured the public liturgical celebrations and preaching described above.[55] The fragmentary evidence at least suggests that Dominic and his monasteries were more involved in public worship than Benedict had envisioned.

Another difference between Benedict's monasticism and Dominic's involves monastic property. Benedict regarded property as a necessary evil (albeit such an important necessary evil that much of the *Rule* is devoted to it). To renounce the world meant to distance oneself from all economic concerns, to place them upon the shoulders of the abbot, who, helped by various monastic officials, was to handle them so that they would impinge upon the monastic routine as little as possible. Benedict did not equate acquisition of property with monastic progress.[56] Later centuries, however, created megamonasteries, great lordships jealously guarded. Leo Mariscanus for Monte Cassino and Gregory of Catino for Farfa wrote monastic histories that were almost narrative chartularies, virtual inventories of properties. Dominic's *lives*, very much a part of this world, glory in lands, lakes, and legal documents. They do find some justification in the economic concerns of the *Rule*. The *Sora Life*, for example, tells how Dominic

54. The only mention of tithes in Dominic's memorials is in *Sora Life* lxxiii, 45, which does not specify when, where, or how Count Berardus II of Marsica had appropriated them unjustly. Tithes in Italy are analyzed in Catherine E. Boyd, *Tithes and Parishes in Medieval Italy: The Historical Roots of a Modern Problem* (Ithaca, N.Y.: Cornell University Press, 1952), 126–27, 140–41, and 157; Constable, *Monastic Tithes from Their Origins to the Twelfth Century*, Cambridge Studies in Medieval Life and Thought n.s. 10 (Cambridge: Cambridge University Press, 1964), 79–82; Toubert, *Structures*, 2:872–81 (who dismisses much evidence for pre-twelfth-century tithes in Lazio by insisting that mentions of "tenths" often refer to seignorial rents paid in that particular fraction); and Andrea Castagnetti, "Le decimi e i laici," *Storia d'Italia: Annali 9*, ed. Giorgio Chittolini and Giovanni Miccoli (Turin: Unione tipografico-editrice torinese, 1986), 512–13. On the customs the Normans inherited, see Vera von Falkenhausen, "Aspetti storico-economici dell'età di Roberto il Guiscardo," in *Roberto il Guiscardo e il suo tempo*, 131 and 137.

55. The unmonastic nature of these ministries was signaled in Boesch Gajano, "Domenico di Sora," in *DBI*, 40:676.

56. de Vogüé, *Commentaire doctrinal et spirituel*, in *RB*, 7:99–115; trans. Hasbrouck, *Rule of Saint Benedict*, 209–27. On the complexity of Benedictine attitudes toward poverty, see Terrence Kardong, "La povertà monastica nei capitoli 33 e 34 della RB," *Benedictina* 30 (1983): 317–40.

carefully chose a monastic site "where namely, according to the mandate of holy father Benedict, within or around the cloister it would be possible to be able to have a garden, a mill, a bakery, and everything necessary for daily life, so that there would be no necessity for the sake of any of these things for the servants of God who would dwell there to make long journeys."[57] But the *Sora Life* soon goes on to boast about how "[Lord] Peter immediately enriched the place with many types of donations, fortifying them with legal documents: he gave farms, villas, mills, pastures, gardens, woodlands, forests, and all other things."[58] Property was praiseworthy per se.

Although monastic materialism characterized the age, it might have been intensified in Dominic's *lives* by the difficulties involved in maintaining monks in the high Apennines. Not all Dominic's monasteries were self-sufficient. The pairing of houses in river valleys and mountains presumes a need to exchange resources. Mountain hermitages located above normal agricultural zones would have required supplies on a regular basis. Even the larger monasteries may have welcomed the food donations so prominent in Dominic's miracle stories. The necessary supply network would have worked against the "separation from the world" that Benedict's *Rule* envisions.

Ultimately there is a contrast in spirit. Whereas Benedict's monasteries seem to have resisted the secular world, Dominic's welcomed it. Benedict's *Rule* tries to strike a balance between the biblically enjoined duty of hospitality and the need to shield the monks: the porter welcomes yet protects; visitors are greeted elaborately but lodged separately; even the monks themselves, if they have to travel, are reintegrated into the community carefully so that the world's pollution does not return with them.[59] Dominic's *lives*, on the contrary, seem less concerned with a narrowly defined monastic family than with a cultic community that includes monks, monastic patrons, rich and poor lay supporters, and the crowds of people who benefit from his preaching and wonders. In the *lives*, monastic communities are just one element of regional "communitas." If this hagiographic perspective actually corresponded to the everyday existence of Dominic's monks, then the world was very much with them.

---

57. *Sora Life* cxxi, 50 and 52. Cf. *RB* lxvi, 2:660.
58. *Sora Life* cxxxi, 52.
59. *RB* liii, 2:616–19. Commentary by de Vogüé in *RB*, 6:1287–89; 7:360–63. Doctrinal commentary in *RB*, 7:360–63; trans. Hasbrouck, *Rule of Saint Benedict*, 259–67.

How then is Dominic's paradoxical "Benedictinism" to be explained? If his monastic system is judged strictly in terms of its adherence to the letter of the *Rule*, it is not very Benedictine. Should it be dismissed as a degenerate form of Benedictine life? If so, then, as the parallels cited above clearly demonstrate, so must nearly all monastic movements of the tenth and eleventh centuries. If Benedictinism is literal adherence to the *Rule*, then the so-called "Benedictine Centuries" saw precious little of it. But is this a fair standard? Western monasticism was always changing. The diverse monastic traditions found in the Late Antique West did not suddenly disappear when Benedict wrote his *Rule*. In the sixth and seventh centuries some Western monasteries gained great wealth, in Carolingian times monastic customaries and more elaborate liturgies appeared, and later "Cluniac" ideals popularized further elaborations. Ecclesiastical historians who presume that Benedictine monasticism is monasticism based on the Benedictine *Rule* are using a static model to describe a continuous, nonlinear process of development.

Perhaps it is our own conceptions about Benedictine monasticism that need to be reexamined. The term "Benedictine" is a seventeenth-century neologism.[60] Although it may seem obvious to us that Benedictine monasticism is monasticism based upon the Benedictine *Rule*, what exactly does this mean? Was the *Rule* a "constitution" for early medieval monasteries? Was it the normative document by which monastic life was to be judged and corrected? Dominic's "Benedictinism" and its many counterparts call this constitutional theory into question. Of course, it could be argued that strict adherence to the Benedictine *Rule* was the ideal, and that the imperfections in actualizing it were the result of ignorance, disorganization, and corruption, but the *reductio ad absurdum* of this line of argument is that it can be used to dismiss an infinite amount of inconvenient evidence. Some scholars have begun to express hesitations about literal definitions of Benedictinism, but they have not dented our reigning certainties very much.[61]

60. Bennett D. Hill, "Benedictine," *Dictionary of the Middle Ages*, 13 vols. (New York: Charles Scribner's Sons, 1982–89), 2:171.

61. Jacques Hourlier, "La Règle de saint Benoît, source de droit monastique," in *Etudes d'histoire du droit canonique*, 2 vols, (Paris: Sirey, 1965), 1:157–68, esp. 157–58; De Vogüé, "Sub Regula vel Abbate: A Study of the Theological Significance of the Ancient Monastic Rules," in *Rule and Life: An Interdisciplinary Symposium*, ed. M. Basil Pennington, Cistercian Studies Series 12 (Spencer, Mass.: Cistercian Publications, 1971), 21–64; and Alain Dierkens, *Abbayes et chapitres entre Sambre et Meuse (VIIe–XIe siècles): Contribution à l'histoire religieuse des campagnes du Haut Moyen Âge*, Beihefte der Francia 14 (Sigmaringen: Jan Thorbecke Verlag, 1985), 332–36.

Current research on literacy and "textuality" may help in reevaluating the assumption that the *Rule* functioned as a "constitution." Brian Stock distinguished himself among historians of literacy by shifting the terms of the debate away from the question of personal literacy toward the question of how the written word functions in society. He has popularized the idea of "textual communities," that is, "microsocieties organized around the common understanding of a script." He sees these as characteristic of the High Middle Ages, part of a new attitude toward literary authority. Not all members of such communities were necessarily literate, but their lives would have been influenced and guided by those who were. The notion presupposes a distinction between "literacy," the ability to read and write at some level, and "textuality," the way particular texts are central to particular individuals and groups. According to Stock, in early medieval Europe verbal discourse existed in interdependence with texts, so that there was a balance between the two; but after the year 1000, he claims, "the written word . . . had once again begun to be widely adopted as a basis for discussion of cultural activity and even as a standard of cultural progress. . . . [T]he rules of the game were radically altered . . . [and] the sole means of establishing a position's legitimacy was assumed to be the discovery of a written precedent." Stock concluded that, while in Western society the tenth century may have been "the highpoint of oral usage," after the year 1000 texts tended to become more important than oral discourse, thus creating a whole variety of textual communities.[62]

Note the conflict between the traditional assumption that early medieval monasteries were communities based on the text of the Benedictine *Rule* and Stock's belief that textual communities achieved ascendency during the High Middle Ages as a result of that period's privileging of text over oral discourse. Were Benedictine monasteries precocious textual communities? Were they the prototypes or even the progenitors of textual communities that would later emerge? Or, more likely, have historians of

---

62. Brian Stock, *The Implications of Literacy: Written Language and Models of Interpretation in the Eleventh and Twelfth Centuries* (Princeton, N.J.: Princeton University Press, 1983), esp. 7–9; and *Listening for the Text: On the Uses of the Past*, Parallax: Re-visions of Culture and Society (Baltimore: Johns Hopkins University Press, 1990), 23. In reaction to Stock's emphasis on later medieval literacy and textuality, the importance of writing in the Carolingian world has been championed by Rosamund McKitterick, in *The Carolingians and the Written Word* (Cambridge: Cambridge University Press, 1989), and in her edited volume on *The Uses of Literacy*. Similar claims for the Merovingian world are made by Yitzhak Hen in *Culture and Religion in Merovingian Gaul, A.D. 481–751*, Cultures, Beliefs, and Traditions: Medieval and Early Modern Europe 1 (Leiden: E. J. Brill, 1995), 21–42. Yet Stock never argued that the Early Middle Ages were "purely oral"—only that oral communication had a more privileged position than in the High Middle Ages.

the Middle Ages been guilty of taking modern assumptions about the centrality of the written word, assumptions that became normative during the
High Middle Ages, and anachronistically imposing them on early Benedictine monasticism?

Most of the puzzling features of Dominic's "Benedictinism" can be
understood if his system and its counterparts are viewed as manifestations of
a largely oral and customary monastic tradition, one for which the Benedictine *Rule* was the most authoritative supporting document but not an
absolute guide. This perspective treats the *Rule* like other important texts of
this period. Historians have gradually come to recognize that early medieval
monastic charters were not "deeds" in the modern sense (not contracts
whose signing was dispositive), but were *memoranda* commemorating
transfers made orally in public ceremonies. What I am proposing here is that
the *Rule* was also a *memorandum*, a document supporting the community's
authoritative customs, rituals, and oral traditions. While it is true that Benedict required a novice to pledge allegiance to the *Rule*, he also required that
same novice to pledge "to observe everything that is commanded him." Benedict's *Rule* closes with the warning that it is a "minimum rule which we
have written for beginners," which, for those "who would hasten to monastic perfection" would have to be supplemented by the Old and New Testament, the works of Cassian, and "the teachings of the fathers." This
open-ended character caused it to be augmented by house traditions, which
could generate their own *memoranda*, that is, monastic customaries.

Yet if the *Rule* itself was seen simply as the most authoritative expression of monastic tradition, then it did not necessarily supersede other
elements of that tradition. Houses following so-called *regula mixta*—
combining elements from the *Rule* of Benedict, the *Rule* of Columbanus,
and other rules—make more sense if they are seen as based on the authority of broad monastic tradition rather than on conflicting constitutions.
The concept of "textual community" is useful in this context precisely because it describes what Dominic's system and its counterparts were *not*—
they were *not* based ultimately upon a text but rather upon customs commemorated by that text. This conclusion was anticipated in some respects
by Jacques Hourlier, who, in a 1965 study on "The *Rule* of St. Benedict as
a Source of Monastic Law," saw the *Rule* as "a reflection of monasticism
as it was then practiced," with a value "more indicative than normative." [63]

63. Hourlier, "Règle de saint Benoît," 161–62.

The import of his warning becomes clearer thanks to the work of historians of literacy and textuality.

Therefore, while Dominic respected and "followed" the Benedictine *Rule*, he was not limited by it. He was also free to adopt whatever he found useful from a broad, amorphous monastic tradition. He had no apparent difficulty in departing from Benedict in regard to the confederation he created, the sub-abbots he appointed, and his attitudes toward monastic stability, hermitism, abbatial residence, pastoral ministries, and openness to the world. Instead of viewing this system as a degraded form of Benedictine monasticism, it might be better to see it as a conservative embodiment of monastic traditions, some of which antedated Benedict, going back to Cassian and other fathers of Western monasticism.

This flexibility may have been the downfall of Dominic's system, since, even during his lifetime, attitudes toward written texts were changing. Centuries before, at the Synod of Aachen in 817, Carolingian ecclesiastics, who represented a civilization more literate than its immediate predecessors or successors, had already attempted to ascribe unique authority to the Benedictine *Rule*. The most decisive and lasting changes, however, were developing out of the centrally directed, legally oriented reform movements of the eleventh century. As early as 1005, for example, Pope John XVIII, writing at a time when the abbot of Subiaco had just died in the dungeon of a neighboring count, wrote to affirm that monastery's right of free abbatial election, "since for a long time we have wanted both to reach out our hand apostolically to the disturbed brothers of the monastery of Subiaco, a monastery which has been disordered with various things contrary to God and to its constitution, and to strengthen by our authority the ancient and rational continuing custom of this monastery out of the precept of the *Rule* of blessed Benedict . . ."; John went on to oppose all things "contrary to St. Benedict and monastic law."[64] Here monastic custom, even though hailed as authoritative, is nevertheless "strengthened" by the "precept" of the *Rule*.

Appeals of this type to written authority were probably particularly effective in the hundreds of new foundations from the late tenth century onward that lacked preexisting traditions and therefore relied more extensively on written guides. Yet scholars who want to see the Benedictine *Rule* clearly animating a "textual community" may need to look to the end of

64. John XVIII, *Epistula*, in *Papsturkunden 896–1046*, 2:801–809, esp. 802.

the eleventh century, to Cîteaux. Cistercian monks radically restructured their lives in order to return to what they saw as the original purity of the *Rule*. Their "constitutional" mentality was closer to our own as well as to that of many other "textual communities" at the start of the High Middle Ages. It would make Dominic's monastic system obsolete.

5

Patrons and Followers

DOMINIC AND HIS MONASTERIES depended on a network of patrons and followers. In this patronage, the counts of Marsica and their allies were so conspicuous that one might be tempted to view Dominic's success as theirs. Yet lesser aristocrats subsidized some of his foundations, the elite of particular *castelli* others. If, as Dominic's *lives* assert, he became a celebrity because of the enthusiasm of "the people," then his most proximate patrons may have been the neighbors of his new monasteries and hermitages. To some extent almost everyone involved in the process of encastellation helped him. To understand who supported Dominic and why can contribute to a better understanding of the dynamism of early ecclesiastical reform.

Dominic's most prominent patrons were members of the lineage of the counts of Marsica, descendents of Berardus the Frank who included the counts of Rieti, the counts of Valva, the "Borelli," the counts of Marsica proper, and other families connected to them by marriage. There are hints that the young Dominic might have dealt directly with two of the sons of Berardus, with Theodinus of Rieti and Oderisius of Valva, but his documented interactions begin with the counts of the third generation, with counts Beraldus, Theodinus, and Randisius of Valva; with their brother Borellus who was creating a new county to the southeast; and with the family of Berardus II of Marsica. By the end of his life, he was dealing with the fourth generation, that is, with the adolescent Count Oderisius II of Marsica and with Doda, daughter of Oderisius I of Marsica, who had married Lord Peter of Sora. These interrelationships are graphed in Genealogical Chart 1.[1]

Dominic was also supported by the Crescenzi, especially by the second and third generations of the Ottaviani Crescenzi. They helped found

1. The complex genealogies of these patrons and their descendents are presented and justified in Appendix B.

GENEALOGICAL CHART I.   Dominic's Patrons from the Lineage of the Counts of
Marsica.

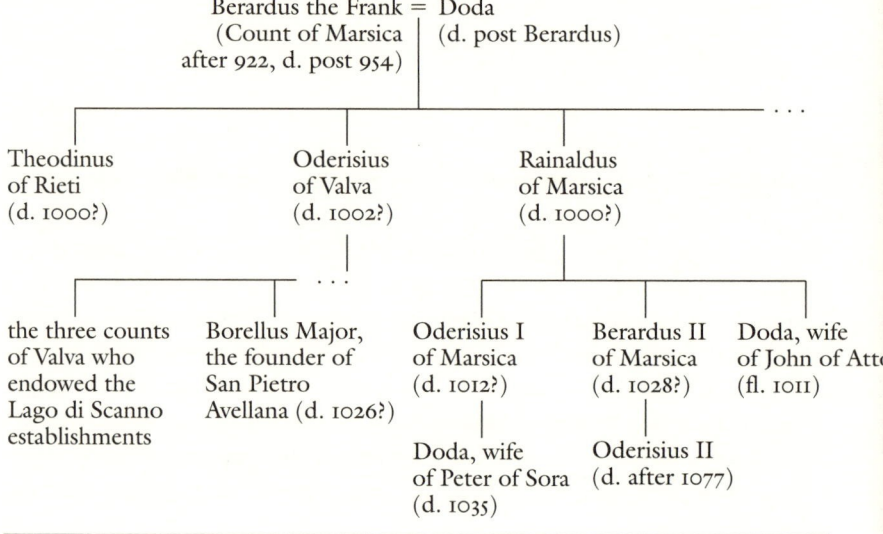

DIRECT PATRONS FROM THE COUNTS OF MARSICA

two houses, albeit ones small enough to be called "oratories." The first
was Sant'Angelo on Monte Cacume, whose requestor, Amatus, Count of
Campania, was connected to the Ottaviani Crescenzi by the marriage of
his son to a daughter of the founding Octavian and by his grand office. The
second was Santissima Trinità on Monte Autore, supported by "John son
of Atto" one of the "illustrious optimates of the land," a grandson of Octavian. How did Dominic come to the notice of the Crescenzi? The link
appears to be John's mother, Doda, a daughter of Count Rainaldus of Marsica and therefore a cousin of his major Marsican patrons. One oratory was
commissioned by her son, the other by the husband of her sister-in-law.
Perhaps Doda was not the only marriage link between the two families: a
generation later the wife of Count Berardus III of Marsica, Rogata, bore
the name of the founding Ottaviani *senatrix*, and thus may have been born
a Crescenzi.[2] Dominic's Crescenzi connections are graphed on Genealogical Chart 2.[3]

2. Rogata is named in Berardus III's 1062 donation of the "Ecclesia S. Manni" in Marsica to Monte Cassino, which is edited, allegedly from an original document in the archives,
in Gattola, *Historia*, 1:241–42. Neither Müller, *Topographische und genealogische Unter-*

GENEALOGICAL CHART 2.   Dominic's Patrons from the Lineage of the
Crescenzi.

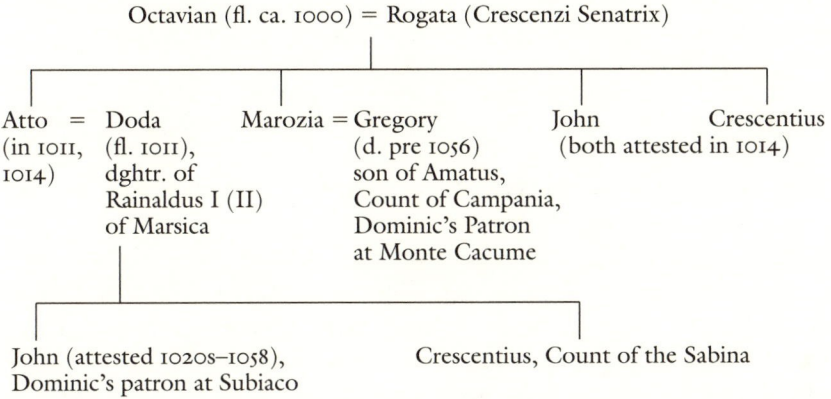

OTTAVIANI CRESCENZI

Octavian (fl. ca. 1000) = Rogata (Crescenzi Senatrix)

Atto   =   Doda   Marozia = Gregory   John   Crescentius
(in 1011,   (fl. 1011),   (d. pre 1056)   (both attested in 1014)
1014)   dghtr. of   son of Amatus,
            Rainaldus I (II)   Count of Campania,
            of Marsica   Dominic's Patron
                                     at Monte Cacume

John (attested 1020s–1058),   Crescentius, Count of the Sabina
Dominic's patron at Subiaco

Dominic dealt tangentially with the Stefaniani Crescenzi, a branch of
the family descended from the Senatrix Stephania, whose power centered
on Rome (Genealogical Chart 3).[4] The Stefaniani cooperated occasionally
with the pope and with the Ottaviani, especially in the period after Dominic's death when, in 1036/1038(?), they all helped Subiaco found Castel
Sant'Angelo (today's Castel Madama). The *Sora Life* relates that "a certain
illustrious Roman woman named 'Imela'," the "wife of one of the optimates of the Romans, a man named Odo ("uxor Odonis")," asked Domi-

---

suchungen, 64, nor Bloch, *Monte Cassino*, 1:363 and 368, establish the precise location of the
church.

3. The Ottaviani Crescenzi genealogy presented here conforms to the relevant parts of
the *stemmae* in Müller, *Topographische und genealogische Untersuchungen*, 27–29 and 33; and
Schwarzmaier, "Zur Familie Victors IV. in der Sabina," 64–79, esp. 74. It differs in not taking
a stand on Schwarzmaier's theories regarding earlier ancestors, in identifying John son of Atto
as Dominic's patron for Santissima Trinità near Subiaco, and in adding data from *Reg. Farf.*,
3:199 (doc. 492), a document which also appears in Manaresi, *Placiti*, 2(2):541–47. Schwarzmaier's reconstruction is largely based on *Reg. Farf.*, 4:15–16, 4:269–70, 4:271, 4:286, 4:
320–21 (docs. 492, 617, 874, 876, 891, 926); *Chron. Subl.*, 10–12; and some necrological
information cited in Schwarzmaier, ibid., 68. However, supplementary evidence survives in
unpublished Subiaco documents signalled by Carosi, "L'abate sublacense Giovanni V," 119–
22; and Hoffmann, "Zur Abtsliste von Subiaco," 881–88.

4. This Stefaniani Crescenzi genealogy corresponds to part of the reconstruction in
Bossi, "I Crescenzi di Sabina," 145–58; and in Müller, 22 and 32. The major document on
which it is based is in *Reg. Subl.*, 72–73 (doc. 34). Bossi, "I Crescenzi di Sabina," 152–54, adds
a hypothetical remarriage for Emilia, but Hoffmann, "Petrus Diaconus," 9–10, disparages this
conjecture.

GENEALOGICAL CHART 3.   Stefaniani Crescenzi.

Senatrix Stefania (fl. late 10th century)

. . .

. . .

Donodeus (fl. 1038) = Emilia (fl. 1038), who begged Dominic for a son?

John, who sent dependent to Dominic's tomb?

nic to pray that she would bear a son, and, even though all her previous children had been daughters, she produced a son within the year.[5] This supplicant may well have been Lady Imilia of the Stefaniani, who was married to Donodeus (fl. 1038). A son named John was born to them, about whom Gaetano Bossi observed, "I must confess that an absolute and profound silence reigns. This might mean either that he had died at a young age or that, having not done anything outstanding, his name went on to be lost among the numerous 'Johns' of the time."[6] Yet it is possible that the child said to have resulted from Dominic's prayers was the same "Lord John," one of "the most illustrious of the Romans," who, many years later, sent a crippled dependent named Azo to seek healing at Dominic's tomb.[7]

"Imela" and "John" are linked not only by their devotion to Dominic but also by the adjective "illustris," rare elsewhere in Dominic's *lives*. It once indicated descent from senatorial stock. The Crescenzi saw themselves as the epitome of the senatorial order, and, even though the old designations of rank and title were hopelessly muddled by this time, "illustrious" might well have been a favored Stefaniani honorific.

A last group of exalted patrons were the lords of Sora, a family of uncertain rank (Genealogical Chart 4).[8] Sora's local historians, perhaps

---

5. *Sora Life* cxliii–cxlv, 54.

6. Bossi, "I Crescenzi di Sabina," 157–58.

7. *Sora Life* ccxxi–ccxxii, 62–63.

8. The genealogy of the lords of Sora begins with an Alexander who is only a name. On his son Rainerius the Gastald, see *Chron. Cass.* II xxxix, 227; and a charter from February of 1021, edited in Alessandro Magliari, "Diplomi, Bolle, Pergamene, ecc." *Bollettino storico volsco* 3 (1899): 33–34. See Bloch, *Monte Cassino*, 2:821. Peter, son of Rainerius, appears, in addition to the *lives* of Dominic, in Amatus, *L'Histoire de li Normant* I xxxiii, 43–44; and in *Chron. Cass.* II lv, 273 and 283. On the full or partial texts of surviving charters he issued, see p. 56. The *exemplum* in the *Sora Life* that places Peter's death three years after Dominic's is the evidence for the 1035 date.

Peter's son Girardus appears in the *Sora Life* cccxxxiii–cccxliii, 73–74, pledging to make a votive offering at Dominic's tomb if the saint will help dislodge from near his eye an arrow-

GENEALOGICAL CHART 4. Dominic's Patrons Who Were Lords of Sora.

Rainerius the Gastald,
son of Alexander "native
of Sora," attested 1004–
1021 (d. before 1024)

Lord Peter, independently   = Doda, daughter   Cofounders of the monastery
attested 1024–(d. 1035)   of Oderisius I   that became San Domenico,
                               of Marsica   at Isola da Liri, near Sora

Girardus
(1035–after 1043), healed at Dominic's tomb

following Jacobilli here, identify Dominic's patron Peter as a count and assume that the region was a county from the late tenth century on.[9] Nevertheless, at the end of the tenth century, Sora, which had been part of the principality of Capua, was at least temporarily under the jurisdiction of the counts of Marsica and their technical overlords, the dukes of Spoleto.[10] The surviving sources do not claim comital rank either for Peter or his family: in Monte Cassino's chronicle, in a section presumably based on a lost document commemorating a donation made in 1004, Peter's father Rainerius is called a gastald; in charters, in Dominic's *lives*, and in the relevant chronicles, Peter and his successor, his son Girardus, bear titles such as "lord of Sora" and "lord of Sora and Arpino." No leader of this region

head acquired at Pandulf of Capua's siege of Naples. The story presents a chronological problem, since that siege is commonly dated to 1027, nearly five years *before* Dominic's death (see Bresslau, *Jahrbücher des Deutschen Reichs unter Konrad II*, 2:297). Dolbeau suggests that the hagiographer rewrote the wonder in order to fit it into the miracles *postmortem*. Farina and Fornari, *Storia e documenti . . . di Casamari*, 158–59; and Antonelli, *Abbazie . . . di Sora*, 158 and 221–22, present a charter text commemorating a donation made by Girardus to San Domenico in 1043.

9. The tradition that Lord Peter of Sora was a count may begin with Jacobilli's *Vita di S. Domenico*, 28. Among the authors who accept it are Alessandro Di Meo, *Annali critico-diplomatici del Regno di Napoli della mezzana età*, 12 vols. (Naples: Stamperia Orsiana, 1795–1819), 7:130; Tosti, "La Leggenda di San Domenico Abate," 315; Lauri, "Origini del distrutto monastero di Santa Chiara," 83; and Antonelli, *Abbazie . . . di Sora*, 157 and 207.

10. Two original documents from 998, preserved in the Monte Cassino archives, reveal attempts by Rainaldus and his son Oderisius and other imperial officials to hold court at Sora. These are edited in Raffaello Volpini, "Placiti del 'Regnum Italiae' (secc. IX–XI): Primi contributi per un nuovo censimento," in *Contributi dell'Istituto di Storia Medioevale* 3, ed. Piero Zerbi, Vita e Pensiero (Milan: Pubblicazioni della Università Cattolica del Sacro Cuore, 1975), 329–35. There was some precedent for Marsican domination of Sora—see Erchempert, *Historia Langobardorum Beneventanorum* xxv, 244.

is unambiguously designated as a count prior to the last quarter of the eleventh century.[11]

Whatever the technical status of the lords of Sora, their prestige was certainly high, for Peter was able to marry Doda, a daughter of Count Oderisius I of Marsica. She, it will be recalled, appears as the cofounder in the charters of Dominic's monastery near Sora. Dominic's relationship with the lords of Sora was established late in his career, only after the family had acquired a marital link to the counts of Marsica.

Dominic's friends included nobles of lesser rank. He received fish from the knight Sanso, a "robustissimus eques," who was "near in blood to the optimates of the Marsi." [12] One of Sanso's colleagues, Rainaldus, was described as "a blood relative of the count." [13] Among the possible reasons why such men who had comital blood nevertheless lacked a comital title are poverty, illegitimacy, or descent from counts' daughters who had been married off into powerful local families. Dominic was sent food by "Falco vicecomes et Dodo Gaze et Pontius frater et Joannes Gezonis, omnes nobiles Arpinates." [14] These men seem to have been part of a civic elite at Arpino, since "John the Judge, son of Gezo," is the presiding official listed on an Arpino charter of 1011. This document is part of a collection of more than two dozen narrow, tapering parchment rolls that illustrate the frugality as well as the legal punctiliousness of the men who commissioned them, inasmuch as each one is made from the skin of a leg of lamb, many having holes where the knee had been.[15] Their joint donation recalls the gifts of the "magnates" of the "terra Credenderii et Zatterii," who commissioned Dominic's easternmost monasteries in the upper valley of the Aventino. Men unable or unwilling to undertake largesse individually

11. Harry Bresslau, *Jahrbücher des Deutschen Reichs unter Konrad II*, 2 vols., Jahrbücher der deutschen Geschichte 14–15 (1879, reprint, Berlin: Duncker & Humblot, 1879), 1:175, guessed that Henry II might have named one of his own followers count over Sora or Comino, but this has not been demonstrated. No comital title is associated with Lando, "lord of Arpino," and his son Landulf, who prospered from the 1050s through the 1070s: see Bloch, *Monte Cassino*, 1:204 and 308–9. It is not clear how Lando and Landulf relate to Lord Peter's family. A "count of Sora" does appear in *Chron. Cass.* IV xiv, 483–84, an "Adenulfus comes" who was captured and chained by the Normans at some time prior to the death of his ransomer, Desiderius of Monte Cassino (d. 1087).

12. *Sora Life* xciv, 47.

13. *Sora Life* lxxvi, 45.

14. *Sora Life* cix, 48–49.

15. "John the Judge, son of Gezo" signed Archivio di Monte Cassino aula II, capsula xxxviii, fasc. 1, no. 6, which is described in Leccisotti, *Regesti*, 7:267–68. On other, similar charters, see ibid., 7:264–78. Unfortunately, the collection does not name more of Dominic's supporters, perhaps because it is largely the work of two judges concerning a single Monte Cassino dependency at Arpino, and thus does not provide a real community cross-section.

could do so collectively. Such joint donations would later become routine in Cistercian circles.[16]

Dynastic motives probably encouraged noble patrons to subsidize Dominic. The counts of Valva, the Borrelli, the Ottaviani Crescenzi, and the lords of Sora asked Dominic to build monasteries for them just when they were in the process of establishing their own recognizable territories and titles. Family monasteries were important. Although in theory counts were imperial or royal officials, in central Italian practice they were those sons of counts who were fortunate enough to possess territorial spheres of influence, residences in *castelli*, and family monasteries. The latter provided territorial focus and patronage duties that could link together subsequent generations of the founding families. Insofar as Dominic's foundations contributed to this sort of family solidarity, they were typical.[17]

Yet Dominic's monasteries, churches, and oratories also helped establish solidarity across a whole group of related families. Dominic appears to have been a monastic "contractor" for the descendents of Berardus the Frank. His work kept these relatives in touch with each other. News would have traveled with him, with the messengers sent to bring him offerings, and with the supplicants who sought his help. He was an occasional house guest, judging from the story of a miracle that occurred when he was visiting the home of the wife of "a certain Marsican named Borrellus."[18] Solidarity would also have been expressed and enhanced when members of the

16. On joint foundations of Cistercian monasteries, see Bouchard, "Knights and the Foundation of Cistercian Houses in Burgundy," in *Erudition at God's Service: Studies in Medieval Cistercian History XI*, ed. John R. Sommerfeldt (Kalamazoo: Cistercian Publications, 1987), 315–22, esp. 317. Bouchard, *Holy Entrepreneurs: Cistercians, Knights, and Economic Exchange in Twelfth-Century Burgundy* (Ithaca, N.Y.: Cornell University Press, 1991), 13–16, cautions, however, that some joint foundations may be illusions created by early Cistercian bookkeeping practices, particularly by lumping together originally separate transactions into *pancartes*.

17. For an overview of the contributions made by German scholars, especially Karl Schmid, to the study of the development of noble family identity and to the role played within this process by the family monastery (*Hauskloster*), see John B. Freed, *The Counts of Falkenstein: Noble Self-Consciousness in Twelfth-Century Germany*, Transactions of the American Philosophical Society 74 (6) (Philadelphia: American Philosophical Society, 1984), 1–11.

18. Dominic's visit to the wife of a man named Borrellus is noted in *Sora Life* cxlvi–cxlix, 55. The text is corrupt. In the original Vallicelliana copy, the master was "Brenlim nomine," an incomprehensible name that a corrector amended to "Borrelli." Spitilli, *Vita*, 22, identified the heroine as the "moglie di Borello," but he could have taken this information from the corrected Vallicelliana copy. Even if the anecdote did refer to one of the *Borrelli* with whom Dominic routinely dealt, it would still be uncertain whether it concerned Ruta, the wife of the Borrellus who was last attested in 1026, or Gervisa, the wife of the next lord, Borrellus II (d. 1083). Whomever the story may concern, it does illustrate that Dominic made housecalls.

lineage donated to foundations Dominic had established in their relatives' territories. In 1062, Count Berardus III of Marsica gave Abbot John of San Pietro Avellana (the house supported by Borrellus and his sons) the "ecclesiam S. Manni" in Marsica "in locum ubi Peteline vocatur."[19] In 1064 he gave the Marsican church of San Ruffino to San Domenico at Sora, a monastery cofounded by his aunt.[20] Similar donations might explain how San Pietro in Lago, founded by Dominic in the county of Valva, acquired properties in Marsica.[21]

Dominic's foundations may even have helped promote solidarity between the counts and their people. The system of military overlordship imposed by the Carolingians did not give counts strong vertical institutional links to their subordinates, placing them at a disadvantage compared to bishops, gastalds, or even urban viscounts.[22] Encastellation, insofar as the counts controlled it, went a long way toward strengthening the necessary lines of authority. But those counts who supported Dominic's projects would have gained an additional opportunity to exercise public leadership in a popular cause and to institutionalize the resulting prestige in their roles as ecclesiastical patrons.

The nobility also used Dominic to gain favors from God. They gave generously, and they expected generosity. While Dominic was alive, counts and countesses sought his prayers, treasured his prophesies, and asked for bonuses such as the birth of a son and a better complexion for a daughter.[23] Even after Dominic's death, they still had requests: Lord Girardus of Sora, Lord Peter's son, invoked Dominic's help for the removal of an arrow point lodged next to his eye; an unnamed blood relative of Count Oderisius II of Marsica tried to get an infection cured; Oderisius himself wanted a hernia fixed.[24] Miracles were also sought by lesser members of the military

19. Edited from an original charter in Gattola, *Historia*, 1:241–42; noted in Bloch *Monte Cassino*, 1:363.

20. Farina and Fornari, *Storia e documenti . . . di Casamari*, 160–61 (doc. vi). Another Marsican church appears in a 1205 confirmation of San Domenico properties made by Innocent III, in a *Privilegium*, ed. Farina and Fornari, *Storia e documenti . . . di Casamari*, 166 (doc. x).

21. Possessions in Marsica are noted in a 1067 donation charter, the original of which has not been located. A copy survives in *Reg. Petri Diac.*, fol. 210r (no. 496); edited in Gattola, *Accessiones*, 1:179–80; noted in Hoffmann, "Chronik und Urkunde," 135. These properties are also mentioned in *Chron. Cass.*, III xxxix, 416. A list of possessions is given in Gattola, *Historia*, 1:237. See also Bloch, *Monte Cassino*, 1:338–42.

22. Delogu, "L'istituzione comitale nell'Italia carolingia," esp. 102, 110, and 114.

23. *Sora Life* lxxi–lxxviii, cxliii–cxlv, cxlvi–cxlix, 44–46, 54, 55.

24. *Sora Life* cccxxxiii–cccxliii, ccclxx–ccclxxvii, ccclxxviii–ccclxxxi, 73–74, 76–77, and 77.

elite, including the knight Albert from Oretino and a "Frank" (Norman?) named Girardus who was a vassal of Count Gregory of Segni.[25]

The extent to which members of the nobility participated in even the most "popular" aspects of Dominic's cult is illustrated by the aftermath of Count Oderisius's hernia cure. He gratefully offered three pounds of silver to be turned into a votive image "of those parts of the body in which ruptures are accustomed to occur."[26] That the monks were less than eager to commission this tasteless sculpture is suggested by their lending of the silver to Bishop Leo of Sora (fl. 1050, d. by 1059),[27] who had it made into a thurible, pledging that after his death equivalent silver would be returned, or, failing that, the thurible itself. After Leo's death, however, "a certain cleric of Sora" (tactfully left unnamed, but perhaps the next bishop) presented as compensation a thoroughly miserable horse (an "equus abjectissimus"). The monks objected, claiming that this settlement covered only about a third of the debt. A few days later a thief carried off the thurible.

What is to be noted here is not the monks' ill-disguised glee at their oppressor's embarrassment, but rather the continuity of piety between the highest and the lowest. Oderisius's gauche benefaction was part of an ongoing exchange of gifts and favors between the people of central Italy and Dominic, an exchange in which the votive offerings of aristocrats differed from those of lesser folk only in the currency used—pounds of silver rather than wax or food. Powerful patrons publicized Dominic, and they were hard to refuse when they instructed supplicants going to competing shrines to visit Dominic's tomb instead.[28]

Yet the desire for salvation may have been the primary motive for supporting Dominic. His noble patrons were violent men whose power came

25. *Sora Life* cccxxi–cccxxxii and cccxliv–cccxlvi, 71–72 and 74.

26. *Sora Life* ccclxx–ccclxxvii, 76. On the antecedents of such votive images, which go back to pre-Christian times, see Mary Lee Nolan and Sidney Nolan, *Christian Pilgrimage in Modern Western Europe*, Studies in Religion (Chapel Hill: University of North Carolina Press, 1989), 46, 71–78, and 350–51.

27. Bishop Leo of Sora is known only through this anecdote and through his signature on the canonization decree (J–L 4219) for Bishop Gerardus of Toul (2 May 1050), transmitted in Widric, *Miracula Sancti Gerardi*, ed. Georg Waitz, MGH SS 4:506–8. He was no longer in office in 1059, since a successor, Bishop Palumbus of Sora (d. 1072/1073), signed the Roman synodal decree on papal elections, edited in Detlev Jasper, *Das Papstwahldekret von 1059: Überlieferung und Textgestalt*, Beiträge zur Geschichte und Quellenkunde des Mittalalters 12 (Sigmaringen: Jan Thorbecke Verlag, 1986), 113 (the name of Palumbus is transmitted, although in slightly different places, in both the original and the altered version of this decree). He is also known through Monte Cassino sources listed in Hoffmann, "Kalender des Leo Marsicanus," 119 and 142.

28. *Sora Life* ccxxii, ccxci–xxxciv, cccx–cccxv, and ccclxxix, 63, 69–70, 71, and 77.

from unsanctioned military force. The counts of Marsica were part of a transalpine warrior class imposed upon Italy by long-departed kings. The Crescenzi were an unholy alliance of Roman factions united by opposition to the emperor. The lords of Sora were in the process of usurping a comital title. These people prospered in a time of anarchy and foreign invasion. It is easy to smile at Rodulfus Glaber's gibe that "today's Italians," unlike their Roman ancestors, prefer to seek "safety in flight rather than in battle,"[29] but this insult is unfair to Dominic's patrons. Members of the extended family of the counts of Marsica were involved in most of the region's early eleventh-century military conflicts.[30] They fought in person: Count Berardus II of Marsica was killed by rebellious subvassals; Lord Peter of Sora died in battle three years after Dominic's death; his son and successor Girardus was hit in the eye socket by an arrow during a siege; Randuisius, son of Count Berardus I of Valva, received a lance wound from which he was miraculously healed at the tomb of Leo IX.[31] They used force liberally within their own territories: Berardus II is said to have ruled his subjects tyrannically; Lord Peter of Sora was sorry for, among his many crimes, his recent execution of a priest; the Sanso who sent Dominic fish may or may not be identical to the later-mentioned viscount of that name, "a man than whom no other could be found crueler."[32] Such men probably traveled with armed retinues, as did Lord Peter of Sora when he witnessed a miracle "cum clercis et militibus."[33] The aristocratic way of life offered no assurance of salvation.

One way to square accounts with God was to secure holy help. Inter-

29. Rodulfus Glaber, *Historiae* I v xvii, ed. France, 32–33; or ed. Cavallo and Orlandi, 39.

30. In 993 counts Rainaldus and Oderisius of Marsica participated in the siege of Capua; in 1021 the counts of Marsica fought with the *Borelli* and the Greeks against the German emperor; in 1026 they were part of another attack on Capua; in 1045 the Marsicans and the *Borrelli* drove the Normans out of the *Terra Sancti Benedicti*. See *Chron. Cass.* II x, xxxviii–xxxix, lvi, and lxxi, 188, 241–43, 274–75, and 310. Additional sources and context can be found in Cesare Rivera, "Valva e i suoi conti," 94–100 and 105–6; and in Wolf, *Making History*, 9–17.

31. *Sora Life* lxxv–lxxvii, cxxxiii, cccxxxiii–cccxliii, 45–46, 52; *Miracula* iii of Leo IX (*BHL* 4821a), edited in *AS* Apr. 2:670.

32. *Sora Life* lxxiii–lxxv, xciv, and cxviii, 45, 47, and 50. Since no explicit cross-reference links the two discussions of Sanso in *Sora Life* lxxv and xciv, 45 and 47, it is uncertain whether or not the Sanso who was Dominic's benefactor is the same man as the cruel viscount Sanso who participated in the killing of Berardus II sometime after 1028. The latter's crime may have paid if viscount Sanso became the later count of that name in *Chron. Cass.* III xvii and lxi, 382 and 442, which mentions his donation of the church "Sancti Angeli in Biturito" to Monte Cassino in 1067/1068, a donation the charter for which was copied into the *Reg. Petri Diac.*, fols. 202r–202v (doc. 469), noted in Hoffmann, "Chronik und Urkunde," 133, and Bloch, *Monte Cassino*, 2:826–27.

33. *Trisulti life* xxxi, 297.

cessory prayers were sought even by the most inveterate sinners, perhaps by them especially. In 959 Campo, the abbot of Farfa who had murdered his predecessor and divided much of the monastery's patrimony among his ten children, handed over a manor and its appurtenances, some taxes, half a mill, and so on, in return for 100 "Kyrie eleisons" each day for his soul.[34] Dominic was specifically asked for his prayers by Doda, the wife of the tyrannical Berardus II of Marsica.[35] The surviving charters for ecclesiastical donations often include general "pro anima" clauses that mention the donor and his or her immediate family, especially deceased spouses and children, but rarely other ascendents or descendents. Yet, if procuring intercessory prayers was the major motive for these donations, it is surprising that the charters rarely take a broader view of family or stipulate particular numbers of prayers or Masses.[36]

Penance may have been more important than intercessory prayer. So suggests the case of Peter, Lord of Sora. According to the *lives*, Peter had sought out Dominic and asked how to atone for "numerous and great crimes." Dominic suggested "fasts and alms and other worthy fruits of penance" and urged Peter to build a monastery in his territory and endow it magnificently. Peter was also asked to put aside his arms, but this was a penance he could not bear—three years after Dominic's death he rode off to battle, disgracefully enough on a horse belonging to his new monastery, and thus met his death.[37] Peter's penitential motive is confirmed in his San Domenico foundation charter. In its long series of prefatory clauses, Peter and Doda describe how:

> . . . one day we began to think within ourselves how we were conceived and born in sin; and how from our infancy day and night, by hours and by minutes, we committed innumerable sins; and how we are to give an account to God in that terrible [day of] judgement concerning all our thoughts and deeds; and how from that most just Judge each person will be rewarded according to his or her works; and further

34. *Liber Largiatorius*, ed. Zucchetti, 1:134–35.
35. *Sora Life* lxvii, 44.
36. Megan McLaughlin, *Consorting with Saints: Prayers for the Dead in Early Medieval France* (Ithaca, N.Y.: Cornell University Press, 1994), 135–36 and 153–65, also raises questions about whether prayers for the dead were the major motive for early medieval noble gift-giving.
37. The judgment that because Peter killed a cleric he should no longer bear arms may reflect contemporary Italian canon law. A famous similar case resulted in the 999 judgment made by Sylvester II, Otto III, and a Roman synod against Marquess Arduin of Ivrea, who had assassinated Bishop Peter of Vercelli, a sentence that begins with the requirement that Arduin may no longer bear arms. An unprecedented legal chapter requiring that anyone who seriously injures an ordained clergyman should undertake a lifetime of penance that includes "bearing no arms" is found in a pre-Gregorian collection of laws made at Farfa, edited in Herbert Hees, "Die *Collectio Farfensis*," *Bulletin of Medieval Canon Law* n.s. 3 (1973): 47–48.

when we began to think how the sinners and the impious, who failed to atone for their sins here, will be damned with the devil in that most feared judgement; and how the just and the elect of God will be glorified in eternal beatitude with the Lord. . . . [O]ur heart was struck with fear and we began to think and to seek council from priests and religious men about how we might be able to atone for our innumerable sins and avoid eternal penalties from the anger of the eternal Judge. We learned from them that, except for renouncing the world, nothing is better than the virtue of almsgiving and to construct, from our own possessions and property, a monastery.[38]

These statements seem less personal when they are compared to the almost identical clauses found in Borrellus's 1026 foundation charter for San Pietro Avellano.[39] But a *topos* may illuminate the penitential mentality of the era even better than a personal revelation.

Dominic's noble patrons were probably motivated by both material and spiritual concerns. New monasteries benefitted their earthly interests inasmuch as they provided focal points for amorphous family holdings and solidarity with relatives and local communities. Dominic's favor was important because he was a powerful holy man with access to the supernatural. Yet, perhaps most of all, the foundation of monasteries was a way to gain salvation, not just through the intercessory prayers of the monks, but especially through the sacrifice of property involved, which was heavy penance per se for grasping nobles. To give resources to monasteries was to take specific steps toward making accounts right with God.

Below the military elite were the substantial free citizens who also helped Dominic. San Bartolomeo was established by the cooperative efforts of six eminent men of Collepardo, their unnamed associates, and all the inhabitants of the *castellum*. They were aided by more than a dozen citizens of the *castrum* of Vico, men who acted by their own will ("propria et spontanea voluntate"), with all other citizens present and consenting. Later the citizens of other surrounding fortified villages became involved, presenting San Bartolomeo with gifts that the *Trisulti Life* has backdated in order to make the foundation appear as the joint effort of four *castelli*.[40] San Bartolomeo is the only monastery for which Dominic is said to have

38. San Domenico foundation charter, edited in Baronio, *Annales Ecclesiastici*, 16:544–45, and edited in Farina and Fornari, *Storia e documenti . . . di Casamari*, 7–8.

39. San Pietro Avellana charter, edited in Gattola, *Historia*, 1:238.

40. *Trisulti Life* xv–xvi, 288–89. The surviving versions of the donations quoted are edited in Taglienti, *Il Monastero di Trisulti*, 88–91 (for the Collepardesi); and edited in Strnad, "Zehn Urkunden," 55–57, and Sechi, *La Certosa di Trisulti*, 81 and 152–53 (for the Vicani).

sought papal guarantees of freedom. Although scholars have traditionally assumed that monastic organizers sought papal support to curtail noble influence and exploitation, the case of San Bartolomeo suggests an alternative explanation. Dominic did not seek papal guarantees as an antidote to noble protection (with which he was quite comfortable) but as a substitute for it, a second-best procedure used when no other powerful protector was available.

Trisulti's story has parallels. San Giovanni e Paolo at nearby Casamari was created by a similar cooperative effort. Around 1036, according to its chronicle:

Some priests living in the city of Veroli [about seven miles from Sora], keeping divine precepts and reflecting on divine judgements, were saying "Woe to us, who have the office of the clergy in name, but lead a life neither canonical nor monastic. What will become of us?" . . . Joining with some pious laymen from their city, they went to the place called Casamari in the territory of Veroli, about three and a half miles from their city, and seeing there the ruins of an ancient edifice, which was said to have been a temple of Mars, they began to work and with divine help built a church in honor of Sts. John and Paul, and after some time four of them, that is Benedict, John, Orso, and Azo—all priests—went to venerable John, abbot of San Domenico, and received from him the habit of holy religion. Returning from there back to Casamari, they elected one of themselves as abbot, Fr. Benedict, a religious man. . . . After some years he crossed over to the eremitical life, leaving the abbacy to a very religious and studious monk named John. . . .[41]

Casamari was founded soon after Dominic's death, but it was part of his world, a daughter house of his monastery near Sora. Perhaps its founders chose to receive their monastic habits at Dominic's tomb because his career had exemplified their own desires for reform, monastic foundation, intermittent hermitism, and so forth. Like Trisulti, Casamari had no single patron but benefitted instead from a multitude of smaller donations; also like Trisulti, it quickly tried to fortify itself with papal guarantees.[42]

The citizens of adjacent *castelli* were the founders of the monasteries of Trisulti and Casamari. Were such city dwellers also important to the

41. A now lost version of the Casamari chronicle claimed that Casamari was founded in 1005, a date still often cited. Yet Baronio, in *Annales Ecclesiastici*, 11:104–105, demonstrated centuries ago that Dominic's death must be a *terminus post quem*, since the founders of Casamari received their monastic habits from his successor at Sora, Abbot John. The 1005 date may be an alteration designed to make Casamari older than its twelfth-century daughter house, San Domenico at Sora (founded in 1010, according to one false tradition).

42. On Casamari's early papal charters, see Kehr, *Italia Pontificia*, 2:166–70; and Luigi de Benedetti, "I Regesti dei romani pontefici per l'Abbazia di Casamari," in *Miscellanea di scritti vari in memoria di Alfonso Gallo* (Florence: Leo S. Olschki, 1956), 325–56, esp. 331–32.

monasteries founded by nobles? San Domenico at Sora, although endowed by the lords of Sora, received support from Sora's citizens, particularly several generations of a family that included "citizen of Sora" Abilonius, his son Bonutius, and his grandson Adenulfus. These must have been prosperous people, since their miracle stories mention a slave girl and other servants, a votive pledge of an amount of wax or oil equal to the weight of Adenulfus; and a "prandium copiosum" to be served to the poor and the needy.[43] Other notable citizens were drawn to Dominic's tomb. One was "a goldsmith named Girolphus from 'Popoli'," in the northeastern county of Valva, who was wealthy enough to promise that if his wife could be freed from a demon he would use his highest skill to craft a silver book cover that he would donate to San Domenico.[44] It is fitting that Dominic's reputation attracted such burgesses, since he himself may have come from their ranks.

This constituency is very difficult to fit into the Lazio described by Toubert in *Structures*. Veroli, Anagni, Sora, and other small urban communities seem to have been continuously inhabited. But what of less-documented Roman, actually pre-Roman, settlements such as Collepardo or Vico, Trisulti's patrons? Were these cities? Or were they simply *castelli* established on former urban sites in order to utilize ruins that could be repaired and recycled? Toubert observed that such communities did not differ much from the newer *castelli*, except perhaps in scale, and indeed he classified Vico and Collepardo as *castra*.[45] This allowed him to maintain that urban remnants "without exception lacked the ferment of renewal that agitated the rural world around them," and to see no sign of dynamism in them until the very end of the eleventh century.[46] But however one classifies Veroli, Vico, Collepardo, and others, their citizens clearly did take the initiative in the early eleventh century in establishing their own religious foundations, projects that paralleled the work of the great nobles. This raises a further problem, because Toubert maintained that there was "nothing spontaneous about encastellation," that things happened "only on seigneural initiative," that there was "no castle without a seigneur."[47] Yet the absence of overlords in Vico, Collepardo, and Veroli is indicated by the way their citizens could endow monasteries without seeking the approval of anyone superior. When the status of these towns can be deter-

43. *Sora Life* cclxii–ccxc, 66–69.
44. *Sora Life* cclviii, 66.
45. Toubert, *Structures*, 1:662.
46. Toubert, *Structures*, 1:659–77, esp. 659.
47. Toubert, *Structures*, 1:xii, 349, 367; 2:791; "Les destinées d'un thème historiographique: 'Castelli'," 24.

mined, in the early thirteenth century, they are independent units owing direct allegiance to no one except the pope.[48] It could be argued that these are not independent *castra* but cities, but then it cannot be argued that the cities lacked dynamism. Dominic's nonnoble patrons were part of a more complex social world than Toubert's original seigneural model suggested. Cases of local initiative documented elsewhere raise similar problems.[49]

Before attempting to analyze why burgesses supported Dominic's monasteries, it is necesssary to establish how these foundations related to the *castelli*. Scholars have tended to assume that the frequent presence in the tenth- and eleventh-century Italian countryside of churches "foris et prope castra" was a holdover from the dispersed settlement patterns of the *curtes*.[50] But Dominic's foundations were new, not survivals. Toubert, looking at them and at other foundations by itinerant hermit preachers, concluded that they were actually eccentric rejections of castral discipline, alternative centers of religious expression that had to be regularized and brought under control.[51] Their topography, however, suggests a more calculated relationship. Dominic's churches were consistently sited so that they were neighbors of the new *castelli*, usually in the mountains above them, often a little higher than the arable land. Many controlled large amounts of forest. They tended to be about three miles away from the *castelli*, far enough to maintain a wilderness character, but near enough to be visited. The line between *cultus* and *incultus* was sharpened as encastellation replaced dispersed settlement, and a separation of three miles or so would probably have put Dominic's churches just outside of the "campanea," the area of countryside tightly controlled by early medieval Italian communities.[52] Dominic's mountaintop oratories were more isolated, but

48. Giulio Silvestrelli, *Città castelli e terre della regione romana*, 2 vols. (Rome: Multigrafica Editrice, 1970), 1:61, 67, 68.

49. Wickham, *Problema dell'incastellamento . . . Volturno*, 58–60, discusses the theoretical problems posed by independent agricultural communities. For particular cases see Wickham, *Studi sulla società degli Appennini*, 86–90, 90–100; and Andrea Castagnetti, "Il potere sui contadini: Dalla signoria fondiaria alla signoria territoriale: Comunità rurali e comuni cittadini," in *Le Campagne italiane prima e dopo il Mille: Una società in trasformazione*, Biblioteca di storia agraria medioevale 2 (Bologna: Editrice CLUEB, 1985), 220–23. In the decades since Toubert wrote *Structures*, scholars throughout Europe have documented the existence of many farming communities which escaped direct involvement with feudal overlords. For a case study and some bibliography, see Bois, *Transformation of the Year 1000*.

50. Settia, "Pievi e cappelle nella dinamica del popolamento rurale," *Cristianizzazione ed organizzazione*, 1:445–93, esp. 476.

51. Toubert, *Structures*, 2:866.

52. Little is known about how well early medieval Italian settlements controlled their surrounding countrysides. For some particular communities, see Andrea Castagnetti, "La 'Campanea' e i beni comuni della città," in *L'Ambiente vegetale nell'alto medioevo, 30 marzo–*

he linked them to ecclesiastical institutions near settlements. Symbiosis, not rejection, characterizes the relationship.[53]

Perhaps monasteries and hermitages gave a heightened sense of stability and community to precariously situated new settlements. The *lives* claim that some of Dominic's foundations were sizeable, particularly San Salvatore at Scandriglia, San Pietro Avellana, San Bartolomeo at Trisulti, and San Domenico near Sora. They remark on the "multitude" of monks assembled, although they more frequently imply size by mentioning "generous" endowments, "apt" or "suitable" for supporting men seeking to renounce the world.[54]

Dominic built in stone. One miracle related in the *Trisulti Life* took place during the construction of San Bartolomeo at a time when he was working with his own hands on the foundation and had men busy burning lime.[55] Given the undeveloped and hostile nature of the countryside, it would be surprising if during Dominic's lifetime his communities were ever larger than a dozen or so monks. Nevertheless, a stone church and cloister occupied by a monastic community of any size would have been impressive in central Italy, where parish churches tended to be even smaller than elsewhere in Europe, often ministering to only about twenty families.[56] Any church and cloister would have enhanced both a mountain valley's microeconomy and its wider contacts.

Dominic's foundations may also have provided a way to regulate natural resources. Prior to encastellation, the forests, fisheries, and pastures of

---

5 aprile 1989, 2 vols., Settimane di studio del CISAM 37 (Spoleto: CISAM, 1990), 1:137–74, esp. 143, 145, and 149.

53. The pairing of rural sanctuaries with adjacent settlements is not unprecedented. The phenomenon antedates Christianity. Rouselle, *Croire et guérir,* 43, after studying pagan cult centers in Late Antique Gaul, concluded that rural sanctuaries owed their success or failure to supporting communities and cannot be treated as independent units ("Le sanctuaire rural n'est pas rural").

54. *Trisulti Life* ii, 283, says that at Scandriglia, Dominic's monks were "multi"; *Valva Life* xxii–xxxi, 73, *Monte Cassino Life* xxii–xxxi, 73, and *Sora Life* xxix, 39, find them a "congregatio" or "multitudo" " . . . non parva." *Sora Life* xxxv, 39, states that in the foundations in the upper valley of the Aventino was collected a "multitudo" of men seeking monastic perfection. The generous endowments given to San Pietro in Lago and San Pietro Avellana were noted in the *Valva Life* xxxviii, 74, the *Monte Cassino Life* xxxviii, 74, and the *Sora Life* xli and lxi, 41 and 43; those of the latter in *Trisulti Life* vi, 284. The *Trisulti Life* xiv, 287, stresses the generous gifts San Bartolomeo received. The *Sora Life* cxvi, 49, mentions the many property deeds given to San Angelo near Patrica. *Trisulti Life* xxii, 293; the *Valva Life* lviii, 76; the *Monte Cassino Life* lviii, 76; and the *Sora Life* cxix–cxxii and cxxxi, 50 and 52, all note liberal endowments for Sora.

55. *Trisulti Life* x, 285.

56. Léopold Genicot, *Rural Communities in the Medieval West,* The Johns Hopkins Symposia in Comparative History (Baltimore: Johns Hopkins University Press, 1990), 94.

the Apennine world would have been subject to a variety of ancient and poorly defined rights of usage. Many conflicts must have arisen when new fortified communities attempted to exploit the countryside more intensively. Government could not arbitrate such conflicts, because the few remaining officials were privatizing all public lands and most political functions. The closest thing left to an independent public sphere was ecclesiastical property, for even proprietary churches had their lands vested in the altar and thus, in theory, had guaranteed territorial integrity. If forests, fisheries, and pastures were given to ecclesiastical establishments, they could be exploited in a regular fashion, opened to individuals in return for rents and offerings.

It sounds far-fetched to suggest that Dominic's little rural churches were intended to function as resource arbitrators, but why else, for example, would San Pietro in Lago have been given five lakes? No one expected Dominic's monks to fish all these lakes, but if they licensed fishermen in return for a certain part of the catch, they could guarantee a steady food supply for themselves and the surrounding communities. A miracle story in which an offering of fish caught on Sunday was rejected by Dominic may indicate not only that fishermen on the monastic lakes provided his monks with food but also that the monks attempted to impose restrictions on them (albeit in this case apparently for religious rather than economic reasons).[57]

The wildernesses around many of Dominic's foundations may have been exploited in similar fashion. Men who donated forests to him would have presumed that they could continue to use them on reasonable terms. This would explain the apparent contradiction between the donations of woodland to Dominic made freely by the citizens of various *castelli* around San Bartolomeo and the way their descendents later insisted on their rights to use these woods, undeterred even by dozens of papal anathemas.[58] Throughout medieval Europe, churches helped civilize forests, not just by

---

57. *Sora Life* lxxxix–xciii, 47.

58. Early papal letters protecting Trisulti's rights to its forest against the residents of the surrounding *castelli* are registered and edited in Strnad, "Zehn Urkunden Papst Innocenz' III," 45–49, 54–55; and in Sechi, *La Certosa di Trisulti,* 77–80, 82–83, 85, 143–51. The most systematic inventory of the relevant bulls is in Hogg, "Charterhouse of Trisulti," xx–xxxi. Disagreements over the rights of the Collepardesi and the Vicani to use the forest of Eici led to vandalism and to actual attacks on the monastery, on which see De Persiis, *Tecchiena,* 170–81; Toubert, *Structures,* 1:250; Taglienti, *Il monastero di Trisulti,* 110–266; and Alfio Cortonesi, "La *silva* contesa: Uomini e boschi nel Lazio del Duecento," in *Il Bosco nel medioevo,* ed. Bruno Andreolli and Massimo Montanari, Biblioteca di storia agraria medievale 4 (Bologna: CLUEB, 1989), 307–12.

promoting land clearance but also by taking title and regularizing the tenancy of the people who lived in them.[59] It is probably more than coincidence that donations of land to monasteries became especially intense in the late tenth century just as the European population began to expand significantly into the wilderness.

The rural church may also have served as a "symbol of the humanization of a landscape."[60] It created a *locus* of the holy in what had been liminal space on the edges of the new settlements. The numinous qualities of caves, mountains, and fountains would have become more disquieting in the late tenth and early eleventh centuries as changes in population, settlement patterns, and wilderness exploitation transformed the relationships between people and countryside. When Dominic's *lives* describe him as "hiding" in the wilderness and then being revealed by herdsmen and hunters, they give the impression that his isolated haunts were becoming more frequented. An eldritch landscape increasingly used by Christians had to be Christianized. It would be safer as a Christian heirophany. It is impossible to know how much Dominic's foundations benefitted from such feelings, which were not necessarily conscious. What is clear is that once an area had been consecrated through mountain monasteries and hermitages, then to that extent its terrors would be abated and the new foundations would themselves become obsolete.

Like the nobles, the residents of the *castelli* also had spiritual motives for ecclesiastical patronage. The groups of citizens from Collepardo and Vico who donated their lands to Trisulti both used the same Alatri notary, who specifies little more than that they hoped for the mercy of Almighty God and the redemption of their souls and the souls of their relatives. For the Collepardesi he adds that at the tribunal of Christ they wanted the Apostle Bartholomew's protection.[61] No charter survives for Casamari.

It is useful, therefore, to look at a related ecclesiastical establishment, San Pietro de Canneto, whose foundation was witnessed on 20 July 1028 by a long list of substantial citizens (judges, blacksmiths, priests, etc.) from the *castello* of Monte San Giovanni, several miles from Sora. San Pietro might appear to have little in common with the monasteries at Trisulti and

59. Wickham, "European Forests in the Early Middle Ages: Landscape and Land Clearance," in *L'Ambiente vegetale*, 2:499, reprinted with revisions in his *Land and Power*, 168; and Bechmann, *Trees and Man*, 52, 82–83, 234, 260.

60. Phrase from Wickham, "European Forests," 520, reprinted in *Land and Power*, 182.

61. Taglienti, *Il Monastero di Trisulti*, 88–91; Strnad, "Zehn Urkunden," 55–57, and Sechi, *Certosa di Trisulti*, 81 and 152–53.

Casamari, since it was a house of canons, not a monastery, and since Dominic's known connections with it are extremely tenuous.[62] Nevertheless, San Pietro de Caneto relates to this discussion not only because it resulted from the same type of popular initiative seen at Trisulti and Casamari, but also because its charter is written in Dominic's charter form!

The same qualms that were said to have animated Borrellus in 1026 and Rainerius and Doda in 1030 are attributed, in slightly abbreviated form, to the citizens of San Giovanni in 1028:

> On a certain day we began to think within ourselves how we were conceived in sin; and how from our infancy day and night, by hours and by minutes, we committed innumerable sins; but how we are to give an account to God in that terrible [day of] judgement concerning our thoughts and deeds; and how each person will be rewarded according to his or her own works. . . . [Therefore,] we took council from priests and religious men, about how we might be able to atone for our innumerable sins and evade the anger of the eternal Judge, and we accepted council from them that there is nothing better within the virtue of almsgiving than to construct from our own possessions and property, a house of canons.[63]

Several scenarios could explain the similarity of this document to those from Dominic's foundations in the lands of the Borrelli and at Sora: (1) the charter form could have been one popularized by Dominic, and then borrowed by other people in his ambient; (2) it could have been developed by a particular notary, whose associates were involved in drawing up all three (different scribes and judges actually signed); or (3) it could have been a standard form, popular in the region. Although two of the greatest scholars of the diplomatic of Lazio, Giorgio Falco and Pierre Toubert, commented on the language of the Monte San Giovanni charter without noting any parallels, the last explanation seems most likely: fragments of these phrases, and even a nearly identical version from a generation later (1066), can be found in documents in the Veroli archives.[64] That

62. *Sora Life* ccci–cccix, 70–71, notes that Abbot Leo of the "monasterii S. Pudentianae, siti in monte Campaniae qui S. Johannis cognominatur," sent a sick resident of Veroli to Dominic's tomb. On Santa Pudenziana, see Caraffa, *Monasticon Italiae*, 1:152. By 1205 the monastery of San Domenico owned property in the *castello* of San Giovanni, noted in the *Privilegium Innocenti III de Libertate Sancti Dominici de Sora*, edited in Farina and Fornari, *Storia e documenti . . . di Casamari*, 165–68, esp. 166, but, since this was the result of a legacy, it probably postdated Dominic's lifetime.

63. Charter from the chapter archives of the Veroli cathedral, edited in Camillo Scaccia Scarafoni, *Le carte dell' Archivio capitolare della Cattedrale di Veroli* (Rome: Istituto di Storia e d'Arte del Lazio Meridionale, 1960), 29–33 (doc. xxxvi).

64. Toubert, *Structures*, 2:927; and Falco, "Note in margine," 201, reprinted in his *Studi sulla storia del Lazio*, 2:711. Falco noted that the *arenghe* from this region in the tenth and

the same penitential language could apply equally well to counts and burgesses shows how religious concerns cut across social divisions.

Individuals from the "populi minuti," although less distinguishable in the surviving records, also played their parts in Dominic's cult. The shepherds, swineherds, and hunters who discovered Dominic in the wilderness had important dramatic roles, but they are largely left unnamed. Some agents of the elite, on the other hand, star in *exempla*. When Giseltrudis, the wife of Count Randisius of Valva, sent her elaborate gifts of food, they came by way of the thieving hands of a certain "Petrum Groctensem" and of another man named Peter.[65] Since the context suggests that the miracle occurred at San Bartolomeo, the first Peter may have come from Grotta near Collepardo. If so, then he was an obvious dependent neither of Dominic, whom he tried to defraud, nor of the counts of Valva, whose property was far away. Rather he seems to have been an ad hoc part of Dominic's messenger system. Other couriers included Peter and John, "servus" and "clientulus" of the Sanso whose relationship to the counts of Marsica has been mentioned, and unnamed "pueri," who carried the offerings of the great men of Arpino.[66] Such agents, although initially thieves, eventually became witnesses to Dominic's power. People of little eminence often benefitted from miracles, but not much can be learned about a "puer from Castro named Leo," an unnamed "rusticus" and his son, "a woman from Collepardo named Maria," "the crippled Azo who was cared for at the house of an illustrious Roman," "a slave girl named Carda" who worked as a laundress in a Sora household, "a certain woman from the lands of Tuscany," "a 'puer' named Simeon who was a citizen of Veroli," a "certain man named Carus from Arsoli," "an adolescent named John from Ancona," "an old man named Adam, son of Albertinus, from the city of Tricole," or many others.[67]

---

eleventh centuries are "rich and diverse" and "deserve to be more attentively studied." For other Veroli parallels, see Scaccia Scarafoni, *Le carte dell'Archivio capitolare . . . di Veroli*, 1–2, 16–17, and 59–61; for a parallel in a 1024 document for Lord Peter of Sora, see Farina and Fornari, *Storia e documenti . . . di Casamari*, 151–53.

65. *Sora Life* lxxix, 46.

66. *Sora Life* xcvi and cix, 47 and 48–49.

67. *Trisulti Life* xiii, 287; *Monte Cassino Life* xlv, 74–75; and *Sora Life* lvii, 42–43, on Leo from Castro. *Trisulti Life* xx, 290–91, on a "rusticus." *Trisulti Life* xix, 290, on Maria. *Sora Life* ccxxi–ccxxxiii, 62–63, on the crippled Azo. *Sora Life* cclxii–cclxxiv, 66–68, on the slave girl ("ancilla") Carda (whose status is anomalous for Lazio in this period, if one accepts the view of Toubert, *Structures*, 1:478–79 and 510–16, that encastellation had largely eliminated slavery). *Trisulti Life* xxxi, 296, on a Tuscan woman. *Trisulti Life* xii, 286–87, and *Monte Cassino Life* lxvii, 76, and *Sora Life* cliii–v, 55, on Simeon from Veroli. *Sora Life* ccxvi–ccxx,

The crowd itself may have more personality than its individual members. A Trisulti description of one of Dominic's Masses tells how all people from all classes ("omnes majores et minores"), "leaping swiftly from their beds, came to the church of San Salvatore with their offerings."[68] Before Dominic could arrive at Collepardo to preach, "The clergy, the men, the women, and the children, all came out to meet him with palms and flowers, singing and offering praises to God, because we merited to have such an overlord and defender in our homeland."[69] The *lives* are filled with phrases such as "universus populus" and "omnis populus et sacerdotes"; a miracle could be confirmed by the testimony of "almost all the people of the *castello*."[70] "Rumor" assembles crowds quickly and efficiently. Intrusive crowds, especially in Alberic's narrative, are what sends Dominic off to new wildernesses.

Although throngs of people are frequent in hagiography, because popular acclaim is a mark of sainthood, crowds seem especially prominent in Dominic's *lives* and other narratives about early-eleventh-century events. In Greek Italy, ecclesiastical reorganization and reform were catalyzed by holy monks preaching to huge audiences.[71] In Latin Italy the reform message affected wider and wider circles.[72] Northern Europe featured mass pilgrimages, the peace and truce of God movements, and popular hermit preachers.[73] Even mass heretical movements reappeared.[74]

R. I. Moore has drawn attention to this reemergence of the "populus," portraying it as a reaction of disenfranchised people, those without

---

62, on Carus from Arsole; ccxci–ccc, 69–70, on John from Ancona; and ccclxxxii–cccxciv, 77–78, on Adam of Tricole.

68. *Trisulti Life* xvii, 289.

69. *Trisulti Life* xvii, 289.

70. *Sora Life* cclxxv, 68.

71. Cosimo Damiano Fonseca, "Particolarismo istituzionale e organizzazione ecclesiastica delle campagne nell'alto medioevo nell'Italia meridionale," in *Cristianizzazione ed organizzazione*, 2:1186–93, esp. 1189.

72. Miccoli, *Chiesa Gregoriana*, 7–20.

73. The importance of crowds in the peace movement was initially analyzed in Loren C. MacKinney, "The People and Public Opinion in the Eleventh-Century Peace Movement," *Speculum* 5 (1930): 181–206. How scholars have developed this theme can be seen in Frederick S. Paxton, "The Peace of God in Modern Historiography: Perspectives and Trends," *Historical Reflections / Reflexions historiques* 14 (1987): 385–404, reprinted in revised form in *The Peace of God: Social Violence and Religious Response in France around the Year 1000*, ed. Richard Landes and Thomas Head, (Ithaca, N.Y.: Cornell University Press, 1992), 21–40. Note also Landes and Head's "Introduction" to that collection, 2–8, 17–18, and the assembled articles. For a warning about this emphasis, however, see Janet L. Nelson's long review of *The Peace of God* in *Speculum* 69 (1994): 163–69.

74. The sources are assembled and published in translation in R. I. Moore, *The Birth of Popular Heresy* (London: Edward Arnold, 1975). For popular religious dissent viewed from an Italian context, see Morghen, *Gregorio VII*, 38–39 and 80–88.

political power, against the *milites*, the violent military elite. He argues that the tension between the two provided the background for the enthusiasm characteristic of ecclesiastical reform.[75] Moore's hypothesis may be sustainable in some contexts, but not necessarily here. The *lives* of Dominic claim that he received enthusiastic support from the comital elite, the solid citizens of the *castelli*, and the socially marginal.

The clergy might appear to be an exception to the universality of Dominic's community. According to his *lives*, he often criticized priests for associating with women. The *Trisulti Life* unflatteringly describes some monks from Monte Cassino.[76] Even the story of the reformed priest Amatus is not wholly positive, since after Amatus had violated his priestly order by, among other things, taking up arms, his repentence required him to move out of the world of secular priests, to dress in sackcloth and ashes and become a hermit—only after time in the desert could he begin his career of fruitful preaching.[77] Yet Dominic did preach to "all the people and priests."[78] When he insisted that the archpriest of Arpino excommunicate the unchaste priests of the city, he was championing the prerogative of an official whose title was relatively rare for Lazio at this time.[79]

Even more strikingly absent from Dominic's community are the highest political and ecclesiastical authorities. The *lives* never mention the German emperors, who were present in central Italy in 967–72, 981–83, 995–1002, 1012(?), 1014, and 1022. They name no popes except for the guarantor of the liberties of San Bartolomeo, even though Dominic spent his whole life on the border of or within papal territory. They take no note of the abbot princes of Cluny, who were in Italy in 967–69, 971–72, 980–81, 983, 986–87, 996–98, 1013–1014, 1022, 1024, and 1026.[80] They ignore

---

75. Moore, "Family, Community and Cult on the Eve of the Gregorian Reform," *Transactions of the Royal Historical Society*, 5th ser. 30 (1980): 49–69, esp. 52–53; "Postscript: The Peace of God and the Social Revolution," in *Peace of God*, 320–21; and "Heresy, Repression, and Social Change in the Age of Gregorian Reform," in *Christendom and Its Discontents: Exclusion, Persecution, and Rebellion, 1000–1500*, ed. Scott L. Waugh and Peter D. Diehl (New York: Cambridge University Press, 1996), 19–46, esp. 28–33. A similar perspective is adopted in André Vauchez, *Les Laïcs au moyen âge: Pratiques et expériences religieuses* (Paris: Éditions du Cerf, 1987), 38–42.

76. *Trisulti Life* xxi, 291–92.

77. *Sora Life* clxxiv–clxxxix, 57–59.

78. *Trisulti Life* xvi and xxvii, 288 and 294.

79. *Sora Life* cxcvi–cxcviii, 60. On archpriests in central Italy in the eleventh century, see Toubert, *Structures*, 2:865; and Loud, *Church and Society in . . . Capua*, 222–23.

80. On the presence of the abbots of Cluny in Italy at this time, see Léon Bourdon, "Les voyages de saint Mayeul en Italie: Itinéraires et chronologie," *Mélanges d'archéologie et d'histoire de l'École française de Rome* 43 (1926): 86–88; and Jacques Hourlier, *Saint Odilon Abbé*

all bishops, except for two witnesses of posthumous wonders who appear in single-sentence afterthoughts toward the end of the Sora *miracles*, in lines that may well be later additions to Alberic's original text. They have nothing further to say about Dominic's original abbot or about any other monastic superior once the young Dominic had received permission from his abbot to enter the desert. The sources give the impression that Dominic anarchically roamed the central Italian countryside, founding churches on his own without any regard for the leaders of state or Church.

Did higher authorities play no role in Dominic's career because they had no power? This thesis can be argued. Perhaps around the turn of the millennium the major impact of the emperors and their armies was confined to the imperial monasteries and palaces they visited and to the military objectives they targeted. Perhaps even their most conspicuous courtiers, such as the abbots of Cluny, had no contact with Dominic and his friends. Although in theory the counts of Marsica ought to have derived their power from the crown and been part of the imperial retinue, in fact their only point of tangency appears to have been sporadic local judicial assemblies, *placita*, which became rarer in central Italy after the tenth century, and which were usually presided over by a *missus* rather than by the emperor himself. These courts made surprisingly little use of the counts Dominic knew, some of whom, such as the counts of Valva, seem to have dropped out of the system entirely. It could be argued that the popes are absent because the noble factions they represented had only Roman concerns (although this seems scarcely credible given the Tuscolaners' interest in expanding their power to the south). Could the bishops be absent because, as Toubert claims, they had little power before the Roman reform turned them into dynamic forces in the countryside?[81] The weakness of central authorities may help explain their absence in Dominic's dossier, but it does not seem to be the whole answer.

A better explanation may be that Dominic's hagiographers deemphasized the world of high politics in order to enhance their own hero. Dominic could discipline and reform to some extent the churches of the *castelli* and the counts who were his patrons. But neither Dominic's own image nor his cult centers' independence would be strengthened by describing his more subservient relationships with higher powers. Such relationships

---

de Cluny, Bibliothèque de la *Revue d'histoire ecclésiastique* 40 (Louvain: Publications Universitaires de Louvain, 1964), 57, 61, 63, 78, 86, 92, and 95.

81. Toubert, *Structures,* 2:930–32.

probably did exist. Dominic's foundation near Scandriglia in the heart of Farfa's territory should have had at least some tacit approval from that great monastery; local bishops must have consecrated some of his new churches and ordained some of his monks. Dominic probably dealt with the popes on occasion. The only documented instance is in regard to San Bartolomeo, whose hagiographer had a vested interest in detailing the papal guarantees that Dominic obtained for it. Yet it may be significant that Dominic's final illness struck while he was on a trip to Tusculo, the hometown of the family then controlling the papacy, a trip known only because of its fatal outcome. How many similar journeys, left unmentioned, might have been part of his administrative career? It is likely that Dominic worked "within the system." The absence of higher authorities in his memorials is a literary reality, significant for the provincial mentality it displays, but not necessarily an objective reality.

Otherwise Dominic's community appears to have been all-embracing, unbounded by monastic cloisters or county lines. His hagiographers delighted in its diversity, in its inclusion of all people "majores et minores." These followers inhabited a broad but coherent geographical range, the world of the Apennine nobility and, in particular, of the counts of Marsica. Although the *Trisulti Life* places most of the miracles it relates in its neighborhood, while the *Sora Life* situates the majority near Sora, both agree that Dominic drew clients from all the lands affected by his monastic system. Map 2 indicates the named homes of the beneficiaries of Dominic's miracles, thus giving a rough idea of his cult's area of influence.

The range of Dominic's cult shown in Map 2 generally parallels the career itinerary delineated in Map 1, except that no devotees came from the area around Foligno—Dominic was not a prophet in his own land. Most came from regions dominated by the lineage of the counts of Marsica. The borders of the cultic area are defined by the great spiritual power centers of Rome, Monte Cassino, and Monte Gargano. Dominic's *lives* denigrate these competitors. The illustrious Lord John of Rome had to send his servant out to Sora to be cured; Dominic had to lecture the monks of Monte Cassino on apostolic comportment; and John of Ancona and Fulco the Frank were both attempting to regain their health at Monte Gargano when they were healed by Dominic while on their way there.[82] Some rivals were closer to home. One story tells how the possessed Sora slave girl, Carda,

82. *Sora Life* ccxvi–ccxx, ccxci–ccc, and cccx–cccxx, 62, 69–70, and 72–73; *Trisulti Life* xxi, 291–92.

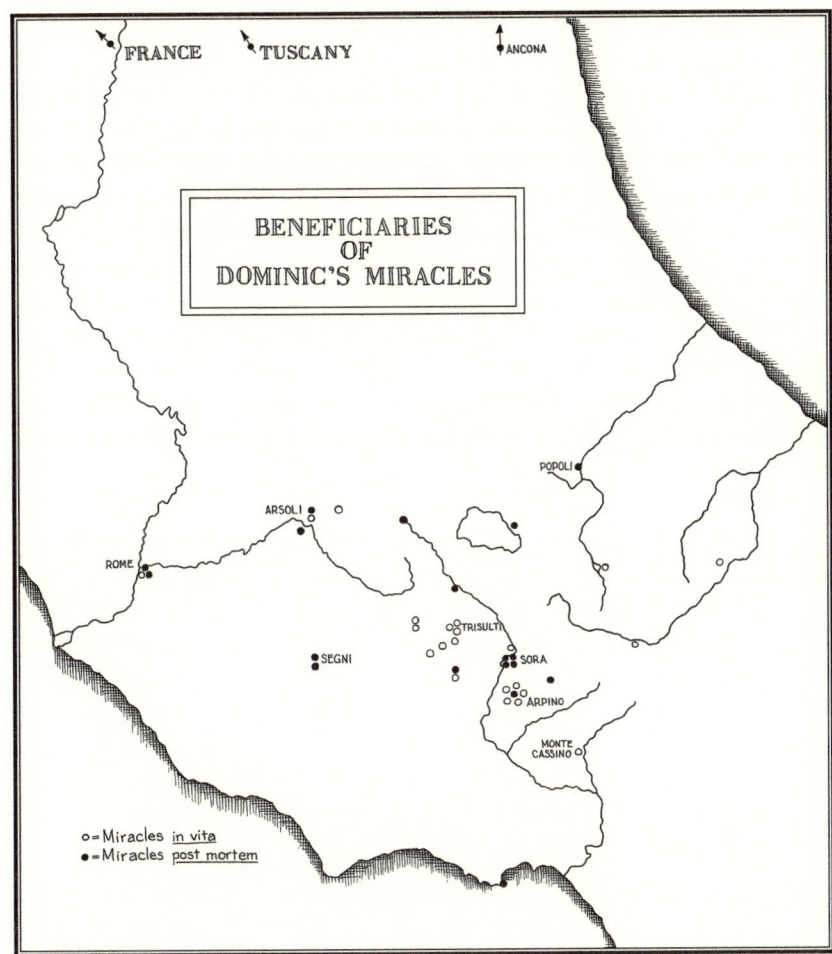

FRANCE TUSCANY ANCONA

**BENEFICIARIES
OF
DOMINIC'S MIRACLES**

POPOLI

ARSOLI

ROME

TRISULTI

SEGNI SORA

ARPINO

MONTE
CASSINO

o = Miracles *in vita*
● = Miracles *post mortem*

Map 2

had unsuccessfully sought exorcism at Sora's church of Santa Restituta prior to obtaining help at San Domenico.[83]

To the east, Dominic's links with lands beyond the Apennine divide were still vital. Supplicants came from the far reaches of the Abruzzi, even from Popoli and Ancona, from areas where, "on the whole, it seems unlikely that the popes had any substantial temporal influence."[84] Yet there are no citizens from nearby coastal cities, such as Salerno and Amalfi. Only Bishop Leo of Gaeta makes a brief appearance in a single, perhaps added sentence near the end of the miracles.[85] This pattern confirms what scholars have already observed on racial, economic, cultural, and political grounds—the coastal commercial centers of Campania, protected by their mountains and volcanic fields, had almost no connections to their rural, mountainous hinterlands.[86] Not even Dominic's cult could transcend this divide.

83. *Sora Life* cclxii–cclxxv, 67–68. This notice should be added to the attempt to edit "the most ample possible collection of notices about Santa Restituta" made in Mauro Ferracuti, "Santa Restituta in Sora: Notizie storiche e trasformazioni architettoniche della chiesa e dell'area ad essa circostante," in *Don Gaetano Squilla: Contributo alla conoscenza della Diocesi di Sora e del suo territorio. Atti del Convegno—Sora, 6 dicembre 1985*, ed. Luigi Giulia (Sora: Centro di Studi Sorani "Vincenzo Patriarcha," 1986), 63–97.

84. Partner, *Lands of St. Peter*, 124.

85. *Sora Life* cccxlvii, 74.

86. Wickham, *Early Medieval Italy*, 150–51, 163; Loud, *Church and Society in . . . Capua*, 15–16.

6

The Great Patronage Shift

DOMINIC'S MONASTIC EMPIRE disintegrated after his death. The sons of the Valva counts who had founded San Pietro in Lago (Theodinus and Oderisius, sons of Count Randisius, and Berardus, son of Count Berardus) gave San Pietro—together with all its possessions in Valva, Marsica, and Chieti, Dominic's hermitage of Prato Cardoso, and its five lakes—to Monte Cassino in 1067 (or 1069).[1] Borrellus Major's son, Borrellus II, acting together with his wife Gervisa and son Walter, gave San Pietro Avellana to Monte Cassino in 1069.[2] Theodinus II and his son Herveus, the grandson and great grandson of the Theodinus who had been count of Rieti when Dominic had entered Santa Maria at Petra Demone and then had founded San Salvatore at Scandriglia, formally donated Petra Demone and San Salvatore back to Farfa in the years 1083 and 1084.[3] No single patrons could alienate Casamari, San Domenico at Sora, and San Bartolomeo at Trisulti, so these houses remained independent longer, but ultimately the

1. The original charter recording the donation of San Pietro in Lago to Monte Cassino is lost. A copy appears in *Reg. Petri Diac.*, fol. 210r (no. 496), edited in Gattola, *Accessiones*, 1:179–80; noted in Hoffmann, "Chronik und Urkunde," 135, and in Bloch, *Monte Cassino*, 1: 338–42. The transaction appears in *Chron. Cass.* III xxxix, 382 and 416.

2. The donation of San Pietro Avellana to Monte Cassino is known through two transcriptions of a charter: one in *Reg. Petri Diac.*, fol. 209v (no. 494), edited in Gattola, *Accessiones* 1:179, and noted in Hoffmann, "Chronik und Urkunde," 135; the other in Archivio di Montecassino, aula II, capsula CXXIII, fasc. 10, no. 96, a 1341 collection of documentary material relative to San Pietro Avellana, published in part in Rivera "Per la storia . . . dei Borrelli," 79–80. Bloch, *Monte Cassino*, 1:364, signals the greater completeness of the later transcript. The transaction appears in *Chron. Cass.* III xxxix, 416.

3. These gifts by the counts of Rieti to Farfa are almost too well documented. In 1083 Count Theodinus [II], the son of Count Berardus [the son of Theodinus I], together with his mother and wife, and with the consent of his son Herveus, gave Farfa the *castella* of Petra Demone and Scandrilia and half of all their possessions there, "including all monasteries and churches," a transaction commemorated in *Reg. Farf.*, 4:78 (doc. 1083); recapitulated in Gregory of Catino, *Chron. Farf.*, 2:169–70. Herveus, the son of the Theodinus mentioned above, in 1084 gave possessions that included his portion "de castello Petra Demonis, et de Scandrilia . . . et de ecclesia Sancti Salvatoris in Scandrilia," a gift recorded in *Reg. Farf.*, 4: 90–91 (doc. 1095); noted in Gregory of Catino, *Chron. Farf.*, 2:170–71. A puzzling restatement of this donation, from 1089 or 1090, is found in *Reg. Farf.*, 5:235–36 (doc. 1255); recapitulated in Gregory of Catino, *Chron. Farf.*, 2:192–93.

popes awarded them in turn to the Cistercians in 1152, the Carthusians in 1204, and the Cistercians of Casamari in 1222.[4] Dominic's system of independent, yet allied, Benedictine houses was gone. Its failure is symbolized by Dominic's cult statue at Sora, which today wears the black and white habit of the Cistercians of Casamari, not Dominic's Benedictine black.

The dissolution of Dominic's monastic empire offers an unusual perspective on the fate of Benedictine monasticism in the eleventh and early twelfth centuries. This is the era central to the scholarly debate about the "crisis of cenobitism," a model that postulates that a new, more eremitical spirituality undermined the power and prestige of the wealthy Benedictine monasteries.[5] Yet scholars have tended to study the "black monks" from the perspective of a few great monasteries, not of the smaller foundations; they have focused on the ultimate fates of winners, even though failures may reveal stress points better than successes. What actually happened to Dominic's little monasteries and to the patronage network that had made them possible stands the "crisis of cenobitism" model on its head, revealing a triumph of the megamonasteries, not of the hermits. It also indicates the seeds of destruction inherent in that triumph.

It is not too surprising that Dominic's monastic system disintegrated. His death dissolved all the links among his foundations that were personal rather than institutional. His allied monasteries were less efficient peacemakers when he himself could no longer preach cooperation to competing

4. The transfer of Casamari to the Cistercians is largely known through late Casamari "chronicles," edited in Farina and Fornari, *Storia e documenti . . . di Casamari*, 175–80. On Innocent III's transformation of Trisulti into the first charterhouse in the Papal States, see Hogg, "Charterhouse of Trisulti," xiii–xxii. The suppression documents for San Domenico include a letter of Honorius III to the monks of Casamari (1 June 1222), a letter to all the Cistercians (11 May 1223), and a confirmation from Frederick II (2 July 1222). See Horoy, *Honorii III . . . Opera Omnia*, 4:179–81 (year 6, doc. 204) and 4:347–48 (year 7, doc. 127), in *Regesta Honorii Papae III*, ed. Presutti, 2:76–77 (doc. 4017) and 2:87 (doc. 4083). Note Kehr, *Italia Pontificia*, 2:169–70; Farina and Fornari, *Storia e documenti . . . di Casamari*, 68; and Antonelli, *Abbazie . . . di Sora*, 231–34.

5. The crisis of monasticism model was most influentially set forth in Jean Leclercq, "La crise du monachisme aux XIe et XIIe siècles," *Bullettino dell'ISIME* 70 (1958): 19–41, with a version in *Aux sources de la spiritualité occidentale: Étapes et constantes* (Paris: Éditions du Cerf, 1964), 175–98, and an English translation in *Cluniac Monasticism in the Central Middle Ages*, ed. Noreen Hunt, Readings in European History (New York: Archon Books, 1971), 217–37. This perspective was merchandized in Norman Cantor, "The Crisis of Western Monasticism, 1050–1130," *American Historical Review* 66 (1960): 47–67. For a critique, see John Van Engen, "The 'Crisis of Cenobitism' Reconsidered: Benedictine Monasticism in the Years 1050–1150," *Speculum* 61 (1986): 269–304. A more sophisticated model of Europe-wide monastic decline, based on the loss of intellectual dominance, is hinted at in Miccoli, "Monks," in *Medieval Callings*, ed. Le Goff, trans. Lydia Cochrane (Chicago: University of Chicago Press, 1990), 37–73, esp. 65–71.

castelli, rebuke tyrannous counts, or compel criminous lords to lay down their arms. Despite the offerings that flowed to Dominic's tomb near Sora, his foundations as a whole were probably less efficient at drawing gifts from all over the Marsican world.

A more significant question is why Dominic's churches and monasteries were handed over to larger monastic entities. The megamonasteries had been rooted for centuries in the lands Dominic helped to develop, but only after his death, as the fate of his houses indicates, did they achieve their greatest predominance. How and why did they acquire Dominic's foundations and patrons? Or did his patrons acquire them? To understand what happened, it is necessary to broaden the scope of the present inquiry, by shifting the perspective from Dominic himself to his patrons and by examining the relationships that existed between the counts of Marsica and the great monasteries both before and after Dominic's lifetime.

Long before Berardus the Frank reached Italy, Monte Cassino was a major Marsican landowner. Charlemagne's conquest of the northern Lombard kingdom, which turned central Italy into a borderland facing the Greeks and the princes of Benevento, made Monte Cassino, San Vincenzo, and other monasteries strategic points. Fragmentary documentation hints at donations made to strengthen Monte Cassino and its ties with the north. Duke Hildebrand of Spoleto (773–89) offered properties, a port, and fisheries on the Lago Fucino.[6] In 835 Emperor Lothar donated a field called "Cervarium," located near the oratory of San Zeno on the northern shore of Lago Fucino, a donation that became much more impressive in the twelfth century when the forger Peter the Deacon, by substituting "pagum" (district) for "pratum" (field), expanded it into a claim on all Marsica.[7] Exchanges in 872 involved Suabilo, gastald of the Marsi, and several Monte Cassino ecclesiastical establishments.[8] Further benefits might have

---

6. *Chron. Cass.* I xiv, 50. A copy of the lost original record is in *Reg. Petri Diac.*, fol. 80–80v (no. 177); edited in Gattola, *Accessiones*, 1:18; noted in Hoffmann, "Chronik und Urkunde," 110–11.

7. Archivio di Monte Cassino, aula III, capsula XIII, no. 4, edited most recently by Theodor Schieffer in MGH *Dipl. Kar.*, 3:96–98; described in Leccisotti, *Regesti*, 2:106. The donation is mentioned in *Chron. Cass.* I xxiii, 68, and copied in *Reg. Petri Diac.*, fol. 49v (no. 111), described in Hoffman, "Chronik und Urkunde," 105. Bloch, *Monte Cassino*, 2:831, locates San Zeno. Peter the Deacon's claim that this donation involved "totum pagum Marsorum"—which has misled historians, such as Rivera, *Conti de'Marsi*, 54—is in *Epitome Chronicum Casinensium Auctore ut Fertur, Anastasio Bibliothecario*, ed. Muratori, *RISS*, 2:365, an altered chronicle Peter falsely attributed to Anastasius Bibliothecarius.

8. Suabilo's lost charter left traces in *Chron. Cass.* I xxxiv, 93. See Bloch, *Monte Cassino*, 1:329–33 and 2:827, and Sennis, "Potere centrale e forze locale, 17."

come in 962 when Prince Gisulf of Salerno (946–77) donated a quarter of
the possessions in the Duchy of Spoleto that had belonged to Emperor
Lambert and then been handed down to him through his grandmother,
but the value of such ancient claims may be questioned.[9] Monte Cassino's
early holdings in western Marsica were certainly extensive.[10] They would
have been vast indeed if they were anything like those further east, in the
counties of Penne and Chieti, which are documented in the unparalleled
Memoratorium of Monte Cassino's Abbot Bertharius (856–83).[11]

After the Muslim raids, after Abbot Aligernus (951–86) had led his
monks back to Monte Cassino and had begun to reclaim the *Terra Sancti
Benedicti*, Marsica again became important. According to the chroniclers,
"Aligernus would most carefully make numerous leases ('libelli quamplu-
rimi'), concerning either the properties of this monastery [St. Benedict's]
or of Sant'Angelo di Barrea [Villetta Barrea, in L'Aquila]."[12] Sant'Angelo,
formerly an independent monastery with many possessions, had been
given to Aligernus in 970 by Otto I, a grant that took it out of the hands
of Bishop Alberic of Marsica.[13] Aligernus leased these disputed possessions

9. *Reg. Petri Diac.*, fols. 90v–100r (no. 224); edited in Gattola, *Accessiones*, 1:80–81;
described in Hoffmann, "Chronik und Urkunde," 115; noted in *Chron. Cass.* II vi, 176.

10. On Monte Cassino's economic involvement in Marsica, see Falco, "Lineamenti di
storia cassinese nei secoli VIII e IX," *Casinensia: Miscellanea di studi cassinesi pubblicati in
occasione del XIV centenario della fondazione della Badia di Montecassino* (Monte Cassino:
Badia di Montecassino, 1929), 538; reprinted in *Rivista storica italiana* n.s. 7 (1929): 409;
reprinted in *Alberi d'Europa*, Biblioteca storica 1 (Rome: Edizioni del Lavoro, 1947), 253. Note
also Luigi Ambrogio Mancone, "Beni di Montecassino nel Ducato di Spoleto," in *Il Ducato
di Spoleto*, 2:887–908.

11. The *Memoratorium* of Abbot Bertharius, a list of possessions in the counties of
Chieti and Penne that depended on San Liberatore, is known from *Chron. Cass.* I xliv, 115–21;
Reg. Petri Diac., fols. 87v–88v, and some of Peter's later forgeries. These sources are amalgam-
ated, edited, and commented on in Bloch, *Monte Cassino*, 2:771–919, esp. 772–76 and 915.

12. *Chron. Cass.* II i–xi, 164–89, esp. 167, 171, 183. For the location of Sant'Angelo, see
Bloch, *Monte Cassino*, 1:369; and Pietrantonio, *Monachesimo benedettino*, 329–32.

13. Monte Cassino's rights to the Sant'Angelo in Barea, as granted in 970, are embodied
in Archivio di Montecassino, aula III, capsula XI, no. 5; edited by Theodor Sickel in MGH
Dipl. Reg. et Imp., 1:538–39 (no. 396); described Lecisotti, *Regesti*, 2:59. A copy is in the *Reg.
Petri Diac.*, fol. 52v (no. 119); noted in Hoffmann, "Chronik und Urkunde," 105.

A charter of doubtful authenticity, dated 19 February 964, that gives Sant'Angelo in
Barrea to Bishop Alberic and his successors, found in the Archiv des bischöflichen Generalvi-
cariats zu Paderborn, Diplom, is edited by Sickel in MGH *Dipl. Reg. et Imp.*, 1:375–77 (no.
263). One problem with this charter is that another exists, written 12 February 964 (a week
earlier), in which Otto confirms the properties of Sant'Angelo without any hint that he in-
tends to establish it as an episcopal possession; the original is Archivio di Montecassino, aula
III, capsula XI, no. 2, ed. MGH *Dipl. Reg. et Imp.*, 1:372–74 (no. 261); described in Leccisotti,
Regesti, 2:57–58.

A 981 confirmation of Monte Cassino's possession is Archivio di Montecassino, aula III,
capsula X, no. 7; ed. by Sickel in MGH *Dipl. Reg. et Imp.*, 2(1):288–95 (no. 254), described in
Leccisotti, *Regesti*, 2:35. Versions altered by Peter the Deacon also exist: Archivio di Monte-

"most carefully" to a variety of holders, none of whom seem to have been Bishop Alberic or his comital siblings.[14]

Alberic's brothers were well aware of Monte Cassino. In 972 Counts Berardus II and Rainaldus presided over a *placitum* in which the monastery successfully vindicated its rights to fisheries on the Lago Fucino.[15] Another brother, Count Oderisius of Valva, sat on the opposite side of the bench when, presumably prior to the death of Otto I in 973, an imperial *missus* ordered him to restore to Monte Cassino some property in the region of Pettorano (about five miles south of Sulmona) and the associated churches of San Stefano and Sant'Eleuterio.[16] By the end of the millennium, Count Rainaldus held much bookland from Monte Cassino. He had leased from Aligernus the monastery of Santa Maria de Luco and its possessions;[17] from Abbot Manso (986–96) San Paulo in the lordship of Comino;[18] and from Abbot John (997–1010) Sant'Erasmo in Pomperano, in a transaction involving some exchanges and additional contracts concerning Santa Maria de Luco and its dependencies.[19] The following generation of counts continued to help with Monte Cassino's judicial proceedings. The sons of Rainaldus, the brothers Oderisius I and Berardus II, presided in November of 1007 (or 1008?) over a judgment recognizing Monte Cassi-

---

cassino, aula III, capsula X, no. 3 is described in Leccisotti, *Regesti*, 2:33; ed. MGH *Dipl. Reg. et Imp.* 2(1):288–95 (no. 254). A copy is found in *Reg. Petri Diac.*, fol. 53r (no. 120), noted in Hoffmann, "Chronik und Urkunde," 105.

14. Some of Aligernus's leases are noted in Inguanez, "Documenti Cassinesi per S. Angelo di Barrea," *Bullettino della R. Deputazione Abruzzese di Storia Patria* ser. 3, 20–21 (1929–30): 13–15; and in Leccisotti, *Regesti*, 2:101 and 6:162–68. These transactions are mentioned in *Chron. Cass.* II iv and viii, 174–75 and 183; and summarized in Bloch, *Monte Cassino*, 1:371–72.

15. The notice of revindication is Archivio di Montecassino, aula III, capsula XII, no. 46, described in Leccisotti, *Regesti*, 2:101. Prior to Lentini's discovery of this document, it had been classified among the "*placiti perduti*" in Manaresi, *Placiti*, 2(2):680–81. The dispute was known through a seven-line summary in *Reg. Petri Diac.*, fol. 104r (no. 233), described in Hoffmann, "Chronik und Urkunde," 116; and through *Chron. Cass.* II vi, 178.

16. *Reg. Petri Diac.*, fol. 104r–104v (no. 233[B]), gives only a sentence summarizing a document Peter knew; noted in Hoffmann, "Chronik und Urkunde," 116. The dispute is reported in *Chron. Cass.* II vi, 179. See Manaresi, *Placiti*, 2(2):679–80. On the churches, see Bloch, *Monte Cassino*, 2:867–68. The literature wrongly dates this *placitum* to the year 972; see Hoffmann, "Die älteren Abstlisten von Montecassino," *QFIAB* 47 (1967): 287; and Bloch, *Monte Cassino*, 2:867–68.

17. The transaction involving Santa Maria de Luco is reported in *Chron. Cass.* II vii, 182–83. On the location, see Bloch, *Monte Cassino*, 1:333–37; and Pietrantonio, *Monachesimo benedettino*, 209–10.

18. The transaction involving San Paulo of Comino is mentioned in *Chron. Cass.* II xiii, 192. On this property, see Bloch, *Monte Cassino*, 2:718–19.

19. The transactions involving Santa Maria de Luco and Sant'Erasmo in Pomperano are mentioned in *Chron. Cass.* II xxvi, 211. On the location, see Bloch, *Monte Cassino*, 2:731; and Pietrantonio, *Monachesimo benedettino*, 210.

no's rights over San Benedetto dei Marsi,[20] and in May 1023, at Oretino, Berardus II witnessed a judgment in favor of Monte Cassino regarding several churches and properties, perhaps former possessions of Sant'Angelo di Barrea.[21]

Despite these connections, Berardus the Frank and his sons did *not* donate property to Monte Cassino. The very few early gifts from the family come from their wives. There is a badly documented series of transactions, probably executed between 954 and 968, whereby Countess Doda, the widow of Berardus the Frank, gave the church of Santa Maria de Luco to the priest Walter (perhaps her own son, the future bishop Walter of Forcona?), who, after it had accumulated many possessions, gave it to Monte Cassino, which then leased it back to Count Rainaldus (Bishop Walter's brother).[22] Between 986 and 996 Jesulfa, the wife of Rainaldus, gave a generous list of properties to Monte Cassino, but these were lands that this daughter of Count Atto of Chieti held in her own right as a result of her first marriage to Count Lando of Teano.[23]

The major philanthropic causes of the sons of Berardus the Frank were their new family monasteries. Although none of the sons of Berardus the Frank is known to have directly given churches or other gifts to Monte Cassino, most of them founded their own monasteries around the year 1000, just before their deaths. On 1 February of the year 1000, the elderly

20. Archivio di Montecassino, aula II, capsula LI, no. 1, described in Leccisotti, *Regesti*, 8:162. Discussed in Bloch, *Monte Cassino*, 1:337; and in Pietrantonio, *Monachesimo benedettino*, 276–77.

21. Archivio di Monte Cassino, aula III, capsula XII, no. 48; noted in Leccisotti, *Regesti*, 2:102. Leccisotti described this as a judgment from Lanfranc, count of the Marsi, commissioned by Henry II. The actual document reveals that Lanfranc was an imperial "comes et missus," a "missus domni imperatoris." It is signed by "Berardus comes . . . in territorio marsicano oretini."

22. The early Marsican transactions are known only through *Chron. Cass.* II vii, 182–83; discussed in Bloch, *Monte Cassino*, 1:333, and 2:1105. If the identifications Bloch hazards are correct, then the *terminus post quem* would be the death of Berardus, who was still living in 954; the *terminus ante quem* would be Walter's elevation to the bishopric of Forcona, a post he already held in 968, as indicated in Gerhard Schwartz, *Die Besetzung der Bistümer Reichitaliens unter den sächischen und salischen Kaisern mit den listen der Bischöfe 951–1122* (Leipzig: B. G. Teubner, 1913), 280–82.

23. Archivio di Montecassino, aula II, capsula XXVI, fasc I, no. 4; described in Leccisotti, *Regesti*, 6:263; edited in Gattola, *Historia*, 1:106–7. Jesulfa donated her properties to Abbot Manso (986–96). Her first husband, Lando of Teano, was still alive in 986, when he commissioned a will prior to leaving on a pilgrimage to Monte Gargano for the remission of his sins: see *Chron. Vult.* IV, 2:317, and Müller, *Topographische und genealogische Untersuchungen*, 84. Sennis, "Potere centrale e forze locali, 35–37, speculates that the property of Marsican wives could have been given to Monte Cassino in order to exchange it for holdings that were more adjacent and defensible.

Count Rainaldus of Marsica established Santa Maria in Cellis (near Carsoli, in the province of L'Aquila).[24] No such clear record exists for his brother Theodinus, who ruled as count of Rieti at the end of the tenth century, but, as has been noted, he may have supported the two Sabine houses associated with Dominic, the monasteries near Petra Demone and Scandriglia over which his descendents had rights in 1083/1084. In 1002 count Berardus II and his wife, countess Gemma, daughter of Count Ademarus, living in Bagnoli, founded San Benedetto in Trigno, presumably as a family monastery; in 1020, after the founders had died without heirs, its abbots gave the property to Monte Cassino.[25] Oderisius, the first count of Valva, in 1001 founded Santa Maria and San Pellegrino di Bominaco on Farfa lands (Bominaco, prov. L'Aquila).[26] The one nonclerical son with no

24. A copy of the lost original charter for Santa Maria in Cellis is in *Reg. Petri Diac.*, fol. 114r (no. 252); edited in Gattola, *Accessiones*, 1:101–2; noted in Hoffmann, "Chronik und Urkunde," 118, and in Inguanez, "Documenti del monastero di S. Maria de Cellis conservati nell'Archivio di Montecassino," *Bullettino della R. Deputazione Abruzzese di Storia Patria*, 3 ser., 7/8 (1917): 128. On the location and records of this house, see Howe, "*Monasteria Semper Libera*," 23–24.

25. For the location of San Benedetto in Trigno, see Bloch, *Monte Cassino*, 1:282–84; and Pietrantonio, *Monachesimo benedettino*, 409–11. The original charter issued by Count Berardus and Gemma is unknown, but there are two copies from the eleventh/twelfth century: one in a Beneventan hand, Archivio di Montecassino, aula II, capsula XLVII, fasc. I, no. 1, described in Leccisotti, *Regesti*, 8:90 (where the indiction should read XV rather than XIV); and one in a northern hand, Archivio di Montecassino, aula III, capsula XII, no. 33, described in Leccisotti, *Regesti*, 2:97 (where the date should read "1002" rather than "1092"). There is also a summary in Inguanez, "Le pergamene della Badia di S. Benedetto de Jumento albo di Civitanova conservate nell'Archivio di Montecassino," *Gli Archivi italiani* 4 (1917): 144.

Despite much scholarly confusion, Berardus can be identified. Rivera, "Origini dei Borelli," 54 and 66, said that in the Triventino area, which Randuisius had gained from the princes of Benevento, Randuisius was succeeded by a Count Berardus, and he presumed that Berardus was the son of Randuisius, since he was unaware of the original charter that identified Berardus as "son of Berardus." Bloch connects Berardus with the Borrelli, which fits the area but is hard to reconcile with Borrelli chronology and with Leccisotti's revelation concerning the paternity of Berardus. A "Bernardus filius cuiusdam Beraldi comitis" was a witness at a *placitum* held in "Campo de Cedici" in 995: see *Reg. Farf.*, 3:90–91 (doc. 388). The founder of San Benedetto in Trigno can be equated with this man, who, if his father had been Berardus the Frank, would have been the brother of Randuisius. He then would have taken charge of Randuisius's sphere of influence after his death. This would also explain the subsequent presence of the Borelli in the region, because, upon the death of Berardus (which, judging from the fate of his monastery, was without heirs), it would have been logical for a nephew, Borrellus, and his sons to take the territory.

26. On the location of Santa Maria and San Pellegrino di Bominaco, see Bloch, *Monte Cassino*, 1:591, and Pietrantonio, *Monachesimo benedettino*, 110–13. The original foundation charter of Oderisius, which was said to be dated to 1001, and which may have contained some dubious elements, appears to be lost; see Celidonio, *La diocesi di Valva e Sulmona*, 3:174; Cesare Rivera, "Le conquiste dei primi normanni in Teate, Penne, Apruzzo e Valva," *Bullettino della R. Deputazione Abruzzese di Storia Patria*, ser. 3, 16 (1925): 46, and "Per la storia . . . dei Borelli," 57–59. Reference to this charter is made in a grant of 1093, ed. in Celidonio, *La diocesi di Valva e Sulmona*, 3:174–76. Oderisius is specified as the monastic founder in a di-

known links to a private foundation is Randuisius, but he seems to have been stinted in honors and property until just before his death.[27]

The grandsons and great-grandsons of Berardus also often founded their own monasteries. As already noted, soon after the year 1000 three of the sons of Oderisius of Valva—Beraldus, Theodinus, and Randisius—gave Dominic the hermitage of Prato Cardoso and extensive lands for the foundation of the monastery of San Pietro in Lago, while another son, Borrellus, helped him found San Pietro Avellana. In 1022, Rainaldus, son of Berardus, presumably a grandson of Oderisius, founded the Benedictine house of San Giorgio in Valva.[28] The descendents of Rainaldus of Marsica were also conspicuous in these endeavors. In 1048 Berardus III, Rainaldus's grandson, was the first benefactor of the monastery of Santa Maria in Valle Porclaneta in Rusconi (Rosciolo dei Marsi, prov. L'Aquila).[29] Another grandson, Oderisius II, after civil wars with his brother Berardus, founded the Collimento branch of the lineage, establishing San Giovanni at Collimento (Collimento, in the neighborhood of Lucoli, L'Aquila).[30]

ploma of 1014 in which Henry II grants the churches of S. Maria and S. Pellegrino to Farfa, which is said to have possessed them in antiquity: *Reg. Farf.*, 3:164 (doc. 484); also edited in Bresslau and Hermann Bloch, in MGH *Dipl. Reg. et Imp.*, 3:350–52. This document was included by Gregory of Catino in *Chron. Farf.*, 2:30, and he later specifies that the "ecclesiam sancti Peregrinus" was a place "in quo comes Oderisius monasterium construxit" (ibid., 2:99).

27. Randuisius, unlike his lay siblings, is nowhere clearly specified as "count." He is absent in 970 from the family group described in *Chron. Vult.* IV, 2:154–58. Rivera, *Conti de'Marsi*, 200, says he appears as a brother of Rainaldus in *Chron. Farf.*, 1:347, but here he is identified only as an advocate. The situation is no clearer in the underlying document—*Reg. Farf.*, 3:99 (no. 397)—where it is a question of "Rainaldum comitem et Randuisium germanos fratres" in a case "de Rainaldo comite et de Randuisio." Randuisius does not appear independently until 997, when Pandulfus II and Landulfus V, the princes of Benevento, gave him the "contado di Trivento," establishing him as one of their "fideles" in a transaction recorded in *Chronicon Beneventani Monasterii S. Sophiae*, ed. Nicola Colet, in *Anecdota Ughelliana*, in *Italia Sacra*, 10:471; registered in René Poupardin, *Les Institutions politiques et administratives des principautés lombardes de l'Italie méridionale (IXe–XIe siècles)* (Paris: Honoré Champion, Éditeur, 1907), 117–18 (no. 145, not no. 45 as in Rivera, "Origini dei Borrelli," 53). On the fate of Randuisius's property, see note 25 to this chapter.

28. Archivio di Montecassino, aula II, capsula I, no. 1; described in Leccisotti, *Regesti* 3:1.

29. *Reg. Petri Diac.*, fol. 200r (no. 460); edited in Gattola, *Accessiones* 1:195, noted in Hoffmann, "Chronik und Urkunde," 133; mentioned in *Chron. Cass.* III lxi, 442. Difficulties in the identification of Santa Maria in Valle Porclaneta (or "in Rusconi") are resolved in Bloch, *Monte Cassino*, 2:825–26; and Pietrantonio, *Monachesimo benedettino*, 212–14.

30. The foundation charter of San Giovanni at Collimento was once in the archives of the bishop of Aquila, from which it was edited in Muratori, *Antiquitates Italiae Medii Aevi*, 6 vols. (Milan Typographia Societatis Palatinae, 1738–42), 5:817–18, 6:493–95; a later copy is partially edited in Cesare Rivera, "L'Abadia di Collimento e una bolla d'Innocenzo III," *Bullettino della R. Deputazione Abruzzese di Storia Patria* 14 (1902): 75 and 81, and also noted in his "Annessione delle terre d'Abruzzo al regno di Sicilia," *Archivio storico italiano*, ser. 7, 6 (vol. 84) (1926): 222. On the monastery, see Pietrantonio, *Monachesimo benedettino*, 210–12.

Yet even though members of the lineage of the counts of Marsica primarily patronized their own family monasteries, they often cooperated with Monte Cassino in military matters. In 1022, during Henry II's Italian campaign, the counts of Marsica and the sons of Borrellus received his enemy, Monte Cassino's Capuan abbot Atenulfus (brother of Pandulfus IV), and helped him flee to Constantinople.[31] In 1025–26, after Henry's sudden death, the counts of Marsica—together with some Normans, Greeks, and others—besieged Capua in order to evict Henry's man and to restore Pandulfus IV, who claimed to be Monte Cassino's friend.[32] After the brief ascendency of Salerno under Guaimar, Pandulfus V was able to return to Capua in 1042, where, in order to ally with the sons of Borrellus, he had to give them a free hand to advance against San Vincenzo al Volturno (whose chronicler claimed that the monastery had not suffered worse from the Saracens). In this exceptional case, the greed of the Borrelli may have worked against Monte Cassino's interests, since Pandulfus was also allied on similar terms with the counts of Aquino, who devastated Monte Cassino.[33] Yet in 1045, when Monte Cassino's Norman "allies" had begun to build forts in the *Terra Sancti Benedicti*, oppress its people, and provoke revolts, the call for help went out to "the counts of the Marsi, the sons of Borrellus, and the other *fideles* of the monastery," who together expelled the Normans.[34] Perhaps it is more than coincidence that at about this time Berardus III, count of the Marsi, received San Salvatore at Avenzano, a former dependency of Sant'Angelo in Barrea, for 300 fish a year.[35] Thus when Pope Leo IX organized the anti-Norman expedition that culminated in his defeat at Civitate in 1053, his forces included those of the counts of the Marsi and of the Borrelli.[36] Such alliances were facilitated by

---

The identity of the founding Oderisius is discussed in Howe, "*Monasteria Semper Libera*," 26–27.

31. *Chron. Cass.* II xxxix, 242–43. Although only the later redactions of the chronicle specify that the sons of Borrellus joined the counts of Marsica in receiving Atenulfus, the route of flight indicated in Leo Marsicanus's autograph version leaves little doubt that the Borrelli must have been hospitable.

32. *Chron. Cass.* II lvi, 274–75; Amatus, *L'Histoire de li Normant* I xxxiiii, 44–46. That the Borrelli were also involved is presumed by Rivera, "Per la storia . . . dei Borrelli," 68.

33. Celidonio, *Diocesi di Valva e Sulmona*, 2:157–60; Rivera, "Per la storia . . . dei Borrelli," 70–71.

34. *Chron. Cass.* II lxxi, 309–12; Desiderius, *Dialog.* xxii, 30(2):1138–39; Amatus, *L'Histoire de li Normant* II xlii–xliii, 108–10.

35. *Chron. Cass.* II lxv, 296, where identification is limited to "count Berardus of the Marsi."

36. Amatus, *L'Histoire de li Normant* III xxiii–xxv, 138–41. Oderisius, son of Borrellus, was present with the papal host eight days before the battle, according to *Chron. Vult.* V, 3:

the fact that the spheres of expansion of the descendents of Berardus the Frank did not impinge as directly on the *Terra Sancti Benedicti* as did those of nearer neighbors, such as the counts of Aquino and the Normans.

Marsican donations of property to Monte Cassino nevertheless remained niggardly. A few years after 999 and prior to the death of Abbot John III of Monte Cassino in 1010, Count Oderisius I of Marsica, a son of Rainaldus, exchanged "Casa Fortini," an important property he had received from his first wife, Gervisa, for the *castello* of Sant'Urbano (now the town of Alvito in Frosinone) and other churches and manors in Comino, which were to be the basis of his family's domain.[37] In 1012, in memory of Gervisa, Oderisius gave to Abbot Atenulfus San Paulo, which Oderisius's father Rainaldus had originally leased from Monte Cassino.[38] All these properties had belonged to Monte Cassino in the first place, and the transactions appear to have been exchanges rather than donations. More profitable may have been a gift in 1014 from Borrellus the Great, who, together with his wife and their sons John, Borrellus II, and Oderisius, donated to Monte Cassino the church of San Eustachio "ad Arcum."[39] Altogether these few Marsican donations are surprisingly unimpressive.

In the late 1050s the relationship between the counts of Marsica and Monte Cassino became warmer. In December of 1055, upon the death of abbot Richerius, a faction of monks backing a Marsican candidate for abbot appeared for the first time (unless one counts Bishop Alberic's conspiracy in 996). Opposing the election of Abbot Peter (1055–57), they championed "Johannes Marsicanus," the prior of San Benedetto in Capua. According to Leo Marsicanus, they failed because they were only "a few

---

86. A long list of forces is given in William of Apulia, *Gesta Roberti Wiscardi* II, lines 148–79, ed. Roger Wilmans, in MGH *SS*, 7:258–59.

37. On "Casa Fortini" and San Urbano, see *Reg. Petri Diac.*, fol. 108r (nos. 239–240), noted in Hoffmann, "Chronik und Urkunde," 117. The transaction appears in *Chron. Cass.* II xxvi, 211–212. Bloch, *Monte Cassino*, 1:203 and 2:875–76, locates "Casa Fortini."

38. On San Paulo, see *Reg. Petri Diac.*, fol. 144v–45r (no. 333); edited in Gattola, *Historia*, 1:327–28; described in Hoffmann, "Chronik und Urkunde," 124. Noted in *Chron Cass.* II xiii, xxxii, 192 and 228. See Bloch, *Monte Cassino*, 2:718–19; Antonelli, *Abbazie . . . di Sora*, 104–11.

39. The location of San Eustachio is discussed in Bloch, *Monte Cassino*, 1:284–87, and 2:1119; and Pietrantonio, *Monachesimo benedettino*, 439–40. The original donation survives in Archivio di Montecassino, aula III, capsula XI, no. 65, described in Leccisotti, *Regesti*, 2:83–84. A version, much improved stylistically and organizationally, appears in *Reg. Petri Diac.*, fols. 100r–100v (no. 225); edited in Gattola, *Historia*, 1:127–18; and noted in Hoffmann, "Chronik und Urkunde," 225. The donation was cited in *Chron. Cass.* II vi, 176 and 181. On the misdating of this donation to 977, and the resulting confusion in reconstructions of the early history of the Borrelli, see Howe, "*Monasteria Semper Libera*," 25.

dissenters" and because John undercut them by swearing on the altar that he would never accept the abbacy.[40] Yet this Marsican faction was strong enough to be noticed.

Very soon afterward, in December of 1057, Monte Cassino was visited by Bishop Pandulfus of Marsica (1056–1094/96). Although scholars have generally overlooked the fact, Pandulfus was a member of the family of the counts of Marsica, like three of his five immediate predecessors and two of his three immediate successors.[41] He was a wealthy and powerful bishop, who, in addition to acquiring the family see, had inherited the castle of Ortona dei Marsi and other properties from his father, Count Berardus II.[42] At Monte Cassino he formally accepted a bull affirming his rule over the whole diocese of Marsica, quashing a long-standing attempt to split it.[43] Leo Marsicanus tells how Pandulfus, having been honorably and lovingly received, offered in return a specially styled chasuble, a silk episcopal mantel with gold fringes, a purple altar facing with fringes and gems, two silver incense burners, a gold chalice and paten, two silver hand-washing basins, one silver censer, a little silver cross with "wood of the Lord," one silver vase for holy water, a great decorative pallium with lions on it, an excellent tapestry, and "other things which it would be superfluous to mention."[44] This is the only list of episcopal donations in the *Chronicle*, which normally itemizes only royal and imperial gifts. When Pandulfus returned home in 1058, he had been admitted into the prayers of the monks and become "extremely close to and devoted to the monastery."[45] His visit cemented a partnership between the Marsican comital lineage and Monte Cassino. Soon the cloisters would be filled with family members and the endowments swollen with their properties.

At least four nephews of Pandulfus became monks of Monte Cassino, the most conspicuous of whom were sons of Count Oderisius II of Marsica. The mother of this Oderisius had been one of Dominic of Sora's benefactors, and Oderisius himself, as an adolescent, had met the saint at Venere

40. *Chron. Cass.* III lxxxix, 341.

41. On the comital ancestry of Pandulfus and other Marsican bishops, see Howe, "*Monasteria Semper Libera*," 28–29.

42. Amatus, *L'Histoire de li Normant* VII xxxv, 334–36.

43. The bull of Stephan IX reuniting the diocese of Marsica (J–L 4377), issued by Humbert of Silva Candida at Monte Cassino on 9 December 1057, is edited in Ughelli, *Italia Sacra*, 1:889–91; reprinted in *PL* 143:875–76. See Kehr, *Italia Pontificia*, 4:241.

44. *Chron. Cass.* II xcv, 354.

45. *Chron. Cass.* II xcv, 354. Inguanez, *I Necrologi cassinesi*, 52 and 92; and Hoffmann, "Der Kalender des Leo Marsicanus," 102 and 143, confirm Leo Marsicanus's testimony that Pandulfus's name was entered into the necrologies.

on the Lago Fucino, an occasion on which Dominic had displayed his prophetic abilities by predicting Oderisius's brilliant future and splendid children.[46] The most illustrious of these would become Abbot Oderisius I of Monte Cassino (1087–1105). Leo Marsicanus identifies him as "a son of Count Oderisius of Marsica"; he tells how, soon after he had been received into the monastery "in pueritia," his future abbacy was predicted by Abbot Richerius (1038–55); and he claims that Oderisius's conduct was so exemplary that he was everyone's choice to succeed Abbot Desiderius (1057–87).[47] If it is assumed that Oderisius had attained the minimum canonical age when he became a cardinal deacon in 1059, then he would have already entered Monte Cassino in the 1040s, in advance of Pandulfus's visit.[48]

Another "son of Count Oderisius of Marsica" was Transmundus, "a splendid adolescent skilled in letters." His career was less fortunate than his older brother's. In 1071, while still very young, he had been made abbot of the monastery of Santa Maria de Mare in the Tremiti Islands (about fourteen miles north of the Gargano peninsula), where, faced with a monastic rebellion, he ordered three of the senior monks blinded and the tongue of another cut out. Because of this scandal he was quickly recalled, but his good connections soon got him the abbacy of San Clemente at Casauria (1072 or 1073), and then the bishopric of Valva. Gregory VII deposed him from that see because he fled from its Norman invaders, but he refused to relinquish his position, held on until his death, and was buried in his episcopal church of San Pelino in 1080 or 1081.[49]

A third son was Atto, a man descended "from the princes of Marsica." He had been bishop at Carsoli, but after his see was quashed in the reunification of the diocese of Marsica (which restored it all to Bishop Pandulfus), he was transferred to the church of Chieti. He later entered Monte Cassino, where he died in 1071, still only 38 years old.[50]

---

46. *Sora Life* lxvi–lxxvii, 44–46.

47. *Chron. Cass.* III lxiii and IV i, 456 and 466–67.

48. *Chron. Cass.* III xiv, 376 (the only source for this papal ordination). On Oderisius's promotion, as well as problems concerning when and where he later became a cardinal priest, see Hüls, *Kardinäle*, 215–16 and 251–52.

49. The major sources for the strange career of Transmundus are *Chron. Cass.* III xxv, 392–93; and Gregory VII, *Epistula* VIII xv, ed. Erich Caspar, *Das Register Gregors VII*, MGH *Epistolae Selectae*, 1:535–36; noted in Kehr, *Italia Pontificia*, 4:254. General accounts and the monastic context can be found in Celidonio, *Diocesi di Valva e Sulmona*, 2:82–88; Leccisotti, "Le relazioni fra Montecassino e Tremiti e i possedimenti cassinesi a Foggia e Lucera," *Benedictina* 3 (1949): 204–6; and Cowdrey, *Age of Abbot Desiderius*, 123–44.

50. Atto is treated in Ughelli, *Italia Sacra*, 6:691. His connection to Oderisius II is established in Amatus, *L'histoire de li Normant* VI viii, 268. Most of what is known about him comes from a poem and an epitaph written by Archbishop Alfanus I of Salerno (d. 1085). These

Thus Count Oderisius II, one of Dominic's patrons and still a grateful pilgrim to his shrine at some time prior to 1059, chose to launch the ecclesiastical careers of at least two of his sons at Monte Cassino, not at any of Dominic's little monasteries. Shortly before 1071 a third son retired there, and after 1077 the ancient count did so himself.[51]

Another nephew of Bishop Pandulfus also entered Monte Cassino, a son of Count Berardus III of Marsica, a brother with whom the bishop was not on the best of terms. Already, in the early 1050s, Berardus III was working at cross purposes with his brothers Oderisius II and Rainaldus II in their attempts to dispose of "Monte Azze," and in 1066/1067 fraternal grievances broke out into full-scale civil war. Berardus III attacked the castle of Bishop Pandulfus at Ortona dei Marsi, and imprisoned him until he renounced his inheritance. Then Oderisius II and Berardus III fought each other in a struggle that disastrously brought Norman and Borrelli auxiliaries into play.[52] Yet in 1063/1064, according to Monte Cassino's *Chronicle*, "Berardus, count of the Marsi" offered Monte Cassino both the monastery of Santa Maria near Monte Marcolano and his son Theodinus, an adolescent "of great talent" who had first entered monastic life at San Salvatore in Rieti, an ancient but more provincial house.[53] Since Berardus III relocated Theodinus to Monte Cassino, he must have judged it more advantageous. The move did advance Theodinus's career, for after Archdeacon Hildebrand, around 1067, asked Monte Cassino for personnel to help staff the papal *curia*, Theodinus became a Roman archdeacon. Theodinus died after 1084, perhaps after 1089.[54]

Thus, by the late 1060s, a brilliant group of young counts of Marsica was ensconced in Monte Cassino (Genealogical Chart 5). Were these cousins a recognizable faction? A strong affirmative answer comes from poems written by a former Monte Cassino monk, Alfanus of Salerno (d. 1085). In

are *Carmina* xvi and xxxi, edited by Lentini and Avagliano, *I Carmi di Alfano I; Arcivescovo di Salerno*, MC 38 (Monte Cassino: Abbazia di Montecassino, 1974), 141–41 and 170. For overviews, see Sennis, "Potere centrale e forze locali," 54; and Howe, "'Fatal Discord' in an Eleventh-Century Noble Family from Central Italy," *Medieval Prosopography* 16 (1995): 11–12.

51. Oderisius's visit to Dominic's tomb prior to 1059 is described on p. 105. His last recorded act took place in the year 1077, when he founded the monastery of Collimento—see Howe, "*Monasteria Semper Libera*," 26–27. His retirement to Monte Cassino, presumably after that date, is noted in *Sora Life* lxxi, 44.

52. Howe, "'Fatal Discord,'" 1–15.

53. *Chron. Cass.* III xvii, 383. On Santa Maria near Monte Marculano, see Bloch, *Monte Cassino*, 2:829.

54. *Chron. Cass.* III xxiv, 391; Hüls, *Kardinäle*, 254. A letter to Desiderius, reporting on "Domnus Theodinus vester monachus," written after the Norman raids of 1066/67, but prior to Theodinus having been called to Rome by Alexander II (d. 1073), is in Hoffmann, "Chronik und Urkunde," 199–201.

GENEALOGICAL CHART 5.   Monte Cassino Monks of the 1060s Who Were
Counts of Marsica.

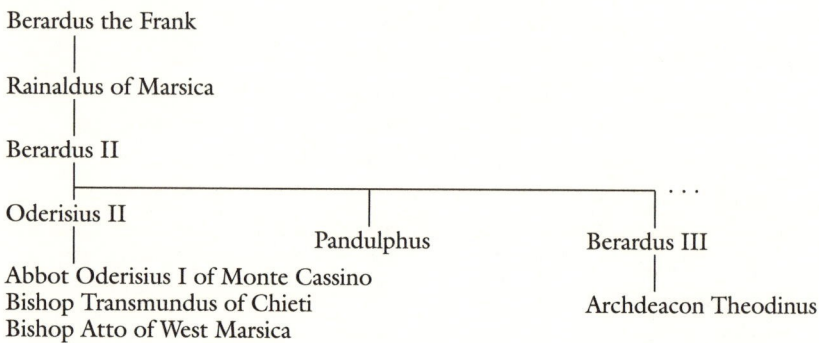

Berardus the Frank
|
Rainaldus of Marsica
|
Berardus II
|
Oderisius II
                    Pandulphus   Berardus III
Abbot Oderisius I of Monte Cassino
Bishop Transmundus of Chieti   Archdeacon Theodinus
Bishop Atto of West Marsica

"To Bishop Pandulfus of Marsica" and "In Praise of the Monks of Monte
Cassino," Alfanus glorifies monks named Oderisius, Theodinus, and Trans-
mundus (or Transmundulus).[55] These names are fairly common at Monte
Cassino, but since one of the poems is addressed to Pandulphus, he would
certainly have identified its subjects as his own Monte Cassino nephews.
Alfanus also wrote a poem "To the Schoolboy Transmundus" that agrees
with what the *Chronicle* said about Transmundus of Marsica's competence
as a student; and another "To Theodinus, Monk of Cassino" that links
Theodinus and Oderisius and specifies the descent of Theodinus from
Marsican nobility.[56] Alfanus liked to write poems to powerful people.
Those that concern the lineage of the counts of Marsica demonstrate that,
despite the discord among the descendents of Berardus the Frank as the
fourth generation yielded to the fifth, the sons of Oderisius II and Berardus
III at Monte Cassino could still be seen by outsiders as a cohesive group.

    Other descendents of Berardus the Frank who lived at Monte Cassino
were remembered because they acquired reputations for sanctity (Genealogical Chart 6). Randisius (d. 1090?), "monk of Monte Cassino and son
of Count Borrellus" (Borrellus II? post 926 to post 983?), was commemorated by Peter the Deacon, who stated that he had "lived a pure life for
thirty years since he had been suffering from dropsy" ("qui per triginta
annos pristinum tenuit cum hydropicus factus fuisset"). Perhaps his father
had sent him to Monte Cassino for a dignified retirement. There Randisius

<hr/>

55. Alfanus of Salerno, *Carmina* i, xiii, and xxxix, 71, 126, and 190.
56. Alfanus, *Carmina* xiv and xxiv, 145–46 and 160–63.

GENEALOGICAL CHART 6.   Monte Cassino "Saints" of the Late Eleventh Century Who Were from the Lineage of the Counts of Marsica.

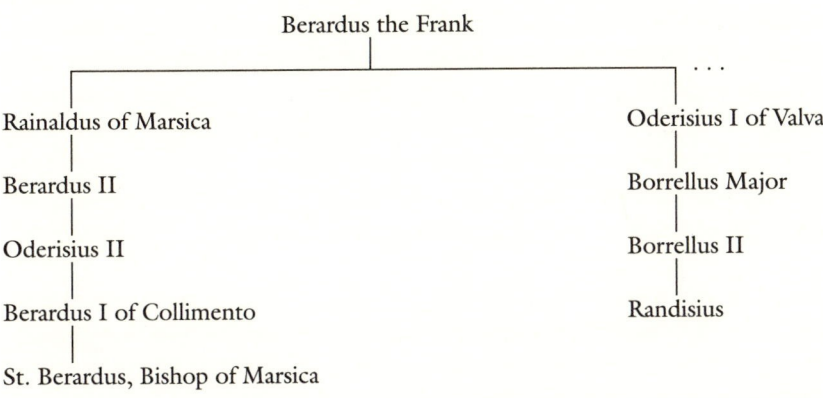

had the spiritual satisfaction of seeing, on his deathbed, the protomartyr Stephen and other holy figures coming for him.[57]

St. Berardus, Bishop of Marsica (d. 1130), is described in the *Vita Berardi* (*BHL* 1176) as a Marsican "from the seed of the great Berardian counts," who, after having been made an acolyte by Bishop Pandulfus, was educated at Monte Cassino, and then became a cardinal priest in Rome.[58] Since the *life* names his father "Berardus" and the family home the *castello* "cui Colli nomen," his father must have been Count Berardus of Collimento and his grandfather the first count of Collimento, Oderisius II of Marsica. This explains why Berardus was a protégé of Pandulfus, since he would have been the old bishop's great-nephew.[59]

Other family members and friends of the counts of Marsica also came to Monte Cassino. In the monastery's calendar, produced at the end of the

57. The sole detailed evidence for this Randisius is in *Petri Diaconi Ortus et Vita Iustorum Cenobii Casinensis* lxvi, ed. R. H. Rodgers, University of California Publications in Classical Studies 10 (Berkeley: University of California Press, 1972), 95. His death is listed under 19 March in the calendar that Leo Marsicanus composed in 1098/1099 (see Hoffmann, "Kalender des Leo Marsicanus," 105 and 145). An *obit* of ca. 1090 is cited by Rivera, "Per la storia . . . dei Borrelli," 81, from the manuscripts of the Abruzzi antiquary Antonio Ludovico Antinori, but Antinori's date may be learned conjecture.

58. *Vita Berardi* (*BHL* 1176), ed. *AS*, Nov. 2 (1):125–35, esp. 129. On his Roman service, see Hüls, *Kardinäle*, 174.

59. *AS* Nov. 2 (1):129. Because of the *life*'s mention of "Berardian counts," Berardus has sometimes been linked to the Berardeschi lineage of Tuscany. For the correct genealogy, see Müller, *Topographische und genealogische Untersuchungen*, 67 and 70; and Zelina Zafarana, "Berardo, santo," *DBI*, 8:775–76. On Collimento, see Luigi Rivera, "L'Abadia di Collimento," 75 and 81.

eleventh century, numerous obituary notices bear the lineage names: Berardus (six, four of whom are described as "comes"); Borrellus (two, one "comes"); Oderisius (three); Rainaldus (two, one "comes"); Rainerius (six); and Randisius (three).[60] The family's Marsican subordinates may have felt encouraged to develop their own contacts with Monte Cassino. One example would be the entrance, between 1060 and 1063, of the chronicler Leo Marsicanus (d. 1115). Within a few years he was joined by his brother John and by his uncle, Archdeacon John of Marsica.[61] Two other Marsican monks at Monte Cassino, both named John, figure among the characters in Desiderius's *Dialogus de Miraculis Sancti Benedicti*, written around 1078.[62]

With the men of Marsica came churches, *castelli*, and land. From about the time of Bishop Pandulf's visit to the close of the eleventh century, the descendents of Berardus the Frank donated great amounts of property to Monte Cassino. Appendix C indicates the magnitude of this largesse by listing, in chronological order, two dozen separate transactions that are discussed in the major studies on Monte Cassino's dependencies by Heinrich Dormeier and Herbert Bloch. Most involve more than one property. Evaluating this evidence is complicated by the fact that subsequent donations to the family monasteries that Monte Cassino acquired become donations to the mother house, thus enhancing the appearance of exponential growth. Nevertheless, Appendix C demonstrates clearly enough that the various branches of the extended family of the counts of Marsica began to give generously to Monte Cassino in the later eleventh century.

Within a generation or two of Dominic's death, the descendents of Berardus the Frank had become an influential part of Monte Cassino's monastic community. Their status was evident in October of 1071 at the dedication of the new basilica built by Abbot Desiderius. The dignitaries who attended the eight continuous days of solemnities included, as Leo Marsicanus proudly noted, the pope, several cardinals, ten archbishops, forty-

60. Hoffmann, "Kalender des Leo Marsicanus," 132, 142, and 145.

61. Leo is sometimes misidentified as belonging to the family of the Marsican counts. For the history of the claim and an analysis of Leo's family, see Newton, "Leo Marsicanus and . . . Monte Cassino 99," 181–205, esp. 194. The date of Leo's entry into Monte Cassino is approximated from *Chron. Cass.* III pref and xxiv, 362 and 387, which establishes that when he entered he was then fourteen years old, and that his novice master was a monk who left for Sardinia around 1063.

62. Desiderius, *Dialog.* I vi and II xvi, 1121 and 1135. The Marsican affiliation is not specified in the first case, which involves the monk who became John V of San Vincenzo al Volturno, but it is clarified in *Chron. Vult.* III, 89.

two bishops, most of the Norman princes, and also "no small crowd of the counts of the Marsi, the counts of Valva, and the sons of Borellus." Some of these were monks and some were *conversi* who had retired into Monte Cassino's splendor, but most would have been visiting guests, the increasingly contentious and closed-packed counts whose donations in recent years had helped finance the basilica. Leo, as a Marsican, gave them a conspicuous place in his list. Despite the internal family feuds of the 1060s, he still saw the counts of Marsica and Valva, and the Borrelli, as a single, unified "crowd." Presumably he, and they, recognized their affinity.[63]

Supreme power in a Benedictine monastery belongs to the abbot. The lineage of the counts of Marsica needed the abbacy to institutionalize its influence. Abbot Desiderius—whose own family, the dukes of Benevento, had been destroyed by the Normans—guaranteed a Marsican triumph when he made Oderisius his provost, and later blessed his election as abbot. The result was signaled more than a dozen years ago by one of the preeminent experts on Monte Cassino, Hartmut Hoffmann, who observed that in the eleventh and early twelfth centuries Monte Cassino's abbots no longer came from the independent Capuan and Beneventan Lombard principalities, but rather from the southern part of the duchy of Spoleto (the Abbruzzi, Marsica, and Chieti), so that there developed a "starke marsische Element" within the abbey, represented most conspicuously by several abbots drawn from its comital family.[64] Yet the strength of this Marsican dominance may have been greater than even Hoffmann suspected.

The Marsicans kept the abbacy. Abbot Oderisius ruled from 1087 until the end of 1105.[65] His reign was followed by an *interregnum* involving at least one disputed election and then the troubled tenure of a sometimes resident papal official, Bishop (Saint) Bruno of Segni, whom Monte Cassino intriguers, turning the pope against him, forced to resign the abbacy and return to his diocese.[66] Those intriguers are left unnamed, but they

63. *Chron. Cass.* III xxix, 398–402. This is largely based on an earlier guest list made by Leo, edited by Leccisotti, "Il racconto della dedicazione della basilica desideriana nel codice Cassinese 47," appended to Angelo Pantoni, *Le vicende della Basilica di Monte Cassino attraverso la documentazione archeologica,* MC 36 (Monte Cassino: Abazzia di Montecassino, 1973), 215–25; annotated in Bloch, *Monte Cassino,* 1:118–21. The context and significance of the gathering is sketched in Nicola Cilento, "Il convegno cassinese dell'ottobre 1071," *Quaderni medievali* 2 (1976): 143–52; and Bloch, *Monte Cassino,* 1:40–42.

64. Hoffmann, "Zur Geschichte Montecassinos," 1–20, esp. 7–8.

65. Hoffmann, "Die älteren Abtslisten von Montecassino," 320–22.

66. The confusing chronology of the early twelfth-century abbots is discussed in Hoffmann, "Älteren Abtslisten von Montecassino," 322–24. How Bruno of Segni was ousted is unclear. *Chron. Cass.* IV xlii, 510–11, a section written by Peter the Deacon, admits nothing

made no trouble during the reign of Bruno's successor, Girardus (IIII–1123), "whose ancestry was from the most noble lineage of the counts of the Marsi."[67] His rise had been aided by his relative, Abbot Oderisius I, who had made him prior of San Nicola in Pica (in the province of Frosinone), a training post for future abbots.[68] Their relationship had been so close that when Girardus was about to die he is said to have been summoned to heaven not by angels but by an apparition of Oderisius.[69]

Girardus maintained familial succession by naming as his prior, at the very start of his reign, Oderisius "from the family of the counts of Sangro," who was probably a great grandson of Dominic's patron, Borellus Major.[70] Oderisius II was elected abbot in 1123, but disputes with the papacy, including an 1126 excommunication, forced him into exile after 1127.[71] His successor, Seniorectus, is viewed as an outsider, a reformer imposed by Honorius II.[72] Yet a closer look at Seniorectus's résumé indicates that he too was closely connected to the counts of Marsica. He had been prior of Santa Maria of Luco dei Marsi, one of their former family foundations, and, subsequently, under the Marsican Abbot Girardus, he had been made prior and then abbot of San Nicola in Pica, marking him as a potential future abbot of Monte Cassino.[73] Although Seniorectus was forced to resign in

more than that a faction in the abbey denounced Bruno to the pope; the *Vita Brunonis*, edited in *AS* Jul. 4:483, makes Bruno's exit sound more violent. On these discrepancies, see Réginald Grégoire, *Bruno de Segni, exégète médiéval et théologique monastique*, CISAM 3 (Spoleto: CISAM, 1965), 43–56; and Loud, "Abbot Desiderius," 325.

67. *Chron. Cass.* IV xlii, 512. For his dates, see Hoffmann, "Die älteren Abtslisten von Montecassino," 324.

68. *Chron. Cass.* IV xliii and lxxvii, 512 and 541. On the prestige of the priors at San Nicola in Pica, see Loud, *Church and Society in . . . Capua*, 126.

69. *Chron. Cass.* IV lxxvii, 541.

70. *Chron. Cass.* IV lxxviii, 542, identifies Oderisius II as "ex Sangrorum comitum prosapia sue originis lineam ducens." The title "count of Sangro" seems to have been first used for Oderisius, one of the brothers of Borrellus II, from the year 1070 on: see Cesare Rivera, "Per la storia . . . dei Borrelli," 80–81. Scholars have presumed that his son Oderisius, i.e., Count Oderisius II of Sangro, was the father of Abbot Oderisius II of Monte Cassino, although the documentary support for this reconstruction is not perfect (ibid.; Bloch, *Monte Cassino*, 3:1500).

The exact year Girardus made Oderisius II prior of Monte Cassino is never stated. However, Oderisius II must have been made a cardinal deacon around IIII–12, judging from the documentation pertaining to other men who were elevated at the same time—see *Chron. Cass.* IV xlii, 511; and Hüls, *Kardinäle*, 227–28. It seems reasonable to infer that the special eminence that made him suitable for the cardinalate was that he was already Monte Cassino's prior.

71. Hoffmann, "Die älteren Abtslisten von Montecassino," 324.

72. Hoffmann, "Petrus Diaconus," 84; Cowdrey, *Desiderius*, 223–24; Loud, *Church and Society in . . . Capua*, 135.

73. *Chron. Cass.* IV xxiv, 554. If it is presumed that Girardus, who had himself been prior of San Nicola, held that position until he became abbot of Monte Cassino, then he must have

1137, a disastrous year of political and military reverses in which four abbots briefly ruled, he was ultimately succeeded by Abbot Rainaldus II (1137 to 1166), "from the family of the counts of the Marsi," from its Collimento branch, most probably a grandson of Count Oderisius II of Marsica, and thus a nephew of Monte Cassino's Abbot Oderisius I.[74] The Marsicans are firmly in control when the *Chronicle* ends.

Although the evidence is far less detailed and conclusive, other great monasteries seem to have received similar attention from the noble families who had formerly supported Dominic. In the years 1083 and 1084, Farfa acquired Petra Demone and Scandriglia from the counts of Rieti, Theodinus II and Herveus, who were the grandson and great-grandson of the Theodinus who ruled the area when Dominic was there. Did such donations correlate with increased family influence at Farfa? From the mid-eleventh century on, most of the abbots of Farfa bore the *Leitnamen* of the lineage of the counts of Marsica: Berardus I (1048–89); Rainaldus I (1089–90); Berardus II (1090–99; Odo, a Lombard monk who reigned briefly in 1099, soon died in disgrace); Berardus III (1099–1119); Rainaldus II (1119); and Berardus IV (1119–23, coterminous with Guido III [1119–25], a low-born abbot supported by the pope).[75] Yet it is not easy to establish a neat correlation, because the little genealogical information available suggests other possible family connections.[76]

The Ottaviani Crescenzi, Dominic's occasional patrons, took over Subiaco, perhaps more by accident than by design. Their original goal had been Farfa. A son of Dominic's patron John, son of Atto, became a monk there. However, in the 1060s, Subiaco's Abbot Humbert was captured in a surprise attack by Lando of Civitella (today Bellegra). When the monks could not negotiate his release, they looked for counterforce. Power in the western part of their sphere of influence was held by the Crescenzi. Therefore, in 1065 a delegation of Subiaco monks fetched John from Farfa and attempted to make him abbot. Lando, probably not eager to battle the

---

been the one who approved the choice of Seniorectus to follow him; by 1115 Seniorectus had become abbot.

74. *Chron. Cass.* IV cxxviii, 604.

75. A list of Farfa's abbots is found in McClendon, *Imperial Abbey of Farfa*, 121–22.

76. Schuster, "L'Abate Ugo I," 624–27, and *L'imperiale Abbazia di Farfa*, 115, connects Abbot Hugo (998–1039) to the counts of Rieti, but cites no evidence. Berardus II was a nephew of Berardus I (ibid., 221). Berardus III was related to Rainaldus II, whom he had made his provost (ibid., 264–67). Yet *Reg. Farf.*, 5:317 (doc. 1324), speaks of "abbas Berardus Florentinus" and "Abbas Beraldus Ascari filius." See Maria Grazia Mara, "Berardo," and Sofia Boesch Gajano, "Berardo," in *DBI*, 8:765–67 and 767–75.

Crescenzi, became "valde contristatus" and let Humbert go. As a consequence of this move, the young Crescenzi abbot returned "in locum
suum" (back to Farfa?). But after Humbert managed to offend the curia
(perhaps by backing the antipope Honorius II?), he was forced to resign.
John triumphantly returned, recognized by the monks and Rome as Abbot
John V (1069–1121). Perhaps it was during John's reign that Dominic's
Santissima Trinità returned to Subiaco.[77] After John's death, the Crescenzi
lost once again to their old nemesis, the counts of Tuscolo, who took Subiaco's abbacy for one of their own. Then, in 1149, Subiaco was bestowed
on Eugenius III's subdeacon Simon, a former Monte Cassino monk who
was descended from the Borrelli.[78]

Why did Dominic's benefactors shift their patronage from small, local
family monasteries to large, "international" ones? Hindsight reveals that
the counts of Marsica profited by exchanging control over their family
monasteries for control over Monte Cassino itself, but they could not have
known in advance that they would triumph so completely. Why did they
originally turn their attention to Monte Cassino?

Political reasons might have encouraged a new patronage strategy.
The Marsican civil strife of the 1060s, for example, could have prompted
Oderisius II to donate Sant'Erasmo and two half churches in 1067 in an
effort to ensure Monte Cassino's good will during his fight with Berardus
III; perhaps some of Berardus III's many gifts to Monte Cassino in this
same period were similarly motivated.[79] Or donations might have been
triggered by the advance of the Normans, a possibility supported by some

77. The genealogy of John V is documented in Hansmartin Schwarzmaier, "Zur Familie
Viktors IV.," 64–77, and "Der *Liber Vitae* von Subiaco," 95–103. Note also Toubert, *Structures*, 2:903–4; Hoffmann, "Zur Abstliste von Subiaco," *QFIAB* 52 (1972): 788; and Ilàri,
"Possessi monastici sublacensi," 432–39. Further context can be found in Delogu, "Territorio
e cultura fra Tivoli e Subiaco," 36–37. The events of his election(s) are recounted, none too
clearly, in *Chron. Subl.*, 9–12. Paolo Carosi, "L'abate sublacense Giovanni V: La duplice elezione (1065 e 1069)," *Atti e memorie della Società tiburtina di storia e d'arte* 42 (1969): 115–
32, offers the most detailed analysis, although his documentary readings receive some correc-
tion in Hoffmann, "Zur Abtsliste von Subiaco," 781–88.
78. For the problems of the Crescenzi, see Partner, *Lands of St. Peter*, 121; and Toubert,
Structures, 2:1069 and 1277. Delogu, "Territorio e cultura fra Tivoli e Subiaco," 50, criticizes
John V for being preoccupied with a relatively limited and provincial agenda; more positive
accomplishments are noted in Martini, "Manoscritti sublacensi e Tiburtini," 199–216. On the
passing of the abbacy of Subiaco among the families of Dominic's former patrons, see *Chron.
Subl.*, 21; and Bloch, *Monte Cassino*, 2:995–96.
79. Dormeier, *Montecassino und die Laien*, 38 and 41; Bloch, *Monte Cassino*, 1:323, 2:
731, 824–26, and 829.

documented examples from southern Italy.[80] The Norman raiders who threatened Marsica, Valva, and the lands of the Borelli from 1067 onward might have encouraged property donation either to exchange indefensible earthly assets for heavenly ones or to protect family monasteries by connecting them to more powerful ones. For example, after Berardus III, between 1067 and 1073, had given Monte Cassino the monastery of Santa Maria in Valle Porclaneta, a Norman occupier, William of Montreuil, refused to surrender it to one of Berardus III's sons, the Monte Cassino monk Theodinus, but did contact Monte Cassino about securing it.[81]

A more inclusive political explanation, advanced by G. A. Loud, is that a great increase in donations to Monte Cassino between 1060 and 1080 resulted from the generosity of the new Norman prince of Capua, Jordan I, which compelled his vassals to follow his example.[82] Yet this does not satisfactorily explain the generosity of the counts of the Marsi, which began before Jordan conquered Capua and continued even after Capuan donations had ceased.[83] Moreover, non-Capuan nobles showered riches on Monte Cassino during this same period—for example, the Tuscolan family under Gregory III (1058–1071) gave ten churches in and around Tuscolo.[84]

Did the Marsican elite liquidate private monasteries because of the Gregorian Reform? By the end of the eleventh century, lay ownership of churches was officially frowned upon, and in many regions of Europe nobles increasingly donated private churches to ecclesiastical authorities, especially to monasteries.[85] Yet reforming pressures may not have greatly

---

80. Dormeier, *Montecassino und die Laien*, 63–67; Vera Von Falkenhausen, "Aspetti storico-economici dell'età di Roberto il Guiscardo," 129; and Loud, *Church and Society in . . . Capua*, 83 and 150–51.

81. *Epistola Guillelmi de Sancta Marie de Roscolu . . .* , edited in Hoffmann, "Chronik und Urkunde," 199–201. On William, see Marjorie Chibnall, "Les moines et les patrons de Saint-Évroult dans l'Italie du sud au XIe siècle," *Les Normands en Méditerranée dans le sillage des Tancrède: Colloque de Cerisy-la-Salle (24–27 septembre 1992)*, ed. Pierre Bouet and François Neveux (Caen: Presses Universitaires de Caen, 1994), 161–63.

82. Loud, *Church and Society in . . . Capua*, 81.

83. Earlier donations by the counts of Marsica have been described here above. Their continuation in a "steady stream," even after Capuan generosity had ceased, is admitted by Loud himself in *Church and Society in . . . Capua*, 129.

84. Hoffmann, "Petrus Diaconus," 10–11 and 60–61; Bloch, *Monte Cassino*, 1:318–19, 2:737–38 and 815–16.

85. On the conciliar and synodal enactments against private ownership of churches, see Rosenwein, *To Be the Neighbor of Saint Peter: The Social Meaning of Cluny's Property, 909–1049* (Ithaca, N.Y.: Cornell University Press, 1989), 8–9; and Tellenbach, *The Church in Western Europe*, 286–93.

affected the wilds of the Apennines where antipopes ruled.[86] In 1083 Farfa
gave a fraction of a church to a group of laymen.[87] In 1102 a priest at Sulmona sold part of a church to a layman.[88] If the prohibitions against lay
ownership of churches did not deter clergymen, would they have influenced lay proprietors? Heinrich Dormeier's examination of donations to
Monte Cassino in the eleventh and twelfth centuries noted only two charters specifically invoking the injunctions against laymen owning churches.[89]
Gregorian ideas do not seem to have greatly affected mountainous rural
lordships "blithely isolated from reforming currents."[90] Even if such ideas
had been influential, since the reformers were quite willing to approve
transfers of ownership into "jus patronatis," owners of private churches
could have regularized them into the new order without donating them to
major monasteries.

Perhaps churches were given to Monte Cassino and other great monasteries in return for retirement packages satisfying the demands of both
piety and annuity. Marsican aristocrats flocked to Monte Cassino right after Desiderius had rebuilt the cloister and the dormitories and had begun
work on his new basilica. Donations were customarily made when would-
be monks entered monasteries, and real estate, including churches, was a
common gift.[91] One donation that was clearly a "dowry" was the monastery of Santa Maria near Monte Marcolano, a gift by Count Berardus III
of Marsica in 1063/1064 which is associated with the entrance of his son

86. The Sabina was dominated by Farfa, a major base for Henry IV and Henry V; for
the pro-imperial politics of its abbots Berardus II (1090–1099) and III (1099–1119), see the
articles on them by Maria Grazia Mara and Boesch Gajano in the *DBI*, 8:765–67 and 767–75.
Cesare Rivera, "Per la storia . . . dei Borelli," 77 and 82, suggests that when the Norman
"allies" of the papal reform party began to advance into the Marsican region from 1067 on,
their opponents naturally preferred the imperially sponsored antipopes.

87. *Reg. Farf.*, 5:31–32 (doc. 1028), commemorates how, in 1077, Count Theodinus of
Valva, "filius randuisi comitis," offered Farfa portions of two churches and a castle and some
land in Marsica. *Reg. Farf.*, 5:66–68 (doc. 1071), contains the 1083 sequel, in which Theodinus
and his son witness Farfa's donation of part of one of these churches to a group of laymen.

88. *Codice Diplomatico Sulmonese*, ed. Faraglia, 31–31 (doc. 21).

89. Dormeier, *Montecassino und die Laien*, 58–62.

90. Loud, *Church and Society in . . . Capua*, 214–15, 235–43 (from whom the phrase is
quoted); Toubert, *Structures*, 2:817–18, 837–38, 897, and 908, partially reprinted with the
same pagination as "Essai sur les modèles hagiographiques de la Réforme grégorienne," in
Études sur l'Italie médiévale (IXe–XIVe s.) (London: Variorum Reprints, 1976); "Monachisme
et encadrement réligieux des campagnes en Italie aux Xe–XIIe siècles," *Le Istituzioni ecclesiastiche della 'Societas Christiana' dei secoli XI–XII: Diocesi, pievi e parrocchie. Atti della sesta
Settimana internazionale di studio Milano, 1–7 settembre 1974*, Pubblicazioni dell'Università
Cattolica del Sacro Cuore Miscellanea del Centro di Studi Medioevali 8 (Milan: Vita e Pensiero, 1977), 428, reprinted with the same pagination in *Études sur l'Italie médiévale*.

91. Lynch, *Simoniacal Entry into Religious Life*, esp. xvi–xvii and 61–81; Bull, *Knightly
Piety*, 115–25.

Theodinus.[92] Entry gifts would also have been made when family members took the monastic habit prior to death.[93] A distant relative, Count Transmundus III of Chieti, offered three of his *castelli* in 1055 because he was "badly infirm and wanting to become a monk."[94]

Tracing the total impact of such gifts is difficult. The elderly nobles who chose to enter the monastery as lay monks are particularly poorly documented. The only evidence that Count Oderisius II of Marsica retired to Monte Cassino is a brief apostrophe in the *Sora Life*, and the only evidence that Maurus of Amalfi, the donor of the abbey's famous bronze doors, retired there in 1071 is a note in Amatus of Monte Cassino's *History*.[95] Yet, although Monte Cassino did not produce necrologies as comprehensive as those found at some Cluniac monasteries, the surviving ones do suggest an unusually high percentage of *conversi*.[96] The high numbers of late entrants probably correlate with the high numbers of gifts. But why did the Marsican counts and other nobles want to retire at Monte Cassino rather than at their own family monasteries?

The best explanation for the shift in monastic patronage is that the great monasteries had become conspicuously superior in their amenities, culture, and spirituality. During Dominic's lifetime, small, local monasteries had no insuperable disadvantages vis-à-vis their ancient, property-rich competitors. Around the time of Dominic's birth, Monte Cassino's monks had only just ended their long and often unedifying exile at Capua. At the time of his death, they were just beginning to rebuild their library,[97] and their buildings were so undistinguished that a generation later Desiderius would not find any of them worth preserving. Farfa was even less advanced, and almost until the end of the tenth century still shocked German emperors by its loose monastic morals, chaotic privatization of property, and competing abbots with large families. Around the year 1000, it will be recalled, local nobles had attacked with considerable success the abbots of Monte Cassino, San Vincenzo, and Subiaco. In these chaotic years, a mo-

---

92. *Chron. Cass.* III xvii, 383. See p. 135 above.

93. On gifts associated with "reception *ad succurrendum*," see Bull, *Knightly Piety*, 143–53.

94. *Chron. Cass.* II lxxxviii, 339.

95. *Sora Life* lxxi, 44; Amatus, *L'Histoire de li Normant* VIII iii, 343.

96. Giles Constable, "Monasteries, Rural Churches," 364–65; and in his review of Dormeier, *Montecassino und die Laien*, in *Speculum* 68 (1982): 494; Dormeier, *Montecassino und die Laien*, 11.

97. *Chron. Cass.* II liii, 265–66, claims that, at the start of the reign of Abbot Theobaldus (1022–35), Monte Cassino suffered from a "maxima paupertas" of books.

nastic pioneer such as Dominic would have found central Italian monasticism a field ripe for development. By the 1050s, however, at the time when Bishop Pandulfus made his triumphal visit to Monte Cassino, it and other great houses absolutely outclassed small local monasteries.

Family monasteries could not compete in terms of physical plant. Abbot princes were creating palaces of Byzantine splendor. In fact, Farfa saw no incongruity in the ancient use of the term "palatium" to describe a monastic guesthouse (one that would include, among other amenities, forty latrines!).[98] The great monasteries vied with each other in creating new basilicas, magnificently decorated by Italian and Byzantine craftsmen. Their consecrations—Farfa in 1060, Monte Cassino in 1071—were attended by the pope, cardinals, and crowds of bishops.[99] In comparison to such splendor, the little stone churches Dominic and his monks had built, in part with their own hands, must have begun to seem small and mean, entirely unsuited to the sons of counts or to counts themselves who wished to retire from the world. Lord Peter of Sora, Dominic's contemporary, retired to the monastery he and Dominic had built in his realm; Count Oderisius II of Marsica, Dominic's far younger contemporary, retired to Monte Cassino.

After the middle of the eleventh century, family monasteries could no longer compete culturally. By then Monte Cassino had expanded its library, welcomed scholars, and reestablished itself as a major center of learning. Abbot Desiderius himself, in his forties, had begun to study seriously the liberal arts, setting an example for his monks. Schoolmasters such as Dominic's hagiographer Alberic were highly esteemed. The Beneventan script achieved its greatest perfection in Monte Cassino's *scriptorium*. Dozens of well-trained monks became central Italian bishops and Roman curialists.[100] Farfa, although not in the same league, had its cultural triumphs.[101] Subiaco's *scriptorium* became active.[102]

---

98. *Liber Tramitis Aevi Odilonis Abbatis*, ed. Peter Dinter, in *Corpus Consuetudinum Monasticarum*, 13 vols., ed. Kassius Hallinger (Siegburg: Franz Schmitt, 1980), 10:205.

99. For Berardus I's consecration of Farfa's new church, see *Reg. Farf.*, 5:291 (doc. 129), reprinted in McClendon, *Imperial Abbey of Farfa*, 134–35, and Schuster, *L'imperiale Abbazia di Farfa*, 216. On Desiderius's consecration of Monte Cassino, see pp. 138–39.

100. On Monte Cassino's "golden age," see Bloch, "Monte Cassino's Teachers and Library in the High Middle Ages," in *La Scuola nell'occidente latino dell'alto medioevo, Spoleto, 15–21 aprile 1971*, Settimane di studio del CISAM 19 (Spoleto: CISAM, 1972), 563–618; Toubert, *Structures*, 2:805–15; and Loud, *Church and Society in . . . Capua*, 46–47. Amatus, *L'Histoire de li Normant* III lii, 176–77, mentions Desiderius's mid-life interest in literary studies. Francis Newton (Duke University) is at work on a monographic study of Monte Cassino's Desiderian and Oderisian *scriptoria*. Lists of bishops and cardinals recruited from Monte Cassino are found in Réginald Grégoire, "Le Mont-Cassin dans la réforme de l'Église de 1049

A sophisticated monastic high culture was developing that contrasted with Dominic's "hands-on" style of abbatial leadership. Dominic's *miracles* tell how his relative, Abbot Benedict, the third abbot of San Domenico, rode out one day to reclaim four cows stolen by a Count Hubert, who, struck ill by divine wrath, quickly returned the three he still had; and how, as Abbot Benedict was driving them back, he was opposed by Hubert's son, who would have stopped him, except that, by divine providence, his horse was bitten by Benedict's.[103] One could imagine Dominic as the protagonist of this homely story, but not Abbot Desiderius, the man who, glorious in square nimbus and ornate chasuble, gazes out at us today from Monte Cassino illuminations and fresco work.

Dominic's little communities could not offer the same spiritual benefits as the resurgent giants. The larger monasteries could promise numerous and elaborate intercessory prayers. When the monks of Farfa requested a confirmation of their privileges from Pope Leo IX in 1049, they identified themselves as about "five hundred praying monks," an impressive figure even after allowances are made for the inclusion of Farfa's subordinate monasteries and perhaps for some exaggeration.[104] These monks could enfief benefactors with their prayers through the use of solemn formulas: "We, all the brothers of the Congregation of Mary Mother of God [at Farfa] . . . , receive you into our society and fraternity and into a sharing of all our good works, namely hymns, all psalms, charitable acts, fasts, sacrifices, and other just acts. May the Lord receive you with us into the society and number of his elect, who live and reign through ages without end, Amen."[105]

The connection between property donations and prayer confraternities is obvious in the charter commemorating Walter of Sangro's 1091 donation to Monte Cassino: "On that day when we [the monks of Monte Cassino] offered our society to Walter, son of Borrellus the Younger, Walter himself together with his son Oddo, restored twelve *casales* to San

à 1122," in *Il Monachesimo e la riforma ecclesiastica (1949–1122): Atti della quarta Settimana internazionale di studio, Mendola, 23–29 agosto 1968*, Pubblicazioni dell'Università Cattolica del Sacro Cuore, Contributi, ser. 3, var. 7; Miscellanea del Centro di Studi Medioevali 6 (Milan: Vita e Pensiero, 1971), 27; and in Cowdrey, *Age of Abbot Desiderius*, esp. 63–71.

101. Paola Supino Martini, "La produzione libraria negli *scriptoria* delle abbazie di Farfa e di S. Eutizio," in *Il Ducato di Spoleto*, 2:581–607.

102. Martini, "Manocritti sublacensi e tiburtini dei secoli XI–XII," in *Atti del Convegno "L'Eredità medioevale . . . tiburtina*," 201–204.

103. *Sora Life* cccxlix–ccclxix, 74–76.

104. *Reg. Farf.*, 4:34–45 (doc. 877).

105. Two versions of Farfa's enrollment formula are quoted in Schuster, "Martyrologium Pharphense," 439.

Benedetto and San Pietro Avellana, placing the charter on the altar of Benedict, for his own soul, his father's, and his grandfather's [i.e., the patrilineal
family back to the founding Borrellus]."[106] Much might be paid for such
spiritual benefits: note, for example, the casually assumed causal sequence
in Gregory of Catino's account of how Henry IV, in the early 1080s, vindicated Farfa's rights over one of its *castelli*: "Since he [Henry] had been
received in a most kindly manner by all the seniors and brethren and been
assured of perpetual prayer by a devoted kiss of peace, and since his name
and the names of some of his faithful followers had been inscribed in the
book of commemoration, he immediately directed his army against the
castello of Fara."[107] Imperial armies were not so readily moved by promises
of prayers from isolated handfuls of monks.

In late eleventh-century Italy, larger monasteries absorbed smaller
ones. It is generally recognized that the Italo-Normans privileged great
monasteries.[108] The history of Dominic of Sora's patrons suggests that in
this policy, as in so many others, they were anticipated by their predecessors. Monastic consolidation was a general movement, motivated by the
attractive power of the great monasteries themselves. Perhaps many of the
monks of the small houses even favored such mergers, although this can
never be known, since the surviving evidence was produced by the elite
institutions. The situation can be described in the jargon favored by the
currently fashionable free-market economists: central Italian monasticism
was developing from a freely competitive open-market situation to a closed
market dominated by giant "mature corporations"; Dominic's old "cus-
tomers," the counts of Marsica and others, traded in smaller monasteries
for shares in the greater enterprises because the megamonasteries offered a
better—or at least more marketable—"product."

106. *Reg. Petri Diac.* fol. 209v–210r (no. 495), edited in Gattola, *Accessiones* 1:179, and
described in Hoffmann, "Chronik und Urkunde," 135. There is an additional medieval copy,
which provides the 1091 date, in a collection of San Pietro Avellana documents copied in 1341.
For discussions, see A. De Francesco, "Origini e sviluppo del feudalismo nel Molise alla caduta
della dominazione normanna," *Archivio storico per le province napoletane* 34 (1909): 668; Dormeier, *Montecassino und die Laien*, 187; and Bloch, *Monte Cassino*, 1:364–66. The donation is
noted in *Chron. Cass.* III xxxix, 416.

107. *Chron. Farf.*, 2:172; Schwarzmaier, "*Liber Vitae* von Subiaco," 122.

108. Lynn Townsend White, Jr., *Latin Monasticism in Norman Sicily* (Cambridge,
Mass.: Mediaeval Academy of America, 1938), 47–54; Von Falkenhausen, "Aspetti storico-
economici dell'età di Roberto il Guiscardo," 128–132; Herbert Houben, "Roberto il Guiscardo e il monachesimo," *Benedictina* 32 (1985): 507, 516–17.

7

Decline and Fall

DOMINIC'S STORY could be read as a tragedy. The enthusiasm he had evoked during his lifetime proved fleeting, and, except in a few small cult centers, he was gradually forgotten. He did not fit into any of the new ecclesiastical categories. Triumphant monastic reformers were educated abbots, grand in the style of Desiderius, or strikingly ascetic hermit preachers, awesome like Peter the Hermit. Now written rules controlled monasteries, and developing canon law governed Christendom. There was little demand for a frontier abbot who followed oral traditions, preached in parish churches, built monastic buildings with his own hands, and acted as a waiter for his guests. Dominic had lived "at that time [when] almost all priests mingled with wives in the manner of laymen."[1] He had fought hard, at least as far as sexual morality was concerned, to separate the clergy from the laity. Yet when a stricter division of clergy and laity triumphed, when theorists and lawyers began to separate out the *vita monastica* from the *vita apostolica*, it undercut his own personal fusion of the roles of hermit, monk, priest, administrator, and popular organizer.

Monastic memory was long, but it was selective, and, even as abbots from the lineage of the counts of Marsica reigned in glory at Monte Cassino, memories of their earlier protégé faded. Dominic was not completely neglected. Monks copied Alberic's *life*, at least in the truncated form here designated the *Monte Cassino Life*. Around 1100 Leo Marsicanus, who had a personal interest in Sora,[2] gave Dominic a single sentence in his chronicle,

---

1. *Trisulti Life* v, 301.
2. Leo's beloved late uncle John had been bishop of Sora (1073–86). Marta and Beranger, "L'Abbazia di S. Domenico in Sora," 196, claim that it was John himself who elevated Dominic's body to the altar in the crypt of San Domenico, but they do not indicate the source of this tradition. On Leo and John, see Hans-Walter Klewitz, "Petrus Diaconus und die Montecassineneser Klosterchronik des Leo von Ostia," *Archiv für Urkundenforschung* 14 (1936): 422–23; Hoffmann, "Der Kalender des Leo Marsicanus," 83–84, 118, 137; and Newton, "Leo Marsicanus and the Dedicatory Text," 186–90, 199–201.

borrowed from one of the *lives* in Alberic's tradition.[3] Leo also inserted Dominic's *obit* into his calendar, written in 1098/1099.[4] From there it was included in the monastery's mid-twelfth-century annals, which may have helped it enter the martyrologies and calendars of central Italy.[5] Yet Dominic's cult was peripheral to Monte Cassino. The monks failed to establish a single "canonical" *Vita Dominici*. They never settled the order of offices for his feast, and, although marks in the surviving Monte Cassino manuscripts indicate that readings were taken from the *Monte Cassino Life*, the hymns were based on a text much closer to the *Sora Life*, one containing some or all of the posthumous miracles. The cult's marginality is confirmed by the fact that, about a decade after Alberic had written his *life* of Dominic, Abbot Desiderius failed to mention Dominic or his miracles in his three books of *Dialogues*, preferring instead to tell stories about monks from Monte Cassino and its dependencies, stable local hermits who stayed in their wildernesses, and priestly reformers such as Leo IX.[6]

After Dominic's death, the monasteries and churches connected with him, even those given over to the megamonasteries, began a sleepy, inexorable decline. His smaller establishments fared worst. Fading into the countryside and leaving few documents behind were Dominic's school, San Silvestro on Monte Subasio; his first monastic home, the monastery of Santa Maria near Scandriglia; his twin monasteries in the province of Chieti; his monasteries and hermitages in the Valley of the Sagiattario; and his oratories associated with the Ottaviani Crescenzi. The Borelli continued to support San Pietro Avellana even after they had donated it to Monte

---

3. *Chron. Cass.* II lix, 283. The sentence on Dominic, bracketed by miscellaneous astronomical observations, echoes the burial notice found in the *Monte Cassino Life* and the *Sora Life*. It is so thoughtless that the city of Sora, which Leo had just mentioned above without any geographical qualifier (*Chron. Cass.* II lv, 283), is here specified, following the wording of the *vitae*, as "in Campania."

4. Hoffmann, "Kalender des Leo Marsicanus," 94–95, 101, and 134.

5. "Annales Casinenses ex Annalibus Montis Casini Antiquis et Continuatis Excerpti," ed. Wilhelm Smidt, MGH *SS* 30 : 1413. A study of Dominic's martyrological tradition remains a *desideratum*. Its solid basis will be the University of Toronto survey of manuscripts written in Beneventan script, directed by Virginia Brown. Dominic's name was frequently included in liturgical texts from his central cult area and even makes isolated appearances in transalpine martyrologies.

6. Desiderius intended to carry on his *Dialogues* further, to have four books like the *Dialogues* of Gregory the Great, a plan described in more detail in Wolf, *Making History*, 72–74. One could speculate that Dominic might perhaps have been included in the fourth book, which was lost or never written, but this is incapable of demonstration and unlikely, given Desiderius's known choice of models.

Cassino, but they found a new patron saint, Amicus of Camerino (d. ca. 1045), a wandering, cave-dwelling hermit who, unlike Dominic, had had the good grace to die near the monastery.[7]

Dominic's larger establishments fared slightly better. San Salvatore at Scandriglia, according to Alberic of Monte Cassino, writing around 1070, had "even today . . . no small number of cenobites." It became one of Farfa's more important possessions. But in an attempt to leaven Farfa's spirituality, it was handed over in the late 1130s to some Cistercian monks, a move whose utter failure is amply documented by the complaints of their prior, Bernard of Pisa (the fiasco did not prevent him from later overseeing even greater debacles as Pope Eugenius III). In 1140 the last descendents of Dominic's counts of Rieti opened a Cistercian monastery on the Rieti plain.[8]

Bitter fighting surrounded San Bartolomeo at Trisulti as citizens of the surrounding towns continually invaded its forests. The *Trisulti Life* already hints at tensions between the *castelli* and the monastery by the ahistorical way it attempts to make all of the *castelli* San Bartolomeo's co-founders and by the care it takes to assert the validity of each of their donations. The townsmen and the monks were soon virtually at war. The condition of the cloister must have been deplored by Innocent III, a native of Segni who had a hunting lodge not far from Dominic's monastery. In 1204 he handed his land and Trisulti's over to the Carthusians, who built a charterhouse that he dedicated in 1211. Although efforts are being made today to identify Trisulti manuscripts, almost all that survive are from the Carthusian era.[9]

7. *Vita Amici* xv–xvii, xix–xxi, xvi, edited in *AS* Nov. 2:96–98.

8. The *Trisulti Life* ii, 283, and the *Valva Life* xxiii–xxxi, 73, comment on the great number of monks Dominic had originally attracted to San Salvatore. When the *Monte Cassino Life* xxviii, 73, and the *Sora Life* xxviii, 39, observe that there were many monks there "even today," this is presumably Alberic's addition, referring to the state of the monastery at the time he wrote, based on information provided by his informants.

Farfa's confirmations of its ownership of San Salvatore include *Reg. Farf.*, 5:95–99, esp. 95 (doc. 1099), and MGH *Dipl. Reg. et Imp.*, 6(2):472–77 (doc. 358); recapitulated in Gregory of Catino, *Chron. Farf.*, 2:173–79. Petra Demone and Scandriglia were given special prayers and protections as their reward for loyalty in time of revolt: see *Reg. Farf.*, 5:317–18 (doc. 1324); used in Gregory of Catino, *Chron. Farf.*, 2:302–4. They were placed among a group of possessions that Farfa's abbots had to swear never to alienate, as described in a decree of Abbot Guido III, preserved in *Reg. Farf.*, ed. 5:313–15 (doc. 1320); also in Gregory of Catino, *Chron. Farf.*, 2:296–300. On the attempt to turn San Salvatore into a Cistercian-style monastic prototype for Farfa, see Schuster, "Il monastero del Salvatore," 40, and *L'imperiale Abbazia di Farfa*, 280–81.

9. On Innocent III's creation of this first charterhouse in the Papal States, see Hogg, "Charterhouse of Trisulti," xiii–xxii. The context is in Brenda M. Bolton, "*Via Ascetica*: A Papal Quandry," in *Monks, Hermits and the Ascetic Tradition: Papers Read at the 1984 Summer*

More dynamism was exhibited by Dominic's monastery at Sora, which developed the panoply of a major pilgrimage center. It is ironic that Dominic, who had little apparent use for relics during his life, amply demonstrated their power after his death. Theatrical miracles occurred at his altar: a goldsmith's possessed wife was cured after being beaten in the church (as part of a ritual?); a slave girl named Carda, who had spent considerable time at San Domenico, fell asleep and was liberated from a demon during High Mass; the withered hand of a boy from the city of Castello was suddenly cured when, while the brothers were singing vespers, he was able to reach out to grab a falling candle.[10] Around Dominic's tomb hung *ex voto* offerings: the spearpoint taken from the hip of a soldier of the count of Segni; the arrowpoint removed from the eye socket of Count Girardus of Sora; and reproductions of body parts made with precious metals, one of which should have been the result of Count Oderisius II's inelegant attempt to commemorate his hernia cure.[11] Candles and other tokens must have been abundant. Present too were living witnesses, supplicants who had been healed and who, after consultation with the abbot, served at the shrine for the rest of their lives.[12] The excited atmosphere is conveyed by the story of the healing of a boy from Sora named Adenulfus:

> The son of Bonutius was a little boy named Adenulfus, whose right side—hand, arm, foot, shin, and thigh—had become paralyzed. Bonutius promised that if Dominic would secure health for his son from the Lord he would give to his holy monastery either wax or oil or some other useful thing equal to the boy's weight, and furthermore would give him to the monks of that holy place if the abbot would be willing to receive him. Dominic's feast day arrived. Bonutius ordered his servants to prepare a tremendous meal so that they could receive poor and needy guests. He himself, taking the boy, hurried to the church dedicated to God in memory of Dominic. At last he reached it. Bonutius situated himself in front of Dominic's im-

---

Meeting and the 1985 Winter Meeting of the Ecclesiastical History Society, Studies in Church History 22 (Oxford: Basil Blackwell, 1985), 161–91. The conflicts between the Trisulti monks and the citizens of the surrounding *castelli* were noted p. 113. On the architectural record, see Giovanni Scaccia Scarafoni, "Un monumento poco notto dell architettura gotica in Italia," *Palladio* n.s. 3 (1953): 115–18; Taglienti, *Certosa di Trisulti*, 41–404; and Giovanni Leoncini, "Arte e architettura alla Certosa di Trisulti," in *La Certosa di Trisulti*, ed. Hogg et al., xcvii–cx. Bibliographical references concerning the Trisulti library are cited in Giulio Battelli, "Un Codice della Certosa di Trisulti recentemente ricuperato (Vallicelliano B 46.)," in *Scire Litteras: Forschungen zum mittelalterlichen Geistesleben*, ed. Sigrid Krämer and Michael Bernhard, Bayerische Akademie der Wissenschaften, Philosophisch-historische Klasse, Abhandlungen n.s. 99 (Munich: Bayerische Akademie der Wissenschaften, 1988), 13–20.

10. *Sora Life* cclvii–cclxi, cclxii–cclxxiv, and cclxxv–cclxxix, 65–66, 67–68, and 68.

11. *Sora Life* cccxxi–cccxxxii, cccxxxiii–cccxliii, and ccclxx–ccclxxviii, 72–73, 73–74, and 75–76. On Oderisius's cure, see p. 105.

12. *Sora Life* cclxxx–ccxci and ccci–cccix, 68–69 and 70–71.

age, and seeing it with bodily eyes, he directed his mind's eyes to him whose image had been made to preserve his memory. He would not stop begging for the health of his son with his whole heart and with deep and frequent groans from within his breast. Meanwhile the boy asked his father if he could climb up onto his neck, saying he wanted to kiss more distant parts of the image being contemplated. Held up on his father's neck, the boy tried to stretch forth each arm to embrace the statue: his left arm, the healthy one, he held out strongly; his right reached with an uncertain and tremulous effort, while his father was calling out loudly again and again the name of Dominic. What else is there to say? The boy grasped the statue with each hand, holding very tightly in his embrace the farther parts of the image he was kissing. And from that hour, the strength of the boy's former health returned to his hand, arm, foot, shin, and thigh. All along the road going home, he was throwing little sticks, this way and that, with the hand which he had not been able to lift to his mouth.[13]

Dominic's cult center was soon graced by a splendid basilica.[14] Its local importance must have increased after it survived the Norman raid of 1103, which destroyed seven churches in Sora proper, and after its consecration by Pope Paschal II on 22 August 1104.[15] Despite this preeminence, San Domenico's monastic community remained undistinguished, its abbots obscure.[16] Although throughout the twelfth-century popes continued to confirm the privileges and properties of the monks,[17] in 1222 Honorius III evicted them, damning them for "living dissolutely, and fattening themselves prodigally upon the goods of the monastery, so that all regular observance had been annulled there and it was like a den of dragons (cf. Isaiah 34:13), and a scandal to many."[18] Were these "scandals" a new collapse of

13. *Sora Life* cclxxx–cxc, 68–69. Jean-Marie Sansterre, "Un saint récent et son icône dans Latium méridional au XIe siècle: A propos d'un miracle de Dominique de Sora," *Byzantinoslavica* 56 (1995): 447–52, draws attention to Byzantine aspects of this story, but I do not follow him in assuming that the words used here to designate the effigy, "ycona" and "imago," necessarily mean a two-dimensional icon in the Greek sense, since the narrative gives the impression of three dimensions, of a cult statue the furthest parts of which Adenulfus had to reach out to grasp. A cult statue the shrine did cherish was destroyed by Napoleon's soldiers—see Luigi Loffredo, *San Domenico di Sora e i luoghi natali di Cicerone* (Casamari [Frosinone]: Edizioni "Terra Nostra," 1981), 69–71.

14. Marta and Beranger, "L'Abbazia di S. Domenico in Sora," 193–210, esp. 198–210.

15. *Annales Ceccanenses* 1103, 1104, ed. Georg Heinrich Pertz, MGH SS 19:281. On the papal consecration of San Domenico, see Carlo Servatius, *Paschalis II. (1099–1118): Studien zu seiner Person und seiner Politik*, Päpste und Papsttum 14 (Stuttgart: Anton Hiersemann, 1979), 99, who relates it to other efforts made by Paschal II to establish his power south of Rome.

16. The disappointingly short list of known abbots is given in Giuseppe Pierleoni, "Per la storia della Badia di S. Domenico di Sora," *Per Cesare Baronio: Scritti vari nei terzo centenario della sua morte* (Rome: Società Editrice Romana, 1911), 661.

17. Papal letters supporting San Domenico are listed in Kehr, *Italia Pontificia*, 8:102–4; and in Antonelli, *Abbazie . . . di Sora*, 222–31.

18. See p. 124n.

standards? Or was part of the problem the loose customary observance of the *Rule* that Dominic had originally instituted? His Benedictines were replaced by the Cistercians of Casamari, who turned the monastery into a priory.

On the material level, Casamari, a daughter house of San Domenico, was the most conspicuous exception to this general tale of monastic woe. It had benefitted early from generous donations.[19] It became extremely wealthy thanks to a location on the coastal plain that had good access to mountain pastures.[20] In the 1140s Eugenius III, citing internal problems and war damage, transferred it to his fellow Cistercians.[21] In 1217 Pope Honorius III brought the whole papal court to dedicate Casamari's new basilica, a building he himself had helped to finance.[22] An additional instance of his support was the 1222 donation of San Domenico mentioned immediately above. Casamari continued to flourish, and even today directs a lively Cistercian subfamily.

Yet prosperous Cistercian Casamari may not have accurately reflected all aspects of Dominic's original monastic ideals. This is suggested by the results of a visit made by Abbot Joachim of Fiore (d. 1202). In a remote sense, Joachim was a spiritual "great grandson" of Dominic (he was abbot of Corazzo, a daughter house of Sambucina, which was a daughterhouse of Casamari, which was authorized by San Domenico). Joachim, debating in 1183–84 whether or not he and Corazzo should affiliate with the Cistercians, accepted Casamari's hospitality. There on Holy Saturday, he had a vision that revealed to him the concord between the Old and New Testaments, an intellectual breakthrough he quickly expressed in the *Concordia Utriusque Testamenti*, the *Expositio ad Apocalypsim*, and the beginning of the *Psalterium Decem Chordarum*. At Casamari he conducted himself so edifyingly that he received a biography from its prior, the future bishop Luke of Cosenza (d. 1224). Yet Joachim—who, in a manner recalling Dominic, preferred to reside on mountaintop hermitages, serve guests, tend the sick with his own hands, and even clean monastic buildings himself—ultimately concluded that Casamari and other Cistercian houses

---

19. Documents cited in Toubert, *Structures*, 2:890; some edited in Farina and Fornari, *Storia e documenti . . . di Casamari*, 117–49.

20. Luigi de Benedetti, *Vita economica dell'Abbazia di Casamari dalle origini al secolo XIX*, Collana di monografie economiche 1 (Frosinone: Camera di Commercio industria agricoltura, 1952), 1–12; Toubert, *Structures*, 1:235 and 272, 2:903.

21. See p. 124n.

22. Jane E. Sayers, *Papal Government during the Pontificate of Honorius III (1216–1227)*, Cambridge Studies in Medieval Life and Thought, 3rd ser., 21 (New York: Cambridge University Press, 1984), 9.

were too rich, too greedy, too involved in the world. He decided to make his prophetic stand at Fiore in the Sila mountains. The charisma that Dominic embodied was no longer obvious at his most successful monastic offshoot.[23]

Dominic's most significant monastic impact, unfortunately, may have been the indirect role he played in the downfall of Monte Cassino. After his death the lineage of counts of Marsica, which he had expertly schooled in ecclesiastical patronage, took over that ancient house. Monte Cassino's fortunes plummeted. In the eleventh century two of its abbots had become popes; in the twelfth three were deposed by popes. In the days of Alberic the Rhetorician and Leo Marsicanus, Monte Cassino may have been the most distinguished intellectual center in Europe; by the mid-twelfth century its preeminent scholar was Peter the Deacon, a forger desperately trying to enhance his own and his monastery's prestige. Lay lords no longer donated lavishly. In a world increasingly dominated by the white monks, Monte Cassino had become an anachronism.

How did this happen? Monte Cassino's successes had been based on a fragile cosmopolitanism. Normally the *Terra Sancta Benedicti* was not one of the world's most sophisticated regions. In fact, Monte Cassino's culture in late Carolingian times, lacking full contact with the universal world of that empire, had been notoriously parochial.[24] The mentality of Southern Italy in the tenth century, and of Monte Cassino in particular, is exemplified by the conservative, pretentious Salernitan Chronicle, whose author still lived in the shadow of Paul the Deacon.[25] Hagiographical ideals remained those of the desert fathers and of Gregory I.[26] Then Monte Cassino

23. Joachim's visit to Casamari is discussed in Stephen Wessley, "'Bonum Est Benedicto Mutare Locum': The Role of the 'Life of St. Benedict' in Joachim of Fiore's Monastic Reform," *Revue bénédictine* 90 (1980): 318–19 and 322; *Joachim of Fiore and Monastic Reform*, American University Studies, ser. 7, 72 (New York: Peter Lang, 1990), 5, 9, 31, and 84; and Robert E. Lerner, "Ecstatic Dissent," *Speculum* 67 (1992): 33–57, esp. 38–40. On his ambivalence about the Cistercians, see Wessley, *Joachim of Fiore and Monastic Reform*, 81–93.

24. Claudio Leonardi, "La cultura cassinese al tempo di Bertario," in *Montecassino dalla prima alla seconda distruzione*, 317–29.

25. For the mentality of the Lombard intellectual milieu, see Cilento, *Italia meridionale longobarda*, 62–64; "La storiografia nell'Italia meridionale," in *La storiografia altomedievale: Atti del XVII Settimane di studio del CISAM (Spoleto, 10–16 aprile 1969*, 2 vols. (Spoleto: CISAM, 1970), 2:521–56.

26. A comprehensive study of the contents of books used for spiritual reading in the world of Monte Cassino remains a *desideratum*. Some seem frightfully conservative. Note, for example, the prominence of the saints of the *vitae patrum* in the cluster of related Beneventan lectionaries from the eleventh and twelfth centuries described in the first volume of Jean Mallet and André Thibaut, *Les manuscrits en écriture bénéventaine de la Bibliothèque capitulaire de Bénévent*, 1–vols., Documents, études et répertoires publiés par l'Institut de recherche et d'histoire des textes (Paris: Éditions du Centre national de la recherche scientifique, 1984).

became more involved in a wider world of competition among Latin and Greek emperors, papal reformers, and various noble factions. Stimulated by and exploiting these rivalries, eleventh-century Monte Cassino was able to produce a splendid Greco-Latin physical plant, an excellent library, the Desiderian *scriptorium*, and great learning. That its achievements were triumphs of ecclectic borrowing is obvious from its library books, its manuscript illuminations, and the diverse backgrounds of the men who became its abbots.

The counts of Marsica upset this delicate balance. The descendents of Berardus the Frank came from a notoriously retrograde region characterized by support of antipopes and private ownership of churches. On occasion the family could produce ecclesiastical heroes. Bishop Pandulfus of Marsica has been alleged to have helped introduce canonical reform into rural central Italy.[27] The reign of Abbot Oderisius I of Monte Cassino has often been rated highly. Bishop Berardus of Marsica provided a clear model of Gregorian activism (although his most-cited accomplishment was to organize local bishops into a united front in order to jointly excommunicate one of his relatives, a count of Marsica).[28] The descendents of Berardus the Frank damaged Monte Cassino not because they were bad but because the pool from which its abbots could be selected had been reduced to them alone.

The deleterious results are illustrated by comparing the reigns of Desiderius and of Oderisius II, the proud scion of the counts of Sangro whom Honorius II derided as a "knight" and deposed for "pride." [29] Desiderius, late in life, embarked on his own personal study of grammar and rhetoric; Oderisius II derided Pope Honorius II for being "full of letters from his head to his feet." [30] Desiderius commissioned the exquisite Byzantine pan-

---

Even during its "golden age," Monte Cassino's most ambitious hagiographical project was Desiderius's *Dialogues*, which only advanced Gregory the Great's *Dialogues* chronologically. See Loud, *Church and Society in . . . Capua*, 73.

27. Toubert, *Structures*, 2:841 and 845, is quick to hail Pandulfus as the pioneer of the *disciplina canonica* in the 1050s, basing this judgment on a passage in the *Vita Berardi* (*BHL* 1176), edited in *AS* Nov. 2(1):895, written about eighty years later. Yet this is not a disinterested tradition inasmuch as Pandulfus was not only the mentor of Berardus but also his great-uncle.

28. *Vita Berardi*, edited in *AS* Nov 2(1):899, the significance of which is stressed in Toubert, *Structures*, 2:837–39.

29. *Chron. Cass.* IV lxxxvi and lxxxviii, 547–50. On the personality conflicts involved here, see Tellenbach, "Der Sturz des Abtes Pontius," 38, reprinted in his *Ausgewählte Abhandlungen*, 4:1049; Hoffmann, "Petrus Diaconus," 75–80; and Bloch, *Monte Cassino*, 2:960–62.

30. *Chron. Cass.* IV lxxxiii, 546. Yet *Chron. Cass.* IV lxxviii, 542, claims that Oderisius II was "trained in the liberal arts."

els of angels and saints for the bronze doors of his new basilica; Oderisius II reversed the panels to create blanks for lists of his monastery's castles and properties, a blazon of feudal power at the entrance to the house of God.[31] The adroit diplomacy of Desiderius had enabled eleventh-century Monte Cassino to survive and even prosper during the dangerous triumph of the Normans; Oderisius II and other arrogant abbots of the twelfth century displayed little finesse in their losing battles with popes and Norman kings.

Marsican control was not limited to the abbacy. In distributing offices, the abbots did not slight their relatives. Oderisius I made his distant cousin Berardus, son of Oderisius Borrellus, advocate and defender of all Monte Cassino's property in the county of Sangro (and of some in Valva); he limited the monastery's right to alienate these lands to any other secular lord.[32] This way of delegating monastic patrimony was Oderisius's personal innovation.[33] Family control is hinted at by the names of some monastic officials. For example, after Oderisius II, who was descended from the Borrelli, had laboriously taken the Rocca d'Arce from the counts of Aquino in 1122, the subsequent castellans whose names are known are a Marius Burrellus in 1155 and a Borrellus in 1191.[34] Another example of nepotism was Simon the Subdeacon, a former monk of Monte Cassino, "de genere filiorum Burrelli de Sangro," the man who persuaded Eugenius III to try to enforce Peter the Deacon's Glanfeuil forgeries, a man who, as Bloch has demonstrated, was related to Abbot Rainaldus of Monte Cassino.[35] Such sinecures were probably especially valued because this was a time when Marsican secular power was waning.[36] The consequences of such appointments were not good. Even Peter the Deacon recognized that monastic organization had deteriorated once the generation of priors appointed by Desiderius had died out, an event he dates to the end of the reign of Girardus (d. 1123).[37]

In 1143, the year when Monte Cassino's treasury was carried off by

31. Bloch, *Monte Cassino*, 1:465–94.

32. *Reg. Petri Diac.* fol. 257r (no. 628), edited in de Francesco, "Origini . . . del feudalismo nel Molise," 670; described in Hoffmann, "Chronik und Urkunde," 145. For other pledges of fidelity in return for property from *Borrelli* relatives of Oderisius, see de Francesco, "Origini . . . del feudalismo nel Molise," 668–69.

33. Grégoire, "Le Mont-Cassin dans la réforme," 52.

34. Hoffmann, "Petrus Diaconus," 68–70. On the location, see Bloch, *Monte Cassino*, 2:728.

35. Bloch, *Monte Cassino*, 2:995–96.

36. Sennis, "Potere centrale e forze locali," 64–68.

37. *Chron. Cass.* IV xciv, 555.

King Roger of Sicily, the monastery was ruled by Rainaldus II (1137–66), "of the most noble race of the Marsican counts." To him Peter the Deacon dedicated Monte Cassino's chronicle. Its narrative ends right after Rainaldus's inauguration, with an account of how the aged monk Albert, who had come from the area of Sulmona, told of a vision in which count Crescentius of the Marsi was being tortured by demons because he had not returned a large silver thurible that he had acquired from Monte Cassino as a pledge during the abbacy of Seniorectus.[38] As the lights go out, the last message from Monte Cassino is that members of the lineage of the counts of Marsica should take care to regularize their affairs with the abbey. Nothing beside remains. Instead of metamorphosing into a new role, as did the monks of Cluny under the scholar abbot Peter the Venerable, the monks of Monte Cassino disappear into provincial obscurity.

Dominic's story could be read as a tragedy. His work as a monastic contractor for predatory aristocrats enhanced their status and cohesion; it refined their skills at ecclesiastical patronage. Although Dominic recognized and rebuked their faults, he did not hesitate to accept their donations. After his death, as his own fame faded, his patrons were able to trade up their properties, including family monasteries he had built for them, for ecclesiastical power that included the biggest prize of all, the monastery of Monte Cassino. He could never have envisioned this triumph or its disastrous results.

But yet, despite the unintended consequences, Dominic had helped to create something new. He had reshaped the wild countryside through which he traveled. His little monasteries on the edges of the *castelli*, his Christianizing of mountains, caves, and ultimately even snake handling, helped bring into existence a world recognizable a millennium later. Although his own Benedictine affiliations have been swept away, the hilltop villages remain along with a few of his churches, hermitages, and fragmented foundations. And somehow he remains. In the drizzle of his feast on 22 January, as snow powders the mountains above Sora, members of the local youth group sing like angels while Dominic's followers, crowded into the basilica of San Domenico, kiss his statue and rub off dust to protect themselves from snake and dog bites. In spring, busloads of pilgrims brave the terrifying roads to Santissima Trinità and gaze in awe at the sheared

---

38. *Chron. Cass.* IV cxxix, 606–7.

rocks of the glacial canyon below. On the first Thursday of May, curious teenagers drive out from Rome to Cocullo, a *castello* now suddenly accessible and prosperous thanks to Autostrada 23. These would-be *serpari*, who know little about Angizia or Christ, seem to sense in Dominic's fascinating mixture of party, piety, and horror a lost dimension, a spiritual ghost limb that still twinges.

Conclusion

A CASE STUDY ought to suggest general hypotheses. Yet Dominic and his patrons are unique, so rooted in the central Italian countryside that it is impossible to imagine them anyplace else. What then can be learned from their monastic adventures and misadventures? Perhaps their very uniqueness. The concept of the "Gregorian Reform" presupposes a Roman center spreading its norms outward by means of papal power and canon law. Yet despite sporadic reform efforts, Rome seems relatively uninfluential in the decades before Leo IX. Thus it is surprising to find some of the themes we associate with the Gregorian Reform already animating Dominic's career: the ecclesiastical building programs, the enthusiastic crowds, the calls to conversion, the attacks on womanizing clerics and on gratuitous violence. All these express a fierce desire to reach out and convert the world. Before there was a center, there was reform, albeit local, popular, messy, frequently disorganized, and put to a variety of uses by different factions and groups. Lay persons, hermits, monks, bishops, nobles, emperors, and popes were all involved, sometimes in contradictory ways. Obviously, no single case study, such as this introduction to Dominic and his patrons, can fully illuminate early reform efforts. But neither can any artificial dichotomy such as Tellenbach's neat division between monastic and Gregorian reform.

Dominic's ecclesiastical activity, like that of other early reformers, was concrete and physical. He built churches, coerced the clergy into non-lay lifestyles, and ministered and preached to large crowds. His hermitages and monasteries witnessed to God in awesome natural locations. This emphasis on the material world reflects the concrete realities of reform: grubby accumulation of ecclesiastical property would make possible the intellectual and spiritual achievements of later generations. Property donations and church building were associated with the increase of arable land, greater exploitation of waste land, and radical restructuring of society that, in its

Italian context, is described as encastellation. Dominic of Sora and his colleagues flourished in the neighborhoods of the *castelli*.

Dominic's story suggests that scholars should pay more attention to charismatic figures. He did not so much teach doctrine as model it. Despite references in his *lives* to the Benedictine *Rule*, and despite Alberic's glosses on the learning of Dominic's appointees, his community seems to have been centered less on any text than on him. He caught the popular imagination by his own personal rendition of *sanctitas*. He was not alone. Thoughout Italy, and indeed throughout northern Europe, the late tenth and early eleventh centuries featured a significant crop of new saints, popular figures who drew communities to themselves. In Italy the generation that included Nilus, Romuald, and Dominic had charismatic leaders. Their qualities can still be seen in Gregory VII, but by the end of his life he was an anachronism. His world had come to be dominated by men such as John Gualbertus, Desiderius of Monte Cassino, and Anselm of Bec, men who, after attempting to become hermits in their youth, ultimately became administrators, organizers, and systematizers. They had inherited the enthusiasm for change and reform of an earlier generation, but their genius, and the genius of the later reformers in general, was to refine and develop these ideas, to work out their implications, to discover ways to implement them on a grander scale. This progression is not unusual. When Max Weber distinguished between individual and institutional charisma, he implied that the former came first; that subsequent generations, lacking charismatic leaders, would attempt to institutionalize divine authority through offices and regulations. Additional studies of early reformers are needed in order to see whether what has traditionally been seen as *the* Gregorian Reform was actually only the last stage of the great millennial reform movement.

To study the early stages of reform requires paying more attention to events in Italy. Of course, anyone who still defines reform primarily in terms of high politics will hesitate to seek its antecedents in early eleventh-century Italy, a world featuring the oft-disparaged Tuscolaner popes, insecure imperial bishops, and great abbots with great problems. Judging from Dominic's story, however, scholars ought to look harder at what was happening just below the highest levels. The comital nobility and their increasingly obtrusive subordinates had their own ideals and goals. The *castelli* and cities of central Italy, defying Toubert's seigneural model, were also players in the game of ecclesiastical patronage, perhaps aping their noble betters but involved all the same. Ecclesiastical leaders such as Dominic would have helped generate the local enthusiasm for reform that would later be vital to the Roman reform party. Such matters cannot be comprehended by traditional transalpine historical perspectives.

Perhaps the most significant lesson from the story of Dominic and his patrons, however, is that studies of ecclesiastical reform must be grounded in social history. Reforms depended on reforming communities. Group movements, paradoxically, not only enable reforms to succeed but also ultimately limit that success. Failure to recognize this leads to the sort of scholarly myopia evident in the contemporary historiography on the downfall of Monte Cassino. Scholars have tried to explain its decline in terms of the global model of a "crisis of Western Monasticism," or of a triumph of newer reform ideologies such as an increased intolerance of monastic wealth and exemptions, or as a result of particular political shifts that might have undercut the monastery's position. These are significant perspectives, but the changes of the early twelfth century were not necessarily more dramatic than those of the eleventh, when Monte Cassino prospered despite tremendous spiritual, ideological, and political upheavals. Why did the monastery lack the leadership to meet new challenges? Scholars need to look not only at abstractions but also at people. Who controlled Monte Cassino? What faction was behind Odersius II and other disastrous abbots? The unexpected and tragic consequences of the way that Dominic's patronage network survived both him and his system, leading ultimately to Marsican domination of Monte Cassino, should provide a caution to ecclesiastical historians. Reforms inhere in people, particularly in people with power enough to make a difference. Their vision, or lack of it, is what finally matters.

Appendices

Appendix A: Dominic's Dossier

The "Introduction" outlines the interrelationships among Dominic's *lives, miracles, sermon*, and hymns. Its reconstruction differs somewhat from the recently published analyses by Dolbeau and Franklin cited there. They themselves disagree on several points. This is not surprising, because in cases such as this where texts are mutually interrelated, influenced by oral traditions, and preserved in late imperfect copies, alternative reconstructions are possible. Debates involve questions of relative probability rather than of absolute certainty.

A reason for some of the divergences is that I have approached this dossier asking historical as well as philological questions. I am willing to draw tentative conclusions about the original form of a name or statement by bringing in additional information from external historical sources, to hazard the assumption that Dominic's records probably originally presented the more correct forms, and to make judgments from this about the relative order of the texts. In this appendix, I express the apparent interrelationships of the texts in the form of a *stemma*, briefly explain how each text came to placed in its position there, and then attempt to date the texts insofar as this is possible.

The lost first written *life* of Dominic would have been composed from oral traditions. Although no previous analyses of the dossier have presented rationales for localizing this hypothetical text, there are strong reasons for believing that its author was connected with San Bartolomeo at Trisulti. All the surviving comprehensive *lives*, even those written to reflect the aims of other cult centers, contain traces of the story of the guiding angel who led Dominic to Trisulti and ordered him to found San Bartolomeo, a unique privileging of that monastery that fits its interests.[1] The only mir-

---

1. Angelic guidance in Trisulti's foundation is suggested in the *Trisulti Life* vi–xxii, 284–92; *Valva Life* liv–lv, 75; *Monte Cassino Life* liv–lv, 75; and *Sora Life* lxiii–lxv, 43–44. The only other establishment with similar claims in Dominic's dossier is the oratory on Monte Cacume, which the *Trisulti Life* xi, 286, uniquely specifies that Dominic founded when "admonished

Dominic's Hagiographic Memorials and Their Interrelationships.

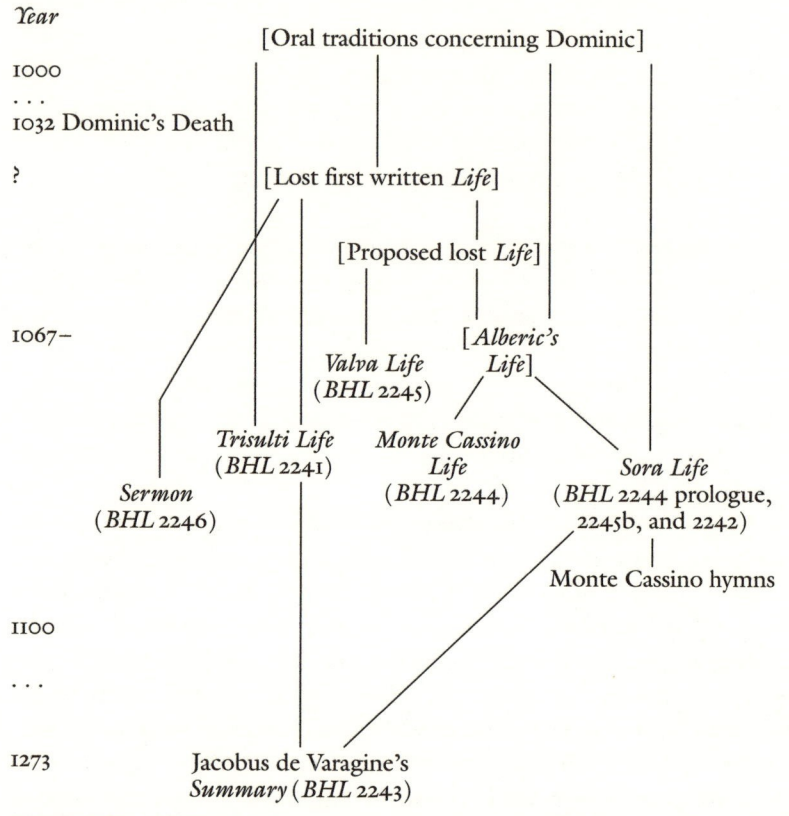

Year

[Oral traditions concerning Dominic]

1000

. . .

1032 Dominic's Death

?   [Lost first written *Life*]

[Proposed lost *Life*]

1067–   [*Alberic's*
                                    Valva Life   Life*]
                                    (*BHL* 2245)

                    Trisulti Life   Monte Cassino
                    (*BHL* 2241)   Life   Sora Life
        Sermon   (*BHL* 2244)   (*BHL* 2244 prologue,
        (*BHL* 2246)   2245b, and 2242)

                                                        Monte Cassino hymns

1100

. . .

1273   Jacobus de Varagine's
            Summary (*BHL* 2243)

acle story common to all the major *lives*—the healing of a fevered boy
named Leo from the city that was called "Castrum"—involves a location
in the immediate neighborhood of Trisulti.[2] Moreover, the priority of the
San Bartolomeo literary tradition is supported by negative evidence. The
prologue to the *Sora Life* specifies that it had been commissioned to replace a known preexisting *life* that it excoriates as "severely defective and

by an angel." This could be a deliberate attempt to make its foundation parallel Trisulti's,
since it appears to have been a Trisulti dependency, built by Dominic while he was based there.
    2. Leo from Castro is featured in the *Trisulti Life* xiii, 287; *Valva Life* xv, 74–75; *Monte
Cassino Life* xv, 74–75; and *Sora Life* lvii–lix, 42. That last *vita*, reacting to an earlier "defective" *life*, protests all too defensively that this and other miracles it describes really took place
while Dominic was still dwelling at San Pietro in Lago. Nevertheless, it still relays Leo's origin
at Castro. "Castrum" was one of the *castelli* involved in the founding of San Bartolomeo (see
p. 50). Thus the anecdote seems to have originated in Trisulti's milieu.

mendacious," words indicating that it was not at all to the liking of the community near Sora and therefore, presumably, not written there. If the original *life* was not from San Domenico, then the most likely alternative would be Dominic's next most important center, the community at which he had lived the longest, San Bartolomeo at Trisulti.

The *Sermon* on Dominic (*BHL* 2246) consists of several paragraphs of a *life* interpolated with moralizing digressions. It covers only Dominic's early years. Dolbeau dismisses it as a text "without any value," amplifying some extracts of *BHL* 2241 and Alberic's work; he places it at the end of Dominic's eleventh-century dossier.[3] Franklin argues, on the contrary, that since its source shared features with different branches of the surviving *lives*, it might have been the original version itself or at least a close relative.[4] My research offers some support to Franklin. Alone among the surviving early texts, the *Sermon* correctly locates Dominic's birthplace in the province of Spoleto, following what appears to have been the original Trisulti tradition, and in regard to the confused forms of the name of San Silvestro on Monte Subasio, the *Sermon* reads more accurately than any other text in the dossier.[5] The only known copy is in a late eleventh- or early twelfth-century collection of hagiography, sermons, and homilies, today Monte Cassino ms. 146, which Francis Newton, the leading student of the Monte Cassino *scriptoria* of this period, attributes to a southern Italian provincial center, not to Monte Cassino itself.[6]

The *Trisulti Life* (*BHL* 2241) must be a product of San Bartolomeo at Trisulti, since its author dwells on that house's rights and privileges, situates most of Dominic's miracles there, and once, while describing the way crowds in that region responded to Dominic, almost seems to involve him-

---

3. Dolbeau, "Dossier de Saint Dominique," 11, and personal communication, 11 April 1994.

4. Franklin, "Restored *Life and Miracles*," 329–36.

5. See pp. 24 and 29–30 above. In theory, a well-informed scribe from the Foligno region could have reintroduced correct geographical information into a derivative text. Yet no such intervention need be postulated if one accepts the *Sermon* as a truncated witness to a source that embodied a somewhat earlier, more correct stage of the tradition than that found in the surviving *lives*.

6. Monte Cassino ms. 146, 431–35, is described in *Bibliotheca Casinensis*, 3:295–301; Mauro Inguanez, *Codicum Casinensium Manuscriptorum Catalogus Cura et Studio Monachorum S. Benedicti Archicoenobii*, 3 vols. (Monte Cassino: Ex Typographia Casinensi, 1925–41), 1:232–34; Faustino Avagliano, "I codici liturgici dell'Archivio di Montecassino," *Benedictina* 17 (1970): 308; Loew, *Beneventan Script*, 2nd ed., 2:72; and Franklin, "Restored *Life and Miracles*," 329–36. Franklin, 329, cites Francis Newton's judgement, made on the basis of decorative elements, that Monte Cassino ms. 146 was not written at Monte Cassino itself but somewhere in its ambient. This hypothesis would help explain how the *Sermon* came to be based on a *life* of Dominic different from those copied at Monte Cassino.

self, slipping into the first person as he tells how they were "singing and offering praises to God, because we merited to have such an overlord and defender in our homeland."[7] The surviving copies present a text whose closing paragraphs appear to have undergone alterations, including the addition of a dubious colophon identifying the author as Dominic's longtime disciple, John.[8] It is known by way of a transcript made in 1597 by a priest of Anagni, copied for two famous hagiographical collectors, Antonio Gallonio (d. 1605)[9] and Constantino Gaetani (d. 1650).[10]

7. *Trisulti Life*, passim, esp. xvii, 289.

8. Suspicion attaches to *Trisulti Life* xxxiii–xxxv, 297–98. This section presents an anachronistic chronological summary of Dominic's career, misdates Dominic's death by seventy years, and claims that the *life* was written by "John, a sinner, who was Dominic's daily disciple and companion," an attribution hard to reconcile with John's role as a source for Alberic's hostile competing *life*. Lentini, "La 'Vita S. Dominici,'" 60–61, itemizes the verbal and stylistic incongruities of the final colophon. There is also a very speculative *argumentum ex silentio* that might be used to attack it: in 1273, when Jacobus de Voragine went to Trisulti and paraphrased the *life* of Dominic that he found there, he appears to have worked from a text identical, except for minor variants, to the *Trisulti Life*, which he summarizes closely except that he does not present the dubious closing paragraph (cf. Bibl. Aless. ms. 91, fol. 353r).

9. Bibl. Vall. ms. H. 12 is one of twenty volumes of hagiographical texts assembled from 1585 on by Antonio Gallonio. Gallonio is a controversial figure, known not only as a hagiographer who wanted to create a project along the lines of the later *AS*, but also as an *éminence grise* too closely associated with Philip Neri. There is an unpublished biographical memorial in *Le Vite . . . de Padri e Fratelli della Congregatione dell'Oratoria*, 3 vols., Bibl. Vall. mss. 0.58–60, 1:fols. 301–312v, which is much more flattering than the hostile treatment in Antonio Cistellini, *San Filippo Neri: L'Oratorio e la Congregazione Oratoriana. Storia e spiritualità*, 3 vols. (Brescia: Editrice Morcelliana, 1989), 1:409, 522, 701, 730–31, and 762; 2:778, 781–86, 790–93, 810, 878, 910–911, 947, 1094, 1167–72, 1262, 1333, 1362–65, 1403; and 3:2130. Gallonio's copy of the *Trisulti Life*, ms. H. 12, fols. 71–78v, ends with the announcement that "Ego D. Johannes Ineus presbyter cathedralis Anagniensis ecclesiae scribebam festo Pentecostes die 25 maii 1597." The manuscript is noted in Albert Poncelet, *Cat. Cod. Hag. Lat. Rom.*, 431; and Dolbeau, "Le dossier de saint Dominique," 8.

10. Bibl. Aless. ms. 91, a volume in a hagiographical collection assembled by Constantino Gaetani, contains the *Trisulti Life* on fols. 326–37v (this copy also includes the 1597 postscript). It is described in Henrico Narducci, *Catalogus Codicum Manuscriptorum praeter Orientales Qui in Bibliotheca Alexandrina Romae Adservantur* (Rome: F. Bocca, 1887), 24; and in Poncelet, *Cat. Cod. Hag. Lat. Rom.*, 135–43, esp. 139.

This work is the ultimate source of the Bollandist edition of the *Trisulti Life*. The nineteenth-century editors had found a copy of Gaetani's manuscript "in . . . schedis majorum nostrum supplementa ad diem 22 januarii continentibus" (p. 298). This copy was apparently lost in the course of the editing process: see Dolbeau, "Le dossier de saint Dominique," 8, and Franklin, "Restored *Life and Miracles*," 290.

The career of Gaetani is described in considerable detail in José Ruysschaert, "Constantino Gaetano, O. S. B., Chasseur de manuscrits. Contribution à l'histoire de trois bibliothèques romaines du XVIIe s: L'*Aniciana*, l'*Alessandrina*, et la *Chigi*," in *Mélanges Eugène Tisserant*, 7 vols., Studi e Testi 231–37 (Vatican City: BAV, 1964), 7:261–319; Ruysschaert, "Trois notes pour une biographie du bénédictin Constantino Gaetano (1568–1650)," *Benedictina* 21 (1974): 215–23; and Dante Balboni, "L'Abate Constantino Gaetani (1568–1650), editore delle opere di S. Pier Damiani (1606–40)," in *Ascetica cristiana e ascetica giansenista e quietista nelle regioni d'influenza avellanita: Atti del I convegno del Centro di Studi Avellaniti, Fonte Avellana 1977* (Fonte Avellana: Centro di Studi Avellaniti, 1978), 110–25.

The *Valva Life* (*BHL* 2245), never edited in its own right, deserves more attention. It contains material found in both the Trisulti and Monte Cassino traditions.[11] Dolbeau thought it derived from the *Monte Cassino Life*, with some interpolations from the *Trisulti Life*; Franklin inclined toward postulating a lost common ancestor.[12] My research offers some support to Franklin. A heretofore unrecognized mutual borrowing from Gregory I's *Dialogues* is rendered more accurately in the *Valva Life* than in the Monte Cassino texts.[13] The *Valva Life* consistently lacks Alberic's rhetorical flourishes—either its author systematically and successfully excised them or, perhaps a simpler proposition, his source was a version of the text that predated Alberic's reworking.[14] Some name forms in the *Valva Life* may be closer to those that would have been found in the original *life* than to those in the Monte Cassino tradition.[15] The manuscripts include two witnesses that could be as early as the eleventh century. One is in a collec-

11. Parallel readings between the *Valva Life* and the *Trisulti Life* are indicated as divergences to the *Monte Cassino Life* in Lentini's edition; more detailed comparisons are in Dolbeau, "Dossier de saint Dominique," 26, and Franklin, "Restored *Life and Miracles*," 320–21.

12. Dolbeau, "Le dossier de saint Dominique," 25; Franklin, "Restored *Life and Miracles*," 321–22.

13. Compare Gregory I, *Dialog.* II i viii, 2:136 ("a multis frequentari coepisset, qui cum ei cibos deferrent corporis, ab eius ore in suo pectore alimenta referebant vitae"), with *Valva Life* xix–xxii, 72 ("coepit a plurimis frequentari, qui dum ei vitae deferrent temporalis subsidia, vitae ab eo referebant perpetuae alimenta"); *Monte Cassino Life* xxii, 72, and *Sora Life* xxii, 38 ("coeperuntque [*Sora* adds "itaque"] eum illorum plurimi, vitae ipsi temporalis deferentes subsidia, frequenter revisere, atque ex eius ore ad perennis vitae cupidinem animos accendentia eloquia intenti audire"). The *Valva Life* offers language intermediate between Gregory and the Monte Cassino tradition. Yet one hesitates to claim it as the source of the latter, because the Alberician texts' "ex eius ore" is closer to Gregory's "ab eius ore" than is the Valva tradition's "ab eo." The evidence suggests a common ancestor rather than direct dependence.

14. In comparison to passages that can be clearly attributed to Alberic because they are shared by the *Monte Cassino Life* and the *Sora Life*, the *Valva Life* offers a simpler, plainer version. It locates Dominic's birthplace in "Tuscia," the more expected name for the duchy of Tuscany, not in "Hetruria," which is presumably an archaism by Alberic (compare *Valva Life* xi, 71, with *Monte Cassino Life*, ibid., and *Sora Life* xi, 36). It lacks the learned etymology for "Petra Daemonis" that is found in the Monte Cassino texts (compare *Valva Life* xv–xvii, 72, with *Monte Cassino Life* xv, 72, and *Sora Life* xv, 37). It lacks the sequence of parallel clauses describing Dominic's monastic way of life (compare *Valva Life* xviii, 72, with *Monte Cassino Life* xvii, 72, and *Sora Life* xvii, 37). Finally, it lacks the tag from Horace (compare *Valva Life* xxiii–xxxi, 73, with *Monte Cassino Life* xxiii, 73, and *Sora Life* xxiii, 38).

15. In regard to the name of Dominic's monastery at Petra Demone, the *Valva Life*, which gives "in monasterio quodam Sanctae Dei genetricis Mariae," is closer to the *Trisulti Life*'s "[in] monasterio sanctae Dei genetricis et virginis Mariae" than to the Monte Cassino tradition, which omits "Mariae" (see p. 34). Since there is a probable parallel with the name of Farfa, the inclusion of Mary is almost certainly correct.

The counts of Valva who patronized Dominic are not named in all texts. The *Trisulti Life* iii, 283, gives no names; the *Valva Life* xxxv, 74, says generically that they were the "comites terrae illius"; yet *Monte Cassino Life* xxxv, 74, and *Sora Life* xxxviii, 40, following Alberic's information from the foundation charter he cites, are able to identify them. The *Valva Life*, therefore, appears closer to the original ignorance.

tion of saints' *lives* written in Beneventan script that was given to the Vatican Library in 1580 by the canons of Corfinio in Valva, whose corporate ancestors originally commissioned it.[16] Another copy, also written in late eleventh-century Beneventan script, survives at Monte Cassino, bearing the *ex libris* of one of its daughter houses, San Nicola "de Turre Pagana" in Benevento.[17]

Alberic of Monte Cassino wrote a *life* and *miracles* of Dominic, a text traditionally equated with the *Monte Cassino Life* (*BHL* 2244). Dolbeau and Franklin have recently presented strong arguments in favor of the theory that what Alberic originally wrote was the *Sora Life*, whose parts had been separately classified as *BHL* 2244 prologue, *BHL* 2245b, and *BHL* 2242.[18] I have reservations about this identification that I will indicate during discussions of the relevant texts. Nevertheless, the *Monte Cassino Life* and probably additional portions of the *Sora Life* are almost certainly Alberic's work. At least where these two sources offer similar wording, one can speak of an "Alberician tradition" and of Alberic's analyses of particular points.

The *Monte Cassino Life* (*BHL* 2244) is known through what may be the earliest surviving copy of a *vita Dominici*, Monte Cassino ms. 101, written in a Beneventan hand characteristic of the *scriptorium* of Abbot Desiderius (1058–87).[19] Because this manuscript prefaces the text with the

16. The *Valva Life* is found in fols. 133–35 of BAV ms. lat. 1197, which begins with a *life* of the patron of the canons of Corfinio, St. Pelinus. It is described in Poncelet, *Cat. Cod. Hag. Lat. Vat.*, 63–66, esp. 65; Marie-Hyacinthe Laurent, *Codices Vaticanae Latini: Codices 1135–1266* (Vatican City: Bibliotheca Vaticana, 1958), 119–23; and Loew, *Beneventan Script*, 2nd ed., 1:76 and 2:143. Note also Vittorio de Donato, "Contributi del paleografo e del diplomatista allo studio delle fonti dell'Abruzzo medioevale," *Abruzzo: Rivista dell'Istituto di Studi Abruzzesi* 6 (1968): 104–5. An eighteenth-century transcript of the *Valva Life*, made from this manuscript, is found in Bibliothèque des bollandistes ms. 104, fols. 149–55v.

17. Monte Cassino ms. 141, fols. 167–70v, described in Inguanez, *Codicum Casinensium*, 1(1):225; Lentini, "La 'Vita S. Dominici,'" 58; Avagliano, "I codici liturgici," 308; Loew, *Beneventan Script*, 2nd ed., 2:71; and Dolbeau, "Dossier de saint Dominique," 28.

18. Dolbeau, "Le dossier de saint Dominique," passim, esp. 11–31; Franklin, "Restored *Life and Miracles*," passim, esp. 285–317.

19. Monte Cassino ms. 101 is described in Inguanez, *Codicum Casinensium*, 1(1):109–11; Avagliano, "I codici liturgici," 305; Lentini, "La 'Vita S. Dominici,'" 58; Loew, *Beneventan Script*, 2nd ed., 1:343, 2:66–67; Sabina Adacher, "L'Età dell'Abate Desiderio: I Codici Cassinesi 98, 442, 147, 101, 116, 444, 314, 83," in *L'Età dell'Abate Desiderio*, 3 vols., MC 59, 60, and 67 (Monte Cassino: Pubblicazioni Cassinesi, 1989–92), 1:159–61; and Franklin, "Restored *Life and Miracles*," 317–18. Franklin quotes Francis Newton as placing Monte Cassino ms. 101 perhaps later than the Desiderian period but "not . . . later than 1100." She also suggests that the title in Monte Cassino ms. 101, attributing the prologue to Alberic, may have been written by a different hand than the original scribe's. Yet the hand looks contemporary.

Franklin, ibid., notes eight more surviving full or partial copies of the *Monte Cassino Life*, but finds no evidence that these later copies have independent authority. The most inter-

unique medieval copy of a "Prologus Domni Alberici Diaconi et Monachi Casinensis," all its editors have identified it as the *life* by Alberic. Since it was probably transcribed at Monte Cassino during Alberic's lifetime, while he was Monte Cassino's schoolmaster, he presumably could have objected if he did not want to claim credit for it. Yet there are problems with identifying the present *Monte Cassino Life* as Alberic's. The version surviving in Monte Cassino ms. 101 appears to have been modified for liturgical purposes: "Lectio VIII" has been written in red at the head of the prologue, and "Lectio VII" at the head of the *life*.[20] It is certainly pared down to some extent, since narrative coherence requires a section it lacks, a passage describing Dominic's journey from "Monte Pizi" to Valva, which is found in related *lives*.[21] Thus the *Monte Cassino Life*, in its surviving form, ought to represent part but not necessarily all of Alberic's original work.

The *Sora Life* (*BHL* 2244 prologue/2245b/2242), was known to seventeenth-century antiquaries through several Latin manuscripts.[22] It subsequently dropped out of sight. At the start of the twentieth century, when the Bollandist Albert Poncelet was inventorying Italian hagiographic manuscripts, he found a copy in Gallonio's collections in the Vallicelliana Library in Rome and a copy derived from it in Naples.[23] In my 1979 UCLA

---

esting may be a closely related copy, lacking the prologue, found in Monte Cassino ms. 110, a manuscript that has also been claimed as "Desiderian." See Inguanez, *Codicum Casinensium*, 1:151–53; Avagliano, "I codici liturgici," 306; Lentini, "La 'Vita S. Dominici,'" 58; and Loew, *Beneventan Script*, 2nd ed., 2:68. But note the cautions of Franklin, "Restored *Life and Miracles*," 318–19.

20. *Monte Cassino Life* i, 70–71 (see also p. 58). Franklin, "Restored *Life and Miracles*," 317–18, observes that these rubrics are in a different hand than that of the text, but the significance of a change of hand is unclear, since red glosses and initials are often added by rubricators other than the original scribe.

21. *Monte Cassino Life* xxxii–xxxiv, 73, where Lentini, recognizing the omission, has added the passage from the *Valva Life*.

22. Jacobilli, *Vita di S. Domenico*, 5, lists among his sources about Dominic a manuscript "nella Catedrale di Sora." Among his often inaccurate marginal citations, there are passages uniquely found in *BHL* 2245b, which he attributes to a manuscript "in cancellaria Sorae" (e.g., 13, 14, 15). He also mentions texts at Atina, Casamari, and Sora, and quotes enough material so that these too can be identified as copies of the *Sora Life*. Franklin, "Restored *Life and Miracles*," 301, was able to verify the existence of a copy at Atina and to specify that it had been written in Beneventan script thanks to a reference in Marcantonio Palombo's early-seventeenth-century unpublished history of Atina (BAV ms. lat. 15184–15187). Franklin and Bloch are editing Palombo's work for *Studi e testi*.

23. Bibl. Vall. ms. H. 18, fols. 407–432v, described in Poncelet, *Cat. Cod. Hag. Lat. Rom.*, 400, 440–42, esp. 441; Franklin, "Restored *Life and Miracles*," 295–300. On Gallonio, see note 9 of this appendix. The Naples copy is in Naples Biblioteca Nazionale Codex Brancaccianus II. B. 1, fols. 315v–332, described in Poncelet, "Catalogus Codicum Hagiographicorum Latinorum Bibliothecarum Neapolitinarum," *Analecta Bollandiana* 30 (1911): 222; Dolbeau, "Le dossier de saint Dominique," 17–18 and 32; and Franklin, "Restored *Life and Miracles*," 295–99.

dissertation, I demonstrated that this *life* was actually the first half of a composition the second half of which was Dominic's *miracles* (*BHL* 2242), published nearly a century earlier in the *Analecta Bollandiana*.[24] Dolbeau and Franklin reached that same conclusion, apparently independently.

Unfortunately, the manuscript tradition of the *Sora Life* is poor. The original scribe or a predecessor had such trouble reading his exemplar that several times he gave up trying, entered an ellipsis, and moved on.[25] One cause of his difficulty was that his source or one of its ancestors must have been written in Beneventan script.[26] Additional problems may have been caused by liturgical alterations, a theory suggested by a reader's mark that the transcriber of the Vallicelliana copy accidently included.[27] As with many other Oratorian documents, the scribe wrote on cheap paper through which his ink bled. A corrector, who inserted a tag in front of the *life* identifying its author as Alberic of Monte Cassino, knew the *Monte Cassino Life* ascribed to Alberic, which he used to "improve" his *Sora Life* transcript, erasing and crossing out so heavily that he often obscured the original.[28] Spitilli's *Vita di S. Domenico*, an Italian translation that appeared in 1604, does not provide as much help as might be expected, for although he claimed to be translating from a Sora exemplar, he based his work at least to some extent on the Vallicelliana version, whose "corrections" he knows, thus indicating that the corrector must have been Gallonio himself or an assistant, since Spitilli published his *Vita di S. Domenico* during Gallonio's lifetime.[29] The *Sora Life*, therefore, has survived only through an early

24. Howe, "Greek Influence," 1:243–57, 2:506–11. The *miracles* were misleadingly appended to the *Trisulti Life* in "S. Dominici Sorani Abbatis Vita et Miracula a Coaevis Conscripta et Nunc Primum Edita," *Analecta Bollandiana* 1 (1882): 298–322.

25. *Sora Life* lxvi, lxxxv, cccxxxviii, 44, 46, 73.

26. One type of error found in the *Sora Life* is the misreading of "i" as "l": e.g., "Borrellus Malore" for "Borrellus Maiore" and "Bernardus Malore" for "Bernardus Maiore" in *Sora Life* lxi and lxvii, 44–45. Loew, *Beneventan Script*, 2nd ed., 1:311, observes that "Errors of this type throw some light on the archetype, for they go back, directly or indirectly, to an exemplar which must have used *i-longa*, i.e., to a MS in . . . Beneventan. . . ."

27. "Lectio iiii" appears in *Sora Life* lxxxix, 47.

28. To illustrate the corrector's dependency on the *Monte Cassino Life*, several examples will suffice. He adds "a simulacro" to *Sora Life* xv, 37, so that it reads with *Monte Cassino Life* xv, 72. He adds "numero" to *Sora Life* xxix, 39, so that it reads with *Monte Cassino Life* xxix, 73. He turns the "columbas" of *Sora Life* liv, 42, into "columnas," harmonizing the text with *Monte Cassino Life* xlii, 74, and other texts of Dominic's *life*.

29. Spitilli's *Vita di S. Domenico*, title page and 5, claims that its translation is "estratta dal Latino originale che si conserva nella Chiesa di Sora." Yet considerable evidence suggests that Spitilli actually used the Oratorian transcript. Dolbeau, "Dossier de saint Dominique," 19 and 37, suggests this possibility; Franklin, "Restored *Life and Miracles*," 299–300, insists on it and itemizes similar errors in the two texts. Yet Franklin's parallels could also result if both the Vallicelliana copy and Spitilli's source had been transcribed from the same defective exemplar. More conclusive arguments can be made from evidence that Spitilli incorporated

modern copyist's imperfect rendering of a now lost Sora manuscript of unknown age.

Dolbeau and Franklin identify this long text as Alberic's original *life* of Dominic, which would once have been preceded by the prologue of the *Monte Cassino Life* (*BHL* 2244).[30] Yet there are problems with accepting today's text of the *Sora Life* as Alberic's:

1. Even those who assume that the present *Sora Life* is Alberic's admit at least one alteration, the loss of Alberic's prologue.[31] Of course, hagiographical texts lose their prologues with great frequency, but this one change supports the possibility that other modifications might have occurred during textual transmission.

2. Some parts of the surviving *Sora Life* seem to be later additions. Alberic ought to have written soon after 1067 (as will be demonstrated below), but the surviving text of the *life* and *miracles* presumes that Count Oderisius II of Marsica had already retired to Monte Cassino (which he had not yet done in 1077).[32] It also refers to the deceased or non-deceased status of bishops Erasmus of Segni and Leo of Gaeta in ways that certainly push the date of the

---

corrections and glosses from Bibl. Vall. ms. H. 18: for example, *Vita*, 7, reads "Curasero o Cuiasero," following the marginal gloss "vel Cuiaseri," after the name "Curasero" (fol. 407); *Vita*, 13, incorporates the interlinear gloss for Trisaltus, "vel Insultus" (fol. 409); *Vita*, 22, amends the incomprehensible "Brenlim nomine" to "Borrelli," following a marginal suggestion (fol. 413v). Spitilli, *Vita*, 8, uses the name form "Donnosus" for Dominic's spiritual father, which is only attested in the surviving manuscript tradition in the hand of the Vallicelliana corrector (fol. 407).

Nevertheless, Spitilli occasionally presents a translation that could be closer to the original than to the readings of the corrected Vallicelliana transcript. For example, of the three ellipses found there, Spitilli's translation fills the first quite credibly (compare *Sora Life* lxvi, 44, with *Vita*, 13); fills the second with a generic phrase that might or might not have been a conjecture (compare *Sora Life* lxxxv, 46, with *Vita*, 15); but handles the third following the Vallicelliana corrector (compare *Sora Life* cccxxxviii, 73, and *Vita*, 42). In the story of the Sunday fisherman (*Sora Life* lxxxix–xciii, 47), Spitilli has translated a line of text that the Vallicelliana corrector could not comprehend and therefore effectively obliterated (*Vita*, 16). The incorporation of the Vallicelliana glosses indicates that Spitilli certainly depends on that copy, which might have been easier for him to read than an original manuscript in Beneventan script; yet he might also, as he claims, have consulted a Sora text.

30. Dolbeau, "Le dossier de saint Dominique," 17–25; Franklin, "Restored *Life and Miracles*," 293–317.

31. Franklin, "Restored *Life and Miracles*," 294–302, attempts to establish on codicological grounds that formerly there could have been a page containing the prologue in front of the Bibl. Vall. *Sora Life*, but she herself finally admits "that there is no positive evidence to support this conclusion."

32. At the time the surviving *Sora Life* was written, Oderisius, son of Count Berardus of Marsica, was a *conversus* at Monte Cassino (*Sora Life* lxxi, 44). Yet he was still active in the world up through at least the year 1077. See Howe, "*Monasteria Semper Libera*," 26.

text after 1071 and most probably beyond 1079/1080,[33] and it presents miracles in a sequence that seems to move in rough chronological order from early to late in a way that suggests that some of
the last miracles may have occurred nearly two generations after
Dominic's death.[34]

3. The claim of Dolbeau and Franklin that there can be "no question" about the derivation of the shorter *Monte Cassino Life* from
the *Sora Life* cannot be sustained without qualifications since the
Monte Cassino Life contains some better readings.[35]

Several scenarios might explain these problems. Perhaps Alberic recognized that what Sora needed was a detailed dossier of local miracles,

33. Lentini, "La 'Vita S. Dominici,'" 64–65, advanced arguments for dating the *miracles* on the basis of the deaths of the bishops named, but the information on their death dates
is more ambiguous than he indicated. The *Sora Life* was apparently written after the death of
Bishop Erasmus, who is identified as having been "at that time bishop of Segni." As Lentini
observed, Erasmus was in office in 1059, and attended the 1071 dedication of Monte Cassino,
but since no other bishop of Segni is known between him and St. Bruno, who took office there
in 1079/1080, the latter date might well be the *terminus post quem* for the *life*: see Ughelli,
Italia sacra, 2nd ed., 1:1235–36.

The next anecdote used by Lentini for a *terminus post quem*, rather less convincingly,
involves the death of Bishop Leo of Gaeta, who held his see in 1071 and was succeeded by
Rainaldus in 1090 (Ughelli, *Italia sacra*, 2nd ed., 1:533–537). Here where to place the *obit* is
even less certain. Moreover, the argument that Leo must already have been dead because he is
not specifically described as still living is unconvincing, since Abbot Benedict of Sora, who
appears in *Sora Life* iii and cccl–ccclxix, 35 and 74–76, and who the prologue indicates was
still living during the time when the *life* was being composed, is not clearly specified as a
contemporary witness when he suddenly reappears, with an awkward repetition of his prologue description, at the close of the *miracles*.

34. The miracles appear to have occurred over a considerable span of time. After presenting separate stories of miraculous events involving three generations of the same family
(Abilonius of Sora, his son Bonutius, and his grandson Adenulfus), stories situated in the
last half of the collection, the author goes on to tell of an adolescent named John from Ancona, who was healed, became a cook at San Domenico, and still lives there "even up until the present time" (*Sora Life* cclxii–ccc, 68–70). The appeal to the authority of eye-
witnesses who knew Dominic, a major theme of Alberic's prologue, is not a prominent part of
the *miracula post mortem*; still-living witnesses to the miracles are rarely invoked, except for
some of the final stories, those apparently involving more recent events.

35. Among the instances in which the *Monte Cassino Life* appears to have superior readings to the *Sora Life* are these:

The original scribe of Bibl. Vall. ms. H. 18., fol. 407, has a lacuna in his text, a skip of a
line of text between "viris" and "constitutus," which is a natural scribal error. An insertion
mark has been added by the corrector's heavier pen, and the line squeezed into the margin,
perhaps on the basis of the *Monte Cassino Life*. The narrative is better if the missing line is
considered part of the original text. Thus its absence in the surviving *Sora Life* suggests that
the *Monte Cassino Life* ought not to come from that text as it stands.

In regard to the muddle that the *lives* make of the name of the monastery of San Silvestro
on Monte Subasio (i.e., "in monasterio Sancti Silvestri subasii," the *Monte Cassino Life* xiii,
71–72, does better in having Dominic sent "in monasterio Sancti Silvestri, cui Aseri cogno-

while what Monte Cassino needed was a short liturgical text, and therefore he wrote or authorized both. Perhaps Alberic himself continued to retouch the *Sora Life*, adding some miracles and making other changes. Perhaps the *Sora Life*'s deficient readings vis-à-vis the *Monte Cassino Life* could be attributed to defects in the manuscript tradition rather than to descent from a common source. Resolving these problems is not easy. Fortunately, it is also not necessary here. For the purposes of historical analysis, it is only necessary to determine whether or not Dolbeau and Franklin are correct in maintaining that the *Sora Life* equals Alberic's original work, and that the *Monte Cassino Life* derives from it and lacks independent authority. The evidence assembled above indicates that, on the contrary, both the *Monte Cassino Life* and the *Sora Life*, as they stand, are independent witnesses to some degree. Both need to be consulted.

Five hymns dedicated to Dominic are known from early witnesses. Two, whose generic and unspecific praises seem to allude to wonders worked at Dominic's tomb, were allegedly found in an eleventh-century Monte Cassino breviary.[36] The other three are found in J. Paul Getty Museum ms. IX 1 (formerly Monte Cassino ms. 199), a manuscript that, probably written at Monte Cassino in 1153, disappeared from the monastery in

---

mentum est"; the *Sora Life*, in Bibl. Vall. ms. H. 18, fol. 407, places him "in monasterio quod Sancti Silvestri Curaseri cognomentum est" (the emendation proposed in *Sora Life* xiii, ed. Dolbeau, 37, simply doubles the misunderstood element).

The *Monte Cassino Life* xv, 72, reads better by adding "a simulacro" to the passage that is *Sora Life* xv, 37.

In regard to the number of monks collected at Scandriglia, *Monte Cassino Life* xxix, 73, reads sensibly as "ex eorundem numero," where "numero" was not given by the original Vallicelliana scribe in *Sora Life* xxix, 39.

In regard to Constantius, the monk whom Dominic put in charge of Scandriglia, the *Monte Cassino Life* xxix, 73, makes him a "virum ad id officii et vita et scientia et lingua pariter commodissimum," which is better than the *Sora Life* xxix, 39, where he was a "virum ad id officii et vita et scientia et lingua peritum."

The *Monte Cassino Life* xxxv, 74, gives a more complete list of the counts of Valva who helped Dominic than does the *Sora Life* xxxviii, 40, which omits a Count Theodinus whose historicity is known from other sources (see p. 46). If the *Monte Cassino Life* were nothing more than an excerpt from the present text of the *Sora Life*, then it would be hard to explain how it contains a better list of the counts of Valva. The sentence presenting the list of counts in the *Monte Cassino Life* also seems more "Alberician" in that it better evokes Alberic's characteristic opposition between Dominic's "beloved hiding places" and the "discoverers" who root him out of them.

It is necessary to conclude that either the *Monte Cassino Life* is not derived from the *Sora Life* or that it was derived from a version of the *Sora Life* that was considerably less corrupt than that which survives today.

36. Guido Maria Dreves, *Hymni Inediti: Liturgische Hymnen des Mittelalters*, 7 vols., Analecta Hymnica Medii Aevi 4, 11–12, 19, 22–23, and 43 (of a total of 55 vols.) (Leipzig: O. R. Reisland, 1886–1922), 5(22):83–84.

the mid-nineteenth century and has only recently resurfaced.[37] Because the first hymn of the three is labeled "In Sancti Dominici Ymnus Alberici ad Vesp.," all three have been assigned to Alberic, an attribution debated by their several editors, but most recently affirmed by Franklin.[38]

A *Summary* (*BHL* 2243) of Dominic's *life* and *miracles* was made in 1273 by Jacobus de Voragine (d. 1298), the compiler of the *Golden Legend*.[39] Except for some readings published by the Bollandists, it remains unedited.[40] It has no independent value as a historical source concerning Dominic, since it is nothing more than a reduced version of the *Trisulti Life* (which Jacobus found at Trisulti) and a rather sketchier presentation of the *miracles* of the *Sora Life*. Yet its readings must have been based on earlier manuscripts than any now surviving. It is known through the hagiographical collections of Constantino Gaetani.[41]

What are the dates of these interrelated texts? They all postdate Dominic's death in 1032, probably considerably since explicit eyewitness references to Dominic are rare. The first solid chronological information comes from the prologue of Alberic's *life*. He explains that he had known a preexisting *life* (which makes his work the *terminus ante quem* of whatever text that was), but that he needed other witnesses, because the text he knew was unpolished and even mendacious.[42] He claims to have visited

37. On J. Paul Getty Museum ms. IX 1, see Avagliano, "Ritrovato il codice Cassinese 199," *Benedictina* 19 (1972): 621–23; Newton, "The Rediscovery of a Lost Monte Cassino MS," *QFIAB* 53 (1973): 457–58; Anton von Euw and Joachim M. Plotzek, *Die Handschriften der Sammlung Ludwig*, 4 vols. (Cologne: Schnütgen-Museum der Stadt Köln, 1979–85), 2: 49–63; and Loew, *Beneventan Script*, 2nd ed., 2:11.

38. Editions of this group of hymns on Dominic, all but the last of which are based on early modern transcripts rather than on Monte Cassino ms. 199, can be found in Mauro Inguanez, "Inni inediti di Alberico ed il codice Cassinese 199," *Bullettino dell'ISIME e Archivio Muratori* 47 (1932): 191–98; Lentini, "Su tre inni in onore di S. Domenico Abate," *Benedictina* 5 (1951): 185–99; and now Franklin, "Restored *Life and Miracles*," 340–45.

39. On Jacob of Voragine and his work, see Barbara Fleith, *Studien zur Überlieferungsgeschichte der lateinischen Legenda Aurea*, Subsidia Hagiographica 72 (Brussels: Société des bollandistes, 1991), 9–16.

40. The Bollandists footnoted readings from Jacobus's *Summary* in their edition of the *Trisulti Life*. Dolbeau, "Le dossier de saint Dominique," 31, promises an edition.

41. Bibl. Aless. ms. 91 (part 2), fols. 347–59v (early seventeenth century), described in Narducci, *Catalogus Codicum . . . in Bibliotheca Alexandrina*, 25. According to Jacobilli, *Vita di S. Domenico*, 62–63, there were still copies of the *Summary* at Casamari and Sora in the eighteenth century. Jacobilli does seem to have known and used a text that was better than that found in the Alessandrina volume, for he gives the date of composition as 1273 rather than as 1233, a date that fits the career of Jacobus de Voragine, the author it names (see Dolbeau, "Le dossier de saint Dominique," 29–31). The readings edited by the Bollandists came from a copy of the Gaetani manuscript that is now Bibliothèque des bollandistes ms. 104, fols. 159–75v (Baudouin de Gaiffier, personal communication, 27 April 1978).

42. *Monte Cassino Life* vi–x, 70; *Sora Life* ii–vi, 35.

Dominic's tomb at San Domenico near Sora in response to the frequent entreaties of a "most dear brother named Dodo."[43] Dodo has never been successfully identified before, but he was very probably the monk of that name who had served in 1037 as provost of San Silvestro in "Valle de Frasso," the Monte Cassino daughter house nearest Dominic's tomb.[44] Alberic says that at San Domenico he met Dominic's relative Abbot Benedict, presumably the third abbot of that house, whose name is found in charters of 1064 and 1077, and who had died before 1097/1098, assuming he is the "Benedictus abbas" whose *obit* on 3 December is listed in the calendar written by Leo Marsicanus.[45] At Sora, Alberic met not only "the revered old men of that place who had been trained under Dominic's tutelage," but even "old John—who had been handed over to Dominic as a disciple while he was still in his boyhood years and who had lived with him even to the very end of his life—now very aged and almost decrepit, stuttering from his toothlessness."[46] Since John is portrayed in the *vita* tradition as Dominic's companion for more than thirty years, one would not expect him or Alberic's other aged informants to have survived Dominic by many decades. Therefore Anselmo Lentini dated the *life* to around the year 1060, locating it at the very start of Alberic's literary career.[47]

Nevertheless, other evidence indicates that Alberic did not write earlier than the very end of the 1060s. Both the *Monte Cassino Life* and the *Sora Life* contain very precise information about the founding of the monastery of San Pietro in Lago, specifying that it was endowed by counts Beraldus, Theodinus, and Randisius, whose generous donations included five lakes, and adding that these gifts were recorded in a legal document. Since none of the *lives* outside the Alberician tradition is so precise, Alber-

---

43. *Monte Cassino Life* iii, 70; *Sora Life* iii, 35.

44. The failures of previous attempts at identifying Alberic's friend Dodo, the original requester of his *Vita Dominici*, are noted in Lentini, "La 'Vita S. Dominici,'" 68. Nevertheless, this Dodo is very likely to have been the monk named Dodo who had served as provost of San Silvestro in 1037. He lived at the right time. He was connected with Monte Cassino as the temporary provost of one of its daughter houses. He was linked to Dominic's cult not only because San Silvestro was near Dominic's tomb but also because the man who had donated this daughterhouse to Monte Cassino was Dominic's final patron, Lord Peter of Sora. Dodo appears in Archivio di Montecassino aul. II, capsulae xxxviii, nos. 23 and 25, described in Leccisotti, *Regesti*, 7:275–76 (nos. 1459 and 1461). On San Silvestro, see *Monasticon Italiae* I:126; Bloch, *Monte Cassino*, 1:305–7; and Antonelli, *Abbazie . . . di Sora*, 170–73.

45. Charters involving Abbot Benedict of Sora are edited in Farina and Fornari, *Storia e documenti . . . Casamari*, 160–62. The little that is known about Benedict's advocacy has been discussed above (p. 83).

46. *Monte Cassino Life* iii and vii, 70–71; *Sora Life* iii and vii, 35.

47. Lentini, "La 'Vita S. Domenico,'" 69.

ic's source of information must have been the foundation charter he cites. Monte Cassino is a long way from San Pietro in Lago, and there is no obvious reason for Alberic to have had access to the charter prior to Monte Cassino's acquisition of San Pietro (and therefore its legal records), an event that did not occur until 1067 (or even, according to the indictional dating of the donation, 1069). Perhaps, although the prologue does not state this, Alberic acceded at this point to Dodo's persistent requests that he write a *life* of Dominic just because Dominic had now entered, by adoption, Monte Cassino's family of saints. Since Alberic's geriatric witnesses could not have lived long after 1067, his work was probably undertaken soon after the acquisition of San Pietro in Lago.[48]

The *lives* that depend upon Alberic have his work for a *terminus post quem*, and there are hints that they had already reached their present forms by the time he died, at some time between 1094 and 1098. As has been noted, the *Monte Cassino Life* survives in an early copy usually assigned to the *scriptorium* of Abbot Desiderius (d. 1087). The surviving *Sora Life* contains elements placing its final form some years beyond 1067, probably into the 1080s. Yet one of the last miracles involves Count Oderisius II, who as an adolescent had met Dominic. Since he is specified as still living at Montecassino at the time the text was written, his longevity becomes increasingly improbable if the *miracles* were not completed well before the end of the 1090s.[49] An additional *terminus ante quem* is provided by the hymns: in the first, the one specifically attributed to Alberic, the claim that Dominic "often found hidden things" evokes the *Sora Life*'s several miracles concerning sequestered food offerings; the mention of Dominic's restoration of the senses of a jealous man who had spoken out against him would appear to refer to the stricken priest in the *Sora Life*'s fifth miracle story; the description of the "pestifer presbiter" who prepared death for the blessed man, but who, as soon as he came near, became dead to the world himself, must be taken from the story of the priest Amatus found in the seventh through ninth paragraphs.[50] If Alberic wrote the first hymn, then

48. *Monte Cassino Life* xxxvii–xxxviii, 74; *Sora Life* xxxviii–xli, 40–41. The foundation of San Pietro in Lago and its later donation to Monte Cassino are discussed on pp. 46–47 and 123.

49. *Sora Life* lxxi–lxxxviii and ccclxx–ccclxxi, 43–45 and 76.

50. Compare the first "Alberician" poem, edited in Franklin, "Restored *Life and Miracles*," 343–44, with the *Sora Life* lxxix–lxxxviii, xciv–cviii, and cix–civ, 46–49 (miracles involving stolen and hidden offerings); ibid., clix–clxvi, 56 (the priest who was "aemulus"); and ibid., clxxii–clxxxix, 57–59 (Amatus, the depraved priest).

at least the first part of the Sora *miracula* had been written before his death prior to 1099.

It is even more difficult to assign precise dates to the texts outside the Alberician tradition. The *Sermon* was written after a lost early *life* of Dominic, which it abbreviates, and must have been composed prior to or quite possibly at the time of the sole surviving late eleventh- or early twelfth-century copy. The date of the *Trisulti Life* has been debated. Pierre Toubert, impressed with its vivid detail, placed it early in the eleventh century. Sofia Boesch Gajano saw it as representative of the local traditions against which Alberic's biography was written. Less sanguine were Anselmo Lentini and François Dolbeau, who considered it of little value, one of the last items of Dominic's dossier to be written.[51] The uncertainty exists because, now that the attribution to Dominic's disciple John has been debunked, the text has no incontrovertible *terminus ante quem* prior to the abbreviation of a similar text (without the present close) made by Jacob of Voragine at Trisulti in 1273. I am willing to accept the *Trisulti Life*, except for the obviously altered conclusion, as an authoritative witness to events of the early eleventh century because it embodies the San Bartolomeo perspective that, as demonstrated above, would have animated the earliest written *life*; because parallels between it and the *Sermon* on Dominic show that the tradition it embodies, at least in its opening paragraphs, is early; and because the texts indebted to the work of Alberic of Monte Cassino seem to be reacting against some of its claims. The *Valva Life* was written after Dominic's lost first *life* and prior to the late eleventh- or early twelfth-century copies in which it appears. More precise dating depends on the difficult question of its relationship to Alberic's work. If it abbreviates it, as alleged by Dolbeau, then it was written after 1067, but if the similarities are to be explained by a common source, then Alberic's work is not a *terminus post quem*.

The lack of precise dates for Dominic's *lives* is disappointing but per-

51. Compare Toubert, *Structures*, 1:45, with Lentini, "La 'Vita S. Dominici,'" p. 67; Sofia Boesch Gajano, "Santità di vita, sacralità dei luoghi. Aspetti della tradizione agiografica di Domenico di Sora," in *Scritti in onore di Filippo Caraffa* (Anagni: Istituto di storia e d'arte dal Lazio, 1986), 191–92, and Dolbeau, "Le dossier de saint Dominique," 26–27. Dolbeau, ibid., 11, argues that the *Trisulti Life* was the source of the *Sermon* on Dominic that survives in a late-eleventh- or early-twelfth-century copy, and thus he presupposes an early-twelfth-century *terminus ante quem* for the *Trisulti Life* (ibid., 27). However, if the *Sermon* actually harkens back to an earlier *life*, as argued above, then it is not possible to derive a *terminus ante quem* from the date of the *Sermon*.

haps didactically useful. Absolute dates might suggest separate traditions that could be neatly compared and contrasted. Dominic's texts are not independent witnesses. They result from the interactions of local communities. Alberic's prologue shows that the monks of Sora knew a *life* that they disliked, presumably from Trisulti. At least by the thirteenth century, as the summary by Jacobus de Voragine indicates, Trisulti had a copy of the *miracles* from Sora. Monte Cassino, perhaps quite early, possessed several versions of Dominic's *life*. Dominic had an ongoing cult, developing in different ways at different centers, of which each surviving text is only a snapshot, a fixed image of Dominic as he appeared at particular instances to particular communities of author and audience. It is impossible to separate the traditions, not simply because the evidence is too fragmentary, but ultimately because the traditions were tangled up with each other like the overlapping responses in a present-day computer-network conversation.

Appendix B: Dominic's Patrons from the Lineage of the Counts of Marsica

Although the lineage of the counts of Marsica is the most prominent extended family group associated with Dominic, exact genealogies are difficult to reconstruct. Its members multiplied titles and continually reused a very small number of names. Even Herbert Bloch, who leaves almost no stone unturned, avoids tackling "the difficult genealogy of the 'comites Marsorum'" (*Monte Cassino* 1:334). Yet, given the importance of this lineage to Dominic's story, it is necessary to summarize and justify the reconstructions assumed here. Genealogical tables follow, which are organized around those family members who had points of tangency with Dominic. These tables often disagree with previously published work, which is to be expected, given that most earlier studies are more than two scholarly generations out of date. To document the changes made, I take as a starting point the most comprehensive previous work, Hermann Müller's *Topographische und genealogische Untersuchungen zur Geschichte des Herzogtums Spoleto und der Sabina* (1930), and indicate, following the chronological order of the tables, the places where Müller and I diverge.

Berardus the Frank, who heads the extended lineage of the counts of Marsica, has his origins described in *Chron. Cass.* I lxi, 153–54. Transactions he conducted from 947 to 954, unknown to Müller, are indicated in the *Liber Largitorius*, 1:102 (no. 139) and 1:113–115 (nos. 158–160). His wife was probably the "Doda" who appears after his death in a property exchange confusingly recorded in *Chron. Cass.* II vii, 182; discussed in Bloch, *Monte Cassino*, 1:333 and 2:1105. Their many children apparently included seven sons, for whom sources are indicated in Müller, 54–71. Not all of these are of concern here: Alberic of Marsica and Walter of Forcona were bishops; two others, Randuisius and Berardus, less influential than their brothers, appear in Dominic's story only in a discussion of Marsican support for family

Dominic's Patrons from the Lineage of the Counts of Marsica.

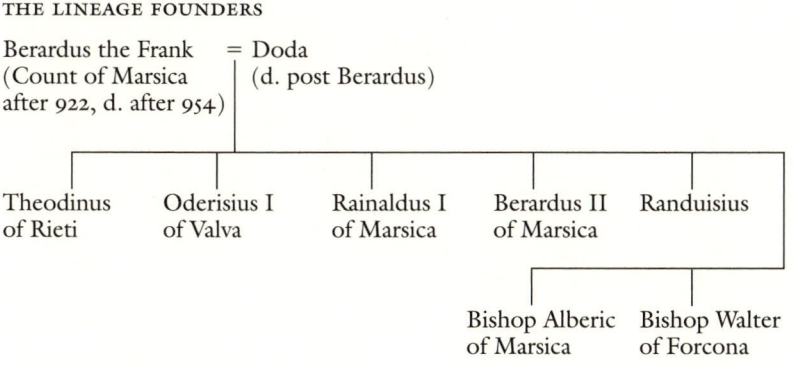

THE LINEAGE FOUNDERS

Berardus the Frank   = Doda
(Count of Marsica   │ (d. post Berardus)
after 922, d. after 954)

Theodinus   Oderisius I   Rainaldus I   Berardus II   Randuisius
of Rieti   of Valva   of Marsica   of Marsica

                               Bishop Alberic   Bishop Walter
                               of Marsica   of Forcona

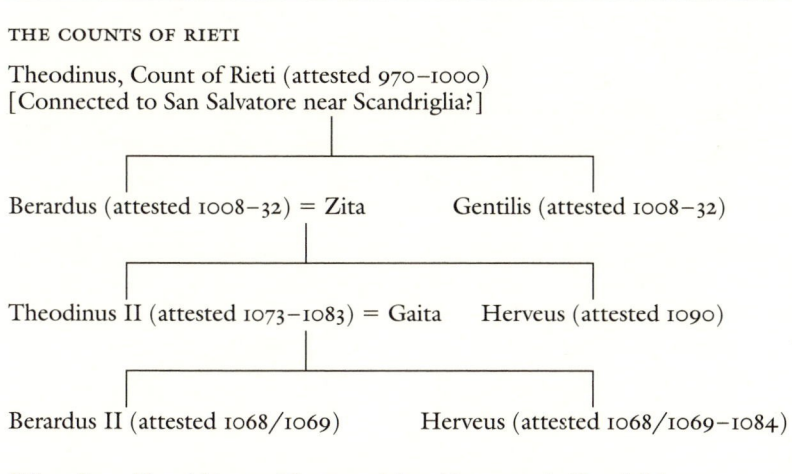

THE COUNTS OF RIETI

Theodinus, Count of Rieti (attested 970–1000)
[Connected to San Salvatore near Scandriglia?]

Berardus (attested 1008–32) = Zita   Gentilis (attested 1008–32)

Theodinus II (attested 1073–1083) = Gaita   Herveus (attested 1090)

Berardus II (attested 1068/1069)   Herveus (attested 1068/1069–1084)

[Theodinus II and his son Herveus claimed interests in Dominic's monastery of San Salvatore in 1083; Herveus in 1084.]

(Continues)

(Continued)

COUNTS OF VALVA

Oderisius I, Count of Valva (attested 972–1001, d. 1002?)
[Possible early patron of the Sagiattario foundations?]

. . . [see Borrelli]

Beraldus I   Theodinus I   Berardus I (attested   Randisius = Giseltrudis
(1002–?   (1002–?, attested   1022, 1024, not   [Pastries to Dominic]
attested   1022–38)   titled count)   (1002–? attested 1038)
1022–38)

[Beraldus, Theodinus, and Randisius
signed the charter of San Pietro in Lago]

Berardus II (attested 1038–67/69)   Theodinus = Oria   Oderisius II = Doda
                                           (attested   (attested
                                           1067/69–1085)   1066–1093)

[Berardus, Theodinus, and Oderisius gave
San Pietro to Monte Cassino in 1067 or 1069]

THE BORRELLI

Oderisius I, Count of Valva (attested from 972 to 1001, d. 1002?)
[See Counts of Valva]

Oderisius Borrellus (Borellus Major) = Ruta
(attested from 1014 to 1026)
[Founder of San Pietro Avellana]

Borrellus II = Gervisa   John (attested   Oderisius   Randisius (attested
(attested 1069–83)   1014, d. between   (attested   from 1035 to 1064)
[Dominated San   1053 and 1057)   1014 to 1070)
Pietro Avellana]

(Continues)

(Continued)

COUNTS OF MARSICA

Rainaldus I, Count of Marsica
(attested 968–1000)

Oderisius I = Gervisa	Berardus II = Doda	Doda = Atto of the Crescenzi
(attested = Gibborga	(attested	(both fl. 1011)
995–1012)	993–1028)	

Oderisius I = Gervisa
(attested   = Gibborga
995–1012)

Doda = Peter, son of Rainerius,	Balduinus (attested after 1028–58)
Lord of Sora	[Involved in the death of Berardus II]
[Dominic's Sora patron]	

Berardus II [Berardus Major] = Doda
(attested 993–1028)   [Sent messages to Dominic,
["Tyrant" whose bad end   begged his prayers]
Dominic had predicted]

Berardus III = Rogata	Oderisius II = Litilda	Sigenulfus
(attested 1048–	[Met Dominic = Gilla	(attested 1060)
1070/1073)	in 1020s; healed	
[Donations to San	at Dominic's tomb	
Domenico in 1064]	before 1059] (attested	
	1020s, d. after 1077)	

Ladolfus	Rainaldus II = Sighelgaita	Pandulphus, Bishop
(attested 1062)	(attested	of Marsica (attested
	1054–1070)	1056–1094/96)

monasteries (see pp. 129–30). However, special attention must be paid to Theodinus, Oderisius, and Rainaldus, who were at least ancestors of Dominic's major patrons (the counts of Rieti, Valva, and Marsica).

Theodinus I of Rieti began the Marsican counts of Rieti. The *stemma* presented here does not differ from that of Müller, 47–53. Most of this reconstruction, including the link between the second and third generation and the names of the wives, is based upon *Reg. Farf.*, ed. Giorgi and Balzani, 5:78–79 (doc. 1083). On Berardus I of Rieti and Todinus in 1014, see Manaresi, *Placiti*, 2(2):541–47 (doc. 285); on Berardus and Gentilis in 1023, see ibid., 659–61 (doc. 319). An additional reference to Berardus in 1028, misidentified as referring to a count of Valva, is in ibid., 3(1):20–22 (doc. 329), and is properly identified in Volpini, "Placiti," 380–81.

Oderisius I of Valva was the progenitor of the counts of Valva. On the second generation counts, whose dealings with Dominic can be documented, see *Chron. Vult.* V, 3:30–34; also ed. in Manaresi, *Placiti*, 2:640–43 (doc. 314). Berardus, the brother not honored as count, appears in *Chron. Casaur.*, 2(2):988–89; photographically reproduced in the *Liber Instrumentorum seu Chronicorum Monasterii Casauriensis* (Aquila: Amministrazione provinciale dell'Aquila, 1982), fol. 180r; also edited in Manaresi, *Placiti*, 2:664–65 (doc. no. 321). An additional record, involving a *placitum* held at Sulmona in 1022, survives in an original document in the archives of the archbishop of Chieti, edited in Volpini, "Placiti del 'Regnum Italiae,'" 381–83. The 1038 attestations of these counts are extremely tentative. A charter secured from Conrad II by Casauria mentions "Bernardo & filius ejus Beraldo & ejus fratribus Comitibus," and if this refers to the second generation count of Valva of that name, his son, and two or more comital brothers, then the only two such brothers known are Theodinus and Randisius—see *Chron. Casaur.*, 2(2):851–52; or *Die Urkunden Konrads II.*, ed. Heinrich Bresslau, MGH *Dipl. Reg. Imp.*, 4:367.

The donation of San Pietro in Lago to Monte Cassino in 1067/1069, by naming the fathers of the donors, ties together the second and third generations of the Marsican counts of Valva better than is indicated in Wickham, *Studi sulla società degli Appennini*, 117. The third generation is otherwise known largely through various donations made to Farfa by Theodinus, son of Randisius, and witnessed by his brothers, which donations appear in *Reg. Farf.*, 5:31–32, 84–85, and 87 (docs. 1028, 1090, and 1092), and are briefly noted in *Chron. Farf.*, 2:170. Secondary scholarship has tended to overlook Nunzio Federigo Faraglia, *Codice Diplomatico Sulmonese* (Lanciano: R. Carabba Editore, 1888), 15 (doc. 9), in regard to

Oderisius, son of Count Randisius, in 1066; and 29 (doc. 20), in regard to his son, Gentilis of Pettorano, in 1098.

Oderisius Borellus (Borellus Magnus), another son of count Oderisius I of Valva, was the patriarch of the Borelli from whom would descend the counts of Sangro. The short *stemma* of the Borelli presented in Chapter 5 adds nothing to Cesare Rivera, "Per la storia . . . dei Borelli," 48–98; H. Enzberger, "Borello," *DBI*, 12 (1970), 815–817; and Bloch, *Monte Cassino*, 1:362–64, 2:996. For additional bibliographic information on the family, see Howe, "*Monasteria Semper Libera*," 24–26; and Luigi R. Cielo, "Porta Bronzea di Montecassino e pertinenze nel Molise: Valori documentari e intenzionalità rappresentative," *Mélanges de l'École française de Rome, Moyen âge* 103 (1991): 228–29.

Rainaldus I of Marsica, another son of Berardus the Frank, headed the counts of Marsica proper. Müller's *stemmae*, 58–71, can be supplemented in various ways. He assumed that the tenth-century references to Count Rainaldus applied to two men, not one (cf. Müller, 60–61, 70). This bifurcation is not accepted in Howe, "*Monasteria Semper Libera*," 23; and "Fatal Discord," 5–7. For much of the documentation on Rainaldus, see the references listed in Manaresi, *Placiti*, 2(2):802. The original document recording a 972 *placitum* at Oretino that involved Counts Beraldus II and Rainaldus I, previously known from the Monte Cassino *Chronicle* and from Peter the Deacon's *Register*, is identified in the Monte Cassino archives in Leccisotti, *Regesti*, 2:101; and edited by Volpini in "Placiti," 260, 310–12. The original document of a 998 *placitum* near Sora that involved counts Oderisius I and Rainaldus I, preserved in the Monte Cassino archives, is edited by Volpini in "Placiti," 329–31. In October 999, Rainaldus leased some Farfa land, as noted in *Liber Largitorius*, 2:303 (no. 2013). Rainaldus in the year 1000 at Carsoli was involved in a papal transaction, now treated in *Papsturkunden*, ed. Zimmermann, 2:736–37 (no. 381).

Oderisius I of Marsica, a son of Rainaldus I of Marsica, is discussed in Müller, 62–63, 67, and 70, which can be supplemented and improved. In addition to the Sora placitum of 998, cited above under Rainaldus I, Oderisius I was at *placita* held in 1007 and 1008 in the Valle di Ortucchio, known through original documents from the Monte Cassino archives, edited by Volpini in "Placiti," 261 and 357–62. Balduinus is identified as a son of Count Oderisius in *Chron. Cass.* III lxi, 442. One should not follow Müller, 67 and 70, and Sennis, "Potere centrale e forze locali," 52, in assuming that Balduinus was a son of Oderisius II, since information from the *Sora Life* lxxv, 45, identifies him as a "nepos" who seized the "vallem

Soranam" from Berardus II before his death (which was soon after 1028). If Balduinus was leading military expeditions this early, then his father was probably Oderisius I. Moreover, that relationship is explicitly required if the *Sora Life*—which owes much to Alberic, who could be a precise writer—uses "nepos" in its literal classical sense as "nephew" (on this terminology, see Toubert, *Structures*, 1:706A). Balsorano, six miles up the Liri from Sora, was actually in Marsica, not in Sora's territory as Müller implied. That Balduinus was the ancestor of the counts of Balsorano is suggested by an early copy of a 1089 charter noted in Leccisotti, *Regesti*, 2:90.

Berardus II of Marsica (Berardus Major), was another son of Rainaldus I of Marsica. Müller, 63–64 and 71, places his death after 1038; Howe, "Fatal Discord," 6, indicates that citations are lacking after 1028. Berardus II was with Oderisius I at *placita* held in 1007 and 1008 in the Valle di Ortucchio, known through original Monte Cassino documents, edited by Volpini in "Placiti," 261 and 357–62. Berardus II was also at a *placitum* held by Count Lanfranc in Oretino in 1022, which is known through Archivio di Monte Cassino, aula III, capsula xii, no. 48, noted in Leccisotti, *Regesti*, 2:102 (where Lanfranc, who was an imperial *missus*, is erroneously identified as a count of Marsica). This document also has been edited by Volpini in "Placiti," 384–87.

The many sons of Berardus II are differently listed in Müller, 64–66 and 71, and Howe, "Fatal Discord," 5–14, as follows:

Berardus III, a son of Berardus II discussed in Müller, 64–66, was also one of the principal parties in a 1061 sale document preserved at San Salvatore on Monte Amiata: *Cartula* (no. 280), edited by Wilhelm Kurze, *Codex Diplomaticus Amiatinus*, 3– vols. (Tübingen: Max Niemeyer Verlag, 1974–), 2:205–7. This identification is supported by the presence of his son there, probably in that year—see *Chron. Cass.* III xvii, 383. Berardus III donated land and a church to San Domenico in 1064, a transaction memorialized in a Casamari copy, edited in Farina and Fornari, *Storia e documenti . . . di Casamari*, 160–61. An inscription in the church of Santa Maria in Valle Porclaneta, honoring Berardus III as its founding patron, is published in Bloch, *Monte Cassino*, 2:285 and 1114. His interrelationships with his brothers are described in Howe, "Fatal Discord," 8–14.

Müller's "Rainaldus III" ought to be "Rainaldus II" if the doubling of Count Rainaldus I is rejected as above.

Sigenulfus, "son of Count Berardus," who resided in Carsoli in 1060 when he donated property to Monte Cassino, is made by Müller, 66 and

71, a son of Berardus III, an identification corrected in Howe, "Fatal Discord," 7.

Oderisius II of Marsica, in addition to the sources listed in Müller, 66–67, is also known from the *Sora Life* lxxi–lxxviii and ccclxx–ccclxxi, 44–46 and 76. This has led to discussions on his dates between Franklin, "Restored *Life and Miracles*," 306–8 (who argues that the documents in Müller must refer to two different men), and Howe, "*Monasteria Semper Libera*," 26–27, and "Fatal Discord," 6–7 (who retains Müller's reconstruction).

On the reasons to add Bishop Pandulfus to the list of the sons of Berardus II, see Howe, "*Monasteria Semper Libera*," 28–29.

Müller, 65 and 70, lists a "Bernardus," "son of Berardus," attested in 1067, as an additional son of Berardus II. The person in question is actually the count of Valva, Bernardus, who belongs on the Valva family tree.

Some additional changes from Müller are incorporated by Sennis, "Potere centrale e forze locali," 75, into his table of the descendents of Berardus II, but in regard to these see Howe, "Fatal Discord," 19–21.

Appendix C: Gifts to Monte Cassino from the Lineage of the Counts of Marsica

The descendents of Berardus the Frank gave lavishly to Monte Cassino from 1057, the year of the visit of Bishop Pandulfus, to 1100. The following list of donations is compiled from the two best recent works dealing with Monte Cassino's dependencies: Dormeier's *Monte Cassino und die Laien* and Bloch's *Monte Cassino in the Middle Ages*. It is certainly incomplete, given the gaps in the surviving records and the lack of a complete register of the documents surviving in the Monte Cassino archive. Yet it ought to give some idea of the magnitude of Marsican patronage.

1057	Berardus, son of John, son of Borrellus Major, gave to Monte Cassino's church of San Eustachio "ad Arcum" (his grandfather's foundation near Pietrabbondante) the church of San Salvatore (Schiavi di Abruzzi, prov.: Chieti). Bloch, 1:286–87.
1058	Count Balduinus, the first count of Balsorano, son of Count Oderisius I of Marsica, together with his wife Theodelanda,

gave Monte Cassino three churches of Comino (prov.: Frosinone), the *curtes* connected with them, and all their dependencies. Dormeier, 34; Bloch, 2:819–20.

1060   Count Sigenulfus, son of Berardus II of Marsica, and grandson of Rainaldus I, who founded Santa Maria de Celle in Carsoli (prov.: L'Aquila), donated to Monte Cassino that monastery and a dependent church near Tivoli. Dormeier, 35; Bloch, 1:323, 334.

1062   Count Berardus III, son of Berardus II of Marsica, together with his wife Rogata and brother Ladolfus, donated to Monte Cassino the "Ecclesia S. Manni," which was in Marsica, "in locum, ubi Peteline bocatur." Bloch, 1:363.

1063/64?   Berardus III, son of Berardus II of Marsica, gave to Monte Cassino the monastery of Santa Maria "in valle Marculana," near Monte Marcolano near Luco dei Marsi (prov.: L'Aquila). Dormeier, 38; Bloch, 2:829.

1067   Theodinus and Oderisius, sons of Count Randisius of Valva, along with Berardus II of Valva, son of Berardus I of Valva, gave to Monte Cassino the monastery of San Pietro in Lago and the hermitage of Prato Cardoso (prov.: L'Aquila), together with five adjacent lakes and all their possessions in Valva, Marsica, and Chieti. Dormeier, 38; Bloch, 1:338–42.

1067   Count Oderisius II, son of Berardus II of Marsica, gave to SS Cosma e Damiano in Tagliacozzo, a "cella" of Monte Cassino, the church of Sant'Erasmo and two half churches, all presumably in the Tagliacozzo area (prov.: L'Aquila). Dormeier, 38; Bloch, 2:731.

1069   Borrellus II, son of Borrellus Major, together with his wife Gervisa and his son Walter, gave Monte Cassino Dominic's foundation of San Pietro Avellana (prov.: Campobasso). Dormeier, 39; Bloch, 1:362–68.

1070   Count Berardus III of Marsica and his son Theodinus, after the latter had entered Monte Cassino, gave to it Santa Maria in the village of Luco dei Marsi (prov.: L'Aquila), together with the *rocca*, its peasants, and all its Marsican possessions. This land, which had been leased to Rainaldus I by Abbot Aligernus of Monte Cassino, had been bookland held held by

	the counts of Marisca for more than a century. Dormeier, 39; Bloch 1:333–34.
c.1070?	Berardus III, son of Berardus II of Marsica, apparently gave to Monte Cassino the castle of Rosciolo and the monastery of Santa Maria in Valle Porclaneta near Magliano de' Marsi (prov.: L'Aquila), a foundation he had endowed in 1048. Dormeier, 41; Bloch, 2:824–26.
1073	Count Oderisius of Sangro, son of Borellus II, gave the church of San Donato in the territory of Bagnoli del Trigno (prov.: Isernia), to San Pietro Avellana. Dormeier, 40.
1077?	The sons of Berardus, son of John, son of Borrellus Major, seem to have given land in Schiavi, near the Church of San Salvatore (Schiavi di Abruzzi, prov.: Chieti), to that church, which their father had donated to San Eustachio in 1057. Bloch, 1:287.
1077	Borrellus II, son of Borrellus Major, offered to San Pietro Avellana, the monastery founded by Dominic that he had donated to Monte Cassino back in 1069, some land near Monte Totino, south of Sessano. Bloch, 1:364.
1080	Borrellus II, son of Borrellus Major, offered to San Pietro Avellana land in the vicinity of Monte Totila (prov.: Isernia?). Bloch, 1:364.
1080	Borrellus II, son of Borrellus Major, offered to San Pietro Avellana land in the vicinity of Pescolanciano (prov.: Isernia). Bloch, 1:364.
1084	Count Rainaldus of Carsoli, son of Berardus III, gave a mill in Capistrella to Santa Maria in Luco dei Marsi (prov.: L'Aquila), the family monastery that his father had given to Monte Cassino in 1070. Bloch, 1:334.
1089	Gentilis, son of count Balduinus, together with his nephew Transmundus, offered to Monte Cassino Santa Maria in Luco dei Marsi, a church already given to Monte Cassino in 1070 by Berardus III. Apparently, claims to this monastery, which had been established by Rainaldus I in the year 1000, had passed down not only through his son Berardus II of Marsica to Berardus III, but also through his son Oderisius I of Marsica to Balduinus. Dormeier, 45; Bloch, 1:334–337.

1089	Gentilis, son of count Balduinus, together with his nephew Transmundus, offered four churches (prov.: L'Aquila) to Monte Cassino. Dormeier, 45; Bloch, 2:823–24.
late 1080s	Count Walter of Sangro, son of Borrellus II, gave to Monte Cassino and San Pietro Avellana the church of San Nicola di Vallesorda (in the territory of Capracotta, prov.: Isernia), an unrecorded donation that is postulated because this church was still independent in 1083 but had to be restored to the above in 1091. Bloch, 1:364–65.
1091	Count Walter of Sangro, son of Borrellus II, restored to Monte Cassino and San Pietro Avellana many properties and six churches, including the church of San Nicola noted above, to which he had made donations in 1083 that his father had approved. Dormeier, 46; Bloch, 1:364.
1093/1094	Oderisius II, count of Sangro, son of Oderisius, gave Monte Cassino Frattura and Collangelo, near Scanno (prov.: L'Aquila). These *castelli* had been in the territory of the counts of Valva, who apparently had lost them during the Norman advance. Bloch, 1:341, 342.
1096	Atelgrima, the widow of Count Rainaldus of Carsoli, the son of Berardus III of Marsica, gave Monte Cassino four *castelli* in the area of Carsoli (prov.: L'Aquila). Bloch, 2:747–48.
1097	A Count Berardus of the Marsi, a son of a Count Berard and Gemma (perhaps this was Berardus V, son of the Berardus captured by the Normans who was the son of Berardus III), gave to Monte Cassino San Martino "in Filimini" on Lago Fucino (prov.: L'Aquila?). Since "Filimini" was land received by Rainaldus, son of Berardus the Frank, in 988 from San Vincenzo Vulturno and in 998 from Santa Maria de Apinianici, this was not exactly a clean title. Dormeier, 48; Bloch, 2:830–31.
1098	Berardus of Sangro, brother of the late Oderisius II of Sangro, confirmed his brother's donations of ca. 1094 and added properties near Castel di Sangro, Monte Chiarano and the plain of Aremogna. Some of these donations are between Scanno and Villetta Barrea and may include territory acquired from the counts of Valva. Bloch, 1:341, 342.

Works Cited

Note: The following works are cited two or more times in the footnotes, with shortened titles appearing after their first reference.

Acta Sanctorum. Ed. Jean Bolland et al. 1st ed. Antwerp and Brussels: Société des bollandistes, 1643–; 3rd ed. Paris: V. Palmé, 1863–69.

Acta Sanctorum Ordinis Sancti Benedicti. Ed. Luc d'Archery and Jean Mabillon. 2nd ed. 9 vols. Venice: Sebastian Colet & Joseph Bettinelli, 1733–40.

Alfanus I of Salerno. *I Carmi di Alfano I, Arcivescovo di Salerno.* Ed. Anselmo Lentini and Faustino Avagliano. Miscellanea Cassinese 38. Monte Cassino: Abbazia di Montecassino, 1974.

Allodi, Leone, ed. See *Regestum Sublacense.*

Amatus of Monte Cassino. *L'Histoire de li Normant.* Ed. Vincenzo de Bartholomaeis as *Storia de' Normanni di Amato di Montecassino volgarizzata in antico francese.* Fonti per la storia d'Italia 76. Rome: Tipografia del Senato, 1935.

L'Ambiente vegetale nell'alto medioevo, 30 marzo–5 aprile 1989. 2 vols. Settimane di Studio del Centro Italiano di Studi sull'Alto Medioevo 37. Spoleto: Centro Italiano di Studi sull'Alto Medioevo, 1990.

Antin, Paul, ed. See Gregory I.

Antonelli, Dionigi. *Abbazie, prepositure e priorati benedettini nella diocesi di Sora nel medioevo (secc. VIII–XV).* Sora: Tipografia Editrice Pasquarelli, 1986.

Ashby, Thomas. *Some Italian Scenes and Festivals.* London: Methuen, 1929.

Aspetti dell'Umbria dall'inizio del secolo VIII alla fine del secolo XI: Atti del III Convegno di studi umbri, Gubbio, 23–27 maggio 1965. Gubbio: Centro di Studi Umbri/Perugia: Facoltà di Lettere e Filosofia dell'Università degli Studi de Perugia, 1966.

Atti del Convegno "L'Eredità medioevale nella regione tiburtina," 26–27 maggio 1979, Villa d'Este, Tivoli. Atti e memorie della Società Tiburtina di Storia e d'Arte 52 (1979).

Avagliano, Faustino. "I codici liturgici dell'Archivio di Montecassino," *Benedictina* 17 (1970): 300–25.

———. See Alfanus I; *Un grande abbazia*; Leccisotti, Tommaso; Lentini, Anselmo; *Montecassino dalla prima alla seconda distruzione.*

Baker, Derek. "'The Whole World a Hermitage': Ascetic Renewal and the Crisis of Western Monasticism." In *The Culture of Christendom: Essays in Medieval History in Memory of Denis L. T. Bethell,* ed. Marc A. Meyer. London: Hambledon Press, 1993, 207–23.

Balzani, Ugo, ed. See Gregory of Catino, *Chronicon Farfense;* Gregory of Catino, *Il Regesto;* Hugh of Farfa.

Baronio, Cesare. *Annales Ecclesiastici.* 26 vols. Ed. Augustino Theiner. Bar-le-Duc: L. Guerin, 1864–83.

Battelli, Giulio, ed. See *Rationes Decimarum Italiae . . . Latium.*

Bechmann, Roland. *Trees and Man: The Forest in the Middle Ages.* Trans. Katharyn Dunham. New York: Paragon House, 1990.

Becker, Joseph, ed. See Luitprand of Cremona.

Benedict of Nursia. *Regula Benedicti.* Ed. Adalbert de Vogüé and Jean Neufville. *La Règle de saint Benoît.* 7 vols. Sources chrétiennes 181–86 bis. Paris: Éditions du cerf, 1971–77.

Benedict of San Andrea di Monte Soratte. *Chronicon.* Ed. Giuseppe Zucchetti. Fonti per la storia d'Italia 55. Rome: Istituto Storico Italiano per il Medio Evo, 1920.

Beranger, Eugenio Maria. See Marta, Roberto.

Bibliotheca Casinensis seu Codicum Manuscriptorum Qui in Tabulario Casinensi Asservatur. 5 vols. Monte Cassino: Ex Typographia Casinensi, 1873–94.

Bibliotheca Hagiographica Latina Antiquae et Mediae Aetatis. Vols. 1–2. Ed. the Bollandists. Vol. 3 (*Novum Supplementum*), by Henri Fros. Subsidia Hagiographica 6 and 70. Brussels: Société des bollandistes, 1898–1901 and 1986.

Bibliotheca Sanctorum. 14– vols. Rome: Istituto Giovanni XXIII della Pontificia Università Lateranense, 1962–70 and 1988.

Bloch, Herbert. *Monte Cassino in the Middle Ages.* 3 vols. Rome: Edizioni di Storia e Letteratura/Cambridge, Mass.: Harvard University Press, 1986.

Boesch Gajano, Sofia. "Domenico di Sora, santo." *Dizionario biografico degli italiani.* 41– vols. Rome: Istituto della Enciclopedia italiana, 1960–. 40:673–78.

———. "Santità di vita, sacralità dei luoghi. Aspetti della tradizione agiografica di Domenico di Sora." In *Scritti in onore di Filippo Caraffa.* Anagni: Istituto di Storia e d'Arte del Lazio, 1986. Pp. 187–204.

Bois, Guy. *The Transformation of the Year 1000: The Village of Lournand from Antiquity to Feudalism.* Trans. Jean Birrell. Manchester: University of Manchester Press, 1992.

[Bollandists.] "S. Dominici Sorani Abbatis Vita et Miracula a Coaevis Conscripta." *Analecta Bollandiana* 1 (1882): 279–322.

———. See *Bibliotheca Hagiographica Latina.*

Bossi, Gaetano. "I Crescenzi di Sabina: Stefaniani e Ottaviani (dal 1012 al 1106)." *Archivio della R. Società Romana di Storia Patria* 41 (1918): 111–70.

Bragazzi, Giuseppe. *Compendio della storia di Fuligno.* Biblioteca istorica della antica e nuova Italia 85. 1858; reprint, Bologna: Forni Editore, 1973.

Braudel, Fernand. *The Mediterranean and the Mediterranean World in the Age of Philip II.* 2 vols. Trans. Siân Reynolds. New York: Harper & Row, 1972.

Bresslau, Harry. *Jahrbücher des Deutschen Reichs unter Konrad II.* 2 vols. Jahrbücher der deutschen Geschichte 14–15. 1879; reprint, Berlin: Duncker & Humblot, 1967.

Brezzi, Paolo. *Roma e l'Impero medioevale, 774–1252.* Storia di Roma 10. Bologna: Licinio Cappelli Editore, 1947.

Brown, Virginia. See Loew, Elias Avery.

Brunhölzl, Franz. *Geschichte der lateinischen Literatur des Mittelalters.* 2– vols. Munich: Wilhelm Fink, 1975– .

Bull, Marcus. *Knightly Piety and Lay Response to the First Crusade: The Limousin and Gascony, c.970 –c.1130.* Oxford: Clarendon Press, 1993.

Caraffa, Filippo. "L'eremitismo nella valle dell'alto Aniene dalle origini al secolo XIX." *Miscellanea Antonio Piolanti,* 2 vols. *Lateranum* n.s. 29–30 (1964). 2: 223–37.

———. *Roma e Lazio (eccettuate l'archidiocesi di Gaeta e l'Abbazia Nullius di Monte Cassino).* Vol. 1 of *Monasticon Italiae.* Pubblicazioni del Centro Storico Benedettino Italiano. Cesena: Badia di Santa Maria del Monte, 1981.

———. *Vallepietra dalle origini al secolo XIX con una appendice sul Santuario della Santissima Trinità sul Monte Autore. Lateranum* n.s. 35 (1969).

Carosi, Paolo. "L'abate sublacense Giovanni V: La duplice elezione (1065 e 1069)." *Atti e memorie della Società Tiburtina di Storia e d'Arte* 42 (1969): 115–32.

Casagrande, Giovanna. "Inventario-regesto delle pergamene della chiesa parrochiale di S. Maria Maggiore a Spello (1187–1844)." *Bollettino della Deputazione di Storia Patria per l'Umbria* 83 (1986): 5–66.

Castelli, Beda. See "Un Monaco benedettino."

Castrum 2: Structures de l'habitat et occupation du sol dans les pays méditerranéens: Les méthodes et l'apport de l'archéologie extensive. Ed. Ghislaine Noyé. Collection de l'École française de Rome 105. Publications de la Casa Velázquez, sér. arch. 9. Rome: École française, 1988.

Castrum 3: Guerre, fortification et habitat dans le monde méditerranéen au moyen âge: Colloque organisé par la Casa de Velázquez et l'École française de Rome, Madrid, 24 –27 novembre 1985. Ed. André Bazzana. Publications de la Casa de Velázquez, sér. arch. 12. Collection de l'École française de Rome 105. Madrid: Casa de Velázquez, 1988.

Catalogus Baronum. Ed. Evelyn Jamison. Fonti per la storia d'Italia 101. Rome: Istituto Storico Italiano per il Medio Evo, 1972.

Cavallo, Guglielmo, ed. See Rodulfus Glaber. *Historiarum Libri Quinque.*

Cecchelli, Carlo. "Note sulle famiglie romane fra il IX e il XII secolo." *Archivio della R. Società Romana di Storia Patria* n.s. 58 (1935): 69–97.

Celidonio, Giuseppe. *Delle antiche decime valvensi (Notizie e documenti).* Sulmona: Tipografia P. Colaprete, 1903.

———. *La Diocesi di Valva e Sulmona.* 4 vols. Casalbordino: Casa Tipografica editrice N. de Arcangelis, 1909–12.

La Certosa di Trisulti. Ed. James Hogg, Giovanni Leoncini, and Michele Merola. *Analecta Cartusiana* 74 (2). Salzburg: Universität Salzburg Institut für Anglistik und Amerikanistik, 1991.

I Ceti dirigenti in Toscana nell'età precomunale. Comitato di studi sulla storia dei ceti dirigenti in Toscana: Atti del 1o Convegno: Firenze, 2 dicembre 1978. Pisa: Pacini Editore, 1981.

Chronicon Casauriense. See "Johannes Berardi."

Chronicon Cassinese. Ed. Hartmut Hoffmann. Monumenta Germaniae Historica Scriptores 34. Hannover: Hahnsche Buchhandlung, 1980.

Chronicon Farfense. See Gregory of Catino.

Chronicon Salernitanum: A Critical Edition with Studies on Literary and Historical Sources and on Language. Ed. Ulla Westerbergh. Acta Universitatis Stockholmiensis, Studia Latina Stockholmiensia 3. Stockholm: Almquist & Wiksell, 1956.

Chronicon Sublacense (AA. 593–1369). Ed. Raffaello Morghen. Istituto Storico Italiano per il Medio Evo, *Rerum Italicarum Scriptores* 24(6). Bologna: Nicola Zanichelli, 1927.

Chronicon Vulturnense del Monaco Giovanni. Ed. Vincenzo Federici. 3 vols. Fonti per la storia d'Italia 58–60. Rome: R. Istituto Storico Italiano per il Medio Evo, 1925–40.

Cilento, Nicola. *Italia meridionale longobarda.* 2nd ed. Milan/Naples: Riccardo Ricciardi Editore, 1971.

Codice Diplomatico Sulmonese. Ed. Nunzio Federigo Faraglia. Lanciano: R. Carabba Editore, 1888.

Constable, Giles. "Cluny in the Monastic World of the Tenth Century." *Il Secolo di ferro: Mito e realtà del secolo X, 19–25 aprile 1990.* 2 vols. Settimane di Studio del Centro Italiano di Studi sull'Alto Medioevo 38. Spoleto: Centro Italiano di Studi sull'Alto Medioevo, 1991. 1:391–448.

———. "Monasteries, Rural Churches and the *Cura Animarum* in the Early Middle Ages." *Cristianizzazione ed organizzazione ecclesiastica delle campagne nell'alto medioevo: Espansione e resistenze, 10–16 aprile 1980.* 2 vols. Settimane di Studio del Centro Italiano di Studi sull'Alto Medioevo 28. Spoleto: Centro Italiano di Studi sull'Alto Medioevo, 1982. 1:349–95.

———. *Monastic Tithes from Their Origins to the Twelfth Century.* Cambridge Studies in Medieval Life and Thought, n.s. 10. Cambridge: Cambridge University Press, 1964.

Cowdrey, H. E. J. *The Age of Abbot Desiderius: Montecassino, the Papacy, and the Normans in the Eleventh and Early Twelfth Centuries.* Oxford: Clarendon Press, 1983.

———. *The Cluniacs and the Gregorian Reform.* Oxford: Clarendon Press, 1970.

———. "The Mahdia Campaign of 1087." *English Historical Review* 92 (1977): 1–29. Reprinted in *Popes, Monks, and Crusaders.* London: Hambledon Press, 1984.

———. *Popes, Monks and Crusaders.* London: Hambledon Press, 1984.

Craven, Keppel. *Excursions in the Abruzzi and Northern Provinces of Naples.* 2 vols. London: Richard Bentley, 1838.

La Cristianità dei secoli XI e XII in Occidente: Coscienza e strutture di una società: Atti della ottava Settimana internazionale di studio, Mendola, 30 giugno–5 luglio 1980. Pubblicazioni dell'Università Cattolica del Sacro Cuore, Miscellanea del Centro di Studi Medioevali 10. Milan: Vita e Pensiero, 1983.

Cristianizzazione ed organizzazione ecclesiastica delle campagne nell'alto medioevo: Espansione e resistenze, 10–16 aprile 1980. 2 vols. Settimane di Studio del Centro Italiano di Studi sull'Alto Medioevo 28. Spoleto: Centro Italiano di Studi sull'Alto Medioevo, 1982.

Cuozzo, Errico. *Catalogus Baronum Commentario*. Fonti per la storia d'Italia 101**. Rome: Istituto Storico Italiano per il Medio Evo, 1984.

Curtius, Ernst Robert. *European Literature and the Latin Middle Ages*. Trans. Willard R. Trask. Bollingen Series 36. 1953; reprinted, with "Epilogue" by Peter Godman. Princeton, N.J.: Princeton University Press, 1990.

Davidson, H. R. Ellis. *Myths and Symbols in Pagan Europe: Early Scandinavian and Celtic Religions*. Syracuse, N.Y.: Syracuse University Press, 1988.

de Bartholomaeis, Vincenzo, ed. See Amatus of Monte Cassino.

de Francesco, A. "Origini e sviluppo del feudalismo nel Molise fino alla caduta della dominazione normanna." *Archivio storico per le province napoletane* 34 (1909): 432–60, 640–71; 35 (1910): 70–98, 273–307.

Delogu, Paolo. "L'istituzione comitale nell'Italia carolingia (Ricerche sull'aristocrazia carolingia in Italia, I)." *Bullettino dell'Istituto Storico Italiano per il Medio Evo e Archivio Muratoriano* 79 (1968): 53–114.

———. "Territorio e cultura fra Tivoli e Subiaco nell'alto medio evo." *Atti del Convegno "L'Eredità medioevale nella regione tiburtina,"* 26–27 maggio 1979, Villa d'Este, Tivoli. *Atti e memorie della Società Tiburtina di Storia e d'Arte* 52 (1979): 25–54.

de Persiis, Luigi. *Tecchiena e il suo statuto*. Frosinone: Tipografia di Claudio Stracca, 1895.

Desiderius of Monte Cassino. *Dialogi de Miraculis Sancti Benedicti*. Ed. Gerhard Schwartz and Adolf Hofmeister. Monumenta Germaniae Historica, *Scriptores* 30 (2:2): 1111–51.

de Vogüé, Adalbert. *La Communauté et l'Abbé dans la Règle de saint Benoît, Textes et études théologiques*. Paris: Desclée de Brouwer, 1960. Trans. Charles Philippi and Ethel Rae Perkins as *Abbot and Community in the Rule of St. Benedict*. 2 vols. Cistercian Studies Series 5. Kalamazoo, Mich.: Cistercian Publications, 1979, 1988.

———. *Règle de saint Benoît 7: Commentaire doctrinal et spirituel*. Sources chrétiennes 186b. Paris: Cerf, 1987. Trans. John Baptist Hasbrouck as *The Rule of Saint Benedict: A Doctrinal and Spiritual Commentary*. Cistercian Studies Series 54. Kalamazoo, Mich.: Cistercian Publications, 1983.

———, ed. See Benedict; Gregory I.

Dictionary of the Middle Ages. 13 vols. New York: Charles Scribner's Sons, 1982–89.

Dierkens, Alain. *Abbayes et chapitres entre Sambre et Meuse (VIIe–XIe siècles): Contribution à l'histoire religieuse des campagnes du Haut Moyen Age*. Beihefte der Francia 14. Sigmaringen: Jan Thorbecke Verlag, 1985.

Di Meo, Alessandro. *Annali critico-diplomatici del Regno di Napoli della mezzana età*. 12 vols. Naples: Stamperia Orsiana, 1795–1819.

Di Nola, Alfonso M. *Gli Aspetti magico-religiosi di una cultura subalterna italiana*. Turin: Boringheri, 1976.

Dizionario biografico degli italiani, 46– vols. Rome: Istituto della Enciclopedia italiana, 1960–.

Dolbeau, François. "Le dossier de saint Dominique de Sora d'Albéric du Mont-Cassin à Jacques de Voragine." *Mélanges de l'École française de Rome: Moyen âge—temps modernes* 102 (1990): 7–78.

D'Onofrio, Cesare, and Carlo Pietrangeli. *L'Abbazie del Lazio.* Rome: Staderini Editore, 1971.

Dormeier, Heinrich. *Montecassino und die Laien im 11. und 12. Jahrhundert.* Schriften der Monumenta Germaniae Historica 27. Stuttgart: Anton Hiersemann, 1979.

Il Ducato di Spoleto: Atti del 9º Congresso internazionale di studi sull'alto medioevo, Spoleto, 27 settembre–2 ottobre 1982. 2 vols. Spoleto: Centro Italiano di Studi sull'Alto Medioevo, 1983.

Egidi, Pietro. *I Monasteri di Subiaco.* Rome: Ministero della Pubblica Istruzione, 1904.

Eizenhöfer, Leo. "Die Feier der Ostervigil in der Benediktinerabtei San Silvestro zu Foligno um das Jahr 1100 nach Ms. 379 der Pierpont Morgan Library, New York City." *Archiv für Liturgiewissenschaft* 6 (1960): 339–71.

Erchempert. *Historia Langobardorum Beneventanorum.* Edited by Georg Waitz. Monumenta Germaniae Historica *Scriptores Rerum Langobardorum et Italicarum, Saeculi VI–IX.* Hannover: Hahnsche Buchhandlung, 1878. Pp. 231–64.

Erdmann, Carl. *The Origin of the Idea of Crusade.* Ed. and trans. Marshall W. Baldwin and Walter Goffart. Princeton, N.J.: Princeton University Press, 1977.

L'Eremitismo in Occidente nei secoli XI e XII: Atti della seconda Settimana internazionale di studio, Mendola, 30 agosto–6 settembre 1962. Pubblicazioni dell'Università Cattolica del Sacro Cuore, Contributi ser. 3, var. 4. Miscellanea del Centro di Studi Medioevali 4. Milan: Vita e Pensiero, 1965.

L'Europa dei secoli XI e XII fra novità e tradizione: Sviluppi di una cultura. Atti della decima Settimana internazionale di studio, Mendola, 25–29 agosto 1986. Pubblicazioni dell'Università Cattolica del Sacro Cuore, Miscellanea del Centro di Studi Medioevali 12. Milan: Vita e Pensiero, 1989.

Fabiani, Luigi. *La Terra di S. Benedetto: Studio storico-giuridico sull'Abbazia di Montecassino dall'VIII al XIII secolo.* 3 vols. Miscellanea Cassinese 33, 34, and 42. Monte Cassino: Badia di Montecassino, 1968–1980.

Falco, Giorgio. "L'amministrazione papale nella Campagna e nella Marittima dalla caduta della dominazione bisantina al sorgere dei comuni." *Archivio della R. Società Romana di Storia Patria* 38 (1915): 677–707.

———. "Note in margine al cartario di Sant'Andrea di Veroli." *Archivio della R. Società Romana di Storia Patria* 84 (1961): 195–227. Reprinted in Giorgio Falco, *Studi sulla storia del Lazio nel medioevo.* 2 vols. Miscellanea della Società Romana di Storia Patria 24 (1–2). Rome: Società Romana di Storia Patria, 1988. 2:705–38.

———. *Studi sulla storia del Lazio nel medioevo.* 2 vols. Miscellanea della Società Romana di Storia Patria 24 (1–2). Rome: Società Romana di Storia Patria, 1988.

Faraglia, Nunzio Federigo, ed. See *Codice Diplomatico Sulmonese.*

Farina, Federico, and Benedetto Fornari. *L'Architettura cistercense e l'Abbazia di Casamari.* 2nd ed. Casamari: Edizioni Casamari, 1981.

———. *Storia e documenti dell'Abbazia di Casamari, 1036–1152.* Casamari: Edizioni Casamari, 1983.

Fasoli, Gina. *Le Incursioni ungare in Europa nel secolo X.* Biblioteca storica Sansoni, n.s. 12. Florence: G. C. Sansoni, 1945.

Fausti, Luigi. "Le chiese della diocesi spoletina nel XIV secolo." *Archivio per la storia ecclesiastica dell'Umbria* 1 (1913): 129–213.

Federici, Vincenzo, ed. See *Chronicon Vulturnense del Monaco Giovanni.*

Feller, Laurent. "Pouvoir et société dans les Abruzzes autour de l'an mil: Aristocratie, *incastellamento*, appropriation des justices (960–1035)." *Bullettino dell'Istituto Storico Italiano per il Medio Evo e Archivio Muratoriano* 94 (1988): 1–72.

Fichtenau, Heinrich. *Lebensordnungen des 10. Jahrhunderts: Studien über Denkart und Existenz im einstigen Karolingerreich.* 2 vols. Monographien zur Geschichte des Mittelalters 30 (1–2). Stuttgart: Anton Hiersemann, 1984. Translated, without the original notes, by Patrick J. Geary as *Living in the Tenth Century: Mentalities and Social Orders.* Chicago: University of Chicago Press, 1991.

Fornari, Benedetto. "I monasteri di San Domenico e di San Nicola presso Trisulti." *Rivista Cistercense* 2 (1985): 127–37.

———. See Farina, Federico.

Fornasari, Giuseppe. "Del nuovo Gregorio VII? Riflessioni su un problema storiografico 'non esaurito.'" *Studi medievali* n.s. 3, 24 (1983): 315–53.

Fortini, Arnaldo. *Nova Vita di San Francesco.* 4 vols. (in 5). Assisi: Edizioni Assisi, 1959 (1960–68).

France, John, ed. See *Rodulfus Glaber. Historiarum Libri Quinque.*

Francovich, Riccardo, ed. See *La Storia dell'Alto Medioevo italiano.*

Franke, Walter. *Romuald von Camaldoli und seine Reformtätigkeit zur Zeit Ottos III.* Historische Studien 107. Berlin: E. Ebering, 1913.

Franklin, Carmela Vircillo. "The Restored *Life and Miracles of St. Dominic of Sora* by Alberic of Monte Cassino." *Mediaeval Studies* 55 (1993): 285–345.

Fumagalli, Vito. *Italia medievale: Il Regno italico.* Torino: UTET, 1978.

Gattola, Erasmo. *Ad Historiam Abbatiae Cassinensis: Accessiones.* 2 vols. Venice: Sebastian Colet, 1734.

———. *Historia Abbatiae Cassinensis per Saeculorum Seriem Distributa.* 2 vols. Venice: Sebastian Colet, 1733.

Geary, Patrick J., trans. See Fichtenau, Heinrich.

Giorgi, Ignazio, ed. See Gregory of Catino, *Il Regesto di Farfa.*

Una grande abbazia altomedievale nel Molise: San Vincenzo al Volturno. Atti del I Convegno di studi sul medioevo meridionale (Venafro-San Vincenzo al Volturno, 19–22 maggio 1982). Ed. Faustino Avagliano. Miscellanea Cassinese 51. Monte Cassino: Abbazia di Montecassino, 1985.

Grégoire, Réginald. "Le Mont-Cassin dans la réforme de l'Église de 1049 à 1122." *Il Monachesimo e la riforma ecclesiastica (1049–1122): Atti della quarta Settimana internazionale di studio, Mendola, 23–29 agosto 1968.* Pubblicazioni dell'Università Cattolica del Sacro Cuore, Contributi, ser. 3, var. 7; Miscellanea del Centro di Studi Medioevali 6. Milan: Vita e Pensiero, 1971. Pp. 21–53.

Gregory I. *Dialogorum Libri Quattuor.* Ed. Adalbert de Vogüé and Paul Antin as *Grégoire le Grand: Dialogues.* 3 vols. Sources chrètiennes 251, 260, 265. Paris: Éditions du Cerf, 1978–80.

Gregory of Catino. *Chronicon Farfense*. Ed. Ugo Balzani as *Il Chronicon Farfense di Gregorio di Catino; precedono la "Constructio Farfensis" e gli scritti di Ugo di Farfa*. 2 vols. Fonti per la storia d'Italia 33–34. Rome: Istituto Storico Italiano per il Medio Evo, 1903.

———. *Il Regesto di Farfa compilato da Gregorio di Catino*. Ed. Ignazio Giorgi and Ugo Balzani. 5 vols. Rome: R. Società Romana di Storia Patria, 1879–1914.

Hamilton, Bernard. *Monastic Reform, Catharism and the Crusades (900–1300)*. Variorum Collected Studies Series. London: Variorum Reprints, 1979.

———. See McNulty, Patricia M.

Hasbrouck, John Baptist, trans. See de Vogüé, Adalbert. *Règle de saint Benoît 7*.

Head, Thomas. See *The Peace of God*.

Herrmann, Klaus-Jürgen. *Das Tuskulanerpapsttum (1012–1046): Benedikt VIII., Johannes XIX., Benedikt IX*. Päpste und Papsttum 4. Stuttgart: Anton Hiersemann, 1973.

Hlawitschka, Eduard. *Franken, Alemannen, Bayern und Burgunder in Oberitalien (774–962): Zum Verständnis der fränkischen Königsherrschaft in Italien*. Forschungen zur oberrheinischen Landesgeschichte 8. Freiburg im Breisgau: Eberhard Albert Verlag, 1960.

Hodges, Richard, ed. See *San Vincenzo al Volturno*.

Hoffmann, Hartmut. "Die älteren Abtslisten von Montecassino." *Quellen und Forschungen aus italienischen Archiven und Bibliotheken* 47 (1967): 224–354.

———. "Chronik und Urkunde in Montecassino. I. Das Register des Petrus Diaconus. II. Gefälschte Herrscherdiplome und Papsturkunden in der Klosterchronik und in den Registern des Petrus Diaconus." *Quellen und Forschungen aus italienischen Archiven und Bibliotheken* 51 (1971): 93–206.

———. "Der Kalender des Leo Marsicanus." *Deutsches Archiv für Erforschung des Mittelalters* 21 (1965): 82–149.

———. "Petrus Diaconus, die Herren von Tusculum und der Sturz Oderisius' II. von Montecassino." *Deutsches Archiv für Erforschung des Mittelalters* 27 (1971): 1–109.

———. "Zur Abtsliste von Subiaco." *Quellen und Forschungen aus italienischen Archiven und Bibliotheken* 52 (1972): 781–88.

———. "Zur Geschichte Montecassinos im 11. und 12. Jahrhundert." Introduction to Heinrich Dormeier, *Montecassino und die Laien*.

———, ed. See *Chronicon Cassinese*.

Hofmeister, Adolf. "Markgrafen und Markgrafschaften im italischen Königreich in der Zeit von Karl dem Grossen bis auf Otto den Grossen (774–962)." *Mitteilungen des Instituts für österreichische Geschichtsforschung: Ergänzungsband* 7 (1907): 215–435.

———, ed. See Desiderius of Monte Cassino.

Hogg, James, ed. See *La Certosa di Trisulti*.

———. "The Charterhouse of Trisulti." In *La Certosa di Trisulti*, vii–xc.

Honorius III. *Honorii III Romani Pontificis Opera Omnia*. Ed. César Auguste Horoy. 5 vols. Bibliotheca Patristica seu Eiusdem Temporis Patrologia 1–5. Paris: Imprimerie de la Bibliothèque ecclésiastique, 1879–82.

Horoy, César Auguste, ed. See Honorius III.

Hourlier, Jacques. "La Règle de saint Benoît, source de droit monastique." *Études d'histoire du droit canonique dediées à Gabriel Le Bras.* 2 vols. Paris: Sirey, 1965. 1:157–68.

Howe, John. "The Awesome Hermit: The Symbolic Significance of the Hermit as a Possible Research Perspective." *Numen* 30 (1983): 106–19.

———. " 'Fatal Discord' in an Eleventh-Century Noble Family from Central Italy." *Medieval Prosopography* 16 (1995): 15–29.

———. "Greek Influence on the Eleventh-Century Western Revival of Hermitism." 2 vols. Dissertation, University of California at Los Angeles, 1979.

———. "*Monasteria Semper Libera*: Cluniac-Type Monastic Liberties in Some Eleventh-Century Central Italian Monasteries." *Catholic Historical Review* 78 (1992): 19–34.

———. "The Nobility's Reform of the Medieval Church." *American Historical Review* 93 (1988): 317–39.

Hubert, Étienne. *Espace urbain et habitat à Rome du Xe siècle à la fin du XIIIe siècle.* Collection de l'École française de Rome 135. Rome: École française de Rome, 1990.

Hugh of Farfa. *Destructio Monasterii Farfensis.* Ed. Ugo Balzani in *Il Chronicon Farfense di Gregorio di Catino; precedono la "Constructio Farfensis" e gli scritti di Ugo di Farfa.* 2 vols. Fonti per la storia d'Italia 33–34. Rome: Istituto Storico Italiano per il Medio Evo, 1903. 1:25–52.

Hüls, Rudolf. *Kardinäle, Klerus und Kirchen Roms, 1049–1130.* Bibliothek des Deutschen Historischen Instituts in Rom 48. Tübingen: Max Niemeyer Verlag, 1977.

Ilàri, Annibale. "I possessi monastici sublacensi in Anticolo di Campagna (Fiuggi) e gli Abati Umberto (1050–69) e Giovanni V (1069–1121)." *Benedictina* 27 (1980): 417–46.

Inguanez, Mauro. *Codicum Casinensium Manuscriptorum Catalogus Cura et Studio Monachorum S. Benedicti Archicoenobii Montis Casini.* 3 vols. Monte Cassino: Ex Typographia Casinensi, 1925–41.

———. "Documenti del monastero di S. Maria de Cellis conservati nell'Archivio di Montecassino." *Bullettino della Regia Deputazione Abruzzese di Storia Patria* ser. 3, 7/8 (1916/1917): 127–58.

———. *I Necrologi Cassinesi, Vol. 1: Il necrologio del cod. cassinese 47.* Fonti per la storia d'Italia 83. Rome: R. Istituto Storico Italiano per il Medio Evo, 1941.

———. "Le pergamene della Badia di S. Benedetto de Jumento albo di Civitanova conservate nell'Archivio di Montecassino." *Gli Archivi italiani* 4 (1917): 141–52.

Jacobilli, Lodovico. *Vita di S. Domenico da Foligno, Abbate dell'Ordine di S. Benedetto.* Foligno: Agostino Alterii, 1645.

———. *Vite de' santi e beati dell'Umbria.* 3 vols. Foligno: Appresso Agostino Alterij, 1647–61.

———. *Vite de'santi e beati di Foligno.* Foligno: Appresso Agostino Alterij, 1628.

Jacobus de Voragine. *De Sancto Dominico Abbati* (1273). Survives in Biblioteca Alessandrina ms. 91 (2), fols. 347–359v (early seventeenth century).

Jaffé, Philip, and Wilhelm Wattenbach. *Regesta Pontificum Romanorum ab Condita*

Ecclesia ad Annum post Christum Natum MCXCVIII. 2 vols. Leipzig: Veit & Comp., 1885–1888.

Jamison, Evelyn. "The Significance of the Earlier Medieval Documents from S. Maria della Noce and S. Salvatore di Castiglione." *Studi in onore di Riccardo Filangieri.* 3 vols. Naples: L'Arte tipografica, 1959. Vol. 1:51–80. Reprinted in Jamison, *Studies on the History of Medieval Sicily and South Italy.* Ed. Dione Clementi and Theo Kölzer. 3 vols. Aalen: Scientia Verlag, 1992. Vol. 2:437–66.

———. *Studies on the History of Medieval Sicily and South Italy.* Ed. Dione Clementi and Theo Kölzer. 3 vols. Aalen: Scientia Verlag, 1992.

———, ed. See *Catalogus Baronum.*

"Johannes Berardi." *Chronicon Casauriense.* Partial edition in Ludovico Antonio Muratori, *Rerum Italicarum Scriptores,* 2 (2): 769–920 and 924–1018. Photo-reproduction of the complete ms. in *Liber Instrumentorum seu Chronicorum Monasterii Casauriensis: Codicem Parisinum Latinum 5411.* L'Aquila: Amministrazione provinciale, 1982.

Kehr, Paul Fridolin. *Italia Pontificia.* 10 vols. Berlin: Weidmann, 1906–75.

Kölmel, Willi. *Rom und der Kirchenstaat im 10. und 11. Jahrhundert bis in die Anfänge der Reform: Politik, Verwaltung; Rom und Italien.* Abhandlungen zur mittleren und neueren Geschichte 78. Berlin-Grunewald: Verlag für Staatswissenschaften und Geschichte, 1935.

Krautheimer, Richard. *Rome: Profile of a City, 312–1308.* Princeton, N.J.: Princeton University Press, 1980.

Kreutz, Barbara M. *Before the Normans: Southern Italy in the Ninth and Tenth Centuries.* Middle Ages Series. Philadelphia: University of Pennsylvania Press, 1991.

Landes, Richard, ed. See *The Peace of God.*

Laudage, Johannes. *Priesterbild und Reformpapsttum im 11. Jahrhundert.* Beihefte zum Archiv für Kulturgeschichte 22. Cologne: Böhlau Verlag, 1984.

Lauri, Achille. "Le origini del distrutto monastero di Santa Chiara in Sora." *Benedictina* 5 (1951): 79–93.

Lazio medievale: Ricerca topografica su 33 abitati delle antiche diocesi di Alatri, Anagni, Ferentino, Veroli. Rome: Multigrafica Editrice, 1980.

Lear, Edward. *Illustrated Excursions in Italy.* 2 vols. in 1. London: Thomas M'Lean, 1846.

Leccisotti, Tommaso. *I Regesti dell'archivio.* 11 vols. Pubblicazioni degli Archivi di Stato 54, 56, 58, 60, 64, 74, 78, 79, 81, 86, 95. Rome: Ministero dell'Interno, 1964–77. (The last three acknowlege Faustino Avagliano as co-author.)

Leclercq, Jean. *La Vie parfaite: Points de vue sur l'essence de l'état religieux.* Tradition monastique 1. Paris: Brepols, 1948.

Lefevre, Renato, ed. See *Tra le Abbazie del Lazio.*

Lentini, Anselmo. *Medioevo Letterario Cassinese: Scritti Vari.* Ed. Faustino Avagliano. Miscellanea Cassinese 57. Monte Cassino: Abbazia di Montecassino, 1988.

———. "S. Domenico Sorano e Montecassino." *Benedictina* 5 (1951): 185–99. Reprinted in his *Medioevo Letterario Cassinese,* pp. 166–84.

———. "La 'Vita S. Dominici' di Alberico Cassinese." *Benedictina* 5 (1951): 57–77. Reprinted in his *Medioevo Letterario Cassinese,* pp. 140–65.

————, ed. See Alfanus I of Salerno.

Leo Marsicanus. See *Chronicon Cassinese.*

Leoncini, Giovanni, ed. See *La Certosa di Trisulti.*

Levi, Guido, ed. See *Regestum Sublacense.*

Liber Instrumentorum. . . . See "Johannes Berardi."

Liber Largitorius vel Notarius Monasterii Pharphensis. Ed. Giuseppe Zucchetti. 2 vols. Istituto Storico Italiano/Istituto Storico Prussiano Regesta Chartarum Italiae 11 and 17. Rome: Hermann Loescher, 1913 and 1932.

Liber Pontificalis. Ed. Louis Duchesne. *Le Liber Pontificalis: Texte, introduction et commentaire.* 2nd ed., by the Bibliothèque des Écoles françaises d'Athènes et de Rome. 3 vols. Paris: E. de Boccard, Editeur, 1955–57.

Loew, Elias Avery. *The Beneventan Script: A History of the South Italian Minuscule.* 2nd ed., by Virginia Brown. Sussidi Eruditi 33 and 34. Rome: Edizioni di Storia e Letteratura, 1980.

Loud, G. A. *Church and Society in the Norman Principality of Capua, 1058 –1197.* Oxford: Clarendon Press, 1985.

Luitprand of Cremona. *Liber de Rebus Gestis Ottonis Magni Imperatoris.* Ed. Joseph Becker as *Die Werke Liudprands von Cremona.* 3rd ed. Scriptores Rerum Germanicarum in Usum Scholarum 41. Hannover: Hahnsche Buchhandlung, 1915. Pp. 159–75.

Lynch, Joseph H. *Simoniacal Entry into Religious Life from 1000 –1260: A Social, Economic and Legal History.* Columbus: Ohio State University Press, 1976.

McClendon, Charles B. *The Imperial Abbey of Farfa: Architectural Currents of the Early Middle Ages.* Yale Publications in the History of Art 36. New Haven, Conn.: Yale University Press, 1987.

McKitterick, Rosamond, ed. See *The Uses of Literacy in Early Medieval Europe.*

McNeill, John Robert. *The Mountains of the Mediterranean World: An Environmental History.* New York: Cambridge University Press, 1992.

McNulty, Patricia M., and Bernard Hamilton. "*Orientale Lumen et Magistra Latinitas:* Greek Influences on Western Monasticism (900–1100)." In *Le Millénaire du Mont Athos, 963 –1963: Études et mélanges.* 2 vols. Chevetogne/Venice: Éditions de Chevetogne, 1963–64. 1:181–216.

Manaresi, Cesare, ed. See *I Placiti del Regnum Italiae.*

Marta, Roberto, and Eugenio Maria Beranger. "L'Abbazia di S. Domenico in Sora." In *Tra le Abbazie del Lazio.* Ed. Renato Lefevre. *Lunario Romano* 17 (1988). Rome: Gruppo Culturale di Roma e del Lazio, 1987. Pp. 193–210.

Martelli, Gisberto. "Le più antiche cripte dell'Umbria." In *Aspetti dell'Umbria,* 323–53.

Martini, Paola Supino. "Manoscritti sublacensi e Tiburtini dei secoli XI–XII." In *Atti del Convegno "L'Eredità medioevale nella regione tiburtina",* 199–216.

Meloni, Pier Lorenzo. "Monasteri benedettini in Umbria tra VIII e XI secolo nella storiografia di Lodovico Jacobilli." *Aspetti dell'Umbria dall'inizio del secolo VIII alla fine del secolo XI: Atti del III Convegno di studi umbri, Gubbio, 23 –27 maggio 1965.* Gubbio: Centro di Studi Umbri/Perugia: Facoltà di Lettere e Filosofia dell'Università degli Studi de Perugia, 1966. Pp. 283–321.

Merola, Michele, ed. See *La Certosa di Trisulti.*

Miccoli, Giovanni. *Chiesa Gregoriana: Ricerche sulla Riforma del secolo XI*. Storici antichi e moderni, n.s. 17. Florence: La Nuova Italia, 1966.

———. "La Storia Religiosa." In *Storia d'Italia*. 6 vols. Torino: Giulio Einaudi Editore, 1972–76, 2 (1): 475–80.

Migne, Jean-Paul. *Patrologiae Cursus Completus: Series Latina*. 221 vols. Paris: Migne, 1844–64.

Miller, Maureen. *The Formation of a Medieval Church: Ecclesiastical Change in Verona, 950–1150*. Ithaca, N.Y.: Cornell University Press, 1993.

Mitchell, John, ed. See *San Vincenzo al Volturno*.

"Un Monaco benedettino" [Beda Castelli]. *La Certosa di Trisulti*. Tournai: Tipografia Notre Dame des Près, 1912.

Montecassino dalla prima alla seconda distruzione: Momenti e aspetti di storia cassinese (secc. VI–IX). Atti del II Convegno di studi sul medioevo meridionale (Cassino–Montecassino, 27–31 maggio 1984). Ed. Faustino Avagliano. Miscellanea Cassinese 55. Monte Cassino: Abbazia di Montecassino, 1987.

Moore, R. I. "Family, Community and Cult on the Eve of the Gregorian Reform." *Transactions of the Royal Historical Society* 5th ser., 30 (1980): 49–69.

Morghen, Raffaello. *Gregorio VII e la riforma della Chiesa nel secolo XI*. 2nd ed. Palermo: Palumbo Editore, 1974.

Morghen, Raffaello, ed. See *Chronicon Sublacense*.

Morini, Enrico. "Eremo e cenobio nel monachesimo greco dell'Italia meridionale nei secoli IX e X." *Rivisti di storia della Chiesa in Italia* 31 (1977): 354–90.

Müller, Hermann. *Topographische und genealogische Untersuchungen zur Geschichte des Herzogtums Spoleto und der Sabina von 800 bis 1100: Inaugural-Dissertation zur Erlangung der Doktorwürde der Philosophischen Fakultät der Universität Greifswald*. Greifswald: Philosophischen Fakultät der Universität Greifswald, 1930.

Muratori, Ludovico Antonio. *Rerum Italicarum Scriptores*. 28 vols. in 25. Milan: Typographia Societatis Palatinae, 1723–51.

Narducci, Henrico. *Catalogus Codicum Manuscriptorum praeter Orientales Qui in Bibliotheca Alexandrina Romae Adservantur*. Rome: F. Bocca, 1887.

Neufville, Jean, ed. See Benedict of Nursia.

Newton, Francis. "Leo Marsicanus and the Dedicatory Text and Drawing in Monte Cassino 99." *Scriptorium* 33 (1979): 181–205.

Noble, Thomas F. X. *The Republic of St. Peter: The Birth of the Papal State, 680–825*. Middle Ages Series. Philadelphia: University of Pennsylvania Press, 1984.

Nolan, Mary Lee and Sidney Nolan. *Christian Pilgrimage in Modern Western Europe*. Chapel Hill: University of North Carolina Press, 1989.

Nolan, Sidney. See Nolan, Mary Lee.

Noyé, Ghislaine, ed. See *La Storia dell'Alto Medioevo italiano*.

Orlandi, Giovanni, ed., trans. See Rodulfus Glaber. *Historiarum Libri Quinque*.

Pantoni, Angelo. *Le Chiese e gli edifici del monastero di San Vincenzo al Volturno*. Miscellanea Cassinese 40. Monte Cassino: Abbazia di Montecassino, 1980.

Partner, Peter. *The Lands of St Peter: The Papal State in the Middle Ages and the Early Renaissance*. Berkeley: University of California Press, 1972.

The Peace of God: Social Violence and Religious Response in France around the Year

1000. Ed. Richard Landes and Thomas Head. Ithaca, N.Y.: Cornell University Press, 1992.

Penco, Gregorio. "L'eremitismo irregolare in Italia nei secoli XI–XII." *Benedictina* 32 (1985): 201–21.

———. *Medioevo monastico*. Studia Anselmiana 96. Rome: Pontificio Ateneo S. Anselmo, 1988.

———. *Storia del Monachesimo in Italia: Dalle origini alla fine del Medioevo*. 2nd ed. Milan: Jaca Book, 1983.

Perkins, Ethel Rae, trans. See de Vogüé, Adalbert. *La Communauté*.

Peter Damian. *Epistulae*. Ed. Kurt Reindel as *Die Briefe des Petrus Damiani*. 4 vols. Monumenta Germaniae Historica, *Die Briefe der deutschen Kaiserzeit* 4(1–4). Munich: Monumenta Germaniae Historica, 1983–93.

———. *Vita Romualdi*. Ed. Giovanni Tobacco as *Petri Damiani Vita Beati Romualdi*. Fonti per la storia d'Italia 94. Rome: Istituto Storico Italiano per il Medio Evo, 1957.

Peter the Deacon. *Registrum*. Archivio di Montecassino ms. 396.

———. See *Chronicon Cassinense*.

Philippi, Charles, trans. See de Vogüé, Adalbert, *La Communauté*.

Phipps, Colin. "Romuald—Model Hermit: Eremitical Theory in Saint Peter Damian's *Vita Beati Romualdi*, Chapters 16–27." In *Monks, Hermits and the Ascetic Tradition: Papers Read at the 1984 Summer Meeting and the 1985 Winter Meeting of the Ecclesiastical History Society*. Studies in Church History 22. Oxford: Basil Blackwell for the Ecclesiastical History Society, 1985. Pp. 65–77.

Picasso, Giorgio. "Monachesimo benedettino in Abruzzo nell'alto medioevo." *Bullettino della Deputazione Abruzzese di Storia Patria* 71 (1981): 5–24.

Pietrangeli, Carlo. See D'Onofrio, Cesare.

Pietrantonio, Ugo. *Il Monachesimo benedettino nell'Abruzzo e nel Molise*. Documenti e storia 5. Lanciano: Editrice Rocco Carabba, 1988.

I Placiti del "Regnum Italiae". Ed. Cesare Manaresi. 3 vols. Fonti per la storia d'Italia 92, 96, 96**, and 97. Rome: Istituto Storico Italiano per il Medio Evo, 1955–60.

Poly, Jean-Pierre, and Eric Bournazel. *The Feudal Transformation, 900–1200*. New York: Holmes & Meier, 1991.

Poncelet, Albert. *Catalogus Codicum Hagiographicorum Latinorum Bibliothecarum Romanarum praeter quam Vaticanae*. Subsidia Hagiographica 9. Brussels: Société des bollandistes, 1909.

———. *Catalogus Codicum Hagiographicorum Latinorum Bibliothecae Vaticanae*. Subsidia Hagiographica 11. Brussels: Société des bollandistes, 1910.

Presutti, Pietro, ed. See *Regesta Honorii Papae III*.

Rationes Decimarum Italiae. Aprutium-Molisium. Le Decime dei secoli XIII–XIV. Ed. Pietro Sella. Studi e Testi 69. Vatican City: Biblioteca Apostolica Vaticana, 1936.

Rationes Decimarum Italiae nei secoli XIII e XIV: Latium. Ed. Giulio Battelli. Studi e Testi 27. Vatican City: Biblioteca Apostolica Vaticana, 1946.

Rationes Decimarum Italiae nei secoli XIII e XIV: Umbria. Ed. Pietro Sella. 2 vols. Studi e Testi 161 and 162. Vatican City: Biblioteca Apostolica Vaticana, 1952.

Regesta Honorii Papae III: Iussu et Munificentia Leonis XIII Pontificis Maximi ex Vaticanis Archetypis Aliusque Fontibus. Ed. Pietro Presutti. 2 vols. Rome: Typographia Vaticana, 1888–95.

Regesta Pontificum Romanorum. Ed. Philip Jaffé, revised S. Loewenfeld et al., under the direction of Wilhelm Wattenbach, 2 vols. Leipzig: Veit & Comp., 1885–88.

Il Regesto di Farfa. See Gregory of Catino.

Regestum Sublacense. Ed. Leone Allodi and Guido Levi as *Il Regesto sublacense del Secolo XI.* Rome: R. Società Romana di Storia Patria, 1885.

Regula Benedicti. See Benedict of Nursia.

Reindel, Kurt, ed. See Peter Damian. *Epistulae.*

La Riforma gregoriana e l'Europa: Congresso Internazionale, Salerno, 20–25 maggio 1985. Studi gregoriani 13. Rome: Libreria Ateneo Salesiano, 1989.

Ring, Richard Raymond. "The Lands of Farfa: Studies in Lombard and Carolingian Italy." Dissertation, University of Wisconsin, 1972.

Rivera, Cesare. "L'Abadia di Collimento a una bolla d'Innocenzo III." *Bullettino della R. Deputazione Abruzzese di Storia Patria* 14 (1902): 75–88.

———. "L'annessione delle terre d'Abruzzo al Regno di Sicilia." *Archivio storico italiano* 84 (1926): 199–308.

———. "Le conquiste dei primi normanni in Teate, Penne, Apruzzo e Valva." *Bullettino della R. Deputazione Abruzzese di Storia Patria* ser. 3, 16 (1925): 7–94.

———. *I Conti de' Marsi e la loro discendenza fino alla fondazione dell'Aquila (843–1250): Cronistoria medioevale dell'Abruzzo e della Sabina de Rieti.* Biblioteca abruzzese pubblicazione periodica 1. Teramo: Giovanni Fabbri Editore, 1913–15.

———. "Per la storia delle origini dei Borrelli conti di Sangro." *Archivio storico per le province napoletane* n.s. 5 (= 44) (1919): 48–92.

———. "Valva e i suoi conti." *Bullettino della R. Deputazione Abruzzese di Storia Patria* 3 ser. 17 (1926): 69–159.

Roberto il Guiscardo e il suo tempo: Relazioni e comunicazioni nelle Prime Giornate normanno-sveve (Bari, maggio 1973). Fonti e studi del Corpus Membranarum Italicarum 11. Rome: Centro di Ricerca Editore, 1975.

Rodulfus Glaber. *Historiarum Libri Quinque.* Ed. and trans. John France as *Rodulfi Glabri: Historiarum Libri Quinque.* Oxford Medieval Texts. Oxford: Clarendon Press, 1989.

Rodulfus Glaber. *Historiarum Libri Quinque.* Ed. and trans. Guglielmo Cavallo and Giovanni Orlandi as *Rodolfo il Glabro: Cronache dell'Anno Mille.* 3rd ed. Scrittore Greci e Latini. Milan: Fondazione Lorenzo Valla, 1991.

Rom im hohen Mittelalter: Studien zu den Romvorstellungen und zur Rompolitik vom 10. bis zum 12. Jahrhundert. Reinhard Elze zur Vollendung seines siebzigsten Lebensjahres gewidmet. Ed. Bernhard Schimmelpfennig and Ludwig Schmugge. Sigmaringen: Jan Thorbecke Verlag, 1992.

Rosenwein, Barbara H. *Rhinoceros Bound: Cluny in the Tenth Century.* Middle Ages Series. Philadelphia: University of Pennsylvania Press, 1982.

Rouselle, Aline. *Croire et Guérir: La foi en Gaule dans l'Antiquité tardive.* Paris: Librairie Arthème Fayard, 1990.

"S. Dominici Sorani Abbatis Vita et Miracula a Coaevis Conscripta." *Analecta Bollandiana* 1 (1882): 279–322.

Santi e demoni nell'alto medioevo occidentale (secoli V–XI), 7–13 aprile 1988. 2 vols. Settimane di studio del Centro Italiano di Studi sull'Alto Medioevo 36. Spoleto: Centro Italiano di Studi sull'Alto Medioevo, 1989.

San Vincenzo al Volturno: The Archaeology, Art and Territory of an Early Medieval Monastery. Ed. Richard Hodges and John Mitchell. International Series 252. London: British Archeological Reports, 1985.

Scaccia Scarafoni, Camillo. *Le carte dell'Archivio capitolare della Cattedrale di Veroli.* Rome: Istituto di Storia e d'Arte del Lazio Meridionale, 1960.

Schimmelpfennig, Bernhard, ed. See *Rom im hohen Mittelalter.*

Schmugge, Ludwig, ed. See *Rom im hohen Mittelalter.*

Schuster, Ildefonso. "L'Abbate Ugo I⁰ e la riforma di Farfa nel secolo XI (998–1030)." *Bollettino della Regia Deputazione di Storia Patria per l'Umbria* 16 (1910): 603–812.

———. "L'Abbaye de Farfa et sa restauration au XIe siècle sous Hugues I." *Revue bénédictine* 24 (1907): 17–35, 374–402.

———. *L'Imperiale Abbazia di Farfa: Contributo alla storia del Ducato romano nel medio evo.* Rome: Tipografia Poliglotta Vaticana, 1921.

———. "Martyrologium Pharphense ex Apographo Cardinalis Fortunati Tamburini O. S. B. Codicis Saeculi XI." *Revue bénédictine* 26 (1909): 433–63; 27 (1910): 75–94 and 363–85.

———. "Il Monastero del Salvatore e gli antichi possedimenti farfensi nella 'massa Torana.'" *Archivio della R. Società Romana di Storia Patria* 41 (1918): 5–58.

Schwartz, Gerhard. *Die Besetzung der Bistümer Reichitaliens unter den sächischen und salischen Kaisern mit den Listen der Bischöfe 951–1122.* Leipzig: B. G. Teubner, 1913.

———, ed. See Desiderius of Monte Cassino.

Schwarzmaier, Hansmartin. "Der *Liber Vitae* von Subiaco: Die Klöster Farfa und Subiaco in ihrer geistigen und politischen Umwelt während der letzten Jahrzehnte des 11. Jahrhunderts." *Quellen und Forschungen aus italienischen Archiven und Bibliotheken* 48 (1968): 80–147.

———. "Zur Familie Viktors IV. in der Sabina." *Quellen und Forschungen aus italienischen Archiven und Bibliotheken* 48 (1968): 64–79.

Sechi, Antonietta Angela. *La Certosa di Trisulti da Innocenzo III al Concilio di Costanza (1204–1414) (Note e documenti). Analecta Cartusiana* 74 (1). Salzburg: Universität Salzburg Institut für Anglistik und Amerikanistik, 1981.

Il Secolo di ferro: Mito e realtà del secolo X, 19–25 aprile 1990. 2 vols. Settimane di studio del Centro Italiano di Studi sull'Alto Medioevo 38. Spoleto: Centro Italiano di Studi sull'Alto Medioevo, 1991.

Sella, Pietro, ed. See *Rationes Decimarum Italiae: Aprutium-Molisium; Rationes Decimarum Italiae nei secoli XIII e XIV: Umbria.*

Sennis, Antonio. "Potere centrale e forze locali in un territorio di frontiera: la Marsica tra i secoli VIII e XII." *Bullettino dell'Istituto Storico Italiano per il Medio Evo e Archivio Muratori* 99 (1994): 1–77.

Sensi, Mario. "Monasteri benedettini in Assisi: Insediamenti sul Subasio e Abbazia di S. Pietro." *Aspetti di vita benedettina nella storia di Assisi: Atti del convegno, 12–13 settembre 1980*, Atti Accademia properziana del Subasio, ser. 6, 5. Assisi: Accademia properziana, 1981, 27–50.

———. "Il patrimonio monastico di S. Maria di Vallegloria a Spello." *Bollettino della Deputazione di Storia Patria per l'Umbria* 81 (1984): 77–149.

Settia, Aldo A. "Pievi e capelle nella dinamica del popolamento rurale." *Cristianizzazione ed organizzazione ecclesiastica delle campagne nell'alto medioevo: Espansione e resistenze, 10–16 aprile 1980*. 2 vols. Settimane di studio del Centro Italiano di Studi sull'Alto Medioevo 28. Spoleto: Centro Italiano di Studi sull'Alto Medioevo, 1982, 1:445–89. Reprinted in his *Chiese, strade e fortezze nell'Italia medievale*. Italia Sacra 46. Rome: Herder Editrice e Libreria, 1991, 3–46.

Shahar, Shulamith. *Childhood in the Middle Ages*. London: Routledge, 1990.

Silvestrelli, Giulio. *Città castelli e terre della regione romana*. 2 vols. Rome: Multigrafica Editrice, 1970.

Skinner, Patricia. *Family Power in Southern Italy: The Duchy of Gaeta and Its Neighbours, 850–1139*. Cambridge: Cambridge University Press, 1995.

Spitilli, Gasparo. *Vita di S. Domenico da Fuligno, Abbate dell'Ordine di S. Benedetto*. Rome: Luigi Zannetti, 1604.

Stock, Brian. *The Implications of Literacy: Written Language and Models of Interpretation in the Eleventh and Twelfth Centuries*. Princeton, N.J.: Princeton University Press, 1983.

La Storia dell'Alto Medioevo italiano (VI–X secolo) alla luce dell'archeologia: Convegno Internazionale (Siena, 2–6 dicembre 1992). Edited by Riccardo Francovich and Ghislaine Noyé. Florence: Edizioni all'Insegna del Giglio, 1994.

Strnad, Alfred A. "Zehn Urkunden Papst Innocenz' III. für die Kartause San Bartolomeo zu Trisulti (1208–1215)." *Römische historische Mitteilungen* 11 (1969): 23–58.

Tabacco, Giovanni. "*Privilegium Amoris*: Aspetti della spiritualità romualdina." *Il Saggiatore* 4 (1954): 324–43.

———. "Regno, Impero e aristocrazie nell'Italia postcarolingia." In *Il Secolo di ferro: Mito e realtà del secolo X, 19–25 aprile 1990*. 2 vols. Settimane di studio del Centro Italiano di Studi sull'Alto Medioevo 38. Spoleto: Centro Italiano di Studi sull'Alto Medioevo, 1991, 1:243–71.

———. "Romualdo di Ravenna e gli inizi dell'eremitismo camaldolese." In *L'Eremitismo in Occidente nei secoli XI e XII: Atti della seconda Settimana internazionale di studio, Mendola, 30 agosto–6 settembre 1962*. Pubblicazioni dell'Università Cattolica del Sacro Cuore, Contributi ser. 3, var. 4. Miscellanea del Centro di studi medioevali 4. Milan: Vita a Pensiero, 1965, 73–121.

———. *The Struggle for Power in Medieval Italy: Structures of Political Rule*. Trans. Rosalind Brown Jensen. New York: Cambridge University Press, 1989.

Taglienti, Atanasio. *La Certosa di Trisulti: Ricostruzione storico-artistica*, 2nd ed. Casamari: Tipografia di Casamari, 1987.

———. *Il monastero di Trisulti e il castello di Collepardo: Storia e documenti*. Casamari: Tipografia di Casamari, 1984.

Tellenbach, Gerd. *Ausgewählte Abhandlungen und Aufsätze*. 4 vols. Stuttgart: Anton Hiersemann, 1988–89.

———. *The Church in Western Europe from the Tenth to the Early Twelfth Century*. Trans. Timothy Reuter. Cambridge Medieval Textbooks. New York: Cambridge University Press, 1993.

———. "Der Sturz des Abtes Pontius von Cluny und seine geschichtliche Bedeutung." *Quellen und Forschungen aus italienischen Archiven und Bibliotheken* 42/43 (1963): 13–55, reprinted in Gerd Tellenbach, *Ausgewählte Abhandlungen und Aufsätze*, 4:1024–66.

Theiner, Augustino, ed. See Baronio, Cesare.

Thietmar of Merseburg. *Chronicon*. Ed. Robert Holtzmann as *Die Chronik des Bischofs Thietmar von Merseburg und Ihre Korveier Überarbeitung*. Scriptores Rerum Germanicarum n.s. 9, 1935, reprint Munich: Monumenta Germaniae Historica, 1980.

Tosti, Luigi. "La Leggenda di San Domenico Abate." In *Scritti Vari*, 2:293–339. Vol. 5 of *Opere complete*. 5 vols. Ed. Loreto Pasqualucci. Rome: L. Pasqualucci, Editore, 1886–90.

Toubert, Pierre. "L'assetto territoriale ed economico dei territori longobardi: Il ruolo delle grandi abbazie." In *Montecassino dalla prima alla seconda distruzione: Momenti e aspetti di storia cassinese (secc. VI–IX). Atti del II Convegno di studi sul medioevo meridionale (Cassino–Montecassino, 27–31 maggio 1984)*. Ed. Faustino Avagliano. Miscellanea Cassinese 55. Monte Cassino: Abbazia di Montecassino, 1987, 275–95.

———. "Les destinées d'un thème historiographique: 'Castelli' et peuplement dans l'Italie médiévale." *Flaran 1: Actes des Premières Journées internationales d'histoire de Flaran (Flaran, 20–22 septembre 1979)*. Auch: Comité départemental de tourisme du Gers, 1980, 11–29; reprinted with the same pagination in *Histoire du haut moyen âge*.

———. *Études sur l'Italie médiévale (IXe–XIVe s.)*. London: Variorum Reprints, 1976.

———. *Histoire du haut moyen âge et de l'Italie médiévale*. London: Variorum Reprints, 1987.

———. "Monachisme et encadrement religieux des campagnes en Italie aux Xe–XIIe siècles." *Le Istituzioni ecclesiastiche della 'Societas Christiana' dei secoli XI–XII: Diocesi, pievi e parrocchie. Atti della sesta Settimana internazionale di studio Milano, 1–7 settembre 1974*. Pubblicazioni dell'Università Cattolica del Sacro Cuore, Miscellanea del Centro di Studi Medioevali 8. Milan: Vita e Pensiero, 1977, 416–41. Reprinted with the same pagination in Toubert, *Histoire du haut moyen âge*.

———. "Pour une histoire de l'environnement économique et social du Mont-Cassin (IXe–XIIe siècles)." *Comptes rendus de l'Académie des Inscriptions et Belles-Lettres, nov.–déc. 1976*. Paris: Académie des Inscriptions et Belles-Lettres, 1976. Pp. 689–702. Reprinted with the same pagination in Toubert, *Histoire du haut moyen âge*.

———. *Les Structures du Latium médiéval: Le Latium méridional et la Sabine du*

IXe siècle à la fin du XIIe siècle. 2 vols. Bibliothèque des Écoles françaises d'Athènes et de Rome 221. Rome: École française de Rome, 1973.

Tra le Abbazie del Lazio. Ed. Renato Lefevre. *Lunario Romano* 17 (1988). Rome: Gruppo Culturale di Roma e del Lazio, 1987.

Tuzii, Francesco. *Memorie istoriche massimamente sacre della Città di Sora.* Rome: Stamperia di Antonio de'Rossi, 1727.

Ughelli, Ferdinand. *Italia Sacra sive de Episcopis Italiae,* 2nd ed. 10 vols. Venice: Sebastian Colet, 1717–22.

The Uses of Literacy in Early Medieval Europe. Ed. Rosamond McKitterick. New York: Cambridge University Press, 1990.

Vehse, Otto. "Das Bündnis gegen die Sarazenen vom Jahre 915." *Quellen und Forschungen aus italienischen Archiven und Bibliotheken* 19 (1927): 181–204.

———. "Die päpstliche Herrschaft in der Sabina bis zur Mitte des 12. Jahrhunderts." *Quellen und Forschungen aus italienischen Archiven und Bibliotheken* 21 (1929/1930): 120–75.

Volpini, Raffaello. "Placiti del 'Regnum Italiae' (secc. IX–XI): Primi contributi per un nuovo censimento." In *Contributi dell'Istituto di storia medioevale* 3. Ed. Piero Zerbi. Vita e Pensiero. Milan: Pubblicazioni della Università Cattolica del Sacro Cuore, 1975, 245–520.

Von Falkenhausen, Vera. "Aspetti storico-economici dell'étà di Roberto il Guiscardo." *Roberto il Guiscardo e il suo tempo: Relazioni e comunicazioni nelle Prime Giornate normanno-sveve (Bari, maggio 1973).* Fonti e studi del Corpus Membranarum Italicarum 11. Rome: Centro di Ricerca Editore, 1975. Pp. 115–34.

Wattenbach, Wilhelm. See Jaffé, Philip.

Weinstein, Donald, and Rudolph M. Bell. *Saints & Society: The Two Worlds of Western Christendom, 1000–1700.* Chicago: University of Chicago Press, 1982.

Wemple, Suzanne Fonay. *Atto of Vercelli: Church, State, and Christian Society in Tenth Century Italy.* Temi e testi 27. Rome: Edizioni di Storia e Letteratura, 1979.

Westerbergh, Ulla, ed. See *Chronicon Salernitanum.*

Wickham, Chris. *Early Medieval Italy: Central Power and Local Society, 400–1000.* 1981; reprint, Ann Arbor: University of Michigan Press, 1989.

———. "European Forests in the Early Middle Ages: Landscape and Land Clearance." *L'Ambiente vegetale,* 2:479–548. Reprinted, with additions, in Wickham, *Land and Power,* pp. 155–99.

———. *Land and Power: Studies in Italian and European Social History, 400–1200.* London: British School at Rome, 1994.

———. "Lawyers' Time: History and Memory in Tenth- and Eleventh-Century Italy." *Studies in Medieval History Presented to R. H. C. Davis.* Edited by Henry Mayr-Harting and R. I. Moore. London: Hambledon Press, 1985. Pp. 53–71. Reprinted, with additions, in Chris Wickham, *Land and Power. Studies in Italian and European Social History, 400–1200.* London: British School at Rome, 1994. Pp. 275–93.

———. *The Mountains and the City: The Tuscan Appennines in the Early Middle Ages.* Oxford: Clarendon Press, 1988.

————. *Il problema dell'incastellamento nell'Italia centrale: L'esempio di San Vincenzo al Volturno.* Studi sulla Società degli Appennini nell'Alto Medioevo 2. Quaderni dell'insegnamento di archeologia medievale della Facoltà di Lettere e Filosofia dell'Universià di Siena. Florence: Edizioni all'Insegna del Giglio, 1985.

————. *Studi sulla società degli Appennini nell'alto medioevo: Contadini, signori e insediamento nel territorio di Valva (Sulmona).* Università degli Studi di Bologna, Quaderni del Centro Studi Sorelle Clarke 2. Bologna: Editrice CLUEB, 1982.

Wolf, Kenneth Baxter. *The Normans and Their Historians in Eleventh-Century Italy.* Middle Ages Series. Philadelphia: University of Pennsylvania Press, 1995.

Zerbi, Piero, ed. *Contributi dell'Istituto di storia medioevale.* See Volpini, Raffaello.

Zimmermann, Harald. "Parteiungen und Paptswahlen in Rom zur Zeit Kaiser Ottos des Grossen." *Römische historische Mitteilungen* 8/9 (1964/65 and 1965/66): 29–88. Reprinted with bibliographical additions in his *Otto der Grosse.* Wege der Forschung 450. Darmstadt: Wissenschaftliche Buchgesellschaft, 1976. Pp. 325–414.

————, ed. *Papsturkunden, 896–1046,* 3 vols. Österreichische Akademie der Wissenschaften, Philsophisch-historische Klasse, Denkschriften 174, 177, and 198. Vienna: Verlag der Österreichische Akademie der Wissenschaften, 1984–89.

Zucchetti, Giuseppe, ed. See Benedict of San Andrea di Monte Soratte.

————, ed. See *Liber Largitorius.*

Index

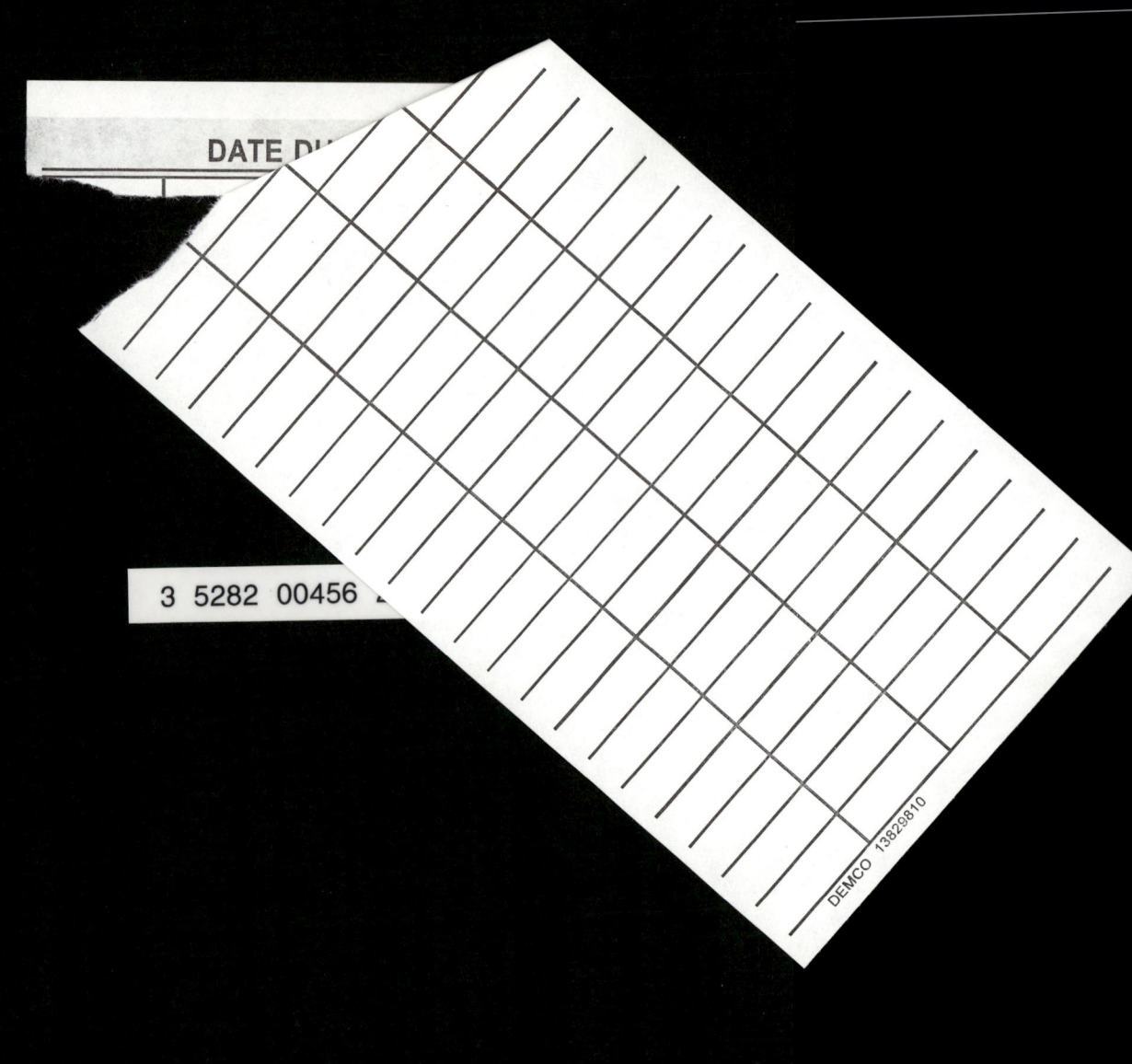

DATE DUE

3 5282 00456

DEMCO 13829810